Luminos is the open access monograph publishing program from UC Press. Luminos provides a framework for preserving and reinvigorating monograph publishing for the future and increases the reach and visibility of important scholarly work. Titles published in the UC Press Luminos model are published with the same high standards for selection, peer review, production, and marketing as those in our traditional program. www.luminosoa.org

A
Philip E. Lilienthal
BOOK

The Philip E. Lilienthal imprint
honors special books
in commemoration of a man whose work
at University of California Press from 1954 to 1979
was marked by dedication to young authors
and to high standards in the field of Asian Studies.
Friends, family, authors, and foundations have together
endowed the Lilienthal Fund, which enables UC Press
to publish under this imprint selected books
in a way that reflects the taste and judgment
of a great and beloved editor.

The publisher gratefully acknowledges the generous support of the Philip E. Lilienthal Asian Studies Endowment Fund of the University of California Press Foundation, which was established by a major gift from Sally Lilienthal.

A Vietnamese Moses

A Vietnamese Moses

*Philiphê Bỉnh and the Geographies of
Early Modern Catholicism*

George E. Dutton

UNIVERSITY OF CALIFORNIA PRESS

University of California Press, one of the most distinguished university presses in the United States, enriches lives around the world by advancing scholarship in the humanities, social sciences, and natural sciences. Its activities are supported by the UC Press Foundation and by philanthropic contributions from individuals and institutions. For more information, visit www.ucpress.edu.

University of California Press
Oakland, California

© 2017 by George E. Dutton

This work is licensed under a Creative Commons CC BY-NC-ND license. To view a copy of the license, visit http://creativecommons.org/licenses.

Suggested citation: Dutton, George E. *Philiphê Bỉnh and the Geographies of Early Modern Catholicism*. Oakland: University of California Press, 2017. doi: http://doi.org/10.1525/luminos.22

Library of Congress Cataloging-in-Publication Data
Names: Dutton, George Edson, author.
Title: A Vietnamese Moses : Philiphê Bỉnh and the geographies of early modern Catholicism / George E. Dutton.
Description: Oakland, California : University of California Press, [2017] | Includes bibliographical references and index.
Identifiers: LCCN 2016035712 (print) | LCCN 2016036930 (ebook) | ISBN 9780520293434 (pbk. : alk. paper) | ISBN 9780520966697 (ebook)
Subjects: LCSH: Bỉnh, Philiphê, 1759-1833. | Catholics—Vietnam—Biography. | Catholic Church—Vietnam—History—18th century. | Catholic Church—Vietnam—History—19th century. | Vietnam—Church history—18th century. | Vietnam—Church history—19th century.
Classification: LCC BX4705.B5195 D88 2017 (print) | LCC BX4705.B5195 (ebook) | DDC 282.092 [B] —dc23
LC record available at https://lccn.loc.gov/2016035712

26 25 24 23 22 21 20 19 18 17
10 9 8 7 6 5 4 3 2 1

For Jessie, Talia, and Miranda

CONTENTS

List of Illustrations ix
Acknowledgments xi

Introduction 1
1. Philiphê Bỉnh and the Catholic Geographies of Tonkin 23
2. A Catholic Community in Crisis 46
3. Journeys: Macao, Goa, and Lisbon 65
4. Arrival in Lisbon and First Encounters 98
5. Invoking the Padroado: Bỉnh and Prince Dom João 119
6. Waiting for Bỉnh in Tonkin and Macao 159
7. Life in Lisbon and the Casa do Espirito Santo, 1807–33 182
8. The Tales of Philiphê Bỉnh 218

Epilogue 260
Appendix 1: Time Line 267
Appendix 2: Cast of Characters 271
Appendix 3: Texts Used by Bỉnh in His Writing Projects 277
List of Abbreviations 279
Notes 281
Bibliography 315
Index 327

ILLUSTRATIONS

MAPS

1. Overview of Vietnam in relation to Macao and the Philippines   5
2. Global demarcation lines dividing realms of Spanish and Portuguese authority, 1493 and 1494   8
3. Important sites of Catholic communities and churches in coastal Tonkin   25
4. Bình's journey from Tonkin to Lisbon, via Macao, the Malay Peninsula, and St. Helena   90
5. Key sites in Portugal where Bình lived or that he visited after his 1796 arrival   100

FIGURES

1. Fields near Bình's home of Ngài Am in 2010   2
2. Waterfront buildings along Macao's harbor, late eighteenth century   72
3. Facade of the former Jesuit church, St. Paul's, in Macao   73
4. Map of Macao, 1795, showing sites of importance for Bình's mission   74
5. Bishop Marcelino, bishop of Macao in the 1790s   77
6. Map of the waterways connecting Macao with Canton, 1748   80
7. The Portuguese enclave of Goa, 1740   82
8. Jamestown Harbor on the island of St. Helena, early nineteenth century   94
9. The Torre de Belem, late eighteenth century   99

10. The Necessidades palace, Bỉnh's residence in Lisbon, 1796–1807   *105*
11. The Portuguese ruler, Crown Prince Dom João, 1799   *111*
12. The Queluz palace on the outskirts of Lisbon   *114*
13. The baths at Caldas da Rainha, early nineteenth-century engraving   *129*
14. Cardinal Pacca, the papal nuncio in Lisbon and Bỉnh's chief opponent   *133*
15. Bishop Manuel Galdino, the Franciscan priest briefly appointed to act as the bishop of Tonkin   *135*
16. Dom Alexandre de Sousa Holstein, the Portuguese court's ambassador to the Vatican   *144*
17. Bishop Caleppi, second papal nuncio to Lisbon during Bỉnh's residence   *146*
18. The Mafra palace compound north of Lisbon, mid-nineteenth century   *152*
19. The Mafra palace in 2006   *155*
20. The prince regent's departure for Brazil in November of 1807   *157*
21. The Casa do Espirito Santo, Bỉnh's home from 1807 until his death in 1833   *185*
22. Map of Lisbon, 1833, showing the Casa do Espirito Santo and nearby churches   *186*
23. Location of Lisbon's Royal Library after it opened in 1796   *206*
24. The Livraria Bertrand, which opened in 1732, the oldest operating bookstore in the world   *207*
25. One of the numerous chronologies that Bỉnh inserted into his notebooks   *234*
26. The last known writing by Philiphe Bỉnh on the final page of his *Tales of Saint Anne*   *259*
27. Family plot purportedly containing the graves of Bỉnh's two sisters and a brother   *265*

ACKNOWLEDGMENTS

The seeds of this project were planted in a conversation with David Marr at the Southeast Asian Studies Summer Institute's 1990 Vietnamese Studies Conference at Cornell. I mentioned that I was interested in working on the Tây Sơn uprising as a possible dissertation project, and he suggested I take a look at a book by a Vietnamese author who had lived through the Tây Sơn era and might offer some insights. I went to the Cornell Library to check out the book, the 1968 photoreproduction of Bỉnh's *Sách sổ*, and almost immediately recoiled. The cramped but fairly neat handwriting stumped me, a first-year learner of Vietnamese, and as I skimmed through the volume's more than six hundred pages there seemed little chance that I would be able to decipher it, much less use it for my work. Then, nine years later, I found myself in the Vatican Libraries, holding a copy of the original in my hands. Now I could read it, and its many companions, and while it proved of only limited use for my Tây Sơn project, I knew that I would have to come back to Bỉnh and his notebooks. This book is the result.

Over the more than a quarter century that has passed between the planting of the seed and the flowering of this book, I've accrued numerous debts to many people in the field of Vietnamese history and beyond who have shaped my scholarship and my career. Some have heard my presentations on Bỉnh at conferences and colloquia at various venues: the Association for Asian Studies in Honolulu, Harvard University, the University of Wisconsin-Madison, the University of California Irvine, Seattle University, the University of California Riverside, the University of California Berkeley, and my home institution, the University of California Los Angeles. Many others have heard my succinct and, at times, less than succinct summaries of Bỉnh's life after asking, "So what project are you working on?"

I'm grateful for everyone's willingness to listen to a story that still fascinates me after years of living with it. While I'll surely leave out some names (for which I apologize), I want to thank my friends and colleagues who've listened and offered suggestions or advice, starting with two very generous colleagues who read the manuscript for the University of California Press. Barbara Watson Andaya and Charles Keith both agreed to read the manuscript and did so with great care, each providing encouraging but useful critical suggestions, many of which were incorporated into the revised book. I am in debt to both of them for their enormous assistance. Hue-Tam Ho Tai invited me to a workshop on Vietnamese biography that was very useful to my thinking about Bỉnh's life and later helped me puzzle over language in Bỉnh's poetry. Roland Jacques answered several e-mail queries with helpful suggestions, as did Liam Brockey when I puzzled over aspects of Bỉnh's story in Lisbon. Nhung Tran allowed me to use her important collection of Bỉnh's writings in photo and microfilm form, a resource of immeasurable benefit. Raul Máximo da Silva sent me numerous articles and files that helped in the final stages of the project, particularly as I translated some of Bỉnh's travel poetry. On my first visit to Lisbon in 2006, Francisco Contente Domingues discussed the Oratorian order with me and confirmed the location of Bỉnh's residence. Over the years, my friend and office neighbor Thu-Huong Nguyen-Vo listened to each of my new discoveries about Bỉnh as I worked my way through his texts and was the first to suggest that his story would make a great movie. Her friendship and support have been invaluable. Among the many people in the fields of Vietnamese and Southeast Asian studies who have listened to my telling of Bỉnh's story and offered insights and suggestions are Peter Zinoman, Mark Bradley, Thongchai Winichakul, Alexander Woodside, Keith Taylor, Anthony Reid, Charles Wheeler, Michael Cullinane, Michele Thompson, Erik Harms, Ben Kiernan, Anh Tran, Judith Henchey, Hazel Hahn, Geoff Robinson, Philippe Papin, Jayne Werner, Olga Dror, Wynn Wilcox, Brian Ostrowski, and Shawn McHale. I am particularly grateful to John Whitmore, who, knowing I was working on Bỉnh, sent me a copy of the 1968 reprinting of his *Sách sổ* notebook, which became a resource and talisman as I came to the end of the project. I also owe a special debt to Vũ Đường Luân, who served as my guide and local contact when I traveled to Bỉnh's home region of Vĩnh Bảo. He made the trip a success, contributing greatly to the final book.

I want also to offer my appreciation to the staff members of the institutions at which I carried out the research for this work: first, to the librarians at the Vatican Library, for allowing me access to their incomparable collections and allowing me to use Bỉnh's original works, and also to the archivists at the Torre de Tombo National Archives in Lisbon, who put up with my atrocious Portuguese while retrieving countless boxes of materials pertaining to the religious house in which Bỉnh had lived for many years. The UCLA Interlibrary Loan office procured a wide range of materials, including the full microfilm set of Bỉnh's notebooks, copies of which have undergirded my research for the past decade. And although my research at the Archives of the Missions Étrangères de Paris was conducted primarily for an earlier project, the notes and materials I collected there were extremely useful for this book, so it seems appropriate once again to acknowledge the assistance of the late Father Gérard Moussay and his extremely helpful assistant Brigitte Appavou.

Finally, I want to express my deep gratitude to my family for their constant love and support throughout the years it took to complete this project. I am especially grateful to my father, Donald Dutton, for listening to my stories of Bình and for reading through an earlier draft and offering his reactions and useful criticism. He has always been an inspiration and a willing sounding board for the many ideas that Bình's story raised for me. My wife Jessie and my daughters Talia and Miranda have brought constant joy into my life and have so often usefully distracted me from my work.

The final product of my many years of research owes much to all of these people, and more whom I've failed to mention, but in the end I take responsibility for the work, its successes and shortcomings. I've told as much of Bình's story as I was able to find, but am always hoping that I or someone else will uncover even more.

INTRODUCTION

In the riverine reaches of the southern corner of greater Hải Phong city, near where the Thái Bình river empties into the Gulf of Tonkin, stands a tiny Catholic church with pale yellow walls and bearing the date of its recent renovation—2005. This simple house of worship, surrounded by fields of wet rice paddy and local water-pipe tobacco (*thuốc lào*), serves a handful of families in the subparish of Địa Linh. In all respects it is an unremarkable site in an area far off the beaten path. Yet this church marks the starting point of a story that linked Vietnam and Europe more than two centuries ago. The sparsely populated hamlet where the church stands is the birthplace of a man whose life bound the religious fate of this coastal region's people with the distant Catholic powers of eighteenth- and nineteenth-century Europe.

This man, possibly born Nguyễn Văn Bỉnh, came of age in the 1770s as European clerics were consolidating their missionary efforts in the region of Tonkin and frequently skirmishing among themselves.[1] It was a time when Catholics in Tonkin, both local converts and their European priests, practiced their faith under the constant threat of persecution by the Vietnamese state. Bỉnh's story, most of it lived under his ordination name—Philiphê Bỉnh—begins in this tumultuous context before shifting to an equally fraught European political and religious landscape. This book chronicles his life and the particular religious community from which he emerged and that he served, and situates both within the larger story of religious and secular politics in Tonkin and Portugal at the turn of the nineteenth century.

Philiphê Bỉnh's story, spanning continents, cultures, and centuries, illustrates the beginnings of Vietnamese engagement with European Catholic conceptions

FIGURE 1. Fields near Bỉnh's home of Ngải Am in 2010. Author's photo.

of their genealogical past and their geographical present. It also suggests their encounter with such conceptions as "East" and "West" and their implications for how Vietnamese now understood their place in the world. It is the story of a Vietnamese priest whose deep affinities with the Portuguese Jesuit lineage caused him to leave a homeland embroiled in civil war on a perilous twelve-thousand-nautical-mile sea voyage to distant Lisbon. His mission, on behalf of a distinctive community of Catholics, was to petition the ruler of Portugal to appoint a bishop for Tonkin to serve their spiritual needs. Bỉnh arrived in Lisbon in 1796 shortly before the Napoleonic Wars began to sweep across Europe, and he watched as these conflicts engulfed the Iberian Peninsula and the Portuguese capital in which he resided. Bỉnh witnessed the Portuguese ruler's hasty departure for a Brazilian exile in 1807, after which he experienced a brief occupation by a Franco-Spanish army followed by an extended British military presence. Thereafter, he lived through the constitutionalist convulsions that swept through Portugal in the 1820s and 1830s. Bỉnh's final years were marked by the Portuguese civil wars of 1832–34, in which monarchists took a last stand against their constitutionalist foes. It was a life lived through turmoil, spiritual and physical, and one of accomplishments and disappointments.

My project is partly a biography, for it focuses on a particular individual and his life story. Yet it is both less and more than this. It is less than a biography because there remains much about Bỉnh that we do not, and perhaps cannot, know. My book relies heavily upon Bỉnh's own telling of his life, a story he recorded quite selectively. He writes nothing about his family background or about growing up, and he provides only limited information about his years as a catechist from the age of seventeen until his ordination as a priest at the age of thirty-four. There is also little quotidian detail about his life after he turns forty-eight in 1807, the year the Portuguese ruler departed Lisbon for Brazil. Consequently, much about Bỉnh remains unclear. We do not even have any idea what he looked like. Bỉnh never thought it necessary to describe himself to an imagined reader, and others who wrote about him never commented on his physical person. In short, there are some fundamental gaps in my story, ones that have frustrated me throughout the writing of this book. I have included as much information as I could find or as much as Bỉnh chose to reveal. Whether the remaining gaps make for a less satisfying life story is for the reader to judge.

Yet this book is more than simply a biography, for Bỉnh's story is also that of the particular community of Vietnamese Catholics whom he served. Indeed, it was Bỉnh's commitment to this community's members and their unwavering dedication to a distinctive way of being Catholic that led him to travel to Lisbon on their behalf. This group of Catholics understood itself to be part of a Christian lineage with its origins in the Portuguese missionary project that had begun in Tonkin in the 1620s. Because this project had been sponsored by the Portuguese court under the auspices of a papal grant—the Padroado Real (Royal Patronage)—the community became known as the Padroado Catholics. For all practical purposes, this "Padroado Community" was also a "Jesuit community," one whose members viewed themselves as sharing an enduring debt to the Jesuits for having brought the faith. This connection remained intact, even as the Jesuit monopoly gave way over the course of the seventeenth century with the arrival of other religious orders, notably the Dominicans (though there were also Augustinians and Franciscans), and secular mission organizations, like the Paris-based Foreign Missions Society (Missions Étrangères de Paris, MEP). Consequently, the Tonkinese mission field become fragmented, and Vietnamese Christians developed affinities for and religious loyalties to particular Catholic traditions represented by the groups or priests serving their specific congregations. When the Jesuit order was formally disestablished in 1773, the Padroado Christians found their community in jeopardy. Told they would have to accept the ecclesiastical authority of the apostolic vicars who supervised Tonkin, these Catholics refused. In concert with some of the remaining Jesuit loyalist European priests, Bỉnh was instrumental in leading the community's defiance. As a consequence, the members of these parishes who defied church authority were labeled as schismatics and barred from access to the

Catholic sacraments. At this point, Bỉnh committed himself to restoring them to the church through his mission to seek a new bishop for Tonkin.

A story of Bỉnh and the community he represented, this book is also an exploration of Catholic geographies and the ways in which these shaped not only the complex ecclesiastical landscape he had to traverse but also the changing mental worlds occupied by Vietnamese Christians. New geographies are a key component to this story of early Vietnamese Catholicism, in terms not merely of spatial dimensions but also of temporal and cultural ones. It was a religious tradition profoundly shaped by place, from the centers of Catholic authority to the territorial division of Vietnamese Catholic communities, to the larger situatedness of Christianity, as a historical religion, in both time and space. This is a story of how Vietnamese Christians positioned themselves within these new spatial, temporal, and cultural geographies. The encounter between local populations and the flows of European Catholic mission work brought about a transformation of certain segments of Vietnamese society and the landscape in which they were situated. It saw a remapping of the Vietnamese territories in which new lines were being drawn, superimposed upon existing administrative territorial demarcations. These lines in some cases extended beyond Vietnamese boundaries, representing threads that connected its Catholic populations to new sites, both in the immediate region and well beyond it.

Vietnamese Catholics of the seventeenth and eighteenth centuries had become members of a global religious community, now linked to other parts of Asia and to Europe via ecclesiastical networks, biblical genealogies, and a shared tradition of revered saints. These networks connected Vietnamese Christians to larger global currents in Roman Catholicism, in real and imagined ways. This transformed world in which Vietnamese Catholics found themselves had both a geographical dimension, featuring trading networks along which European missionaries traveled, and a hierarchical one, manifested in the larger Catholic church structures in which the Vietnamese were now embedded. The geographies that mattered to Vietnamese Catholics were often defined less from Thăng Long or Phú Xuân than from Macao, Manila, Goa, and ultimately Rome. At the local level, the parameters of the struggle were set by European missionary groups and their relationship to their Vietnamese followers. While the Vietnamese state (highly fragmented at times in the seventeenth and eighteenth centuries) had an impact on Vietnamese Catholics in terms of its oppression of and/or tolerance toward the faith, it had no particular stake in the battle pitting Jesuit loyalists against secular or Dominican priests. Thus both subnational and transnational politics were at work. At one level the contest between Catholic groups was very much a Vietnamese issue, yet at another level it transcended the Vietnamese in significant ways. In short, this book argues that these geographical factors profoundly shaped the contours of early

MAP 1. Map showing an overview of Vietnam in relation to Macao and the Philippines.

modern Vietnamese Catholicism and that examining such geographies through Bînh's mission helps explain the development of Christian communities and their relationship to Catholic centers of power and authority.

The story of Bînh and the Padroado community, while strongly influenced by Catholic geographical factors, is also profoundly shaped by complex national geographies. Scholarship on Vietnamese linkages to Europe has largely focused on France's growing involvement over the course of the eighteenth and then nineteenth centuries, first through its missionaries and later through its military forces. Before the French, however, the Portuguese were the predominant European presence in the Vietnamese lands and left a significant mark through their Jesuit missionaries as well as their trading factories. Moreover, they sustained their religious connections through the proximity of their outpost on Macao. Roland Jacques makes an eloquent case for the importance of Portuguese missionaries not only in giving Catholicism its early roots among the Vietnamese but also in developing and popularizing the new romanized script, which would become the primary written system used by the Vietnamese Catholic community.[2] Bînh was very much part of this particular thread of Vietnamese history, one that held considerable significance for a notable population in the northern Vietnamese realm for more than two centuries.[3]

Although these spatial and national geographies were profoundly important for Vietnamese Catholics, other geographies were in flux around them, including ones of temporality, as Vietnamese Catholics became members of a universal religion. Vietnamese, like other Christians around the world, came to see themselves as descendants of individuals whose genealogies were traced through the Old Testament. Consequently, not only the legacy but also the history of these figures became that of later generations of Christians, no matter where they might be located. In this manner Vietnamese become linked to an entirely new set of ancestors, a shared past that tied them to fellow Catholics in Europe and beyond. The figures of the Old Testament became the spiritual ancestors of the Vietnamese Catholics. They became points of reference that represented a marked shift in how at least some Vietnamese regarded the past. Where literate Vietnamese had once looked back to China's past and its Confucian ideological landscape for ways to understand and articulate their present, some now turned instead to stories of the Bible and the figures that peopled its landscape. In short, Vietnamese Catholics had been exposed to and were developing a new worldview, both in a conceptual sense as they saw their world through new ideological lenses and in a literal sense as their view of the physical world was transformed and expanded to include a vast range of unfamiliar places associated with their faith's past and present. The referents of this worldview were tales of the biblical patriarchs, accounts of the saints, and stories of the Jesuit missionaries, rather than tales of Sinic sages, worthy ministers, and loyal generals.

This transformation explains why Father Binh represented himself to members of his community as Moses and in turn portrayed them as the Israelites in Egyptian exile. He was their advocate and mentor, whether speaking up for them with the pharaohs or urging their patience while he was atop Mount Sinai to receive the Ten Commandments. Binh saw his journey to Lisbon as analogous to both of these Old Testament episodes, for he traveled to a royal court to beseech help for his people, hopefully returning with the source of their ultimate salvation. Members of the Padroado community thus came to regard him as their Moses, and although Binh never succeeded in coming down from the mountain, or returning from the royal court at which he was their champion, his use of these Old Testament analogues suggests some of the new genealogies and geographies that had taken root among Vietnamese Catholics over the seventeenth and eighteenth centuries. They were a changed people, and Binh's life and mission reflected these changes.

DRAWING LINES ON THE GLOBE

The prominence of Portuguese Jesuits in Tonkin can be understood only through examination of the geopolitical context in which European Catholic powers were engaging in a global evangelization project. The transmission of Roman Catholicism to the Vietnamese lands was in part the product of a division of the globe articulated in two significant fifteenth-century papal directives designed to regulate the missionary projects of the most powerful Catholic states of the time, Spain and Portugal. The first was a pair of grants known as the Padroado Real and the Patronato Real (grants of royal patronage) issued by Pope Nicholas V in 1452. This concordat constituted an arrangement between the Vatican and the two Iberian Catholic monarchs, in which the papacy recognized the authority of Portuguese Catholic rulers over both missionary work and the administration of newly created churches in Asia and Africa, while giving the Spanish crown responsibility for churches in the Americas. In a significant exception to these general guidelines, the Philippines were attached to the Americas, thus falling under the jurisdiction of Madrid.[4] The second papal decree, issued by Pope Alexander VI in 1493, grew out of the first and in response to Columbus's explorations in the New World: it drew a line on the globe, assigning newly discovered lands east and west of the line to either the Spanish or the Portuguese crown. Unlike the earlier Padroado and Patronato grants, this papal directive divided the territories of the globe for the purposes of exploration and subsequent political authority rather than evangelization. Like the first papal grant, the second had its ambiguities and points of territorial conflict. Less than two years after it was promulgated, the two parties met to revise the line of demarcation. By the terms of the 1494 Treaty of Tordesillas, portions of the Americas, notably what would become the Brazilian

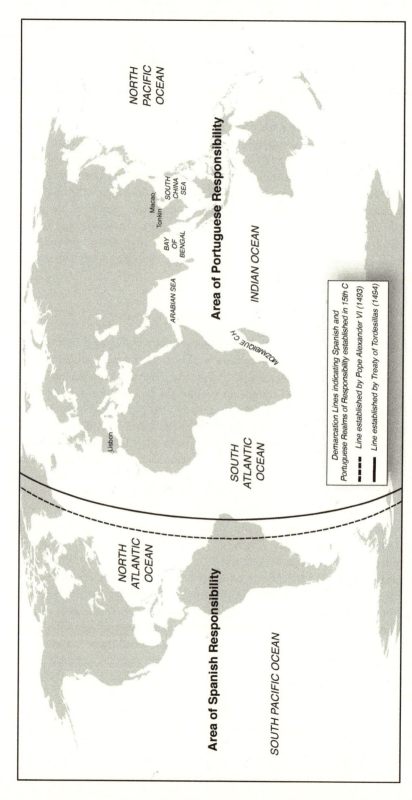

MAP 2. Global demarcation lines drawn by the 1493 papal directive and the 1494 Treaty of Tordesillas for the purposes of dividing ecclesiastical authority and responsibility between the Spanish and Portuguese crowns.

territories, were shifted from Spanish to Portuguese control. The papal grant of the Padroado and the later territorial divisions spelled out in the Treaty of Tordesillas thus ostensibly demarcated the realms of Iberian influence around the globe and shaped the expansion of Catholicism into Asia and the Americas.

While these geographical delineations were established to head off territorial and ecclesiastical disputes between the powerful Iberian monarchs, the situation in the mission fields themselves was, not surprisingly, much more complicated. The superficially neat division of the globe gave way to the realities of distance and limited oversight, and this administrative structure was frequently adjudicated in an ad hoc manner. This resulted in imprecise boundaries, disputed regions of control, and differing interpretations of territorial and ecclesiastical responsibility. In the first place, agreements reached in and directives sent from Europe carried less weight in the remote corners of the globe where actual mission activity was occurring. Communication was irregular, unreliable, and time-consuming. Equally important, there were few enforcement mechanisms in place, meaning that local decision making was frequently the primary method either for resolving disputes or for creating them in the first place. The fact that the initial division of the globe had stemmed in part from squabbling between the Portuguese and the Spanish meant that each sought ways to interpret (or ignore) these agreements to their own advantage.[5] The complexities and the challenges they presented grew over the course of the sixteenth and seventeenth centuries. The rising power of other (non-Iberian) European states and the growing desire of subsequent popes to more directly influence the expansion of the global Catholic Church meant that both the Treaty of Tordesillas and the Padroado and Patronato grants came under increasing pressure.[6] In many ways, both sets of agreements gradually became obsolete, even as their terms were not explicitly overturned.[7] Yet they continued to be invoked by their respective Iberian claimants as they engaged in a fierce rivalry played out in mercantile and missionary activity.[8]

A brief survey of the early European Christian contacts suggests the complexity that defined the Vietnamese mission field. The first Christian missionary efforts in the Vietnamese territories occurred in the early sixteenth century when a small group of Spanish Dominicans arrived at the important trading port of Hội An along the central coast. Their presence was short-lived and no permanent mission was established, nor were any churches created. In the 1550s a Portuguese Dominican, Father Gaspar da Cruz, passed through Hà Tiên in the far southern reaches of what would become the Vietnamese realm, presumably on his way to the mission field in Cambodia.[9] Somewhat later, in 1583, a pair of Spanish Franciscans, Bartolomeo Ruiz and Francisco Montilla, arrived in the southern Vietnamese realms known as Cochinchina.[10] None of these visits, however, yielded any tangible results, and while another Franciscan priest arrived in Đà Nẵng in 1583 and managed to reside there for two years, he too was unsuccessful in establishing an enduring foothold in Vietnamese territory.[11] Trương Bá Cẩn's comprehensive survey of the Christian missionary presence on Vietnamese soil prior to the seventeenth century speaks also of Augustinian priests visiting the southern realm and mentions Portuguese and French priests among those who were active in these initial contacts.[12]

As this list of early mission visits—featuring Dominicans, Franciscans, and Augustinians—suggests, the Padroado authority notwithstanding, the Vietnamese realm was a site of nascent competition for converts. Indeed, this active rivalry was a defining element of the global propagation of Catholicism that had begun in earnest in the fifteenth century.[13] These contests played out both on the ground among squabbling missionaries and their followers and in the corridors of Catholic power in Rome and the capitals of Europe. Unsurprisingly, national allegiances were a significant component of this contest, for missionaries represented not only particular orders but also distinct national backgrounds that further shaped their view of the mission. The seventeenth- and eighteenth-century mission field in the Vietnamese realms included not only Portuguese and Spanish missionary priests but also Italians, Germans, and Frenchmen. Contests between these men reflected doctrinal disagreements but also, to an extent, geopolitical differences playing out in the Europe from which they had come. As a nation whose fortunes had been in decline in Asia since the sixteenth century, Portugal was particularly jealous of its remaining claims to authority, especially those articulated in the Padroado Real. During the seventeenth and eighteenth centuries, its rulers fought a protracted rearguard action to defend these rights, though with limited success.[14]

NEW GEOGRAPHIES FOR THE VIETNAMESE

The geographies of Vietnamese Catholicism were thus significantly shaped at the global level in terms of the fifteenth-century territorial divisions between Spain and Portugal. Such higher-order geographies, however, remained abstractions for Vietnamese Catholics. For most Tonkinese Christians the local manifestations of religious geographies had more immediate relevance. When European Catholic missionaries arrived in Tonkin, they found an already elaborated administrative geography at work, one largely arrayed along geopolitical lines. People were grouped into villages; villages were in turn grouped into districts, which were collected into prefectures, which were finally aggregated into provinces.[15] While the villages had coalesced over the centuries to reflect locally determined forms of self-organization, the larger groupings of villages were fixed by the state, which periodically surveyed its realms and examined these territorial arrangements. At times adjustments were made: territorial units were merged to create larger units or divided to create smaller ones. Occasionally such actions were accompanied by name changes for regions or subregions, either to reflect the combining of units or for less tangible reasons such as to improve local fortunes or to punish regions for political transgressions.¹⁶ Such changes were rarely made with reference to local interests, and in some ways the alterations made little difference to people whose lives revolved around the largely immutable village-level structures. In short, social collectivities, whatever their reconfigurations, were determined chiefly by political and administrative concerns.

The arrival of Roman Catholicism initially did little to alter this organizational system. In the early years of the mission project the numbers of converts remained small, and their social and geographical realm of influence was still marginal. However, as the numbers of Vietnamese adherents increased, missionaries began to address the logistics of organizing their growing congregations. Estimates for the number of early converts vary substantially, but some suggest that by 1639 there were already nearly 80,000 Christians in Tonkin, a figure that increased more than fourfold to 350,000 by 1663.¹⁷ As it had done elsewhere, the Roman Catholic Church introduced new geographies representing realms of religious authority and responsibility, including parishes and subparishes, but also larger areas of responsibility in the form of dioceses under the authority of more senior religious authorities. Vietnamese found themselves embedded within these territorial divisions. Missionaries began by creating congregations (or subparishes) as the smallest ecclesiastical unit. This was eventually followed by the creation of parishes that grouped communities with sizable Christian populations. Eventually, even larger aggregates of Catholics were created in the form of vicariates, which grouped parishes across large geographical territories. Unlike the existing political administrative boundaries of the Vietnamese state, the boundaries drawn by the church—whether for congregations, parishes, or vicariates—had less to do with land than with those who inhabited it. The concern of the priests was for the communities of people under their spiritual authority rather than for the territories in which they lived. For Vietnamese Christians, these divisions, whether at the level of vicariates or parishes, represented a radical new organization of space and a fundamental reorientation of their relationship to their fellow Vietnamese. For the first time, Vietnamese populations were being grouped with reference not to local political administrations but to ecclesiastical hierarchies being set by European religious leaders. Vietnamese Christians found in this new territorial template a different form of group identification. One now belonged simultaneously to a civic territorial structure and to an ecclesiastical territorial arrangement, and the two sometimes had little to do with one another. One's sense of territorial belonging could now be expressed in very different terms than had been the case previously.¹⁸

Vietnamese Catholics were now subject to both civic and Catholic authority. This simultaneous exercise of civil and religious authority represented a significant departure from traditional forms of religious organization. Where Roman Catholicism brought with it these kinds of territorial and ecclesiastical structures, existing Vietnamese religious practices had featured no such institutional framework. Folk religious practices were centered on the village, and people's obligations to these rituals and to their follow villagers were understood and enforced by custom. Buddhism, which existed in tandem with folk practices (and indeed frequently merged with them), was also noninstitutional as far as villagers were concerned. The practice of Buddhism was personal, again centered on local temples, with little reference to temples in other villages or places.[19] In short, the overlapping forms of authority created a newly complicated geopolitical landscape for Vietnamese Catholics. Sometimes these multiple layers of authority had little importance for Tonkinese Christians, but at other times they loomed large, as when church leaders imposed binding religious regulations upon those who lived in their particular jurisdictions.

As these lines of ecclesiastical authority were being laid out across the Vietnamese lands at multiple scales, new configurations were emerging, along with new claims upon Vietnamese living within these newly bounded spaces. At some level this project could be seen as a form of religious colonialism, not merely because of the territorial claims, but also because the claims were being contested among and between competing groups of religious orders and powers, as well as nations. This new mapping taking place in Đại Việt has not drawn the attention of scholars, yet it bears examination, for it also had considerable implications for at least some of the peoples living in these spaces. Historians and geographers have tended to look more at the ways in which European states or their military agents carved up the world on behalf of their territorial claims, but few have considered the ways in which religious groups created their own claims in similar fashion.

A good example of the focus on secular state authorities' projects to delineate territorial space is Thongchai Winichakul's *Siam Mapped* (1988), an examination of the emerging "geobody" of Siam. The nineteenth-century European race for colonies was bound up with a determination to draw lines of demarcation across the surface of the globe.[20] Thongchai demonstrated how such lines, drawn, in the Siamese case, by British and French surveyors along the western and eastern frontiers of the Thai realm, had enormous implications for the royal court in Bangkok and also for the peoples through whose territories these lines were drawn. Prior to these aggressive mapping projects, divisions among the various mainland Southeast Asian political realms had largely been a function of centralized state power and its projection, rather than arbitrary and unenforceable border lines. This had begun to change over the eighteenth and early nineteenth centuries with the growth of increasingly bureaucratized mainland states and an awareness of territorial divisions. Nonetheless, as Thongchai's examination of the Thai case makes clear, nineteenth-century colonial geographic imaginings dramatically reshaped the political and territorial landscape of Southeast Asia, underscoring the implications of the delineation of political authority.

Thongchai's examination of Siam shows very clearly the import of such line-drawing enterprises and their consequences in the later nineteenth century. While his study focuses on a small portion of mainland Southeast Asia, it could readily be extended to cases in Africa and the Middle East as well. What Thongchai does not discuss, however, is that Europeans had already been drawing lines on Asian lands for some time, and in ways that had little to do with colonial territorial or economic claims. The case of Catholicism in Asia generally, and in Tonkin more particularly, represents a significantly earlier manifestation of the European impact upon territorial divisions. It also makes clear that those who inscribed such lines were not always European colonial officials (or their agents), nor were they always at hand when the lines were being drawn like the French surveyors carefully demarcating the space of French Indochina from that of Siam. Whether we consider the remote and completely arbitrary demarcation of the Treaty of Tordesillas, or the more direct divisions of the Vietnamese realm into vicariates and parishes in the later seventeenth century, we see significant interventions with local consequences.

On the one hand, the Vietnamese territorial example is demonstrably different from that of Siam. Its rulers and officials had adopted the Chinese administrative structure with its territorial structures and hierarchies and had applied it (to the extent that they had the capacity to do so) across the Vietnamese landscape. The result had been a relatively elaborated system of fixed (if not always fully demarcated) boundaries between administrative units of increasingly smaller sizes, from provinces through districts to prefectures to villages and hamlets. In short, the Europeans could teach the Vietnamese little about the practice of establishing territorial boundaries. What they could do, however, was introduce the notion that the world might be divided into administrative hierarchies and that peoples could be grouped in ways that made no reference to centralized, secular political authorities. The Catholic missionaries in the Vietnamese realm, and their superiors at an increasingly distant remove (whether in Macao, Goa, or remote Rome), created new structures of division that brought with them a politics of their own. At one level, these structures were designed to organize Vietnamese for purposes of ecclesiastical authority. At another level, and one that perhaps superseded the first, they were designed to divide territory specifically between various missionaries and missionary organizations in order to avoid the conflicts that had broken out and would continue to do so among the contending proselytizers. Indeed, the globalized mission project was built upon the foundation of precisely such an objective. The Treaty of Tordesillas had been drawn up, not to benefit Asian or American converts-to-be, but to keep the Spanish and Portuguese from outright warfare over their claims to mission work and ecclesiastical authority.

Clearly, there were profoundly significant differences between the mapping described by Thongchai on the nineteenth-century mainland and that which took place between the fifteenth and eighteenth centuries among various global missionaries. Yet as Thongchai has so eloquently argued, historical accounts of Asia, and Southeast Asia in particular, cannot ignore the profound consequences of such mapping, The maps were not necessarily the proximate causes of subsequent events, but they nonetheless determined some of the trajectories of local histories, whether these concerned the crafting of Siam as a modern nation or the contestation among Vietnamese Catholics about religious traditions and transnational affiliations.

SHIFTING VANTAGE POINTS

While my book will explore these complex geographies and the ways in which they were created and then shaped the lives of Vietnamese Catholics, its primary focus remains Philiphê Bỉnh. This allows me to consider the life of an earlier Vietnamese Catholic in great detail and to argue for the agency of Vietnamese converts in this early modern period. Much existing scholarship on Vietnamese Catholicism has, to varying degrees, focused more on the perspective of the European missionaries than on that of Vietnamese Catholics themselves. This is a product of the available sources, which are largely letters, reports, and other accounts written by missionaries. While the voices and considerations of Vietnamese do sometimes appear, they are rarely foregrounded. Because of the enormous body of writings Bỉnh left behind, we can view at least a portion of the history of Vietnamese Catholicism from a different vantage point, that of a Vietnamese Christian.

This question of perspective was memorably raised by John Smail half a century ago in his seminal article "On the Possibility of an Autonomous History of Southeast Asia" (1961).[21] In it, Smail argued that a basic problem with much of the historical writing about Southeast Asia was its privileging of the Europeans' vantage point. This had rendered Southeast Asian figures largely indistinct and undifferentiated and had given lesser weight to their concerns and participation in history. In short they lacked any kind of historical agency. I was reminded of Smail's assertion when I happened upon Charles Boxer's passing comment about Bỉnh in his monumental study of the Portuguese overseas realm, *The Portuguese Seaborne Empire, 1415–1825* (1969). In it, Boxer described Bỉnh as "a rather pathetic figure" who represented the last gasp of the Vietnamese tradition of Portuguese-inspired Catholicism.[22] From the vantage point of the large Portuguese empire, or that of the Vatican surveying its global missionary project, Bỉnh might indeed be regarded as insignificant and "pathetic." The battle over a new bishop for Tonkin, of paramount significance for Bỉnh, was for European church authorities merely a minor skirmish between Lisbon and Rome. From the Vietnamese perspective, however, Bỉnh does not look "pathetic." Rather, he appears heroic and daring, undaunted in the face of long odds. While Bỉnh's story cannot represent an "autonomous history" as envisioned by Smail—indeed, the interconnections of global historical forces like religions make such projects chimerical—it does offer a legitimate alternative to existing accounts and a new way to think about how historical forces affect and are engaged with by Southeast Asian actors.

This new vantage point not only enables me to reveal the agency of Vietnamese Catholics and their ability to contend with the power of the institutional church but also suggests the emergence of new forms of Vietnamese identity that became possible in the early modern era. Both Li Tana and Keith Taylor have suggested that this period saw the emergence of "new ways of being Vietnamese," which involved the physical movement southward of Vietnamese settlers into territories that later became known as Đàng Trong (the Inner Region) or Cochinchina.[23] The case of Vietnamese Catholics, whose emergence coincides temporally with the demographic shift Li and Taylor discuss, also represented an opportunity to be Vietnamese in a different way. In their case, however, it required no physical relocation to begin anew; instead, their own geographical shift was mental and ideological, though with equally profound consequences. Thus the introduction of Roman Catholicism brought with it alternative conceptualizations of the world and the place of Vietnamese in it. Bỉnh's writings reveal these complex possibilities in which Vietnamese thought-worlds were being transformed and expanded to include Europeans, the religion they brought with them, and the larger world encompassed both by the concrete realities of missionary networks and by the imagined geographies of ancient Christianity. Religious needs and circumstances drove some Vietnamese to leave their homeland and to travel along the missionary networks that had emerged since the early sixteenth century. These networks linked Europe and Asia, and while they served primarily to bring European missionaries of various religious orders to Asia, they also enabled Vietnamese to reverse the direction of this travel.

STRUCTURE OF THE BOOK

This work has been organized in roughly chronological fashion, tracing the course of Bỉnh's life from his birth in Tonkin in 1759 to his death in Lisbon in 1833. At the same time, it addresses the shifting Catholic geographies that structured both why and where he traveled. It uses Bỉnh's later writings to reveal the larger changes that occurred in the worldview of Vietnamese Catholics. While Bỉnh's life provides the overall arc of the story, at times the historical and geographical elements will be more prominent. This is particularly true in the opening chapters of the book, in which I establish and contextualize the ecclesiastical geographies that determined the course of Bỉnh's actions. Bỉnh's life can be understood in terms of three broad time periods: the early years, in which he emerged as a seminarian and grew to become a representative of his Catholic community; the middle years, in which he became an active champion of this community and traveled to Lisbon on its behalf; and the later years, in which he took up his pen to leave behind a significant literary legacy. This tripartite division is somewhat temporally imbalanced, with the greatest amount of fine-grained detail available only for the period between 1793 and 1807. But thinking of Bỉnh's life in this way allows us to consider the distinctive geographical dimensions of each period of Bỉnh's life, from the fundamental geographical structures that shaped the global and Tonkinese mission fields, to the ecclesiastical political landscape in Europe and Lisbon that determined the course of Bỉnh's project in Europe, to the mental landscapes and new geographies that Bỉnh addressed through his writings while he was in the Portuguese capital. In doing so, I suggest the profound importance of geography, not only because of how it shaped the direction of Vietnamese Catholic lives, none more so than that of Bỉnh himself, but also because of the invaluable lens it offers for helping us to understand the transformations that Vietnamese Christians experienced, ones chronicled by Father Bỉnh in his later writings.

The first section of the book introduces Bỉnh and his emergence as a singularly important figure for his community of Portuguese Jesuit loyalists. At the same time, however, it includes a necessary detour to explore the complicated geographies of Catholicism that defined the Tonkinese experience of the faith and its ecclesiastical authority. This helps situate Bỉnh and his community within a very specific context that shaped what would follow. I describe aspects of his religious training and service from 1775 until his ordination in 1793. I then examine the period between 1793 and 1796, during which Bỉnh planned and made his journey to Europe. This is followed by a description of Bỉnh's six-month ocean voyage from Tonkin to Lisbon, sailing on an English vessel from Macao across the Indian Ocean to St. Helena in the South Atlantic before boarding a Portuguese boat to reach Lisbon in July of 1796.

The second part of the book marks a shift in focus, for it details both Bỉnh's efforts to secure a new bishop for Tonkin and the new political and ecclesiastical landscapes that shaped his mission. While Bỉnh's immediate target was the ruler of Portugal, Dom João, he quickly came to understand that there were multiple audiences for his campaign. These ranged from local clerics to Portuguese officials, and from the Vatican envoy in Lisbon to the pope himself. Moreover, larger geopolitical factors intruded upon Bỉnh's efforts, most notably the Napoleonic Wars, whose threat frequently distracted Dom João's attention, and the eventual Franco-Spanish invasion that ultimately forced the Portuguese ruler to flee the country in 1807. Bỉnh was initially treated as an exotic addition to the royal court, which bolstered his early efforts. However, the passage of time and the frequent intrusion of more serious matters of state weakened his influence and the likelihood of success. I follow the trail of disappointment that marked Bỉnh's efforts as he shuttled between the court and numerous bureaucratic offices seeking support. Chapter 6 then offers a different vantage point and examines the aftermath of Bỉnh's departure from the perspective of those left behind in Macao and Tonkin. It shows the importance of the letters exchanged by the two sides for providing updates of their respective circumstances and for conveying urgent messages. It concludes by discussing the impact of the arrival of a new bishop for Macao in 1803, which marked the last chapter in the Padroado community's long resistance effort.

The last section of this book begins with chapter 7 after the departure of the Portuguese ruler for Brazil in 1807, when Bỉnh's life took a new direction. With the Portuguese ruler no longer accessible, and with Portugal alternatively under French and British military authority, Bỉnh could no longer pursue his mission. Instead, he began to devote his time to service as a priest and to writing. I begin this section of the book by using Bỉnh's notebooks as a window into the quotidian aspects of his life in Lisbon. He wrote of his living arrangements, the kinds of foods he ate, the sorts of clothing he wore, the forms of medical treatment he and his friends received, the kinds of employment they found, and the financial arrangements that sustained them. In this section I also discuss Bỉnh's many observations of life in early nineteenth-century Portugal. I conclude with a lengthy chapter examining Bỉnh's literary undertaking. While he produced several written volumes prior to 1807, most of this early output consisted of copies of existing texts in Portuguese and translations of a small amount of liturgical material. The vast majority of his written output dates from the second and third decades of the nineteenth century, reflecting the time now available to him. These texts are significant in themselves but also provide insights regarding Bỉnh's worldview and his religious sentiments.

SOURCES AND LIFE WRITING

It is possible to tell Bỉnh's story only because his writings, comprising at least twenty-four bound notebooks totaling more than ten thousand pages, were somehow preserved in the Vatican Library. Sometime after his death in 1833, virtually all of Bỉnh's notebooks were deposited in the Vatican Library and attached to the Borgia collections, which originated with the historian and antiquarian manuscript collector Cardinal Stefano Borgia (1731–1804). There they sat, unremarked upon, for a century, before being discovered in the late 1940s by Father George Schurhammer, a German Jesuit priest and scholar. Perhaps the twentieth century's preeminent historian of the Jesuits, Schurhammer had scoured the Vatican and other archives for materials on the order's past. During his research he came across Bỉnh's writings and published an article on them in 1951. After this several Vietnamese Catholic researchers began to explore these materials.[24] In writing about Bỉnh, I have been forced to draw largely on his own literary output, which constitutes the most comprehensive guide to his life. I have read through most of his own notebooks, focusing in particular on his journals and observations about life in Tonkin and Portugal. But for his writings, Bỉnh would barely represent a buried footnote in the history of Vietnamese Catholicism or Vietnamese encounters with Europe. Consequently, any account of Bỉnh must rely, to a seemingly inordinate degree, on the writings of the subject himself. Without his writings it would be virtually impossible to write about Bỉnh at all, and in many respects it is because of his writings that Bỉnh is worth examining in the first place.

My heavy reliance on Bỉnh's writings means, in some respects, that this story is as much autobiographical as biographical. Its broad narrative is recorded by Bỉnh himself. His notebooks and observations provide much of the content and some of the structure of this work. My interventions are to contextualize, reorder, and amplify Bỉnh's own record. My approach to Bỉnh's life is inspired in part by a work about another ordinary person of the eighteenth century, albeit one geographically and culturally remote from him. Laurel Thatcher Ulrich's *A Midwife's Tale: The Story of Martha Ballard* is an account of an ordinary person that draws heavily from her subject's diary, which describes the travails and joys of life as a midwife in colonial New England.[25] The diary provided Ulrich the narrative structure, to which she added external detail to contextualize her subject's life.[26] Ulrich argues that her book is unlike a great deal of the new "social history" because she looks at a particular and distinctive individual rather than a larger agglomeration of people. At the same time, and in the tradition of social history, she tells the story of Ballard within the context of the community in which she lived and worked. Like Ulrich I am not simply channeling Bỉnh and offering an unmediated retelling of his life experiences; I am also examining him as an individual, seeking to understand what motivated him, why he reacted to events and circumstances the way he did, and how he was able to sustain his commitment to a mission that dragged on for years, seemingly without an end.

In a recent study of Southeast Asian life writing, Roxana Waterson argues for the importance of considering the life stories of ordinary people in the region's history. As she points out, "The lives lived by ordinary people have . . . in fact been endlessly extraordinary. It is not that such lives merely reflect the history that was in the making, for their actions and experiences were also helping to shape it."[27] I would argue that Bỉnh exemplifies this point, as a person who was simultaneously ordinary and extraordinary, and who actively engaged with the history through which he lived. Bỉnh's was a life deeply shaped by a succession of large-scale movements, conflicts, and ideologies, and as such it reveals how these events affect an individual person. Yet his is also a story of the ways in which an individual self-consciously responds to these kinds of historical structures, for Bỉnh's writings make clear that he understood the larger forces that were directly affecting his life. Moreover, while at some level he could be considered more a victim than a shaper of these forces, and ultimately one of history's "losers," Bỉnh defied the dictum that history is written by the victors, recording his own story in a tone that alternated between humility and defiance.

There remain, of course some significant limitations to what these notebooks can tell us about Bỉnh's life. The first is that they constitute Bỉnh's own view of the trajectory of his life and thus have both the advantages and disadvantages of an insider's account. Some of the information contained in his notebooks can be verified through references in other sources, but much cannot. The second limitation, as noted earlier, is that Bỉnh offers very little detail about his life prior to the 1790s and only limited glimpses of his life after the Portuguese ruler's departure for Brazil in 1807. And what he did record of his life appears all to have been compiled many years after the events being described, representing an organized reminiscence more than a journal. Consequently, these writings have all of the benefits and drawbacks of hindsight, recorded with the knowledge of where they fit into the trajectory of his life.

While Bỉnh's own writings represent the primary raw materials for this work, I have supplemented them with a wide range of other contemporary sources. Most notably, I have drawn on missionary letters contained in the archives of the Missions Étrangères de Paris (MEP) in Paris, whose priests were active in Tonkin during Bỉnh's lifetime. I have also relied on published volumes of letters from other MEP and Jesuit clergy working in Tonkin and in Macao and numerous letters from the bishop whom the Portuguese ruler eventually sent to Macao. Further, I have drawn on a range of contemporary published accounts by travelers to Lisbon in an attempt to sketch life in that city during Bỉnh's time there. Portugal was a prominent destination for European travelers of the eighteenth and early nineteenth centuries. Many English visitors were drawn to Portugal for its climate and its reputed cultural charms, but travelers from Germany, France, and Spain made the trip to Lisbon as well. To some degree, Bỉnh belongs to this group of early nineteenth-century foreign visitors to Portugal, and his observations of daily life in and around Lisbon have much in common with the travel accounts written by Europeans. Eyewitness accounts of the Peninsular Wars (1807–14) during which the British battled Napoleon's forces for control of Portugal are also useful for giving a sense of that particular moment in Bỉnh's life as he lived through the French occupation of Lisbon and the subsequent British encampment there.

To supplement the written record, I have collected visual depictions of people with whom Bỉnh interacted and of places he visited. While I was unfortunately unable to locate a portrait of Bỉnh himself (if one was ever composed), I have included images of the numerous individuals who figured prominently in his life and whom he met at one time or another. These include portraits or engravings of a diverse cast of characters from the bishop of Macao to the patriarch of the Portuguese Catholic Church to the man briefly appointed as bishop to Tonkin.

Other images include those of Bính's patron the prince regent of Portugal and future king Joao VI, as well as the papal nuncios in Lisbon who challenged Bính's efforts at every turn. And I have collected a combination of contemporary maps of Macao, Goa, St. Helena, and Lisbon and engraved scenes from some of these same places, which I have supplemented with my own photographs of sites in Bính's home village, the ecclesiastical landscape in Macao, and the two residences Bính called home during his years in Lisbon.

Finally, while much of my time was spent in archives and libraries, I also traced Bính's footsteps from his home village in the coastal province of what is today northern Vietnam to Macao and finally to Lisbon. In 2005 I spent a day walking the streets of Macao, visiting the numerous churches or remains thereof that Bính would have seen and worshipped at in the 1790s. That same year I spent several weeks in Lisbon to gain a sense of the place in which Bính spent nearly half of his life. Although much has changed in the past two centuries, the broad contours of the old city remain, as do many of its structures. In my peregrinations through Lisbon, I attempted to see Lisbon through Bính's eyes—the vistas, the churches, the markets—and I hope that some of this sense of place comes through in this account. Finally, in 2010 I was able to visit Bính's home village and parts of the region of coastal northern Vietnam in which he grew up and first served as a priest. This allowed me to understand the riverine landscape that so shaped his travels and to picture his regular movement between different communities in the 1790s.

While this book explores larger issues of globalizing Catholicism and Vietnamese engagements with its political networks, and at times must set aside its main character to do so, my primary objective throughout is to tell a story of Bính as a person. The inspiration for this book, and the motivation that carried me through this long project, was my desire to humanize an ordinary Vietnamese man who lived in the early modern period. History is only as important as the people who inhabit and experience it, for it is these individuals who play primary roles in shaping the grand patterns and the complex interactions of the world. Stripped of distinct people, history provides only limited understanding and questionable relevance. In the end I am convinced that history must be about individuals. All the descriptions and analyses of larger patterns, movements, and trends matter only to the extent that they reflect or shape the courses of real people's lives. We need to articulate the life stories of people, both famous and ordinary, because it is in such stories that larger historical themes are made real. As Waterson notes about the process of collecting and recording life stories, "We see in these stories the self, however variably culturally constructed, confronting a set of historical circumstances, and making a life out of the opportunities available. Such narratives shed light not only on particular historical events or conjunctures lived through, but in a more general sense, have things to tell us about the nature of the human experience."[28] The abstractions of European missionary work, transcontinental cultural interactions, political violence and turmoil, and linguistic evolution become concrete in particular individuals, who are themselves engines of historical change, sometimes consciously and sometimes unwittingly. Bỉnh is one such man, and his story is important for what it tells us about these themes, even as it is significant for what it tells us about a single human being.

A NOTE ON PLACE NAMES: TONKIN, ANNAM, ĐẠI VIỆT, ĐÀNG NGOÀI

Throughout this book I am speaking about a country that today is known as Vietnam but that in the eighteenth and early nineteenth centuries bore a complex and shifting set of labels, applied by insiders and outsiders. Using *Vietnam* would be anachronistic before the term came into formal (albeit infrequent) use with its adoption by the Nguyễn state in 1804. Consequently, in this book I use a number of different labels that change as the context in which they are used changes. At times I use *Tonkin* for convenience in referring to the northern Vietnamese realms under the control of the Trịnh lords until at least 1786. I do so in part because Bỉnh himself frequently used this Europeanized version of *Đông Kinh* (Eastern Capital). But he also used the more generic term *Annam*, which might encompass the entire Vietnamese territories, this time using a label imposed by the Chinese and also taken up by Europeans in the seventeenth and eighteenth centuries. When I wish to speak of the country in a larger sense removed from Bỉnh's vantage point or that of European missionaries, I use the name *Đại Việt* (the Great Việt), used by the state in its diplomatic encounters or in state documents until the dawn of the nineteenth century. On occasion I also use the local vernacular terms employed by Vietnamese to refer to the two separated realms of the Trịnh and Nguyễn lords, *Đàng Ngoài* and *Đàng Trong* respectively. Bỉnh used these to label his two-volume history of Vietnamese Catholicism, though he used the terms only sporadically elsewhere in his writings. While I realize this is potentially confusing, I believe it is more historically precise, and in any case context should almost always make the labels clear.

1

Philiphê Bỉnh and the Catholic Geographies of Tonkin

Philiphê Bỉnh, who would later also style himself as Felippe do Rosario, introduced himself to an imagined future reader in the preface to his notebook of miscellany, *Sách sổ sang chép các việc* (Notebook that transmits and records all matters):

> I am the priest Philiphê Bỉnh, of the province of Hải Dương, prefecture of Hạ Hồng, district of Vĩnh Lại, village of Ngải Am, hamlet of Địa Linh. I was born in the year 1759, the same year that King Jose of the country Portugal destroyed the Order of the Virtuous Lord Jesus in his realm. When I reached the age of seventeen in the year 1775 and entered my teacher's home, the order had already been destroyed two years previously in Rome, because the Virtuous Pope Clemente XIV disbanded the Order of the Virtuous Lord Jesus on the 22nd of July in the year 1773. However, prior to disbanding the order, and at the beginning of that year, eight members of the order arrived in Annam: Master Tito and Master Bảo Lộc [Paul] had gone to Quảng [Nam], and the rest of the missionaries, Masters Ni, Thiện, Phan, Luis, and Cần traveled to Đàng Ngoài ["Tonkin"]. Thus, in that year [1775], I went with Master Luis and left my home.[1]

This brief introduction precisely situates Bỉnh in a particular place and at a distinct moment in time, while also foreshadowing the complex trajectory his life would eventually take. It is noteworthy for how Bỉnh positions himself geographically both locally and globally. He begins by describing the location of his home village, using a standard Vietnamese formulation that proceeds from the province through lower levels of administrative organization all the way down to the hamlet. He then shifts registers from a localized Vietnamese geographical articulation to a globalized one, one that speaks to the new geographical realities of his Catholic community. He writes of Portugal—his community's point of origin—and of Rome, the center of global Catholic authority but also the locale from which the order to disband the Jesuits emerged. Bỉnh also refers to the larger Vietnamese context in which Vietnamese Catholics and European missionaries lived and worshipped—the land of Quảng (Cochinchina) and the northern region of Đàng Ngoài (Tonkin) in which he lived.

From this introduction, we learn that Bỉnh was a native of Hải Dương, which lay to the southeast of Thăng Long (present-day Hà Nội) and was part of the coastal region drained by the Red River and its branches. A network of canals and rivers crisscrossed his home district of Vĩnh Lại, which lay directly on the coast.[2] While otherwise unremarkable, Bỉnh's home village of Ngải Am did merit mention in nineteenth-century geographical texts as the site of a temple dedicated to a thirteenth-century Chinese empress dowager, famous for having committed suicide by drowning rather than risk capture by pursuing Mongol troops. Her spirit later manifested itself in Ngải Am, and several miracles were attributed to it, prompting locals to erect the temple.[3]

Bỉnh's hamlet itself was fairly ordinary, but the larger prefecture in which it was situated had a certain historical reputation. According to Phan Huy Chú's early nineteenth-century gazetteer, the *Hoàng Việt địa dư chí* (Geographical records of the imperial Việt), Hạ Hồng prefecture was noted for its production of upright Confucian scholars.[4] Bỉnh's home district of Vĩnh Lại made two notable contributions to their ranks. One of these, Đào Công Chính, was a child prodigy who passed the local civil service examination at the age of thirteen, the *tiến sĩ* (presented scholar) examination in 1661 at the age of twenty-three, and later served on an embassy to China.[5] The other was one of the most famous Vietnamese scholar-officials of the premodern period, Nguyễn Bỉnh Khiêm (1491–1585), a man whom Keith Taylor has described as the "moral center" of sixteenth-century Đại Việt.[6] Khiêm first served the Lê dynasty and then, when it was overthrown in 1527 by the Mạc family, agreed to serve the new rulers. After several years of service to the new dynasty, Khiêm retired to his home village, where he spent most of his time composing poetry.[7] After his death, a temple to Khiêm's memory was erected in Vĩnh Lại. This temple has been refurbished numerous times during the succeeding centuries and is today a popular tourist destination. Indeed, it is probably the only real tourist attraction in this small corner of Vietnam.[8]

Although it produced a few notable scholars, the region was primarily known for its agriculture, as the land was well watered by its numerous rivers, which deposited rich topsoil along their courses. Sericulture was particularly important, with many households involved in raising silkworms and selling their cocoons. Many families also cultivated areca palm, cotton, and water-pipe tobacco, as an early nineteenth-century gazetteer records.[9] Today residents continue to produce tobacco, which can be seen along the roadsides during the harvest season spread out on drying racks, smoldering fires lit under them to speed the curing process.

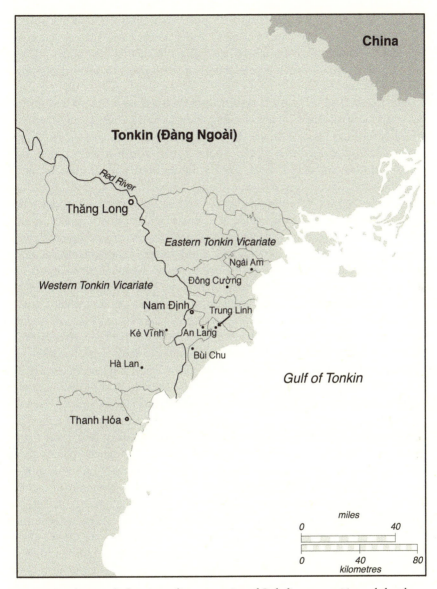

MAP 3. Map showing the locations of important sites of Catholic communities and churches in coastal Tonkin. It also shows the dividing line between the Eastern and Western Vicariates of Tonkin as of 1678.

These tobacco crops are alternated with paddy rice production as the seasons change, offering the area some measure of crop diversification. These practices are probably not greatly altered from the late eighteenth century, and Bỉnh undoubtedly witnessed the rituals of tobacco drying and rice transplanting during his early childhood years.

Vĩnh Lại was also very close to the sea, to which it was connected by a wide river, and given its coastal location it was among the sites to which Roman Catholicism spread in the early years of the mission. Many of the early Portuguese Jesuit missionaries landed along this section of Tonkin's coast, which stretched southward from the modern city of Hải Phòng. The coastal denizens, poor farmers, but especially those practicing maritime occupations such as fishing and trading, became the primary targets of conversion efforts.[10] During the seventeenth century this region of Tonkin became a stronghold of Vietnamese Catholicism, and the coastal landscape quickly became dotted with modest wooden churches, religious houses, and schools. The European missionaries took advantage of the easy travel afforded by the region's many rivers to spread their message and subsequently to minister to scattered communities, many of whom did not have their own permanent clergy.

The arrival of these Portuguese Jesuit missionary priests in Tonkin had been an outgrowth of the order's very successful evangelizing project in Japan, initiated by Francis Xavier in the 1540s. This Jesuit mission to Japan had been dominated by Portuguese priests (later joined by smaller numbers of Spaniards), but when the Japanese ruler abruptly cracked down on the new religion and its adherents in the 1590s these missionaries were forced to look elsewhere in Asia to continue their mission. They turned their sights to the still largely unexplored lands of Đại Việt. For logistical reasons these first Vietnamese Portuguese missions were formally carried out under the auspices of the Jesuit "Province of Japan," and it was to this existing ecclesiastical territory that the newly opened Vietnamese church territories were appended.[11] Consequently, the earliest Vietnamese Catholics, guided by Portuguese Jesuit priests, found themselves classified as an annex to the distant and culturally dissimilar Japanese Province, evidence of the peculiarities of Catholic ecclesiastical geographies that would persist in the following centuries. For Vietnamese converts, however, it was not this Japanese connection but the one to Portugal, the homeland of their new priests, that was significant. Indeed, the Portuguese connection led many Vietnamese to refer to the newly introduced religion as "Đạo Hoa Lang"—the Way of the Portuguese, a label that survived the subsequent national diversification of the mission field.[12]

Although it did not have the initial success enjoyed by the Jesuit ventures in the southern Vietnamese territory of Cochinchina, the mission to Tonkin slowly took root after some hesitation on the part of the Trịnh rulers, seigniorial lords who controlled a kingdom nominally ruled by the Lê dynasty. By 1626 the first priests were permitted to reside in the capital Thăng Long.[13] The Jesuits' primary successes, however, lay in the coastal regions, which provided both easier access by boat and relatively safe distance from potentially hostile authorities at the more inland capital. In these areas, and particularly the stretch between what are today the cities of Hải Phong and Thanh Hoá, Jesuit missionaries established communities of Catholics. Estimates for the number of early converts vary considerably, but some suggest that the number of Tonkinese Christians stood at around 80,000 by the year 1639 and had increased more than fourfold to 350,000 by 1663.[14]

Ironically, the man who emerged as the most prominent figure in this early wave of Padroado Jesuit missionaries was not Portuguese but a Frenchman from Avignon, Father Alexandre de Rhodes. De Rhodes first traveled to Cochinchina in 1624 and undertook two years of language study in preparation for his missionary work. After completing his studies, in 1626 he traveled to Tonkin and quickly became active in this territory. De Rhodes had arrived at a critical juncture in modern Vietnamese history, for only three years after his arrival in Vietnam the seigniorial families who controlled the northern and southern Vietnamese territories commenced a civil war that would play out episodically over the next forty-five years. During this time both camps were highly sensitive to outsiders, whom they regarded as potential agents of the enemy—an attitude that complicated the status of resident Europeans. Under the circumstances, de Rhodes's position became increasingly precarious, and in 1630 he was expelled by the northern rulers and forced to retreat to Portuguese Macao, where events forced him to remain for the next decade. When he was finally able to return to Vietnam in 1640, de Rhodes traveled to the southern realm of the Nguyễn rulers. He remained there for seven more years until his presence sufficiently irritated the southern rulers that he was condemned to death in absentia and thus finally forced to leave the Vietnamese territories for good.

De Rhodes returned to Europe in 1649 convinced of the rich possibilities for conversion presented by the Vietnamese territories. He tried to persuade Pope Innocent X to send large numbers of Jesuits to Đại Việt to take advantage of this opportunity.[15] The pope, however, proceeded cautiously, unwilling to endorse de Rhodes's project without further study. Frustrated, de Rhodes was forced to look elsewhere for support. In 1652 he traveled to Paris, where he found considerably more enthusiasm for his project and as well as several seminarian candidates deemed ready to make the journey to Asia. This effort caught the attention of the Portuguese, who vowed to block any French interference in their Padroado mission domain in Asia. "The Portuguese ambassador [to the papal state] made it known to the Pope that no French missionaries could be sent to Vietnam; that Portugal would be responsible for the nomination and maintenance of any Vietnamese clergy; and that should French missionaries be sent, there would be war against them."[16]

The Jesuit was not discouraged, however, and appealed next to the cardinals of the Congregation of the Propaganda Fide. The Propaganda Fide had been established in 1622 in an effort to impose direct papal authority over the global Catholic Church that was being created in historically non-Catholic regions. While it took de Rhodes some time to persuade its leadership, the Propaganda Fide eventually endorsed the project, which had the secondary benefits of eroding the power of the Portuguese and the Jesuits, each of which was viewed with antipathy by the Propaganda leadership.[17] In the spring of 1658, the members of the Propaganda Fide agreed to take two interrelated steps. The first was to designate the mission territories across Indochina as apostolic vicariates, an act of geographical legerdemain designed to sidestep Padroado authority. The move effectively created a new form of ecclesiastical jurisdiction, one whose leaders were answerable to the papacy rather than to the Iberian monarchs or their delegates.[18] Apostolic vicariates were created in various corners of the globe typically as temporary measures covering regions that did not yet have sufficient numbers of Christians to justify the creation of formal dioceses that would be part of the global Catholic hierarchy. The apostolic vicars were appointed to titular bishoprics of previously established but often defunct Christian communities, typically ones located in parts of the Middle East. Such appointments gave them the necessary ecclesiastical authority to oversee these communities but nevertheless brought them into direct conflict with the existing bishops appointed by Portuguese rulers under the Padroado system. In the Vietnamese case this was the bishop of Macao, whose diocese extended well into the Vietnamese realms.[19]

The second step taken by the Propaganda, in close cooperation with de Rhodes, was to create an entirely new missionary apparatus, the Foreign Missions Society of Paris (Missions Étrangerès de Paris, MEP).[20] The MEP rapidly become a central institution in the story of Vietnamese Catholicism and more generally in the specifically French Catholic mission project across Asia. Unlike religious orders such as the Jesuits, whose members were united through vows that created a particular brotherhood, the MEP was founded as a congregation. Such an organization, whose members were referred to as seculars, was composed of a body of priests bound by a common commitment to a particular missionary objective. Once the apostolic vicariates and a new secular mission society had been created, the only remaining step was to link the two, and in 1660 two Frenchmen affiliated with the MEP were selected as apostolic vicars. François Pallu was named to head the mission responsible for Tonkin, Laos, and five provinces in southwestern China, while Pierre Lambert de la Motte was given authority over Cochinchina, four southeastern Chinese provinces, and the island of Hainan.

The appointment of the apostolic vicars, as Georg Schurhammer has pointed out, marked the beginnings of open conflict pitting those representing the Padroado-based community, which owed its origins and political allegiance to the

Portuguese and Spanish rulers, against the Propaganda-based community, whose loyalty was to the papacy and in particular the institution of the Propaganda Fide.[21] Whether or not de Rhodes had anticipated it, the appointment of the French non-Jesuits Pallu and de la Motte to a mission area long dominated by Portuguese Jesuits represented the opening salvo in what would become a long-running contest for ecclesiastical authority in Đại Việt. It was a battle whose course was determined partly by doctrinal differences, partly by a pursuit of power for its own sake, and partly by complex national politics, which in seventeenth- and eighteenth-century Europe were still closely bound to religious affairs. Eventually Philiphê Bỉnh would find himself caught up in this contest in the late eighteenth century.

THE BEGINNINGS OF CONFLICT: MEP BISHOPS TRAVEL TO ANNAM

The seeds of the Catholic conflicts in Đại Việt having been planted in the 1650s during de Rhodes's discussions with the Propaganda Fide, their fruits first appeared when the two newly minted apostolic vicars set off for Asia.[22] The two men traveled overland and separately, with de la Motte reaching Siam in the spring of 1662, followed by Pallu in 1664. Ironically, the two men spent almost no time in their assigned territories. Pallu himself never once set foot on Vietnamese soil: his sole attempt to reach Tonkin was foiled by a storm that forced his ship to divert to Spanish Manila, where he was captured and deported back to Europe. For his part, Father de la Motte made a brief trip to Tonkin in 1670, then another short trip to Cochinchina in 1677, but spent most of his time in Siam, where he died in 1679. Thus, while the two men had been sent to Southeast Asia as agents of the pope to gain a foothold in the Vietnamese mission field, their personal impact was limited to the largely symbolic status of forerunners, even as other MEP clerics were making their way to the Vietnamese realms. Among them was François Deydier, who arrived in Thăng Long (Hà Nội) in August of 1666, earning the distinction of becoming the first MEP missionary to set foot on Vietnamese soil.[23] By the time Deydier arrived in Tonkin as the forerunner of the new Paris mission organization, forty-eight Jesuit missionaries under the auspices of the Portuguese Padroado authority had already been active in Vietnamese territory over a period of four decades.[24] Deydier's arrival set the stage for a confrontation with the Jesuits as he moved rapidly to establish MEP authority across all Christian communities in the Vietnamese realms by drawing on the power of the newly established apostolic vicariate.

When de la Motte finally arrived in Tonkin four years later, he too acted with alacrity. In January of 1670 he ordained seven new priests and conferred minor orders on forty-eight Vietnamese converts, elevating them to positions as assistants to the Catholic community and the priests who served it. The following month de la Motte convened the first synod to be held in Vietnam. The synod, a general gathering of clerics to discuss church matters, was designed in part to put an MEP stamp on the nature of the Christian mission in Vietnam, and also to address the still unresolved demarcation of clerical authority over the Vietnamese territories.[25] The synod's resolutions were formally accepted by Pope Clement X in 1673 with only minor modifications, and the pontiff issued a formal brief stipulating that Padroado authority was no longer in force in territories not under direct Portuguese control.[26] But the pope's declaration was not the final word on the relevance of the Padroado in Asia, whose power continued to be invoked in the battles over ecclesiastical jurisdiction in Asia. Indeed, more than four decades later in 1717, Pope Clement XI was forced to acknowledge that the Padroado authority still held sway over three of the Chinese bishoprics, including that of Macao.[27] Thus the tension that had existed between Padroado and papal authority since at least the beginning of the seventeenth century continued well into the eighteenth. It was a battle pitting the French "Sun King" against the Portuguese "Grocer King," as he was derisively labeled by his opponents, and Portuguese priests continued to travel to the Vietnamese and other Asian mission realms, where they contested the orders of the French clerics.[28]

While the MEP synod had not definitively resolved the question of ecclesiastical authority, it forced the Jesuits to fight a rearguard action to reassert their own control over northern Vietnamese Catholics. The Jesuit Filipe Marini left Macao in February of 1671 bound for Tonkin, where he was to represent his order's interests in the face of this challenge. He was captured by Vietnamese authorities, however, as his boat traveled up the Red River, and found himself imprisoned at Hưng Yên, halfway between the coast and the Vietnamese imperial capital at Thăng Long.[29] From his cell, he wrote a forty-nine-page letter to Father Deydier in which he challenged MEP claims of authority in Tonkin and reasserted the rights of the Jesuits and of the Portuguese in controlling this particular mission field.[30] His epistolary challenge to the authority of the apostolic vicars represented the first explicit Jesuit rejection of MEP claims as apostolic vicars.

FURTHER GEOGRAPHICAL DIVISIONS: TONKIN PARTITIONED

The dispatch of the two apostolic vicars to Vietnam in the 1660s accelerated the divisions of Catholicism in Vietnam, pitting the forces of the pope against those of the Portuguese crown and those of the secular MEP against the Jesuit order. Not long after the synod called by the MEP and the pope's endorsement of its conclusions, the Tonkinese mission field was subjected to a further, and this time geographical, division. In 1678 Tonkin was formally separated into two large dioceses, Eastern Tonkin and Western Tonkin, a move intended to simplify logistics for organizing a mission that encompassed a large geographical territory. The dividing line was drawn roughly along the course of the Red River, though, as Alain Forest points out, not entirely along the primary branch of the river, but partially along one of its more southwestern secondary courses.[31] As the apostolic vicar designate Jacques de Bourges wrote: "No division could be more fair and more convenient than that which nature herself has created, along the river which follows a straight line from the north through the kingdom of Bao (which is currently submitted to the authority of the Chua), to the royal city, and from which equally is a straight line toward the south, which enters the sea at a river mouth called Luc-va."[32] The Eastern Tonkin Vicariate consisted of the coastal region from the Chinese border to Nam Định, while the Western Tonkin Vicariate extended southward of the river, from the mountains to the west along the coast as far as modern-day Hà Tĩnh.[33] This dividing line would have considerable significance for Bình, for it ran through the heart of the Jesuit communities that were clustered to the north and south of Nam Định. Thus, in his later struggles in support of this community, Bình found himself frequently crossing this line as he served Padroado Christians who fell on both sides of it. This meant he would be doing battle with the leaders of both apostolic vicariates, complicating what was already an enormous challenge.

While the division of Tonkin into two vicariates was geographical, it brought with it significant national and religious institutional implications. The Western Tonkin Vicariate was left in the hands of the MEP, while the Eastern Tonkin Vicariate was to be placed under Dominican control upon the death of its incumbent, the trailblazing MEP priest François Deydier, which occurred in 1693.[34] The partition of Tonkin reduced French MEP authority in the northern Vietnamese territory to that region's western half, which was contiguous with their existing MEP-controlled mission fields in Cochinchina further to the south. The Dominican eastern half, meanwhile, was readily accessible by boat from the order's outpost in the Philippines, where large numbers of its missionaries were helping to evangelize the islands and to secure Spanish control. The appointment in 1696 of an Italian, Father Raimondo Lezzoli, as apostolic vicar of Eastern Tonkin, marked the beginning of a Dominican control of the region that would endure for more than two and a half centuries. Although Lezzoli was an Italian, the position would soon be taken on by an unbroken succession of Spaniards that would last until the middle of the twentieth century. The first Vietnamese was not appointed to the post until 1953, and the first non-Dominican bishop did not occupy the position until 1960.[35]

The introduction of Dominican ecclesiastical authority in Tonkin must have been particularly galling to the Jesuits, for the Order of St. Dominic represented perhaps their most ardent theological and missiological foe. The Dominicans had been established by St. Dominic in the early thirteenth century as one of the first Catholic missionary orders. Since its founding, the order had established a reputation as a champion of Catholic orthodoxy and a critic of what its members regarded as heresy. It had also been one of the first orders to send missionaries to Asia, doing so before the Jesuits. With the establishment of the Jesuits in 1540, and that order's venture into the Asian mission fields, it was perhaps inevitable that the two orders would come into conflict. Indeed, they were already engaging in theological disputes only a few decades after the founding of the Jesuits. True to their traditions, the Dominicans attacked what they regarded as overly accommodating attitudes of the Jesuits toward local practices. This dispute accelerated in the seventeenth century when the Dominicans took issue with the Jesuit tolerance of Chinese rituals such as ancestral veneration, which the older order regarded as inimical to Catholic beliefs. The Dominicans brought the matter to the Vatican, which was initially unwilling to take sides. Pressed by the Dominicans, however, Pope Clement XI ultimately ruled in favor of their position, which had the consequence of dramatically reducing the influence of Christianity in China, and with it that of the Jesuits themselves.[36]

With the appointment of Spanish Dominicans to oversee the Eastern Tonkin Vicariate, the Spanish Philippines colony and its capital, Manila, became of increasing importance for Vietnamese Catholicism. The Philippines was the center of Spanish Dominican activity in Asia, and the region of Spanish responsibility in Vietnam was treated as an adjunct to the project based in Manila. As such, from the Dominican perspective the Vietnamese Christian territories were merely an extension of the "Provincia dominicana de Nuestra Señora del Rosario."[37] Manila remained an abstraction for the vast majority of Vietnamese Christians, but for a few it became concrete as a training site for aspiring catechists seeking to enter the priesthood. Such Vietnamese with connections to Dominican missionaries were sometimes given the opportunity to study in Manila at the College of San Juan de Letran, the University of St. Tomas, or sometimes both. The first Vietnamese to attend the College of San Juan de Letran was Jose Huyen de St. Tomas (1730–56), who came to Manila as a teenager in the later 1740s. He attended both institutions, slowly rising in the ranks from acolyte to sacerdote. Although he apparently intended to return to his community of Bùi Chu, he died in Manila before being able to do so.[38] He was followed by five other Vietnamese students over the next half century, most of whom attended on a scholarship established by the Spanish king in 1738. The most notable among these was Vicente Liêm de la Paz (1732–73), who studied in Manila between 1752 and 1758 and then was ordained as a Dominican priest. He returned to Tonkin, where he served as a priest for the next fourteen years before being arrested in an anti-Christian crackdown in 1773. Not long after his arrest, he was executed by Trịnh authorities, becoming one of the most commemorated Vietnamese martyrs of the eighteenth century.

While the division of Tonkin between the Dominicans and the MEP reduced the potential for conflict between the two groups, it conspicuously ignored the still predominant Jesuit presence in the region. The Jesuit priests and their communities were ostensibly answerable to the authority of the bishops who presided over the two parts of Tonkin, but in practice they retained a substantial measure of autonomy, and members of the order ministered to communities on both sides of the new partition line. Unsurprisingly, the Jesuits had been fiercely opposed to any such division of the territory in which they had invested so much time and effort. In their challenge to the division, some Jesuit priests had invoked the biblical tale of King Solomon, whose solution to a dispute between two women over a child had been to threaten to cut it in half, giving each woman a portion of the baby. The Jesuits regarded the Tonkinese mission field as their baby and saw its dismemberment as a death blow to their project rather than an equitable solution to a dispute.[39]

RECALL OF THE JESUITS: 1678–1696

The dispatch of the new MEP apostolic vicars in the early 1670s and then the partition of Tonkin were the first blows to be felt by the Jesuits in Tonkin, but the most damaging fell a little more than ten years later in 1682, when the entire contingent of Jesuits was ordered to leave Tonkin and report to Rome. The impetus for this order was the Jesuits' continued resistance to their new ostensible overseers. The MEP apostolic bishops had been sent with papal briefs declaring their ecclesiastical authority over the Vietnamese territories and had insisted that the existing Jesuit missionaries accept their jurisdiction. Hardly surprisingly, the Jesuits refused to yield, continuing to exercise their religious functions without reference to the MEP bishops.[40] The Vatican sided with the apostolic vicars; in 1682 Pope Innocent XI recalled all of the Jesuits in both Vietnamese realms, Đàng Trong and Đàng Ngoài, and banned the order from sending any further missionaries to the region.[41] The Jesuit missionaries were forced to abandon their mission fields and their communities to make the lengthy and arduous journey to Rome, their future entirely uncertain.[42]

With the forced departure of their Jesuit priests in 1682, Vietnamese Catholic communities who had been under their religious leadership were confronted with a choice. Their members could either attempt to continue their religious practices and rituals on their own, maintaining the Jesuit-influenced approach to Catholicism, or they could shift their allegiance to one of the other orders or to the secular missionaries of the MEP. This choice was made in an atmosphere of great uncertainty about when or even whether the Jesuits might be permitted to return. Indeed, the recalled Jesuits themselves did not know what the future held. Thus the communities who held out hope that they might see their Jesuit priests again did so in the face of considerable challenges. As Bỉnh later wrote, many of the local Catholics yielded to the appeals of the other religious communities, and the ranks of those in the Padroado community shrank dramatically. Bỉnh compared the situation of the Vietnamese Christians in this period to that of the Jews awaiting

Moses after his ascent of Mount Sinai to receive the Ten Commandments.[43] Bỉnh argued that just as uncertainty about the return of Moses had driven the waiting Jews to turn to worship of the golden calf, so many Vietnamese Christians, unwilling to wait for an uncertain Jesuit return, had agreed to submit to the authority of the apostolic vicars and their affiliates. Later in his life, Bỉnh would return to this same Old Testament analogy.

Meanwhile, in Europe, the Jesuit leadership forcefully argued for permission to return to Tonkin and eventually prevailed upon Pope Innocent XI to issue another papal brief dated January 7, 1689, authorizing their return. At the same time, however, the pope made it clear that he now expected the Tonkinese Christian communities to obey the orders of the apostolic vicars.[44] This message from the pontiff meant that any future rejection of the apostolic vicars' commands would constitute direct defiance of an explicitly stated papal order. Even with the permission to return, it would not be until 1696 that the first Jesuit missionaries finally returned to Tonkin and began to restore their communities.

THE PORTUGUESE AND GLOBAL DISSOLUTIONS OF THE JESUIT ORDER

Despite the pressures brought about by the partition of Tonkin, the brief recall of its missionaries, and the naming of apostolic vicars, the Jesuit-led Catholic community remained intact and its numbers stable. New Jesuit missionaries continued to arrive, still vying with the Dominicans and the MEP for Vietnamese adherents. The situation, however, changed dramatically in the middle of the eighteenth century, as Bỉnh made clear in his self-introduction: "I was born in the year 1759, the same year that King Jose of the country Portugal destroyed the Order of the Virtuous Lord Jesus in his realm." Although Portugal had been the driving force establishing mission communities in Tonkin in the early seventeenth century, it was also the instigator of the Jesuit order's destruction. The agent of its demise was the Portuguese prime minister Sebastiao de Carvalho e Melo, the Marquis de Pombal.

Pombal's rise to prominence came in the aftermath of a massive earthquake in Lisbon in 1755, when he became the chief administrator of the Portuguese court's recovery and rebuilding efforts.[45] One of Pombal's major undertakings was to strengthen the royal court along absolutist lines, which required reducing the influence of nonroyalist forces both upon the court and upon politics in Portugal more generally. Among his primary concerns was the influence of the religious orders, particularly the Jesuits, whose power was both political and economic. Their political power lay in their schools and their role as confessors to the court, while their economic power came from the hundreds of thousands of acres of prime farmland that the order controlled in Brazil. Seeing what he regarded as the pernicious influence of the Jesuits, Pombal set out to destroy the order in Portugal and beyond. He did this through the expedient of alleging Jesuit involvement in a plot to kill the Portuguese monarch, which allowed him to commence a systematic dismantling of the Jesuit order first in Portugal and then in its overseas possessions in Brazil and the Far East. By 1759, Pombal had succeeded in shutting down the Portuguese Jesuit order houses and banning the order from religious and secular affairs.[46] With this success under his belt, he turned to extirpating the Jesuit influence in Portugal's global outposts, including Goa and Macao. Pombal sent a ship to Macao, the Portuguese enclave off the southern Chinese coast, to collect both the Jesuit priests and their movable property and bring them to Rome. Among these men was an unnamed Vietnamese priest who refused to abandon the order and similarly rejected a return to Annam. Consequently, like the other Macao-based Jesuits, he found himself being shipped to exile in Rome. This sojourner never returned from his Italian exile and became the first Vietnamese to die in Europe. Bỉnh later cited a European account of this man as having been "a person of humanity and virtue."[47]

After learning of the order's destruction in Portugal, in 1760 the Jesuit father superior in Tonkin, François Antoine (?–1773), sent Father Onofre Villiani to Rome to request additional Jesuit missionaries. Villiani, known to the Vietnamese as Cố Hậu, was an important and senior leader of the Vietnamese Jesuit community, having arrived in Tonkin in 1750.[48] The Vatican agreed to the request, sending several priests to Tonkin and a few to Cochinchina as well. Upon arriving in Tonkin, the delegation's members learned that the Jesuit father superior, François Antoine, had just died. This led Father Villiani to take on the position as the Padroado community's senior clerical leader. He was supported in his work by several other veteran European Jesuit clerics, notably the Portuguese Father Tulano (Augustin) Carneiro (1722–1802), who had arrived in Tonkin in 1748, and the Neopolitan Father Nuncio Horta (or D'Orta; 1722–1801), who had arrived in 1760.[49] Of the three, Father Carneiro was of particular significance both for the length of his service to the Padroado Catholics and for his being Portuguese, and Bỉnh, in his later writings, would refer to him as "our spiritual father."[50] Indeed, Tulano Carneiro would eventually outlive his counterparts to become the final European Jesuit priest to serve the Padroado Catholics.[51]

In the meantime, however, Pombal was not satisfied with dismantling the Jesuit order in Portugal and its overseas territories. He remained convinced that the continued existence of the Jesuit order as a global institution represented a grave threat to royal authority not only in Lisbon but also in other parts of Europe, where the order controlled many educational institutions and where its priests often served as royal confessors. Indeed, Pombal regarded religious orders more generally as corrosive of monarchy in Europe, at one point threatening to break the Portuguese Catholic Church from papal authority entirely. Seeing what he regarded as the inherent dangers of the Jesuit order, Pombal mounted a vigorous anti-Jesuit campaign among leaders of the other European Catholic states, which gradually began to take their own steps against the order. The combination of Pombal's aggressive pressure and the possibility of a Portuguese break from Rome led a reluctant Pope Clement XIV to accede to Pombal's demand that the Jesuit order be outlawed in its entirety. The pope issued a brief to this effect in 1773. Thus, substantially as a result of Pombal's efforts, the Jesuit order found itself disestablished around the world, and communities formerly under the ecclesiastical guidance of its priests were now adrift.[52] Among these communities was Philiphê Bình's. It was a community that had been shaped by Jesuit practices and approaches to Christianity for more than a century and a half, and the order's demise came as a profound shock.

The dissolution of the Jesuits represented a golden opportunity for their rivals in Tonkin. The French MEP and Spanish Dominican apostolic vicars acted quickly, urging the members of the local Jesuit-led Catholic communities at long last to accept the vicars as the leaders of the local Catholic hierarchy. This proved not to be a simple matter. Although news of the Jesuit dissolution apparently reached Tonkin by 1774, the Jesuit loyalist priests did nothing to spread this information, which they tried to keep a secret as along as they could.[53] When the news finally did trickle down to the Jesuit-led communities, many refused to accept this change in church regimes, preferring to retain their autonomy and relying on their own resources to support themselves. Bình's community was among those that refused the overtures from the MEP and the Dominicans, seeking instead to find ways to preserve their distinctive community identity and their particular forms of ritual and practice.

The decision to reject the authority of the apostolic vicars was not an act of stubborn caprice but hinged on factors both historical and cultural. In the first place, these communities had witnessed the disappearance of their Jesuit priests before (in the 1680s), only to see them return once the politics of the situation had been sorted out. It is likely that many believed, or hoped, that the latest attack on the Jesuits would also prove but a temporary setback. Indeed, at some level the situation was not quite as dire as it had been during the earlier Jesuit recall. This time the Jesuit priests had not been withdrawn, so their ties to their congregants remained largely intact. Moreover, though their order no longer existed, the men had been instructed to continue to function as ordained priests for their respective communities. This meant that the Padroado community initially experienced little disruption to its distinctive ritual and cultural traditions, and the continuing presence of sympathetic priests made the community's defiance of MEP and Dominican pressure easier to sustain. Although the presence of a large contingent of priests in the Jesuit lineage was comforting, it was not in itself a guarantee of the community's survival. Not content to rely solely on the hope that the Jesuit order might somehow be restored, the Padroado community's members also began to take active measures to reverse this setback.

FOLLOWING "FATHER LUIS": LIFE AS AN ITINERANT CATHOLIC CATECHIST

A major part of the community's strategy to ensure its survival consisted of supporting training for its native sons, who might eventually be ordained to continue to serve the Padroado faithful. Philiphê Bỉnh was one of these, and he began his religious training in 1775 at the age of sixteen. As he noted in his introduction, "In that year, I went with Master Luis, and left my home." This was a crucial moment in his life, as it marked a new direction that would guide him for the rest of his days. It was the beginning of a long period of apprenticeship, study, and service. It was also the start of a frequently itinerant existence that would take Bỉnh up and down the heavily Catholic coastal reaches of Tonkin between Thanh Hóa and Hải Phong.

Philiphê Bỉnh's new mentor, the man he referred to as "Father Luis," was an Italian Jesuit by the name of Alexandre-Pompée Castiglioni who had recently arrived in Tonkin as part of the contingent Villiani had brought back from Europe. Castiglioni was a member of an Italian noble family from Milan and a close relative of Cardinal Valenti Gonzaga (1690–1756). When he was still a young man, his father had identified a suitable spouse for his son and made arrangements for their marriage. Castiglioni, however, had other plans, informing his father that he had no intention of marrying her, for he was preparing to enter the priesthood. Shortly thereafter, at the age of twenty-two, he joined the Jesuit order and began training for a career as a missionary.[54] Thus, when the Vatican authorized an additional group of Jesuits to be sent to Tonkin in the company of Father Villiani, Castiglioni was ready. The young Italian prepared to head into the mission field with enthusiasm and resolve but also more than a bit of trepidation, as reflected in a farewell letter to a favorite aunt written in December 1772:

> Finally, you no doubt would like to know, my dear aunt, what sort of a place this Tonkin is. It is a country covered with swamps, where one finds neither bread, nor wine, nor oil, nor butter, nor milk, nor meat, nor game, nor eggs, nor poultry, nor birds, nor vegetables, nor pastures, nor fruit: in a word, one finds there absolutely nothing but rice, sun, and hot water: hot, because cold is considered harmful. They also have bandits, whose objective is to capture men in order to sell them. There is a price on the head of Europeans and, when they are captured, they are certain to be hanged. The Christians number to three hundred thousand, constituting 11 percent of the inhabitants: the rest are idolaters. The country is extremely poor and the climate very hot. The difficult thing is getting there. There are various winds, various patrol boats, and various reefs that one encounters along the coast that do not allow anyone to pass unmolested. But what is all this to me? Onwards![55]

Shortly after dispatching this letter with its bleak view of his destination, Father Castiglioni, now thirty-six years old, departed for the Tonkin mission as a member of Father Villiani's delegation, prepared to serve the Padroado community.[56]

Less than two years after his arrival in Tonkin, Castiglioni was approached by a young Vietnamese, Philiphê Bỉnh and was asked whether the priest would be willing to provide religious training. The Italian Jesuit agreed, and Bỉnh became his companion in the years that followed. Bỉnh's notebooks say little about the nature of his training during the twelve years he spent, intermittently, with Father Castiglioni, though from his scattered comments it likely consisted of what Peter Phan has described as "on-the-job training."[57] Father Castiglioni and his young protégé spent much of this time traveling around the region, during the course of which the Italian Jesuit instructed Bỉnh in Catholic teachings, while in return his new catechist would have served as a cultural, geographical, and linguistic mediator. By serving as Father Castiglioni's catechist, Bỉnh would have been educated in Catholic ritual, history, and practice, while also becoming steeped in the history and traditions of the Tonkinese Jesuit community. Their relationship was typical of that between European missionaries and the young men who had been identified as promising candidates for serving the church and its communities. Rather than immediately immersing themselves in academic study in a religious school, these men often began their training as apprentices to the European clergy, serving as their assistants in conducting rituals and caring for local church communities. These apprentices were labeled as "catechists" and would engage in years of learning by doing and observing the actions of their mentor priest.[58] Most would never be formally ordained, instead remaining in the ranks of a kind of liturgical support staff. A few, like Bỉnh, would eventually demonstrate the skills and intelligence to be ordained as Catholic priests. But the necessary training would often take years or decades. At the same time, while Bỉnh learned from his mentor, the priest learned much from a young man who amounted to a kind of "native informant." Bỉnh knew the area in which he had grown up, its people, and, perhaps most importantly, their language. He would have helped the priest navigate the cultural and geographical terrain of coastal Tonkin as the European slowly learned the language and came to understand that perhaps Tonkin was not quite the desert he had described in the letter to his aunt.

Although Bỉnh did most of his training with Father Castiglioni, circumstances sometimes forced him to leave his mentor and spend time with others. Indeed, not long after beginning his apprenticeship, Bỉnh had to leave Castiglioni temporarily, while the Italian was traveling so extensively he could not support Bỉnh's training. Bỉnh moved in with a Father Tước in Xứ Đông until Castiglioni returned from his travels and Bỉnh was able to rejoin him for parts of 1776 and 1777. Soon, however, Bỉnh was forced again to leave his teacher temporarily, for 1777 was a year of enormous social upheaval that was spawned by a widespread famine followed by a large-scale rebel uprising, both of which caused enormous hardship and population displacement.[59] Castiglioni sent Bỉnh to stay in the residence of an MEP cleric, Father Chính Trung, where the young catechist spent time copying out books before eventually rejoining Father Castiglioni.

Not long after reconnecting with his student, Father Castiglioni brought Bỉnh with him to a meeting at the small village of Hà Lạn at the end of March of 1779. Others at the gathering included the remaining Jesuit loyalist missionaries in Tonkin and the recently appointed apostolic vicar of Eastern Tonkin, Bishop Manuel Obelar. The bishop likely had called the meeting to discuss his vision for how to address the lingering tensions between the Dominican and Jesuit loyalist communities. The discussion centered on the precise nature of their support for the Padroado community and what role these priests would continue to play. Bỉnh was there as an observer and companion to Father Castiglioni, and in his later histories of Tonkin he recorded the meeting's key issues as best he could remember them. The discussions among the clergymen left a considerable number of questions unresolved, and it was decided that further clarification would be required from Rome, which would necessitate sending a delegation to the Vatican. In June, Father Villiani sent a letter to Father Castiglioni inviting him to a meeting to discuss the trip. At the gathering the senior cleric told Castiglioni that they had decided to send a delegation to the Vatican that would include Villiani himself and two of the community's more advanced catechists, John Thiều and Paul Cuyền.[60]

As the delegation's departure was delayed, Castiglioni became increasingly apprehensive about the state of the Padroado community, and toward the end of 1779 he began to make plans of his own to return to Europe, where he also hoped to recruit additional priests. As he was preparing to travel to Macao, however, he fell ill, first with malaria and then with an intestinal virus caused by drinking unboiled water, and so was unable to leave.[61] Castiglioni continued to worry about the state of the mission and about training additional Vietnamese catechists. In particular, he wanted to find a way to train them without having to send them to the seminaries run by the MEP or the Dominicans. He wrote to Rome requesting permission to establish such a school, and while he received a reply it did not address the question of the schools. At some point in 1781 he determined to follow up his request in person and once again made plans to travel to Europe, going so far as to assign Bỉnh to take care of his religious property in his absence. This trip, too, stalled, and Castiglioni remained in Tonkin, where he continued to mentor his protégé. By this time Bỉnh was apparently becoming quite skilled in using the romanized alphabet, likely writing in Latin, for he regularly drafted letters for Castiglioni in his correspondence with the apostolic vicars.[62]

Meanwhile, even as Castiglioni made repeated unsuccessful efforts to leave Tonkin, in July of 1780 Father Villiani and his Vietnamese companions, Thiều and Cuyền, finally set off on their long journey to Europe.[63] After making its way to

Canton, the delegation had to wait some time before finding a Portuguese vessel destined for Lisbon. The journey suffered a second lengthy delay when their boat stopped in Mozambique off the eastern coast of Africa for several months before eventually resuming the voyage to Portugal. When the small delegation finally arrived in Lisbon sometime in early 1781, its members spent a month recovering from their long journey while Father Villiani met with friends in the local clergy to talk about their situation. These consultations completed, the small group set out for Rome, where they hoped to use Father Villiani's connections to recruit more priests for the community. Unfortunately, upon reaching Rome they learned that Villiani's primary contact in the Holy See had died, and although Villiani presented his appeal directly to Pope Pius VI he received no commitments. When it became clear that there was little he could do, Father Villiani opted not to return to Tonkin choosing instead to stay behind in the hopes that he could persuade other clergy to join the Tonkin mission. Although unsuccessful in gaining any commitments from the pope, Villiani did manage to secure places at a local seminary for his two Vietnamese companions to continue their education.[64]

Over the next four years, Thiều and Cuyền studied Italian and then completed their training for the priesthood, after which both men were ordained.[65] At this point, they presented a formal petition to the pope requesting that he appoint a bishop to their northern Vietnamese community.[66] The pope responded by stating that such an appointment lay outside of his authority and that responsibility for making it rested with the king of Portugal, who still held the Padroado grant.[67] The pope's disingenuous reply allowed him to deflect responsibility for the matter while effectively trapping Thiều and Cuyền. When the two Vietnamese clerics requested permission to travel to Lisbon to put their request directly to the Portuguese ruler, their petition was denied. Meanwhile, the apostolic vicar for Western Tonkin, Father Jean Davoust, tried to force their return. He wrote a letter to the Holy See claiming authority over the men but also promising to assist them in completing their clerical training upon their return.[68] His requests to have the men sent home were, however, turned down by Vatican authorities.

When their departure could no longer be put off, the men were finally given permission to leave Rome. But they were still not allowed to travel to Lisbon. Instead, Thiều and Cuyền were diverted to Paris, where they were housed at the MEP headquarters on Rue du Bac, one of the strongholds of anti-Padroado sentiment in Europe and Tonkin. After roughly two years, the men were permitted to leave Paris but were once again denied permission to travel to Lisbon and were forced instead to return home to Tonkin. When Thiều and Cuyền at last reached Tonkin again in late 1787, they had gained valuable experience of the European world and, even more importantly, had returned as ordained priests. They had not, however, moved the community any closer to its objective of securing a formal bishop for Tonkin. Also, unfortunately for the Padroado community, although these men had left as strong supporters of the Jesuit loyalists, they returned with an affinity for the French MEP, likely a result of their time spent in Paris at the congregation's seminary, and opted to side with these rivals of the Padroado community.[69]

SEMINARY TRAINING AT BÙI CHU

Although Fathers Thiều and Cuyên had not secured the bishop they had sought, they did not return entirely empty-handed. They carried a letter from the pope directing the apostolic vicars of both Eastern and Western Tonkin to enroll students from the former Jesuit communities in their seminaries and to train them to serve the Padroado community. This looked like a hopeful compromise that would secure at least some measure of autonomy for the Jesuit loyalist Catholics in sustaining their sense of community. A small number of seminarians were thus taken in for tutelage to prepare them for the priesthood. Among those was Bỉnh. His on-the-job training with Father Castiglioni had been an indispensible aspect of his religious education, but to advance to the priesthood he would eventually have had to receive more formal education in the context of a school or seminary. As it happened it was an ideal, if bittersweet, moment to make this transition, as Bỉnh had just lost his longtime mentor after a protracted illness. Bỉnh writes that Castiglioni had fallen ill in October of 1786, suffering from an unrelenting headache that local Catholic doctors were unable to resolve. A non-Christian doctor was then called in, presumably to apply Vietnamese medicine, but this also failed to cure Castiglioni's condition. After struggling with this illness for six months, Castiglioni died on April 19, 1787.[70] Bỉnh entered the seminary at Bùi Chu shortly thereafter.

In entering a seminary, Bỉnh was joining an institution with deep roots in the European missionary project in Tonkin. From the outset, European missionaries sought to do more than merely baptize Vietnamese into the faith. While they were the primary force for conversion among the Vietnamese populations, both Jesuits and secular missionaries of the MEP understood that ordination of local priests or at least the training of ritual assistants would be essential if the new Catholic communities were to survive. Thus European missionaries to Tonkin had begun to establish religious communities for committed laypersons, as well as schools to provide religious training. These schools would become the mechanism by which to produce both small numbers of ordained native priests, as well as much larger numbers of lay catechists trained to carry out a variety of support activities, from maintaining church buildings to procuring ritual objects, and even performing certain sacraments for members of the community.[71] The first Vietnamese catechists were trained at an MEP seminary established at the Siamese capital of Ayutthaya in 1665.[72] Siam was a relative safe haven for European missionaries, who were not regarded as a threat to the Siamese monarchy, and it became an outpost for missionary activity in other parts of mainland Southeast Asia during its first decades. Missionaries in the Vietnamese realm, however, were determined to create such colleges closer to home, and by 1682 a number of "petits collèges" had been established in Tonkin, including in Nghệ An, Sơn Nam, and Kinh Bắc. While the colleges at Sơn Nam and Kinh Bắc were temporarily downgraded to "schools" after the death of their founder, by 1724 they had once again been upgraded, and all three served as centers of religious training for catechists as well as for indigenous priests. Persecution by the Vietnamese court occasionally threatened these schools and their pupils, and the notable college at Kẻ Vĩnh (in Sơn Nam province) was razed in a crackdown in 1773 and not restored until seven years later.[73]

Bình appears to have entered a smaller seminary located in the Eastern Tonkin Vicariate at Bùi Chu. Bình's course of study at the Bùi Chu seminary likely consisted of a combination of language and religious subjects. Most of his fellow students would have studied as catechists, to play a supporting role in the church communities, while a smaller number, like Bình, would have pursued more rigorous training to enable their eventual ordination as priests. Their religious training would have involved both reading texts and memorizing portions of them, since students might well not be able to carry texts with them, or even have access to them, after the completion of their studies. European missionaries were often astounded at the capacity of their Vietnamese students to memorize large sections of these texts, prayers, and catechisms, a reflection no doubt of a society in which the transmission of "literature" had of necessity been oral.[74] The texts included those composed in Chinese by Jesuits active in the China mission field. The students would almost certainly also have studied locally produced catechisms either in the romanized alphabet or in *chữ nôm*. It is possible that draft or hand-copied versions of Alexandre de Rhodes's *Cathechismus* might have been in use, though it is unlikely that the version printed in Rome in 1651 was in circulation in Tonkin at the time.[75] Indeed, students who were engaged in the more rigorous course of study to be ordained as priests would also have studied Latin, giving them access to European religious books in that language. Among the texts they would have read were *The Lives of the Saints*, Thomas Aquinas's *The Imitation of Christ*, and St. Frances de Sales's *Introduction to Devout Life*.[76]

As the catechist of a devoted Jesuit loyalist, Father Castiglioni, Bình was preparing himself to serve the Padroado community, which would have placed him in a significant tradition of locally trained and ordained Vietnamese clergy in the Jesuit lineage. Over the course of the first 130 years of their presence in the Vietnamese territories (1626–1752), the Jesuits had admitted thirty-one Vietnamese men into their order. Of these, eleven were ordained as priests, while the other twenty were admitted as lay brothers. Twenty-five of these men had entered the order in Tonkin, while the remaining six had done so in Cochinchina.[77] During his own time at the seminary, Bình became well acquainted with several of the other seminarians who were also advancing toward full ordination. He became particularly close to Manuel Xavier Trêu, a student from Nghệ An. Bỉnh would later describe their relationship as being like that between King David and Jonathan, men who shared a common soul and kindred spirit. While Bỉnh would go on to serve the Padroado community in Tonkin and then as an envoy to Europe, Father Trêu would serve in the southern reaches of Tonkin, where he would be closer to his home in Nghệ An. There he was captured by the Tây Sơn regime during a crackdown on Christianity, probably in the course of 1798. Later, in the course of his research in Lisbon, Bỉnh would learn that his friend had been martyred for the faith in the Tây Sơn capital at Phú Xuân in 1800 and would recall that he had last seen his friend and classmate in April of 1794, when Bỉnh had left their common house.[78]

In addition to Trêu, several other supporters of the Jesuit community were entering local seminaries during the years of Bỉnh's own training. The year after Bỉnh began his studies, a young man by the name of Xuân entered the seminary at Kẻ Là. He had previously been a catechist working with Father Cuyển, one of the two men who had returned from Rome the previous year. Upon entering the seminary, Xuân decided to change his name to better reflect his commitment to the Padroado community and its clergy. He adopted the name Trung, meaning "loyalty," to show his support for the community. Not long thereafter, a young man from the southern region of Nghệ An by the name of Quỳnh followed his mentor priest to the coastal Tonkin region and entered the seminary at Kẻ Vĩnh. He too opted to change his name, choosing Nhân, or "humaneness," to indicate his commitment to the order as well. It is striking that both names, used to indicate adherence to a particular Catholic religious community, are ones with deep resonance for Confucianism, as loyalty and humaneness are among the core virtues espoused by Confucianist scholars.[79]

BỈNH'S ORDINATION: A MOMENT OF JOY AND DISAPPOINTMENT

The project to train the new catechists specifically for the Padroado community was dealt a distinct setback in 1789 with the deaths in rapid succession of the apostolic vicars of Eastern and Western Tonkin. The project had been very much tied to these two leaders, and there was little assurance that any successors would continue it. At the same time, however, the apostolic vicars' deaths did represent something of a reprieve for a community under increasing pressure, for they left the leadership of the vicariates in flux. In Western Tonkin Father Jacques-Benjamin Longer (1752–1831) took up the post as apostolic vicar, but as he had not yet been consecrated as a bishop he could not ordain a successor for the apostolic vicariate in Eastern Tonkin, nor did he have the standing to ordain new priests. Consequently, his authority was less then complete. Furthermore, the political situation in Tonkin remained highly uncertain in the aftermath of a series of invasions and counterattacks between the Tây Sơn armies and their Trịnh/Lê rivals, and then a large-scale Qing invasion in the summer of 1788. While the Tây Sơn had succeeded in driving out the Qing army in early 1789, it would take some time to secure Chinese recognition of the new regime. In addition, loyalists of the former regime resisted the authority of the new government, and some went into rebellion against Tây Sơn rule. Not until the summer of 1792 did the situation calm down enough to allow the members of the Catholic community to move about with some ease. Father Longer was then finally able to travel to Macao, where in September of 1792 he was formally consecrated as a bishop by the bishop of Macao, Marcelino José da Silva. During this three-year interval, the priests serving the Padroado community, and those training for the ministry, could carry out their duties within this Catholic population without having to answer to religious leaders hostile to their project. Although the numbers of their priests was diminishing, the community was still able to function according to its own practices.

However, Father Longer's consecration as bishop significantly altered the ecclesiastical landscape, for upon his return to Tonkin in early 1793 he was invested with the authority to consecrate his counterpart in Eastern Tonkin to the episcopate as well. Father Feliciano Alonso had been serving as the "vicar general" of Eastern Tonkin since the death of Bishop Manuel Obelar in 1789. Prior to his promotion, Father Alonso had served as a missionary priest in coastal Tonkin, where he had arrived from his native Spain in 1766. During his years as a local priest he had gained a reputation as a compassionate and understanding man, attributes that earned him the nickname "El Simpático" (the congenial one).[80] Like his predecessor, Father Alonso was based in Trung Linh, a few miles southeast of Nam Định and less than ten miles from the coast. On March 10, 1793, Father Longer formally consecrated his counterpart as bishop, with the nominal title of bishop of Fez (Fessee).[81] Consequently, the two vicariates were once again under the formal authority of bishops. The newly ordained bishops in Eastern and Western Tonkin, now secure in their authority as both apostolic vicars and bishops, were determined to assert their vision of the ecclesiastical chain of command and were no longer willing to tolerate the autonomy of the Padroado priests and their community.

This development prompted the Padroado community leadership, including both its European priests and its Vietnamese clergy and catechists, to hold a meeting to decide on a course of action. The attendees decided at this time that they would send a three-man delegation to Macao to request a bishop of their own, one dedicated to the needs of their particular community.[82] This had important implications for the community's future, as its members had been pinning their hopes on the small cohort of men who had begun their religious training at the Kẻ Bùi seminary in 1787 after the return of Fathers Thiều and Cuyên from Rome. By the time that the two bishops had been ordained and had begun to sketch out plans for their respective vicariates, the seminarians were finishing their training and would soon be ready for ordination as priests. The bishops decided to hold a collective ordination ceremony for the men and selected an auspicious date for the event, the Feast Day of St. Andrew, November 30. So on that day in late November 1793 the six seminarians were formally ordained in a ceremony conducted by the two apostolic vicars at the seminary in Kẻ Bùi. The six represented a variety of regions, for Bỉnh reported that two were from more southerly areas, one from Phú Xuân and a second from Nghệ An, three others were from Xứ Nam (around Nam Định, near the seminary itself), and one, Bỉnh himself, was from slightly further north in Xứ Đông (the area of Hải Dương).[83] Philiphê Bỉnh had finally become a priest, sixteen years after beginning his religious training with Father Castiglioni and six years after entering the seminary.[84] This represented a crucial moment for the Padroado community, for Bỉnh was one of their own. He understood their commitments and their history; he was sympathetic to their determination to remain loyal to their traditions; and he was a dynamic and activist priest, willing to speak his mind and to defend the community even against long odds.

It was, however, a bittersweet moment, for what might have been a celebration to welcome half a dozen new priests into the ranks of those serving the community saw not a single one assigned to serve the Padroado Catholics. Instead, the apostolic vicars designated them to serve either the French MEP or the Spanish Dominican communities.[85] Bỉnh was intensely frustrated by this turn of events, for as he understood it he and the other five men had been trained specifically to help the underserved Padroado Christians. He saw this redirection of the new priests' appointments both as a violation of the Vatican's intentions in setting up this arrangement and as a repudiation of the promises made by the two earlier apostolic vicars. As he wrote in his later notebooks: "Our Christians [Padroado] were thus abandoned to hunger and thirst; they forced our Christians to bow to their priests, just as when the pharaoh forced the offspring of Jacob to become his subjects in the country of Egypt and to forget about the undertakings of Joseph."[86] It was clear that the only way to improve the situation for the Padroado community would be to secure a bishop of their own.

2

A Catholic Community in Crisis

Bình's ordination in 1793 had been the culmination of nearly two decades of apprenticeship and training, and yet, as we saw in the previous chapter, this important step had done nothing to improve the situation of the Padroado Catholics. Their sense of community and ability to defy the apostolic vicars was continuing to crumble under the relentless pressure of the MEP and the Dominicans, which only increased because of the efforts of the newly ordained Bishop Alonso. The community's desperation would eventually drive them to dispatch first a small delegation of catechists and then a group led by Bình himself overseas to seek support for their efforts. This chapter surveys the increasing challenges that the community faced, most notably the efforts by Bishop Alonso to restrict or alter their liturgical rituals and practices. These new regulations, meticulously critiqued in Bình's writings, ultimately forced the Padroado Catholics to choose between surrender or continued defiance at the cost of being labeled as schismatics and denied access to the sacraments.

HARDSHIPS FOR TONKINESE CATHOLICS

Bình's theological training, first with Father Castiglioni and then in the seminary at Kẻ Bùi, had taken place against a complex and often dangerous sociopolitical backdrop. The populations in Tonkin generally faced great hardships that began in the middle of the 1770s, just as Bình had begun to serve as Father Castiglioni's catechist. The Christian populations specifically had to deal with periodic and often unpredictable persecution and state repression. This was a time of accelerating political upheaval highlighted by the death and bitterly disputed succession of the

Tonkinese ruler Trịnh Sâm (r. 1767–82). This took place against a backdrop of ongoing environmental crises—floods, droughts, and related crop failures—through much of the 1770s and becoming more severe in the 1780s. At times, such crises sparked large-scale popular uprisings, such as the one in 1777 that disrupted life for Bình and Father Castiglioni.[1] The climax of these troubles was the famine of 1785–86, which killed anywhere between 150,000 and 600,000 people according to one European eyewitness, and which Bình's mentor, Father Castiglioni, discussed in a series of letters written to Europe and Macao in the summer of 1786.[2]

The already horrific situation in Tonkin was only magnified that summer as the region endured the first of a series of invasions from Cochinchina carried out by armies of the Tây Sơn rulers. The Tây Sơn movement had begun in 1771 as a popular uprising against the Nguyễn rulers in the southern Vietnamese territories and had grown rapidly over the 1770s and early 1780s, at which point its leaders sought to extend their political gains northward. Not long after the Tây Sơn attacks from the south, in the fall of 1788 Tonkin was invaded from the north by a Chinese army numbering as many as half a million soldiers. This attack was followed by yet another Tây Sơn invasion in early 1789, which succeeded in driving out the Chinese but further added to the woes of the local population. The Tây Sơn triumph also brought an end to the more than three-hundred-year reign of the Lê dynasty, creating considerable rifts in northern society, as well as enormous uncertainty.

In addition to these substantial political and at times existential threats, Tonkinese Catholics had to contend with persistent state suspicion of Christians and their European priests. Persecution of Vietnamese Catholics had been a regular occurrence since the introduction of the faith in the early seventeenth century. This persecution was not, however, continuous, or always vigorously enacted; it varied substantially depending on political and military circumstances, as well as the inclinations of local officials to carry out the ruler's orders. It also varied between the two Vietnamese realms, that of the Trịnh rulers in the North and that of the Nguyễn in the South, though not in a predictable fashion. There had even been periodic executions of Christians in Tonkin (both European priests and local converts) during the eighteenth century, including five during Bình's lifetime in the relatively short span of seven years from 1773 to 1779, just as Bình was beginning his religious training.[3] For Vietnamese Catholics, persecution or its threat was a constant reality, and the uncertainty surrounding state attitudes toward the faith was a defining element of their lives and religious practices.

Fortunately, after the disasters in the 1770s and 1780s caused by contested political transitions, famine, and multiple invasions from both south and north, by the early 1790s, as Bình was finishing his seminary training, the situation in Tonkin stabilized and some semblance of order slowly returned. After defeating the Qing armies in 1789, the Tây Sơn regime had slowly taken steps to restore the economy, return peasants to their villages, and encourage cultivation, though there continued to be sporadic crop failures and famines caused by weather and the lingering effects of years of displaced populations.[4] The new rulers, Emperor Quang Trung (r. 1788–92) and his son and successor, Emperor Cảnh Thịnh (r. 1792–1802), were generally tolerant of, or at least indifferent to, the Catholic communities and their European clergy. In the summer of 1791, a European missionary was able to report that "all of our dear confederates in northern Cochinchina are in good health, and our blessed religion is completely free from persecution. I have been told that it is active and with a greater liberty than ever before."[5] In subsequent years European missionaries continued to comment on the considerable religious freedom they enjoyed. One letter of June 1793 reported that there was much greater religious liberty than had existed under the earlier Trịnh and Lê regimes,[6] while another noted that "since Tonkin has been under the domination of the Cochinchinese, there is no talk of persecuting the religion."[7] A year later, an MEP missionary compared the religious situation in Tonkin favorably to that in his native France, then in the throes of the French Revolution. He wrote that the two situations of civil war were similar, but for the fact that "our rebels [the Tây Sơn] do not touch the religion at all and on the contrary, they have given more freedom than it has ever had before."[8] Another, writing in 1794, observed, "We enjoy a peace and a tranquility that is truly great in terms of that which concerns religion, and we celebrate the solemn feasts with the permission of the governor of the province where I now found myself (Xứ Nam)."[9] Although the situation of Christians was not without difficulty in this period, it was certainly better than it had been. Catholics in Tonkin were not typically singled out by national authorities in this time, though they were occasionally the victims of local officials' avarice and other kinds of sociopolitical pressure, such as kidnapping to extort money from their coreligionists or their European clerics.[10] More generally, Christian populations suffered alongside their non-Christian neighbors through the crises of political conflicts, marauding armies, and weather-induced crop failures.

THE ECCLESIASTICAL LANDSCAPE SHIFTS

The Tây Sơn regime's political consolidation in Tonkin in the early 1790s was matched by an ecclesiastical consolidation and a strengthening of the two mission organizations headed by the apostolic vicars. While the Padroado community saw the number of its priests continue to dwindle—in 1786 only three of the original six Jesuit loyalist priests remained, and by 1793 there were only two—the French MEP and Spanish Dominican contingents began to grow. In 1790, the MEP had just four priests active on the ground in Tonkin: Philippe Sérard, Jean François Le Roy, Charles de la Motte, and Pierre Eyot. Then, in May of 1791, the MEP's ranks doubled with the arrival of four additional missionaries: René Tessier, Jean-Jacques Guérard, Joseph Le Pavec, and Pierre Lemmonier de la Bissachère.[11] Not long after the MEP presence was bolstered, the Spanish Dominicans also expanded their ranks. Despite their nominal authority over the entire Eastern Tonkin Vicariate, only three Spanish priests had served the area for much of the 1780s and into the early 1790s. This changed beginning in 1795, when four new Spanish priests arrived. They were joined by three more missionaries who arrived the following year. The Dominican delegation now dwarfed even that of the French MEP and finally represented a significant presence in their sphere of influence. In addition to these ten European missionaries, there were sixteen Vietnamese Dominican priests serving the region in 1793.[12] The expanding French MEP and Spanish Dominican presence in conjunction with the declining number of Jesuit loyalist priests dramatically increased the pressure on the Padroado holdouts.

Although they had not gained the services of any of the recently ordained native priests, the Padroado community's members continued to cling to the hope that Father Bình might come to their aid. He would do so, but not immediately. After Bình's ordination, Bishop Alonso appointed the new priest to serve as the manager (*quản lý*) for his office at Kẻ Bùi, where Bình had studied and then been ordained.[13] Kẻ Bùi was located in the coastal area of the province (*trấn*) of Sơn Nam Hạ, where a lower branch of the Red River emptied into the Gulf of Tonkin. Significantly, this branch of the river served as a boundary between the two vicariates, so Bình found himself in a space feeling the impact of both sets of apostolic vicars. Kẻ Bùi was a day's journey southwest of Nam Định and, more importantly for Bình, was only thirty miles south of his home in Vĩnh Lại.[14] This meant that he could periodically return to visit his family. Bình's new post brought with it responsibility for overseeing the mission's property and finances. Bishop Alonso's decision to assign Bình to this position suggests that the recently ordained priest may have distinguished himself by his intelligence and honesty, and perhaps also by his ability to work with numbers and important written documents, something already indicated by his having served as Father Castiglioni's secretary in the early 1780s. The degree to which Bình's later writings reveal an obsession with finances and a proclivity for exacting and systematic record keeping also suggests he was well chosen for such a position.[15]

Whatever the apostolic vicar's initial trust in Bình, before long their relationship began to deteriorate. Indeed, there had been signs of strain between the men even before Bình's ordination, hinting that there were limits to Alonso's reputation as a sympathetic and understanding figure. Bình later recalled that in July of 1793 people were referring to Bishop Alonso as "Herod," invoking the biblical king who had ordered the death of all firstborn boys in an effort to kill the infant Jesus. Bình also reported that some people were calling one of Alonso's associates "Pilate," a reference to the man who oversaw Jesus's crucifixion.[16] Although these were apparently not Bình's own characterizations, his apparent sympathy with these labels reflects his growing frustration with the pressures these men were placing upon his community and the fact that he was feeling trapped in the Dominican community, when his desire was to serve the Padroado Christians.[17] It did not take long for the tension between the two men to grow intolerable for Bình, and he decided to leave Kẻ Bùi. In part, Bình may have been inspired by the resolve of his fellow seminarian and friend Father Trệu, who around this time announced his own unwillingness to accept the bishop's orders, rejecting instructions to travel to minister to a community of Dominican Christians.[18] Thus, on April 19, 1794, less than four months after taking on the position at the Dominican bishop's office, Bình decided to set off on his own. The date of his departure was probably chosen deliberately; it was the seventh anniversary of the death of Bình's mentor, Father Castiglioni.[19]

NEW PRESSURES ON THE PADROADO CHRISTIANS

The primary source of the growing tension between the men was Bishop Alonso's aggressive implementation of a range of new regulations and restrictions that were binding upon all Christians living in his vicariate but that to Bình appeared to fall most heavily upon the Padroado community. These represented a test of the community's will, whether its members were prepared to reject direct ecclesiastical instructions to preserve their autonomy. The question of submitting to or rejecting the ecclesiastical authority of particular bishops was not simply one of abstract loyalties to a certain religious order. There was a strong sense among the members of Bình's community that the Dominican bishops and to a lesser extent the MEP missionaries were directly interfering with the ways in which they carried out their religious practices. They objected not merely because the MEP or Dominican bishops were not Jesuits, and as such should not be obeyed, but because these new bishops were demanding changes to long-established religious practices. In doing so, the bishops were both articulating their own interpretations of correct ritual and practice and reasserting their authority over these Jesuit loyalists whose congregations had once dominated the Catholic landscape in Tonkin. The changes the apostolic vicars were requiring of their followers were clearly designed to integrate the Jesuit loyalists into the larger Catholic communities and to erode the sense of separate identity that Padroado Catholics had been able to retain even after the dissolution of the Jesuits.

While some of Bishop Alonso's new regulations were of only limited significance, others threatened fundamental elements of Padroado identity. Bình later enumerated the objectionable regulations in the opening pages of one of his notebooks, prefacing the list of complaints by writing: "First of all, I will speak of the various reasons why the Christians of the Jesuit order in the country of Annam refused to accept the two 'temporary' bishops and went to request an official bishop."[20] The first and most modest of Bishop Alonso's restrictions was a ban on Christians' selling or wearing a type of hat Bình refers to as a *mũ bàng*. Bishop Alonso had determined that such hats were associated with rites for local spirits and thus were linked to indigenous religious practices he and his MEP counterpart were trying to eliminate. Bình complained about this new ban, arguing that this style of hat had traditionally been worn for civic events such as the ritual ceremonies to welcome examination laureates back to their villages. Thus, he insisted, the hat was not merely worn for "venerating the spirits." Moreover, Bình wrote that local Christians had long worn such hats when carrying out church rituals at the central altar or when bowing at the altar of the Virgin Mary.[21] Clearly, the new directive was regarded as an unwarranted interference in long-established ritual practice.

A second policy of considerably greater significance barred Christians wishing to confess their sins from looking for sympathetic priests or ones whom they might regard as more likely to uphold their community's practices. Instead, they were required to confess only to their local parish priest. Practically speaking, this meant that Catholics striving to remain loyal to the Jesuit tradition and the Padroado community's peculiarities could not seek out Bình or the other two remaining European Jesuit loyalist priests to hear their confessions. Bình denounced this restriction as "contrary to the laws of the blessed church and contrary to nature, and also contrary to the ideas of all of the doctors [of philosophy] who have written books about sins, because in these [books] the authors set forth [the idea] that if a person has a problem with any priest, then he need not say his confession to that priest, but should go to confess his sins to another priest."[22] Elsewhere Bình offered an extended version of this critique, emphasizing in particular that the right to select any priest to hear confession was universal but that in his homeland the apostolic vicars had illegally curtailed it.[23] He also pointed out that the dire shortage of priests routinely experienced by Vietnamese Catholics meant that they often had to wait for itinerant priests to make an appearance or, alternatively, travel some distance to find a priest to hear their confession or baptize their children. In short, by restricting their access to potentially sympathetic priests, the new regulation made it much more complicated for the community's members to resist the pressures of the apostolic vicars.

THE PADROADO CHRISTIANS AND THE SAYING OF GRACE

While restrictions on hats were frustrating, and a ban on shopping for priests to hear one's confession was considerably more troubling, it was the bishop's third injunction that provoked Bình and his community's most determined resistance to his authority. This was a seemingly innocuous restriction on how Catholics in the Eastern Tonkin vicariate were expected to pronounce the word *grace*.

The question of language and of translation was obviously a central concern of the so-called world religions from the moment they began to move beyond their point of origin. Those who spread them had to find a way to make their message accessible to new populations operating in different linguistic and cultural realms. This required translating core texts or at least summaries of those texts into local languages, as well as creating local versions of subsidiary commentaries, popular writings, ritual materials, and so forth. Those charged with such projects were confronted with the complex challenge of selecting terminology that would have meaning in the target language but at the same time would convey the ritual significance of concepts, names, and terms that originated in another historical, cultural, and linguistic context.

The issue of language and religious discourse among early Asian Catholics has been explored at length by Vicente Rafael in *Contracting Colonialism* (1988), his study of the seventeenth-century Philippines. Rafael demonstrates the ways in which control over language, and assumptions about hierarchies of language, enabled Spanish Dominican missionaries to assert authority over their Filipino Catholic converts. As Rafael points out, the linguistic hierarchies claimed by European Catholic missionaries reflected not merely the presumed superiority of European languages for the expression of Catholic truths but also hierarchies of European languages themselves. In the Spanish case described by Rafael, the Dominican missionaries asserted a privileged status for their Castilian Spanish as an intermediary between biblical Latin and the Tagalog vernacular spoken by their erstwhile converts.[24] Moreover, while some measure of translation had to occur, this was carefully controlled because of the importance placed on proper transmission of the Word of God.

The Vietnamese case was far more complex. Unlike the monolingual Spanish evangelizing project in the Philippines, the Vietnamese mission was populated by priests from a range of European nations, each of whom brought his own language to the mission field. This created a complex linguistic stew that mixed spoken Vietnamese with Latin and the national (or even subnational) languages of the missionaries, including German, French, Spanish, Portuguese, and Italian. Here the lingering influence of the early Portuguese Jesuit missionaries mattered substantially to the Vietnamese. When the Portuguese arrived in Vietnam and began to communicate basic ritual language to their new converts, they had naturally relied upon Portuguese pronunciations of key terms. The profound influence of Portuguese in this early linguistic project was preserved in Alexandre de Rhodes's *Portuguese-Latin-Annamese Dictionary* (1651), the first published work to link Vietnamese terms and their pronunciations to a particular European language.

But while de Rhodes's dictionary captures some of the terminology in use by Vietnamese Catholics and European missionaries, it does not even hint at the bitter debates that preceded its creation. While some discussions must have happened among priests on an informal basis, at times such debates were conducted in formal dialogue seeking to create standardized terminology. One notable effort to hammer out agreements took place in Macao in 1645 among Jesuits hoping to agree upon a common language for the critically important pronouncement in the course of the ritual of baptism, "I baptize you in the name of the Father, the Son, and the Holy Spirit." As Tara Alberts has shown, while a phrase was formally agreed upon, numerous participants remained unhappy with the outcome, and missionaries from other orders were not necessarily willing to accept the resolution.[25] In short, efforts to find common ground often faltered across national or religious order lines.

Some of the debate hinged on finding the best terms to convey the essence of the religious message or ritual. But another important aspect of the discussion centered on the issue of the pronounceability of ritual terms. Successful completion of Catholic rituals depended upon the correct pronunciation of their sacred words. Thus at times the key question facing the missionaries was not how to translate particular terms but whether to translate them at all. In short, was it better to attempt a translation of a term or ritual phrase or to opt for the somewhat simpler path of transliterating the original Latin? Often missionaries chose the latter course, and many liturgical terms were conveyed into the local vernacular in an approximation of their sound rather than their meaning. Examples of this preference for sound abound, but good ones for the Vietnamese case are found in the collections of tales written in the local vernacular script, *chữ nôm*, by Geronimo Maiorica in the middle of the seventeenth century. Maiorica's works included many examples of sound-based transliteration of the Latin rather than translations of terms into the local vernacular:

sacrament	sa-ca-ra-men-tô
sacerdote (priest)	sa-se-đo-tê
communion	cô-mô-nhong
cross	câu-rút
sacrifice	sa-ghê-ri-phi-xi-ô[26]

At one level, the phonetic rendering of these terms neatly sidestepped any complicated effort to determine local terminology that might convey the significance of the relevant concepts. At another, however, it was a nod to the focus on sound, rather than meaning, which in turn emphasizes the spoken rather than written apprehension of this information. Maiorica's use of *chữ nôm* was thus very closely linked to the spoken word within Catholic communities.[27]

But even finding local approximations for liturgical terms by using Vietnamese or Chinese characters did not always resolve these issues. The MEP apostolic vicar of Western Tonkin, Bishop Longer, for example, lamented the widespread variability in pronunciation of Chinese characters. In a letter of 1796, he bemoaned the fact that "[each character] is pronounced differently in each province in China, and in a manner yet again different in Cochinchina and in Tonkin," and this being so, "What sort of uniformity can we hope to have among our preachers as they follow the liturgy?" In the same letter he mentioned that a decade earlier the new Tây Sơn ruler had issued a list of thirty tabooed characters, each of which was now required to be pronounced slightly differently from its conventional form to preserve the sacred nature of the names of members of the royal family.[28] The practice of tabooing words, requiring both the modification of how they were written and of their pronunciation, was a standard practice among new dynasties and suggests that Vietnamese themselves had long been aware of the complex politics of language and the idea that how a word was pronounced could carry more than abstract linguistic significance.

The issue of pronunciation became a bone of contention not merely because of questions of the physical difficulties in saying words but also because of the historical background to the ways in which they were said. The word *grace*, which lay at the heart of this controversy, is pronounced "grasa" (*graça*) in Portuguese, but the early Portuguese missionaries discovered that their Vietnamese converts had difficulty pronouncing the initial consonant digraph "gr," a sound combination that did not exist in their spoken language.[29] To overcome this problem, the Portuguese clerics permitted their followers to interject an "a" into the diagraph, resulting in the more manageable pronunciation "garasa." As Bỉnh later wrote: "The Jesuit teachers taught the Christians of the eastern region to read it in the Portuguese language, thus *Graça*. But it was difficult for the Annamese Christians to say the word *graça*, so they added the letter 'a' in order to make it easier to say, and thus it was read as 'garasa,' which is just like the word *graça* because they have the same meaning."[30] Indeed, this pronunciation was conveyed into the written vernacular, for the demotic script *chữ nôm* rendered the term using the characters for the sound—"ga-ra-xa."[31]

After his appointment in 1793, Bishop Alonso waded into the turbulent waters of pronunciation politics when he ordered the Vietnamese in his vicariate to change their pronunciation of the word *grace*. He now demanded that they all pronounce it in the Spanish manner as "gracia," thus removing the "a" that had been added by the Portuguese as a matter of linguistic convenience. Bishop Alonso insisted upon this altered pronunciation because in his native Spanish the word *garasa* referred to "the grease of a fat pig" and so could not possibly double as a sacred word.[32] The bishop announced that failure to pronounce the term in the proper way would prevent Vietnamese Christians from participating in the sacraments of the church. Since these sacramental rituals are obligatory for Catholics, the effect of this decree was to separate the members of this community from their religion. Bỉnh regarded the bishop's order as a scheme to depopulate the Padroado community: "The Dominicans wished to take all of the sheep of the Jesuit order, and were preventing the Christians from reading the word *garasa*, [stating] that anyone who did not give in could not have their confessions heard, nor could they have their children baptized, and thus it was that our Christians did not wish to accept the priests of the Dominican order."[33] Indeed, Bishop Alonso later wrote a letter in which he specifically identified the issue of the pronunciation of the term *grace* as one that served to demarcate this community: "Only in the regions of the already-disolved Jesuit area, comprising thirteen parishes [*giáo xứ*], do the coreligionists read it as 'Ave Maria đầy Garasa' [Hail Mary, full of grace], for in all of the other regions in this diocese they read it as 'Ave Maria đầy Gratia.'"[34]

This episode suggests the degree to which language had become a central issue for Vietnamese members of this community and how in this case it served as a marker of a particular subset of Vietnamese Catholics. In his study of the Philippines, Rafael comments that the need to pronounce words correctly was motivated by the Tagalog people's desire to avoid being laughed at: "The danger involved in the mispronunciation and misapprehension of Spanish words stems from a real physical threat—that of incurring the laughter of the Spaniard with whom one speaks."[35] For the Vietnamese Christian community, the threat was not physical but spiritual. The inability (or perhaps refusal) to pronounce the words correctly meant being denied access to the sacraments that lay at the heart of Catholic sacred ritual.

Bỉnh angrily denounced what he regarded as an onerous and unnecessary requirement, one he argued was causing many to die without receiving last rites and preventing the community's children from being baptized.[36] It was, Bỉnh argued, quite unfair that these devout Christians should be punished for their literal inability to conform their tongues to this tricky new pronunciation. Bỉnh also pointed out that the Vietnamese had been using the word *garasa* for *grace* since 1627, and said he could not understand how it had only now become a problem 170 years later. Indeed, while Alonso made the argument that *garasa* was unacceptable because of its objectionable referent in Spanish, he did not explain why this had never been addressed by any of his Spanish predecessors. Four different Spanish apostolic vicars had occupied this position during the course of the eighteenth century, and none had raised any concerns about how the Padroado community members had been saying *grace*. While it is conceivable that the issue hinged on the particular dialects of Spanish spoken by these successive bishops, it is more likely that Bishop Alonso's aggressive policy was a deliberate strategy calculated to bring the community to heel by taking advantage of its declining number of priests and growing vulnerability to pressure from higher church authorities.

Bỉnh mounted a vigorous challenge to the apostolic vicar's pronouncement on the word *grace* using the essential logic that while all languages are distinct from one another, and use different words, these words all have the same referent. Thus, while the term might be *garasa* in Vietnamese, *graça* in Portuguese, *gracia* in Spanish, and even *gratia*" in Latin, "all carry the same meaning, because each country has its own language."[37] He then cited the varying terms used for

God across different languages: "In Spanish it is *Dio*, in Portuguese it is *Deos*, in Chinese it is *Thien Chua*, and in Annam it is *Đức Chúa Blời*." Again, Bỉnh noted, while these might be pronounced very differently in each language, in every case the pronounced word referred to the same thing. In making this argument, Bỉnh was echoing the logic of a participant in the 1640s Jesuit debate in Macao about rendering the baptismal formula and other terms into the local language. The priest observed that while the number 100 "is said 'Cien' in Castilian, 'Cem' in Portuguese, 'Cento' in Italian, and 'Centum' in Latin . . . the significance of the thing is the same, even if the vocables are diverse."[38]

Like the case described by Rafael, the episode illustrates the ways in which European geographies and nationalisms impinged on Asian Catholic practice. What was being transmitted to Asia was not a single Catholicism but multiple versions of this faith shaped by numerous factors ranging from the nationality and language of a given missionary to the religious order or community with which they were affiliated. Bỉnh's very practical argument stemmed from his knowledge of European and Asian languages and reflected the pragmatism of at least some of the Jesuit priests who had introduced Catholicism at the beginning of the seventeenth century. While the erosion of Jesuit and Padroado authority was something about which people were concerned for historical and perhaps emotional reasons, their resistance to these intrusions into their long-held and valued practices would have provided a much more powerful motivation for resisting the authority of the new apostolic vicars.

While Bỉnh spoke of the difficulties for Vietnamese of pronouncing the "gr" of *grasa*, and suggested that the precise term being used did not really matter, since all served as referents to the same concept, the reality was that his community clung to *their* pronunciation of grace precisely because it was *theirs*. It had become an important marker of identity, and their stubborn refusal to change to accommodate shifting ecclesiastical leadership was precisely about preserving this part of who they were. If Bỉnh was correct in arguing that all pronunciations of the word *grace* pointed to the same referent, then his community should not have so strenuously objected to this seemingly simple request from Bishop Alonso. Although the pronunciation might have been challenging, it was not inherently impossible, as many others apparently accepted the new requirement. That the Padroado community so strongly resisted reveals that the battle was for them a much larger one—a dedicated commitment to their heritage. The saying of *grace* became an issue upon which to take their stand against the apostolic vicars.

The dispute about pronouncing the term *grace* clearly lay at the heart of Bỉnh's conflict with his bishop and seems to have been intractable. At some point in 1794 (the precise date is unclear), Bỉnh was staying with the bishop and requested permission to return to his home village to say masses there. To this the bishop replied: "You, Bỉnh, are the young priest who does not accept the pronunciation of *gracia*, but if you will go to instruct [the members of your community] to pronounce it [as such], then you may return [home]." This stipulation was unacceptable to Bình, who responded: "My only intention is to return home to perform a burial ritual for my family ancestors, nothing more. When I go to perform this mass there will be many nonbelievers who come to watch me. If I rebuke and scold the Christians in front of these people, then it will set a very bad example. Thus I will return to Xứ Nam instead and will not go back to my home." Challenged in this fashion, the bishop relented and told Bình that he had permission to go back to perform the services, and that if the congregants were to say "garasa" he could leave them alone and not scold them. At this Bình responded that he would accept the bishop's compromise and go back to his village.[39]

When he returned to the village, the people feared that he had come to force them to conform. He reassured them, however, saying: "I have come back, but not to create difficulties for you, because the Virtuous Teacher has already given permission for me to return to perform the ritual, and those who wish may read the term as 'garasa.'"[40] Members of his family and others were relieved that he had not come to reproach them on the matter of pronunciation. For Bình, however, this was not the end of the problem, for the bishop's dispensation as to how the term could be pronounced extended only to Bình himself and not to other members of the community, despite the one-time exception described above. Bình wrote of his unhappiness at this state of affairs and noted that it brought to mind a biblical parallel during which God was using Moses as a spokesperson to the Egyptian pharaoh to persuade that ruler to release the Israelite people. Moses, Bình observed, enjoyed the benefits of living in the ruler's palace while he communicated God's message to the pharaoh, even as the Israelite people continued to suffer as the Egyptian ruler's slaves.[41] As Bình later wrote,

> Thus my situation also looks like this, because I do not wish to be content on my own, for when all of the priests and all of the Christians of the Jesuit order must endure hardships, we must abandon the home of the Virtuous Teacher and go forth. When the blessed Moses left the palace, he went directly into the wilderness and guided the sheep for forty years, as he had the intention of passing the days and months, because he did not know how to bring the people of Judah back to their ancestral home.[42]

Bình did not wish to enjoy this privilege alone and felt it only fair that if his people were suffering he should suffer along with them.

SCHISMATICS AND RELIGIOUS EXILE

The centrality of the issue of saying *grace* is reflected in two aspects. First, as the above account suggests, the ways in which people pronounced the term became seen as a marker of Catholics' ecclesiastical loyalties. The issue divided Vietnamese

Christians into two camps: those who said the word *grace* "correctly" and those who continued to pronounce it in the older Portuguese-Jesuit fashion. Thus whatever labels the community in the Padroado tradition had borne before were now replaced by one classifying its members as "those who read it as 'Ave Maria đấy Garasa.'" From the perspective of the Tonkinese ecclesiastical hierarchy, this demarcated them in a particular fashion. From a broader perspective, of course, this was simply a new designation for a particular community of people, long at odds with the apostolic vicars, but the label served to put the contest into even starker relief.

The second element of this dispute was that it caused yet another new label to be attached to the Jesuit loyalist community, namely that of "schismatics." The failure to accept the apostolic vicar's decree regarding the pronunciation of *grace* brought with it not merely criticism but a much more severe penalty, that of formal separation from the church. In Roman Catholic doctrine, schisms emerge when an individual or a collectivity of Catholics refuses to accept the authority of their episcopal leader, rejecting his commands or his interpretations of doctrine or ritual. Those who reject episcopal authority are formally labeled as schismatics, understood to be Catholics causing a rift in the body of believers and thus eroding its unity. This is considered a severe breach, for it threatens the integrity of the church. Catholic leaders were acutely aware of the possible repercussions of such disagreements, whatever their scale. The historical disputes within the Christian Church dated back to the early centuries of the Common Era and had given rise to multiple denominations, alternative hierarchies, contending interpretations, and so on. Schisms, however small, had the potential to produce unpredictable and dangerous consequences.

The direct refusal of the community of Jesuit loyalists to accept the pronouncements of their ostensible clerical authorities was thus seen as a dangerous development. The response of the Tonkinese religious leadership was forceful. The community's members were declared to be in schism and were formally barred from access to any of the holy sacraments of the church. This meant that they could not have their confessions heard. They could not attend mass to partake of Holy Communion. They could not have their children baptized, nor could they be given last rites. Each of these sacraments was considered obligatory for remaining a Catholic in good standing. Denial of the sacraments was an extreme measure with severe consequences but was regarded by the apostolic vicars as the step most likely to move the community to accepting their authority, for its members were now forced to rely upon their few remaining clergy, among them Bỉnh himself, who refused to accept the apostolic vicars' ruling and continued to minister to as many as possible. The community was too large, however, for this small cohort of priests to serve its needs, and the reverberations of the schism declaration were felt immediately. Bỉnh wrote about its heartbreaking effect, particularly upon those hoping to have their children baptized, often before their premature deaths.[43] Just as significantly, the label of "schismatics" was now attached to the Padroado community and became part of the shorthand used by its rivals.[44] By his own association with the Padroado community, Bỉnh himself would later be labeled by the Dominican apostolic vicar as the "leader of the schismatics."[45]

One of the profound consequences of the labeling of the community as schismatic was that its members were cast into a form of ecclesiastical exile. The defiant Padroado Christians had been separated from the body of believers through the declaration of schism and were now outside the church. Thus, by not budging—either physically or theologically—the community of Padroado believers suddenly found itself spiritually distanced from the larger church community and its sacraments, subjected to a spiritual exile from which they could return only by submitting to the authority of the apostolic vicars. The idea of the community's members as being in exile took root in their imaginations, as was evidenced in Bỉnh's later writings. In numerous letters to the community, and then in his later histories of Vietnamese Catholicism, Bỉnh drew upon the analogy of the Israelites in captivity in Egypt. This was a community of religious exiles, desperately seeking a way to return to their ancestral land. Bỉnh represented his community as the exiled Israelites and, by extension, himself as their Moses whose journey to the distant Portuguese court was designed to resolve their exile and to bring them back to their spiritual home—not in a physical sense, but in a theological one. Thus, just as Bỉnh himself would eventually become an exile in distant Portugal from which he would never return, so to his community found itself in exile—a place of separation—even though it had never moved.

FICTIVE BISHOPRICS

The unhappiness of the Padroado community with the restrictions on dress, speech, and confession was compounded by yet another issue, stemming directly from the peculiarities of Catholic geography in Tonkin. Since the pope had not dared to overturn Portuguese Padroado authority to appoint formal bishops to Asia, he had, as we saw in chapter 1, used the device of apostolic vicariates to assign his own bishops to the Vietnamese territory. These were religious leaders whose authority lay in fictive (technically defunct) bishoprics. As a consequence, Vietnamese Catholics found themselves under the authority of the bishops of such places as Fesseë, Gortyna, Milopotamus, Ruspae, Hierocaesarea, Ceramus, and Gaballa. By this device Vietnamese Christians were linked to a complex, historical geography of early Christianity, which, while largely abstract, had contributed to shaping the kinds of lineages to which they were the heirs. Bỉnh was clearly unhappy about the apostolic vicar designation in general, but he also objected to the vicars' nominal appointment to religious seats of long-dead or abandoned religious communities in the Middle East. To him, it was absurd that Vietnamese Christians should be overseen by the bishop of Ruspae or Fesseë, rather than a bishop of Tonkin or Annam. In his writings Bỉnh constantly fulminated about these "temporary bishops" (*tám giám mục*), as he called them, whose status he did not respect and whose appointments to fictive Christian communities seemed an insult to Vietnamese Catholics.

Bỉnh and his community saw the solution to their woes in the appointment of a formal bishop to Tonkin. Bỉnh couched his arguments in terms that cast the incumbents in a negative light while impugning the entire system more generally, as this was the most likely means by which to gain sympathy and support for his point of view. In his arguments, Bỉnh underscored the need to create an "official bishopric" for the Vietnamese territories, like those that already existed for other Asian mission areas, among them Goa, Malacca, Bombay, and Peking. Engaging in some hyperbole, Bỉnh spelled out the reasons for his community's unwillingness to accept the authority of the apostolic vicars, distinguishing temporary from official bishops not merely by official status but by a difference in emotional commitment:

> First of all, I will speak about reasons why the Christians of the Jesuit order in the country of Annam do not accept the two temporary bishops and why they are requesting official bishops. [It is] because the official bishops are the masters of their sheep, and they love their sheep, and when they are hungry they give them food, and when they are thirsty, they give them drink, and they also [are willing to] risk their lives for their sheep and they hold and take them when they suffer poverty.... And as for the temporary bishops, when their priests perform rituals they neither read nor pray for us because this is not their territory. And as for those who are not the masters of their sheep, they do not risk their lives for their sheep, but rather carve and loosen and squeeze to reshape them. When they are hungry, they do not give them food, and when they are thirsty, they do not give them drink, and they also beat them to cause hardships for them, and thus [the Christians] fear them, and do not dare to follow them, and they immediately turn and run away and search for their [own] masters. Thus it is with animals, just as Christians are the sheep of the Virtuous Lord Jesus, who has already died on behalf of his sheep, and when they were lost, he went to find them and bring them back.[46]

Thus Bỉnh suggested that because these men were not primary bishops they did not care for their flocks in a suitably conscientious manner. Although Bỉnh's argument seems specious, it is clear that he did not like the particular apostolic bishops who were nominally in charge of his community of Christians, precisely because they were not looking out for this group in the way that Bỉnh would have liked. In short, his objection to them seemingly had less to do with their being temporary or fictive bishops than with the long-running feud between the apostolic vicars and the Padroado community. In any event, whatever Bỉnh's unhappiness about the situation, it would be nearly another century and a half before the apostolic vicariate system was finally disestablished for Tonkin. Only in November of 1960 was Bishop Joseph-Marie-Pierre Khuất Văn Tạo ordained as the first man to carry the formal title "bishop of Haiphong" rather than the designation "vicar apostolic."[47]

BÌNH STRIKES OUT ON HIS OWN AND THE COMMUNITY DECIDES TO ACT

With his community now regarded as being in schism, Bình was determined to dedicate his efforts to supporting their religious needs as best he could. Having left the Dominicans' office in Kẻ Bùi, Bình began an itinerant ministry in the area around his home district, serving only those in the Padroado community and declaring that he would not minister to Christians in MEP or Dominican parishes.[48] Bình was apparently an extremely popular priest, both because of his dedication to the community and because he was known as a local man who understood the region and its people. He wrote, with considerably less humility than was characteristic, that he was held in higher esteem than the other two newly ordained Vietnamese priests who were now also serving in the Dominican-controlled area: "I did not have a salary, but truly the people loved me more than Father Duệ or Father Trêu because I was better acquainted with the Christian communities of Xứ Nam and Xứ Đông than these two fathers were."[49] The community's attitude was reflected in its treatment of Father Bình. He wrote, for instance, that each local priest was typically allocated four bottles of sacramental wine every year; if they ran into problems with purchasing additional amounts, they might be given two further bottles. Bình, however, was told that no such limits applied to him and that when he ran out of wine he could simply take more (presumably from the central stores). Moreover, he was even told to drink it himself if he wished. He also wrote that the villagers would send someone to do his marketing every day, buying whatever food or even clothing that he might need. Finally, people looked out for Bình even when he later found himself under orders of excommunication for failing to accept the apostolic vicar's authority. For example, Father Paul Cuyên, a long-standing acquaintance and one of the two men who had returned from Rome, continued to hear Bình's confessions and did so even after having been told that the only persons permitted to hear Bình's confession were the local bishop or the pope himself.[50]

Supported by Bình and their remaining European clerics, the community refused to relent in the face of the apostolic vicar's draconian actions. But it was now clear that the ecclesiastical pressures, most notably the declaration of a schism, threatened the very existence of the Jesuit loyalist community. Time was running out, as Fathers Carneiro and d'Orta were both in their seventies, and Bình alone could not possibly handle the spiritual needs of all of the Padroado Catholics. The community concluded that decisive action was needed to address this crisis. Its members now understood that their earlier 1781 mission to Europe had failed because of church politics and because it had apparently been misdirected to Rome rather than Lisbon. The community and Fathers d'Orta and Carneiro now came together once again to consider their options. The gathering decided to draw up plans to dispatch another delegation, this time directly to Portugal, whose ruler, the pope had claimed, held the authority to grant their request. The community also had to select a man to lead this mission.[51]

Given his reputation, accomplishments, and dedication to the community, as well as his recent ordination, Binh was the logical choice to head the delegation. In selecting him, the community chose one of the very few ordained priests who continued to serve them and to stand up for their particular interests against the pressure of the apostolic vicars. In voting to send Binh, the community was taking a significant risk, facing the distinct possibility that he would either die somewhere en route or run into some of the same challenges that had turned back the earlier delegation. Dispatching Binh to Europe meant hoping that he would manage to safely negotiate his passage across several oceans, then bring himself to the attention of the Portuguese ruler and somehow persuade that man to send them the bishop and the priests that they needed to retain their autonomy. The community could, of course, have decided that Binh was simply too valuable to lose and selected instead someone more junior to represent their interests. But sending someone more junior, without the status of a priest, and lacking Binh's experience and language skills, would have greatly reduced the likelihood that the mission would succeed. Thus they decided that the gamble, however great, was worth taking.

The Padroado community's decision to send a delegation represented an assertive response to a desperate situation. It suggests the degree to which Vietnamese Christians were not merely the passive "sheep" of their European clerics but active participants in their own religious lives. Binh underscored this agency among the Vietnamese when he observed in one of his journals: "Because we are not animals who lie down and hide, we have risked death for the Lord and for the teachers and for our Christian brothers."[52] Clearly, Binh regarded himself and his companions as actively engaged participants in this drama rather than merely observers subject to larger historical forces. Binh's forceful statement of the risks that he took echoes the Vietnamese tradition of Catholic martyrs, men and women who gave their lives in defense of their religious convictions. At another level, the passage appears to be an implicit criticism of the many former Jesuit loyalists who had given in to the pressure of the apostolic vicars and had chosen to abandon their Jesuit roots. Whereas those Christians had taken the easy route, unwilling to challenge the authority of the non-Jesuit bishops, Binh and his community had chosen the difficult path of resistance, clinging to their traditions and practices even in the face of threats of excommunication.

BEYOND VIETNAM: MACAO, MANILA, MALACCA, AND GOA

With the development of plans to send delegations to Macao and then Europe, the Padroado community began an active, direct engagement with the larger geographies of global Catholicism. Nodes of Catholic authority and logistics that had developed at places such as Macao, Manila, Malacca, Goa, and beyond had long been remote abstractions for Vietnamese Catholics. Indeed, it is likely that the number of Vietnamese Catholics even aware of their existence remained small and that fewer still understood their prominence within their religious world. Those aware of them knew that their missionaries had come from or through these locales. They knew that these places represented sites of European influence and understood them as places where more advanced religious instruction could be found. Consequently, these sites became part of an emerging and transforming geography for Vietnamese Catholics who now understood themselves to be linked to these new religious sites beyond their homeland.[53]

The most obvious manifestation of these new linkages, of course, was the fact of a transnational ecclesiastical hierarchy within the Roman Catholic Church that extended beyond the bishops who administered the parishes under their authority. This hierarchy involved multiple levels of administration that stretched from the papal seat down to the subparishes in far-flung lands. First and closest among these sites was Macao. Until the creation of the apostolic vicariates in Tonkin, Vietnamese Catholics had been subject to the authority of the bishop in Macao. Once the vicariates were created, Macao was no longer a site of religious power over Tonkin, but it continued to loom large as the primary site through which missionaries passed on their way to and from Tonkin. It also served as a safe harbor for those who were expelled from Đại Việt from time to time. Furthermore, from an administrative perspective, Macao represented the nearest active bishopric (as distinct from a vicariate) and the closest city in which a papal nuncio was stationed. A handful of Vietnamese Catholics apparently traveled there for additional religious education at the Macao College as early as 1644, though little is known about these earlier travelers.[54] Finally, some, like Bình and his companions, traveled to Macao to act as advocates for their communities with local church officials.

Further afield within the Catholic ecclesiastical hierarchy of Asia lay the remote archbishopric in Goa on the southwestern coast of the Indian subcontinent. Archbishoprics held ecclesiastical authority for often vast territories, particularly in the mission fields of Asia and the Americas. Archbishoprics were territorially delimited, thus having a distinct geographical component. In the Asian case, a single metropolitan archbishopric was established by the Portuguese in the early part of the sixteenth century at the enclave of Goa on the western tip of the Indian subcontinent. This tiny Portuguese toehold in India thus represented a

Catholic center that extended at least some measure of jurisdictional authority over Catholics across Asia.[55] Goa had been established as an archdiocese in 1533, at which time its jurisdiction stretched across vast swathes of Asia and the Americas, and in 1576 it was made a suffragan diocese linked to Macao.[56] While this did not formally give the archbishop jurisdiction over the independent bishop of Macao, it did create an administrative connection. In any case, the archbishop of Goa was himself, like all other Catholics, subject to the authority of the pope in even more remote Rome.

For some Vietnamese Catholics, these new linkages to the wider world and to Catholic church hierarchies represented a substantial broadening of their sense of the globe, yet it was an uneven transformation. Many Vietnamese Catholics, particularly those less caught up in the politics that had ensnared the Padroado community, retained an older outlook in which neither Europe nor much closer Catholic nodes mattered much. As some European missionaries observed, their Tonkinese parishioners often continued to view the world through a lens still substantially shaped by their connections to the Chinese realm. As late as the 1790s, a French missionary in Tonkin was writing to Europe requesting maps depicting the four parts of the globe to demonstrate that other lands lay beyond the Chinese realm. He noted that his congregations understood the world to be composed of the *thap bat cuoc* (十八國), or the "Eighteen Kingdoms," which were tributaries to the Chinese and "which are now almost all reduced to provinces or governorships, with the exceptions of Korea and Tonkin."[57] This suggests that the spread of modern geographical knowledge and the Roman Catholicism to which it was linked did not have a uniformly transformative effect on the Vietnamese exposed to it. But, enough Vietnamese Catholics understood, or hoped, that the world was now indeed a much larger place and one in which they might find their spiritual salvation. The missions that Bỉnh and his fellow envoys planned to lead would test that hope.

3

Journeys

Macao, Goa, and Lisbon

Once the members of the Padroado community and their remaining European priests had decided to direct an appeal to Portugal, Bình's life moved in a new direction, both figuratively and literally. Rather than merely advocating for his community within the increasingly hostile ecclesiastical environment in Tonkin, Bình and a small coterie of companions left Tonkin to engage with those remote sites of Catholic authority that represented both the source of their difficulties and potentially their solution. These men would travel first to Macao, then to Malacca and Goa, and eventually to Lisbon in their effort to resolve their community's religious crisis. Once he reached Europe, Bình's story intersected with the agents of other major powers on the continental stage. The papal envoys to the Portuguese court were players in the drama that unfolded in Lisbon, as were the combined military forces of the French and Spanish, allied in their efforts to topple the Portuguese throne in the Napoleonic Wars. These European actors and the geographies within which they operated were also of great significance in shaping how events unfolded for Bình after he left Tonkin for the last time in late 1795. Consequently, his story shifts geographically from the immediate divisions on the ground in Tonkin to the larger sphere of global Catholic networks and distant European power structures. This chapter and those that follow trace these journeys that eventually led Bình to Lisbon, while also considering the ways in which he retained ties to his homeland. New spatial geographies, once distant, now became the stage on which Bình's story and that of his community played out. Resolving the problems facing the Padroado Christians in Tonkin required traveling the paths of European Catholic expansion in reverse.

BÌNH AS A VIETNAMESE EMISSARY

Although Bình's departure from Tonkin for distant shores was an uncommon occurrence in a country where such journeys were theoretically closely regulated, it was hardly unique. Porous borders, to the extent that such existed, and even more importantly a long, unregulated coastline made leaving Vietnam for foreign lands a relatively straightforward proposition. Indeed, soldiers, merchants, traders, and political exiles of various stripes had for centuries been departing Vietnamese soil, some only for brief periods and others for good. While many left of their own volition, significant numbers departed under duress: as soldiers in the ranks of Vietnamese armies attacking their Chinese or upland neighbors; as figures in tributary missions of artisans and craftsmen to the Chinese court, such as those sent to the Yuan in the fourteenth century; or as prisoners captured by Chinese or Cham armies with whom the Vietnamese clashed over the centuries. Still others left as political exiles to distant lands. Notable among earlier political refugees were members of the Lý dynastic family, which was ousted by the Trần family in the early thirteenth century. Led by Prince Lý Long Tường, hundreds of Lý clan members and their entourage boarded ships and sailed northward along the Chinese coast, eventually reaching the Korean peninsula, where they were granted refuge by the ruler of the Koryŏ dynasty. They settled there, and their descendants can still be found in both Koreas.[1] Later examples include the literatus Lê Tắc, who sided with the Mongols during their invasion of Đại Việt in the late fourteenth century and then retreated with the Yuan troops to live and write in China, and Tuệ Tĩnh, who at about the same time had been forcibly resettled in China, where he continued his career as a noted physician. Later still, many more Vietnamese became exiles in the nineteenth and twentieth centuries, some forcibly extracted by the French and shipped off to exile in remote corners of the French Empire, others fleeing the political turmoil and warfare of the mid-twentieth century. In short, departure from Vietnamese soil, for a wide range of reasons, is an occurrence of long standing.

Most Vietnamese who left their homeland received little or no mention in the historical record as individuals. The chief exceptions were officials serving as envoys of the court and traveling north to the Chinese capital on tribute and investiture missions. These officials were carefully selected by Vietnamese emperors for their literary skills, knowledge of diplomatic protocol, and understanding of the nuances of Chinese culture and etiquette. Such an appointment was also a way for rulers to acknowledge and reward scholar-officials for loyal service to the court. As representatives of the Vietnamese court, these men were expected to demonstrate that the Vietnamese also belonged to the cultured world whose parameters were defined by their northern neighbors. In making such a journey to the Chinese kingdom, these envoys took part in what amounted to a kind of cultural pilgrimage, as Liam Kelley has demonstrated.[2] Their journey would take them across geographies that were simultaneously alien, since these men had never previously traversed them, and familiar, since these routes were marked by geographical, historical, and cultural monuments with which the scholars were already well acquainted, having encountered them in historical or literary works. At their destination, the Vietnamese envoys would find themselves at the center of the Confucianized world of which they were a part and from which its forms and patterns emanated. The experiences of these men reinforced their understanding of their own belonging to this cultural and philosophical realm.

Just as these elite Confucian scholars served as envoys, so too Philiphê Bỉnh now undertook a mission on behalf of others. Rather than representing the Vietnamese state, however, Bỉnh was a representative of another entity, a particular community of Vietnamese Catholics. His mission was not one of tribute but rather of appeal. Like the Confucianists who served the Vietnamese court, Bỉnh had been selected for his literary skills and his ability to function effectively within a foreign, but not alien, cultural milieu. For Bỉnh, as for the elite Confucian scholar envoys, such a journey would have constituted a pilgrimage to the center of the religious and cultural world of which he had become a part. His journey—to the European West, rather than the Chinese North of the Confucian envoys—would take him a great distance from his homeland and would afford him the opportunity to visit sacred sites associated with his particular worldview, one centered on Roman Catholicism and its ideological and institutional history. Thus both the Confucian scholar journeying to the Chinese capital and the Catholic priest making his way to Lisbon were traveling to a place in which they were simultaneously outsiders and insiders. Each would have been a delegate from far-off "Annam" (or in Bỉnh's case "Tonkin"), but at the same time each belonged to a particular "universal" tradition, whose belief systems extended to some within the Vietnamese lands. As such, while geographical outsiders, both were ideological insiders who, on reaching their destinations, were capable of speaking at least the ideological language (Confucianism or Catholicism) of their hosts, even if they could not always speak their hosts' vernacular tongue.[3] Like the Confucian scholars dispatched by the Vietnamese court, Bỉnh traversed geographical networks that bound his home to a distant ideological heartland. Also, like those scholars, he sought to be recognized and accepted by the distant ruler who lay at the end of the long journey, in the hopes of returning with something that would justify his effort.

Bỉnh shared another significant trait with the Confucian scholars who traveled to China, namely that he, like they, recorded his journey in poetry. Vietnamese scholars had long used poetry to commemorate their feelings, impressions, and personal experiences, for they regarded verse as the supreme form of literature. The genre of Vietnamese travel poetry is a rich one, providing many insights into the mental worlds of those who composed their verses en route.[4] Demonstrating his own origins in this cultural milieu, Philiphê Bỉnh too produced travel poetry along the course of his journey, recording his emotions in response to the experiences of a difficult voyage. Like his Confucian envoy counterparts, Bỉnh wrote verses about the landmarks he reached, the events of his trip, his arrival at key waypoints, and his encounters with people at his destination. He continued to write his "travel" poetry even after arriving in Lisbon, now to mark significant events either immediately or tangentially relevant to his mission. Like the poetry of the envoys to China, Bỉnh's surviving poetry was all written in a seven-syllable regulated Tang form, favored as a verse structure by generations of Vietnamese scholars. Where Bỉnh's poetry departs from that of the China-bound scholars is that he wrote it in the romanized Vietnamese alphabet (*quốc ngữ*), which had come into increasing use among Vietnamese Catholics, rather than in the classical Chinese used by the Confucian scholars. This, as well as the content of his poetry, marked Bỉnh as a distinctive literary voice whose verse suggested a man straddling two cultural worlds. His poetry also makes clear that Bỉnh was not simply a well-schooled Catholic seminarian but also a man acquainted with the larger Sino-Vietnamese literary traditions to which his verse belongs. That he chose to record his travel experiences in poems situates him firmly in the lineage of envoy poets, attempting to capture his feelings and encounters in a form that transcended unexpressive prose.

MACAO: FIRST STEPS

The first phase of the Padroado community's ambitious project to seek outside assistance took the form of a small preliminary mission to Macao, one that would not yet involve Bỉnh. Members of the community had heard a rumor that some European priests were still resident in the Portuguese enclave's Jesuit order house, and they hoped that a direct appeal might persuade some of them to come to serve the community in Tonkin.[5] Thus three of the community's catechists, Brother Lịch and Bỉnh's two seminary acquaintances, Brothers Trung, and Nhân, left Tonkin on September 8, 1793. After a lengthy journey on a small Chinese vessel the men reached Macao on November 13.[6] The tiny peninsula of Macao, situated on the southwestern coast of China, had been a crucial nexus between Asia and Europe since the first Portuguese had arrived there at the beginning of the sixteenth century. Its location and deep-water ports made it a natural stopping-off point for vessels passing between Southeast Asia and the Chinese coast. Macao was ceded to the Portuguese by the Ming court in 1557 and would remain under Portuguese control for the next 440 years. When the Portuguese took possession of what was then an island (landfill and a growing sandbar transformed it into a peninsula over the seventeenth century), it represented one in a long string of Portuguese portcitadels along the perimeter of the Indian Ocean stretching from the eastern coast of Africa to Malacca and then to the southeastern corner of the Chinese realm. Although Macao had initially been established as a trading center, the growth of Jesuit missionary work in Asia, first in Japan, and later in China and Tonkin, made the city an administrative center for Catholic expansion into Asia as well. As Bỉnh would later observe: "The king of Portugal established the city of Macao in the land of the Great Ming [China], not only for all of those who came to carry out commerce, but also with the intention that it [be used] by all of the priests coming to spread the Gospel, for this city would assist them. Thus boats from Macao regularly transported priests of the Jesuit order to Japan, to China, to Annam, to Siam, and to India."[7]

Upon arriving at the Portuguese outpost, the men quickly learned that their hopes had been misplaced. The rumors about Jesuit loyalist priests had been entirely false. Moreover, they saw that the former Jesuit properties had either been taken over by other religious orders or been allowed to fall into disrepair. In the aftermath of this dispiriting discovery the men had to look for a place to stay, as their plans to sleep at the local Jesuit residence had fallen through. Eventually the men found a religious residence willing to take them in, but they were told that they would have to pay for their lodging and meals—a significant hardship, as they had virtually no funds between them.[8] Disappointed in failing to find any priests, the men were determined to salvage something from their journey and so decided to contact the bishop of Macao, Father Marcelino José da Silva, to get a better understanding of how their plight was regarded among the outpost's church leaders. The fact that no one in their delegation spoke either Portuguese or Cantonese placed them at a distinct disadvantage, particularly when the only interpreters they could find were Macao-based priests of the rival Dominican and MEP communities. Hardly unbiased intermediaries, the delegation's interpreters introduced the Tonkinese men to the bishop of Macao by identifying them as renegade Catholics who refused to accept the authority of the apostolic vicars, thus ensuring the bishop's antipathy.[9]

Shortly after their disastrous meeting with Bishop Marcelino, the group's fortunes suffered another blow when Brother Lịch abruptly abandoned his colleagues. The journey to Macao had been much more difficult than he had anticipated, particularly after it became clear that they would not be welcomed into the homes of local clergy and provided for. His group had little money and no connections, and Lịch bore significant responsibility for looking out for the others. He had found them food and shelter, but both were of extremely poor quality and the men were very uncomfortable. Macao was nothing like he had expected, or perhaps hoped. Shortly after his group's unsuccessful meeting with the bishop, Brother Lịch went to call on the local MEP procurer, Claude-Françoise Letondal (1753–1813).[10] When the Vietnamese catechist saw how well stocked the French MEP residence was, and that its priests lacked for nothing, he promptly defected to the enemy camp. It was,

Bình later reported, precisely like the temptation that Eve had experienced in the Garden of Eden when the serpent drew her to the alluring apple against which she had been warned.[11] Not long after entering the MEP residence, Lịch succumbed to yet another temptation, this time seduced by the lure of commerce after falling in with a local trader. The merchant had persuaded the young Vietnamese cleric of the profits to be found in the sale of rosary beads. These were readily available in Macao, and there was a pent-up demand for them in Tonkin, where they were very scarce, so Lịch and his new companion set sail for Tonkin to take advantage of this opportunity.[12] Brother Lịch's defection made it necessary to find a replacement, and the community sent Brother Phanchico (Francisco) Ngân to Macao to join the others. Ngân set out from Tonkin on June 2, 1794, and reached his destination in early August. As Bình later wrote, "This was just like Saint Matthias replacing the traitor Judas," a reference to the man who was added to the group of Jesus's disciples in place of Judas, who had just betrayed Jesus to the Roman authorities.[13]

Brother Ngân's departure left only two members of the Padroado community's overseas recruitment project in Tonkin, Bình and his friend Brother Liên. Bình had been traveling frequently since leaving Bishop Alonso's offices in the spring of 1794, ministering to small Padroado communities while raising money for his own upcoming trip to Macao. The latter was crucial because of the anticipated expenses of the journey to Macao, residence and sustenance in the Portuguese outpost, and then the enormous cost of passage on the months-long trip from Macao to Lisbon. Furthermore, if members of this group did manage to reach Lisbon they would face the expenses of a potentially prolonged residence in the Portuguese capital.

Bình's financing for the trip appears to have come from two primary sources: direct contributions and commercial activities. Many members of Padroado communities in coastal Tonkin made donations, large and small, to pay for Bình's journey to Macao and eventually on to Europe. This was clearly regarded as a kind of spiritual investment, one that would hopefully yield the long-desired bishop to preserve their community. Some of the donations were outright gifts with no specific expectations or stipulations on the part of the givers. Others appear to have been loans, the repayment of which was contingent on Bình's safe return, though where the funds to repay the loans would come from remains unclear. There was also a third category of donations, which involved a quid pro quo. The gifts were made in exchange for promises to say masses on behalf of the donor. Similarly, some donors who had given their money as a loan stipulated that if they were to die before Bình's return, since he could not repay the money, he should instead say masses for their souls. Bình meticulously recorded the names and home villages of these donors, and his notebooks contain lists of these people, along with annotations about the nature of the gifts, whether they were contingent or unrestricted.[14] Everywhere he traveled, Bình found significant support for his fund-raising efforts. In some villages people were desperate to offer something even if their own resources were severely limited. Bỉnh writes of a poor man in one village who had to borrow money to make a donation, while in another an extremely poor woman made a donation, a portion of which Bỉnh felt compelled to give back, judging that she could not spare the entire sum. The enthusiasm of the community and the outpouring of generosity that his project inspired allowed Bỉnh to raise considerable amounts of money for his group's travels.

While donations were a key source of funds, once he reached Macao Bỉnh supplemented this revenue with modest profits derived from small-scale trading, mostly in textiles. Bỉnh's involvement in commercial trade was a logical outgrowth of his Jesuit heritage, for the Jesuits had historically engaged in commerce and other ventures to support their missionary work. Unsurprisingly, the apostolic vicars, most notably Bishop Alonso, seized on Bỉnh's commercial ventures to criticize him, though they also condemned him for the donations he was collecting, claiming that he was misusing the funds or misrepresenting the likelihood of loans being repaid.[15] Bỉnh was acutely aware of these accusations against him. His subsequent detailed and methodical accounting of money received and spent was clearly a means to deflect these criticisms. Moreover, Bỉnh supplemented his balance sheets with extensive justifications for his expenses, particularly while in Lisbon, where he had to explain expenditures (hiring carriages, purchasing clothing) that might have seemed extravagant to those unfamiliar with the cultural context, while also highlighting his own attempts to cut costs wherever possible.[16]

With the flurry of travel and fund-raising completed, Bỉnh was finally ready to depart. In late September, he and Liễn set sail from the small riverside town of An Lang for the Chinese coast. The two men reached the mouth of the Pearl River on October 19, 1794. From there, Bỉnh had a choice: he could either hire a private boat for himself and his companion or travel by regularly scheduled boats that followed certain routes and stopped at intermediate ports en route to their final destination. While the private boat would have been faster, making the journey in a day and a night, Bỉnh opted for the slower but cheaper and likely less conspicuous public boat. It took Bỉnh and Liễn three days and nights to reach Macao, a trip that required stopping at numerous ports to take on and disembark other passengers, and required changing boats several times. Via this convoluted path, the men finally arrived in Macao on Monday, October 27, and were reunited with their three companions.[17]

BỈNH IN MACAO

Bỉnh's first visit to Macao must have had an enormous impact on him. When he set sail from Tonkin for Macao on this first overseas journey in early fall of 1794, Bỉnh left behind a country where Christianity existed in a semiclandestine state, subject to varying degrees of official proscription, its followers constantly uncertain

FIGURE 2. Late eighteenth-century engraving showing the waterfront buildings along Macao's harbor as they would have appeared to Bỉnh upon his arrival. Author's collection.

about the church's status during the political turmoil of the era. Its religious edifices were for the most part humble wooden structures, subject to the whims of anti-Christian officials and readily dismantled for concealment when necessary. In Macao, Bỉnh found a thriving, European-inflected port city deeply steeped in Catholicism.[18] After commerce, religion was the most prominent institution in this city of twenty-five thousand. Indeed, from its founding, Macao had been a city strongly associated with the Roman Catholic Church, as reflected in its formal name: "City of the Name of God, Macao." Several priests had been among the first Portuguese settlers and had established small churches soon after their arrival. These churches were gradually transformed into larger, more enduring edifices, so that by the time Bỉnh visited in the 1790s he would have seen a city dotted with religious structures running along a line in the western part of the hilly peninsula. These included three modest chapels, eight large churches (including the cathedral), the Jesuit Seminary of St. Joseph, and the Jesuit College of St. Paul. There were also several convents housing orders of Catholic sisters.

Of the city's numerous religious edifices, the most dramatic was the Church of the Jesuit College of St. Paul, which stood atop a hill with commanding views across the city.[19] Reached by a wide, steep staircase climbing the hill upon which it was perched, the structure must have amazed Bỉnh. The St. Paul's Church had been erected between 1620 and 1627 and featured a highly carved, four-tiered facade, as well as a richly painted wooden interior. The church's interior was described in a 1637 account as "carved in wood, curiously gilt and painted with exquisite colours,

FIGURE 3. Facade of the former Jesuit church, St. Paul's, which was destroyed by fire in 1835. Today it stands as an icon of Macao. Author's photo.

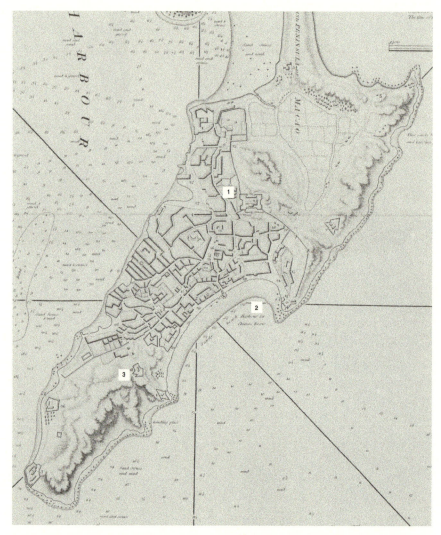

FIGURE 4. Map of Macao from 1795, the year of Bỉnh's passage through the city on the way to Europe, showing sites of importance for his mission: College of St. Paul (1), Macao's harbor (2), and likely location of MEP residence (3). Library of Congress.

as vermilion, azure, etc. divided into squares; and at the joining of each square, great roses of many folds or leaves, one under another, lessening until all end in a knob."[20] The affiliated College of St. Paul was itself noteworthy for the historical role it played in the spread of Catholicism in Asia. Matteo Ricci and Johann Adam Schall von Bell, famed Jesuit missionaries to China, had both studied Chinese language and customs at this Jesuit college before beginning their mission work in China. St. Paul's was also a significant point of pilgrimage, for it served as a repository for the bones of martyrs from around Asia. By the 1790s its subterranean crypts already contained the remains of Jesuit martyrs from Japan and, more importantly, from Tonkin. Bỉnh would certainly have visited the church's ossuary, particularly given the significance of these martyrs' remains for the early history of the Vietnamese church and his own awareness of this history.

While such Jesuit vestiges suggested the order's historical importance in Macao, by the time Bỉnh and his friends had arrived the order was already fading into memory. Most of its property and structures had been seized or allowed to fall into disrepair, and the order's priests had been forcibly returned to Europe. The Jesuit seminaries and churches had been taken over by rival religious organizations, and the order's once-powerful presence in Macao had been reduced to a handful of Jesuit loyalist priests and some sympathetic Portuguese merchants. Despite the disruption of the Jesuit tradition, the sight of former Jesuit strongholds such as the Church and College of St. Paul, now slowly decaying from neglect, must have stirred Bỉnh's determination to continue his advocacy for the order's legacy and devotees in the Tonkin he had left behind.[21]

THE ABORTIVE TRIP TO EUROPE: 1795

The first thing Bỉnh did on arriving in Macao after reuniting with his friends was to deliver letters written by Father Nuncio Horta to Bishop Marcelino and to the Holy See's representative in Macao, papal nuncio Giovanni Baptista Marchini. After delivering these letters, Bỉnh and his four companions went in search of accommodation large enough for the five of them. They were fortunate to find lodging in the home of a fellow Tonkinese, a merchant who had settled in the Portuguese colony and married a Macanese woman. Once housing had been arranged, the men visited the local markets to stock up on provisions. In his later writings, Bỉnh described the cost of food, calculating that the men had enough money for supplies to sustain them for a month. As it turned out, the men would be in Macao nearly three times that long and must have undertaken some significant economies or relied on the charity of local religious organizations. Bỉnh reported that in Macao (unlike Tonkin), women neither sold nor purchased goods in the markets, but that men handled such matters. Unfortunately for the Vietnamese visitors, these merchants would not deliver their purchases to their residence as Bỉnh had expected, and while most others hired local youths to deliver purchases to their homes, Bỉnh's group saved money by carrying their own.[22] Bỉnh also reported that during their stay in Macao the men were fortunate to find a taste of home in the form of a type of dried fish (*ngão*) imported from Đồng Nai in Cochinchina. They ate this with fresh rice as one of their regular meals.[23]

After arranging lodging and purchasing supplies, Bỉnh turned his attention to finding a way to travel to Europe. He immediately encountered several difficulties. The first was that there were no European vessels anchored at Macao, making it impossible to book direct passage to Portugal. Bỉnh reported that European ships had been scared off by the threat of French pirates then operating in the Southeast Asian seas.[24] He would either have to wait until European vessels did appear—a time-consuming option with no guarantees except the high cost of lingering in Macao—or, alternatively, consider traveling on a vessel that might carry them along only a portion of their intended route. While contemplating these unpalatable choices, Bỉnh ran headlong into his second hurdle. This stemmed from the same ecclesiastical politics between the MEP and Dominican apostolic vicars and the Jesuit loyalists that had driven Bỉnh and his companions to Macao in the first place. The MEP procurator, Father Letondal, was on good terms with the local Spanish Dominican representative and was prepared to coordinate with the Dominicans to prevent the Vietnamese delegation's departure. Aware that Letondal might prove an obstacle to their efforts to find passage out of Macao, Bỉnh tried to secure local allies who might assist in overcoming the MEP procurator's efforts. Most notably, he contacted the Portuguese governor of Macao, Jose Manuel Pinto, to speak on their behalf with Bishop Marcelino. The governor was sympathetic to the men's plight and promised to help by arranging and attending a meeting between the Vietnamese men and the bishop. Unfortunately, Pinto fell ill on the day of the meeting and sent along two other officials in his stead. At this meeting, the bishop sought to erode the governor's support for the Vietnamese by laying spurious (according to Bỉnh) accusations against the men and their larger community, dredging up the case of a Vietnamese Jesuit who had taken a wife as evidence of the community's moral shortcomings. Consequently, when Pinto's two delegates reported back to him, Pinto accepted the bishop's accusations and dropped any efforts to assist Bỉnh.[25]

The meeting's outcome was a setback, though it did not deter Bỉnh from continuing to plan for their departure. The larger problem remained the shortage of transportation options: it took Bỉnh another two and a half months to find a boat for their journey. Unfortunately, when he finally located the boat on January 15, 1795, it was sailing only as far as Goa. Although this was only partway toward their destination, the prospect had a certain appeal because Goa was the seat of the archbishop whose authority extended across all of Asia's bishoprics.[26] Bỉnh paid the boat's captain 120 Portuguese *patacas* in advance for himself and for Brother Nhân, who would accompany him. Brothers Liễn, Trung, and Ngân would remain behind to await their return and to look out for the community's interests in Macao.[27] Having made their payment, the two men boarded the vessel. Bỉnh must have felt considerable relief as their boat slowly made its way out of Macao's inner harbor in preparation for the long voyage to Goa.

But the boat had just cleared the harbor when it stopped to await the arrival of its captain, who was completing some last-minute business on shore. The delay proved

FIGURE 5. Bishop Marcelino, bishop in Macao in the 1790s, was the man who blocked Bỉnh's first attempt to travel to Europe and whom Bỉnh had to escape to succeed in his second. Portuguese National Digital Library.

disastrous for Bỉnh's carefully laid plans: Father Letondal had learned of Bỉnh's impending departure and took advantage of the opportunity to block the Vietnamese from traveling. Letondal spoke with the boat's captain and persuaded him to remove his Vietnamese passengers in exchange for an additional payment.[28] Seeing an opportunity to increase his profit by being paid for a passage he would not have to provide, the captain agreed to this arrangement. But when he visited Letondal to collect the promised compensation, the MEP cleric could not provide it. Letondal had been counting on the Dominicans to provide half of the sum, since they also had a stake in blocking Bỉnh's journey. When the Dominicans refused to help fund the scheme, Letondal was unable to pay the captain, who angrily denounced him as a cheat and vowed never again to transport MEP clergy. With the arrangement dissolved, the captain invited the two Vietnamese priests back aboard his vessel.[29]

Just as it seemed that the Vietnamese group's plans were back on track, however, Bishop Marcelino himself intervened and formally barred the captain from transporting Bỉnh on his vessel.[30] Blocked from traveling on the boat, Bỉnh went to see the captain and insisted that his initial payment be refunded. The captain, however, told him that he had already spent the money and thus could offer no refund. Bishop Marcelino then suggested a compromise in which Liễn would replace Bỉnh, as the captain would still be providing passage for two priests.[31] In the end, Bỉnh reluctantly agreed to this wholly unsatisfactory compromise and was forced to swallow the bitter disappointment of watching his companions sail to Goa without him. Bỉnh lamented his travails in Macao in a poem, composed on January 24, 1795, several days after seeing his friends depart:

Obstacles Preventing the Priests from Traveling
We are stupefied at being fated to weakness, how dare they block us?
Grieved at our departure being prevented by one in a position of
    high saintliness.
The chasing wolf herds the sheep [through] the confusing storm;

Chasing the bees, and crushing the ants, causing both so much
    hardship.
I have been blocked by the generous Lord, so that I do not become
    too proud
All my labors have been for naught as they've all been turned back.
But our envoy's banner hurries forward and still waves ever onward
Aiding the sacred hours and minutes whose duration we cannot know.[32]

Why did Bishop Marcelino first block Bỉnh's departure and then suggest such a compromise? If he was determined to halt the project in its tracks, it would have been far simpler for the bishop to prevent any of the Vietnamese from leaving for Goa. The bishop's compromise appears to have a ruse calculated to allow the men to use up their limited financial resources while he took steps to sabotage the project and its chances of success. When the Vietnamese men needed a Portuguese translation of the petition they intended to bring to the ruler in Lisbon, they had turned to a local priest who spoke and read Chinese and who had frequently served as an interpreter for visiting Chinese delegations. This man had drafted a Portuguese version and had then innocently shown it to Bishop Marcelino in the hopes of securing his assistance. The bishop, on seeing the petition, and perhaps for the first time clearly understanding the import of the Vietnamese Jesuit loyalist project, had seized the translated version and refused to return it.[33] This meant that when the two men finally set off for Goa they were forced to leave without a key element in their appeal to the Portuguese ruler.

RETURNING TO TONKIN

Forced to remain behind in Macao while his companions sailed to the west, Bỉnh planned his next steps. He had given most of the group's money to the two men who had set out on the long journey to Goa, meaning that those who stayed behind would have to monitor their remaining funds very carefully. Accordingly, the first thing he did was to find cheaper lodging for himself and Brothers Trung and Ngân. He managed to secure apartments with a local Chinese man whom Bỉnh identified as Simon, possibly a fellow Christian. After that, Bỉnh began to make plans to return to Tonkin, where he needed to conduct additional fund-raising in preparation for possible future journeys, while leaving Brothers Trung and Ngân behind to look out for the community's interests in Macao and await the return of Liễn and Nhân.[34] Fortunately for Bỉnh, the same Chinese boat that had earlier delivered him to Macao had just returned from its run up the coast to Teochew and was on its way back to Tonkin. Bỉnh had come to trust the captain and was pleased to be able to use his services again. The captain must also have trusted the young Vietnamese priest, for he lent Bỉnh fifteen silver coins (đồng bạc), which Bỉnh then gave to the men who would stay behind.[35] Bỉnh also purchased food for his own journey: dried fish, stored in bottles. Finally, on the evening of January 24, 1795, Bỉnh and the captain's two sons boarded the small boat to begin their journey to Tonkin. Their trip would first take them up the Pearl River to Canton, where the captain had some business to conclude before continuing the journey to their destination in Tonkin.

Bỉnh's return to Tonkin almost ended before it began. Immediately upon leaving the docks at Macao, the boat was stopped by Chinese customs officials who boarded the vessel and began to search it for opium, an extremely valuable but illegal cargo whose smugglers were subject to severe penalties. Opium had become a major concern for Chinese authorities along their southeastern seaboard, and the Qing government had begun to police harbor traffic much more aggressively. Bỉnh's boat was indeed transporting opium, which was now on the verge of being discovered. Thinking fast, however, the boat's captain offered the customs inspectors several of Bỉnh's bottles of dried fish as "samples" of the freight he was carrying. Fortunately, the inspectors were satisfied at this apparent proof of the captain's cargo, and the ship was permitted to resume its journey to Canton.

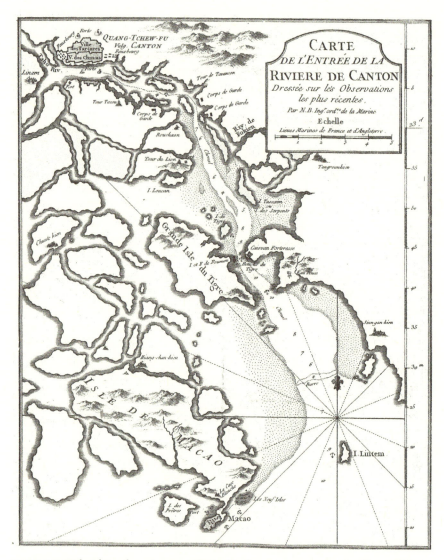

FIGURE 6. Mid-eighteenth-century map illustrating the waterways connecting Macao with Canton, along which Bỉnh traveled in 1795 during his return to Tonkin after his first journey to Macao. Author's collection.

Once the boat reached Canton, Bỉnh's voyage stalled. He was forced to endure a two-week wait while the captain conducted business on shore and awaited the arrival of additional Teochew vessels with whom they could convoy for safety as they headed to Tonkin. Bỉnh took the opportunity afforded by the unexpected delay to explore the city and its environs. He reported that "during these fifteen days while I was in Canton, I visited all of its streets and even went outside the city walls, in order to attend mass and to visit a small community of Christians who engage in goldsmithing."[36] A few members of the community spoke a bit of Vietnamese, enabling Bỉnh to converse with them during his visit. The captain finally completed his onshore business, and the boat set out once again. It was an excruciatingly slow trip, taking more than a month to cover the roughly one hundred kilometers from Canton to the mouth of the Pearl River.[37] The sluggish pace was caused in part by low water levels and weak winds, which forced the boats to rely on oars, rather than sails, for propulsion. The journey was also slowed by the boat's repeated stops to visit the numerous small shops along the riverbanks selling items that might be profitable for Tonkin-bound merchants.

The final leg of the journey was marked by the threat of pirates who the captain had heard were attacking coastal towns. Although Bỉnh's boat was not traveling directly through the area where the pirates had been reported, their course would take them along the edge of it. Bỉnh later wrote that although he had no personal property to lose in such an attack he was still frightened and prayed to God for protection. The captain took more mundane precautions, counseling Bỉnh that in the event of an attack he should fend off any attackers with a heavy wooden staff, and all the while telling him "not to worry."[38] Fortunately, their ship passed through the area unmolested, finally reaching its destination, the Vietnamese port of An Lang near the confluence of the Red and Ninh Cơ rivers, on May 20, 1795.[39] Bỉnh's return journey, with its repeated delays, had taken nearly four months.

THE JOURNEY TO GOA AND BACK

As Bỉnh was slowly making his way back to Tonkin, Brothers Liên and Nhân were on a lengthy journey to Goa and hopefully beyond. The inauspicious start to their journey, marked by Father Letondal's schemes and Bishop Marcelino's interference, was a harbinger of what lay ahead, for the two men encountered one complication after another in the course of their trip. The first major problem occurred when Liên and Nhân's boat arrived at the Portuguese outpost of Malacca just around the tip of the Malay Peninsula. Instead of making a quick stop to resupply the vessel, the ship's captain abruptly announced that he had decided to make an extended stay at the port. In addition to delaying their journey, waiting for the boat to resume its course would have meant the considerable expense of temporary residence in Malacca, so Liên and Nhân reluctantly left the boat to find onward transport. Fortunately, they were able to find a ship on the verge of departing for Goa and arranged to come aboard.[40] Having resumed their journey after the unexpected delay in Malacca, Brothers Liên and Nhân finally reached Goa in May of 1795. Like Macao, Goa was one of Portugal's major fortified outposts along its

FIGURE 7. The Portuguese enclave of Goa, which the two Tonkinese envoys visited during their 1795 attempt to reach Europe. It was here that the archbishop of Goa turned them back to Macao. Engraving, 1740. Portuguese National Digital Library.

Indian Ocean trading routes. It had been taken over by the Portuguese in 1510 and represented their primary base on the west coast of the subcontinent. Like Macao, Goa was an ecclesiastical as well as a trading center. The archbishop of Goa exercised nominal oversight of bishoprics throughout South and East Asia, including that in Macao, and was thus potentially a significant figure in the church politics shaping the lives and experiences of Vietnamese Christians.

To their great relief, upon their arrival, the archbishop, Manoel de Santa Catarina, a member of the Carmelite order, welcomed the two men into his residence.[41] Brothers Liễn and Nhân's joy at reaching Goa and being welcomed by the archbishop was soon tempered by yet another setback on their ill-starred journey, one that echoed the problems that had stalled their earlier departure from Macao. As had been the case in Macao, there were no European vessels at the port in Goa. This threatened to halt their journey or to delay it indefinitely. While the absence of Europe-bound vessels was a distinct problem, the men faced an even bigger and equally familiar obstacle, namely the complex church politics they hoped to have left behind in Macao. In short, the men were not granted the necessary ecclesiastical authorization to continue their onward journey to Europe. They discovered that although Bishop Marcelino had allowed them to make the journey to Goa, he had simultaneously taken steps to sabotage any attempt to reach Europe itself.

Unbeknownst to the two Vietnamese, they had carried with them the instrument of their undoing: a letter from Bishop Marcelino addressed to the Goan archbishop. The bishop's missive requested that the two men be sent back to Macao and assured the archbishop that he could himself deal with their concerns, making a trip to Europe unnecessary. The archbishop, letter in hand, informed the men of the bishop's instructions and assurances. The Vietnamese envoys protested that it was this bishop who had already made their journey so difficult and who was now once again interfering with their efforts. The archbishop, clearly unaware of the nuances of the situation, and having no reason not to trust the bishop's word, told the men that he was confident that matters would be different upon their return.[42] Although they were understandably skeptical of the bishop's ostensible change of heart, Liễn and Nhân had no choice but to accept the archbishop's directive.

So it was, that after just a week in Goa, Brothers Liễn and Nhân were forced to begin their return journey. They first made the eight-day passage by boat up the coast to the British port of Bombay to increase the likelihood of finding a ship making the trip to Macao. Even there, however, finding passage proved difficult, and they spent three weeks in Bombay before eventually securing berths on a Macao-bound English vessel. Unfortunately for Liễn and Nhân, their journey home proved yet another ill-fated ordeal, one that made their earlier problem-filled journey pale by comparison. After forty days of traveling, first down the western coast of the subcontinent and then across the Indian Ocean, the men finally came within sight of the Malay Peninsula. Just as their vessel entered the Straits of Malacca, however, it was attacked by a fleet of six French pirate ships. The pirates seized the boat's passengers and crew and began to pillage their vessel. After being held captive for three days along with the rest of the ship's passengers, Liễn and Nhân were finally put ashore at Malacca, while the pirates sailed away not only with everyone's possessions but also with the boat they had traveled on. The men were now destitute. All of their money was gone and their worldly possessions had been reduced to the clothes on their backs. The two Vietnamese men had reached the nadir of their misfortunes.

At this point, desperate and marooned, Liễn and Nhân finally saw their fortunes slowly begin to improve. Some sympathetic locals guided the two men to a resident Dutch merchant known to provide assistance to those in difficulty. True to his reputation, the Dutchman, who lived outside of the city walls with his concubine, agreed to take in the stranded Vietnamese clerics and to provide them with food and clothing. Finally, after three weeks of searching, the Dutchman managed to find a Dutch boat on its way to Macao and convinced its captain to provide the Vietnamese free passage back to their starting point.[43] By this time it must have been early September of 1795. The men boarded this vessel and after a further forty days at sea finally reached Macao, probably sometime in the second half of October.[44] Their adventure had lasted more than ten months and had covered more than eight thousand nautical miles, but at its end the two men found themselves back where they had started, and with less than nothing to show for it. They had lost virtually everything they owned in the pirate attack, and, perhaps even more dispiriting, their mission had been a complete failure.

BỈNH'S FINAL MONTHS IN TONKIN

While Brothers Liễn and Nhân were struggling to overcome their many challenges, Bỉnh had been back in Tonkin, once again engaged in a whirlwind of activity. Upon his return in May, he visited dozens of communities, where he met with people ranging from local Christians to high-ranking Tây Sơn officials to Nguyễn military spies curious about conditions in Macao. His primary task was continuing to raise funds for a return trip to Macao and for the men he had left there, who would need additional financial support. His efforts to secure donations continued to be quite successful. In one village a local catechist welcomed Bỉnh and then announced to the gathered villagers: "This man is not like the others, and we should thus welcome him, for he is a person undertaking the task of the order. He has already traveled to Macao and has returned, and having gone there and met with the people there, he will again be going back to Macao, and thus anyone who feels compassion for him should make offerings to him that he might be able to eat."[45] Hearing this speech, many people came forward to present gifts to Bỉnh. Bỉnh also continued his work as a priest, saying mass in numerous communities, meeting with local Christians to discuss religious matters, and continuing to defend the Jesuit loyalists against the pressures of the apostolic vicars.[46] Fortunately for Bỉnh, this period of frenetic activity coincided with a time of relative political calm in Tonkin. Although warfare was raging in Cochinchina, where the Nguyễn armies were slowly encroaching upon Tây Sơn positions on the south central coast, the situation in Tonkin was somewhat more tranquil. Tonkinese Catholics had been briefly shaken by an aggressive anti-Christian edict proclaimed in February of 1795, but by the time Bỉnh returned in late May it had already been revoked and the official who had issued it had been dismissed in disgrace.[47] European missionaries reported that while they faced some problems, they and their communities were generally being well treated and some of the property seized from them during earlier crackdowns was being returned.[48] It was also a time in which Vietnamese Catholics could travel openly, meeting with almost no interference.

While Bỉnh was able to move about freely, he still faced challenges, not from political but from religious authorities. On learning that Bỉnh had returned to Tonkin, Bishop Longer wrote to Bỉnh, probably criticizing his actions (Bỉnh does not say), but Bỉnh refused to reply to the bishop's letter, seeing no point in doing so.[49] Soon thereafter, Bishop Alonso also renewed his effort to rein in his onetime subordinate. Indeed, the bishop issued an order that anyone who came across Bỉnh was to seize him and turn him over to the apostolic vicariate.[50] The dynamic of their complicated relationship is captured in a pair of letters Bishop Alonso wrote to Bình in mid-1795, after the latter returned from Macao. In the letters, the bishop expressed strong affection for Bình and offered to bring the newly ordained priest under his personal tutelage. In the first letter, dated June 27, 1795, Bishop Alonso wrote, "There is no one in this world who holds you in greater affection than I do, and there is also no one who does favors for you like I do, and so I must express clearly my feelings of affection for you."[51] Despite these obvious marks of regard, the bishop expressed exasperation with Bình for his stubborn refusal to place himself under the care and guidance of his superior. He referred to the young Jesuit priest as a "lost sheep" and tried to convince him to return to the fold, urging him to come to meet to discuss their differences and expressing hope that Bình would return to "correct your earlier mistakes." In his reply Bình stated that he was very busy with a number of important tasks and would be unable to visit until they were completed. In short, the young priest felt no obligation to accept the bishop's invitation to talk, likely convinced that their differences of opinion were irreconcilable.[52]

Bình obviously continued to resist appeals from the solicitous bishop, for a second letter followed a few months later in September 1795. Written shortly before Bình's final departure for Macao, this letter summarized Bình's ecclesiastical transgressions and repeated the bishop's call for a meeting to address his outstanding concerns. In the letter, Bishop Alonso added to his earlier accusations against Bình, now claiming that the Vietnamese priest had been hearing confessions and saying masses without authorization. The letter also reiterated charges that Bình was illegally engaging in commerce, a transgression for which the bishop threatened to excommunicate him once again.[53] As in the previous missive, the bishop revealed a mix of fondness for and frustration with Bình. While his affection may partly have stemmed from his natural affability, Alonso was also known as a strong supporter of the indigenous clergy, among whom he had worked for more than three decades, and he likely held Bình's demonstrated abilities in high regard.[54]

As the bishop's letters and Bình's own writings make quite clear, Bình was a man of determination bordering on obstinacy. The threats and pleadings of his religious superiors had little impact on him, for he did not hold figures of authority in awe. Indeed, the pressure placed upon him only prompted Bình to write ever more vigorous defenses of his actions in letters and journal entries. When necessary, he was not above engaging in a measure of sophistry based on his knowledge, or at least his interpretation, of canonical law and practice. For example, he contended that the order of excommunication against him had not been properly implemented and as such was not in force. After having received the order, Bình was saying mass in a local church when a person asked how he could be doing this when he had been excommunicated. Bình replied that had he truly been excommunicated, a notice to this effect would have been posted on the church door barring his entry and informing people that Bỉnh was not permitted to say masses there. He argued that since this procedure had not been followed, it was logical to conclude that he had not actually been excommunicated.[55] He made much the same argument when he arrived in Macao and immediately went to say mass at a local church, despite still being under the order of excommunication.[56]

RETURN TO MACAO

Having completed another round of successful fund-raising and having eluded the bishop's grasp, Bỉnh left Tonkin for the final time on November 15. After a journey complicated by Chinese authorities who were carefully screening vessels in response to the heightened threat of pirates, Bỉnh reached the coast of Guangdong on January 23, 1796, and three days later arrived once again in Macao.[57] Here he was reunited with Brothers Liễn and Nhân, who by now had been reduced to begging on the streets to survive. When Bỉnh met them he was shocked at what he saw: "When I arrived in Macao and saw Brother Liễn and Brother Nhân I was very startled, because their clothing was in tatters, their faces were yellowed, and they were confused [chẳng biết ý nào]."[58] Initially, the two men were reluctant to share their story, as they did not wish to dishearten their friend, but Bỉnh pressed them for details, and eventually they poured out their litany of woes, in particular describing the ruse used by the bishop of Macao to block their onward journey in Goa.[59] The bishop's actions infuriated Bỉnh, who must have wondered whether the Macanese religious leader had permitted the men to travel as far as Goa simply to deplete their limited resources, fully confident that his letter would reel them back in. Although angered by this deception, Bỉnh was obviously already well versed in the complex religious politics surrounding his community and its efforts. Indeed, on his own return to Macao he had slipped ashore on a tiny boat rather than continuing to the main docks on the vessel bringing him from Tonkin, fearing that his arrival might once again attract the unwanted attention of the religious authorities.[60]

Now reunited with his friends, Bỉnh immediately began to organize a second attempt to reach Europe, this time hoping to travel as a group of five. His travel companions were people he knew and trusted, men now tempered by the experience of sea journeys and of living abroad. He hoped to divide his delegation into two groups that would journey separately before reuniting in Europe if all went according to plan. Traveling in the company of others brought several advantages. Were one man to fall ill, his companion could care for him while continuing to handle any necessary travel arrangements. Another factor might simply have been to increase the impact of their arrival on the court in Portugal, where a delegation, rather than a solitary envoy, might attract more attention and underscore their seriousness. Furthermore, all of the Vietnamese who had previously traveled to Europe had done so in small groups, never alone. A last consideration might simply have been the emotional need for company during the months-long journey. While Bỉnh likely had the mental fortitude and linguistic facility to travel by himself, the subsequent journey suggests that traveling in the company of others brought numerous advantages. Dividing the delegation into two groups was motivated by the very practical consideration that it would increase the odds that at least one team would survive the journey.

Before these plans could be finalized, however, Brother Liễn's health suddenly deteriorated. He had fallen ill after returning from his arduous trip to Goa and had never fully recovered. Bỉnh was concerned that Liễn might not survive the long and difficult journey to Europe and decided to leave him behind in Macao to represent the Padroado community's interests and to serve as a conduit for information between Tonkin and Europe. Because Liễn's health was still poor and he needed care, and because Bỉnh did not wish to leave this important position in the hands of a single invalid, he made arrangements for another man, Brother Bảo Lộc (Paul) Thuyên, to travel to Macao to stay with him.[61] Meanwhile, accompanying Bỉnh, now thirty-seven years old, would be Brother Trung, also thirty-seven, Brother Nhân, who was thirty-six, and finally Brother Ngắn, the youngest member of the delegation at just twenty-six.

After deciding on the composition of his delegation, Bỉnh turned to arranging the logistics of their departure. As before, he found himself under the watchful gaze of local Catholic authorities, notably the bishop of Macao, who continued to seek ways to block Bỉnh's departure for Europe. Since his arrival in Macao, Bỉnh had already twice been called to the bishop's residence, and a third summons soon followed. Bỉnh was certain that at this meeting, scheduled for February 14, the bishop would formally order the Vietnamese to return to Annam and finally submit to the authority of the apostolic vicars.[62] Wary of the bishop's intentions, Bỉnh hastened his preparations for the journey, hoping somehow to evade the prelate's grasp. The first step he took was to cut his plait of hair, an act, he noted, that would prevent his being able to go through, much less return to China, where the plait (queue) was required by law.[63] After cutting his queue, Bỉnh's final task was to clean out his group's rented quarters. Once this was completed, the small company fled, with Bỉnh noting that "otherwise [the bishop] would throw me into prison, because I do not go along with his ideas."[64] It was February 11, 1796.

Bỉnh carefully guided his group to the waterfront, where he had previously made arrangements with the owner of a small boat who would help them to look for a European vessel for their long journey. The men boarded the boat and soon left the city's harbor behind, their crew rowing in the direction of nearby islands where their search for sailing vessels would begin. Their preliminary efforts on the afternoon and early evening of that day were unsuccessful, and, with night falling, the men decided to chance a brief return visit to the city. Trusting that darkness would shelter them from the eyes of the bishop or his agents, they directed their captain to head back to the harbor. Once their boat had anchored, Brother Ngân slipped ashore and made his way to Brother Liễn's apartment. Ngân visited with his ailing friend for a few hours and then retraced his steps to the harbor, still under the cover of darkness, and reboarded the vessel, which promptly set out to sea once again.[65]

The group spent the next several days in an increasingly anxious search for a boat to take them to Europe. The seas around Macao were dotted with islands, making the search extremely difficult. There were any number of anchorages where European boats might be located but not readily visible to the searchers. Bình's boat periodically pulled ashore at one of these islands so a crew member could climb to its highest point to scan the horizon for boats or the telltale signs of masts protruding over the tops of islands. As their search dragged on Bình became increasingly fearful and exhausted. He knew this was a highly uncertain and perilous venture, not only because of the threat of pirates who infested these waters, but also because of his suspicions about the trustworthiness of the crew of his own boat.[66] As he wrote in his later account of the episode: "I was frightened of the sailors on our ship that they might kill me and seize my possessions."[67]

Then, on the morning of February 14, after three days and nights of fruitless searching, the men finally spied a cluster of six English vessels anchored off the coast of Guangdong and preparing to set sail for Europe.[68] Their crew immediately began rowing hard in the direction of these ships. They approached the English vessels in turn, but at each of the first five their request for passage was rejected. The crew of Bình's vessel were rapidly tiring and becoming extremely discouraged. They had been rowing all morning and into the early afternoon without pausing to eat or drink. Bình was also deeply disheartened, for he had no idea where they would go if they were unable to secure passage to Europe. The thought of a humiliating return to Macao and its waiting bishop was more than he could bear.[69]

With growing desperation, the men rowed toward the last remaining prospect, the most distant boat of the anchorage. Here their luck finally turned. The men hailed the captain of the vessel, requesting permission to come aboard as passengers. The captain, seeing a boat full of men, asked how many were seeking passage and on learning that it was just four men welcomed the Vietnamese aboard. Having attained his objective, Bình pulled out his purse to pay the crew of their small boat. The men expressed their surprise at Bình's apparent wealth. Since the four Vietnamese were not travelling with the kinds of luggage normally carried by passengers for distant lands and had been rather shabbily dressed, the sailors had assumed they were poor. Bình later wrote that he suspected only this misperception had protected his group from harm and he attributed their survival to divine intervention.[70] Bình's delegation now climbed aboard the British vessel, which they learned was called the *St. Anne*. Bỉnh took this as a sign that this saint (the mother of the Virgin Mary) had rescued them by providing the miracle of a ship that would take them to Europe.[71] Since it was already afternoon, the captain provided his new passengers with what must have been immensely welcome food after several days of nervous travel on a tiny boat.[72]

Now that they were aboard the *St. Anne,* Bỉnh was understandably eager to depart. The more distance between himself and the Macanese bishop who had been attempting to prevent his departure the better. Unfortunately, the winds were calm and the ship was unable to move away from shore. At the mercy of the tides, it began drifting slowly back in the direction of Macao. This greatly alarmed Bỉnh, who could do nothing but fret and pray. Finally, the late afternoon winds slowly began to pick up, filling the vessel's sails and gradually pushing the boat out to sea. Soon Bỉnh could no longer see Macao, and finally he began to relax, confident that he had escaped the bishop's reach.[73] The boat set full sail around noon of the following day, February 15, 1796, in the company of the other five English vessels, three of which were also headed to Europe, while the other two were destined for Bombay.[74] Soon their boat passed within sight of the Chinese island of Hainan, a sure indication that they were now truly under way.[75] And, as the boat sailed slowly southward, Bỉnh celebrated his good fortune and departure with a poem.

> *Rejoicing at Having Begun the Journey to the West*
> The year has just commenced, the sixth day of the month that be-
>   gins the spring,
> The will of the saints has brought about a completed wholeness.
> We are in the northern seas, and even though we still have thousands
>   of miles to cross,
> The western sky seem already a bit nearer.
> Ahead lies the virtue of the Lord of Heaven above,
> Behind lies the support of a myriad people below.
> The times of hardship will become a period of joy
> For truly his hand distributes each wisely and equitably.[76]

EN ROUTE TO EUROPE

For the next five weeks the *St. Anne* traveled through the South China Sea and along the Vietnamese coast. The boat then rounded the southern tip of the Vietnamese territory and crossed the Gulf of Tonkin to the Malay Peninsula, whose eastern coast it followed southward, stopping only briefly at an unnamed location between the fifth and seventh of April to take on food and water in preparation for the longest and most dangerous leg of their journey.[77] Once the ship passed the tip of the

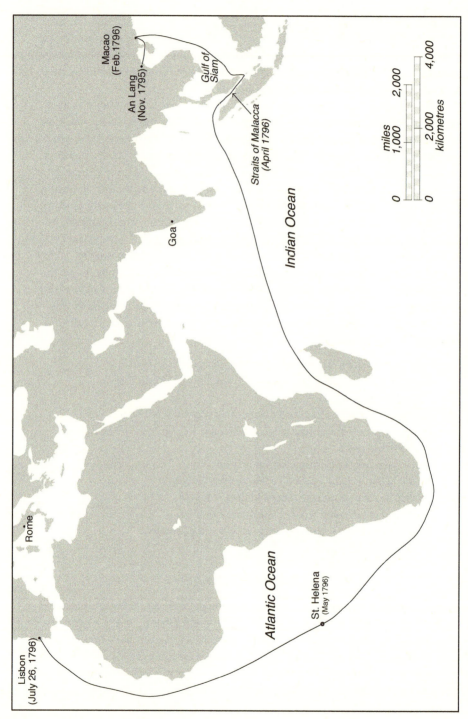

MAP 4. Map showing the route of Binh's journey from Tonkin to Lisbon, via Macao, the Malay Peninsula, and St. Helena. The dates shown are for his departures from various locales, except for St. Helena and Lisbon, which are arrival dates.

peninsula, its course would take it northwestward through the Straits of Malacca and then across the Indian Ocean. The first part of the trip would be particularly hazardous because the islands that lay between Sumatra and the Malay coast were, like those around Macao, infested by pirates, both Southeast Asian and European. It was here that Nhân and Liễn had been beset by pirates on their return from Goa. In preparation for this part of the trip, Bình and his three friends received instruction on how to load and fire the vessel's cannons and, like the other passengers and crew, had their names randomly assigned to form eight-man teams for each cannon. The *St. Anne*'s crew was a diverse multiethnic group composed of people from numerous countries, so communication was a challenge. Bình feared that acting in concerted fashion in the face of a pirate attack would be difficult at best.[78] He and his companions participated in repeated cannon-firing drills during this part of the voyage but fortunately never faced an attack.[79]

Finally, on April 19 the *St. Anne*'s crew and passengers were relieved to clear the straits and find themselves at last in the open waters of the Indian Ocean. Here the men traded the threat of pirates for the open ocean's potential for dangerous storms. While Bình had fortunately avoided a pirate attack, he was not so lucky in escaping the perils of the unprotected seas. Ten days into their voyage across the seas below the subcontinent, the *St. Anne* was struck by an enormous storm.[80] The tempest's ferocity was such that their captain ordered the lowering of the masts and sails to avoid their being ripped off by the raging winds. For three days and nights the boat pitched and rolled, completely at the mercy of the sea and winds. Like many on the ship, Bình was certain that they would all perish, and he and other Catholics aboard confessed their sins and prepared to die. After three days of terror, however, the storm finally blew itself out, and Bình commemorated the event and their escape with a poem.

A Poem on Encountering a Storm on the Open Seas
As evidence of the vast immensity in the distances of the ocean
The angels of heaven blew up a powerful storm.
The squalls of rain rose up like mountains of water,
The peaks of the waves rose as high as the rooftops of houses.
As for those holding the sails, and those holding the rudder,
They regretted their crimes, and called out with laments.
It was three days before the storm ceased and we were fortunate to
    be given help
As the brightness before us to the east emerged once again.[81]

The storm finally behind them, the four Vietnamese managed to eat some dry bread, the first food anyone had been able to hold down since the storm began. Although the ship had survived the storm, the gales had pushed it far off course and had caused it to become separated from the other ships in its convoy. This raised renewed fears about the possibility of pirate attacks on the open seas.

The captain sought to offset their greater vulnerability by increasing their speed and traveling more aggressively at night. Once again, Bỉnh and his friends were called on to assist with a variety of shipboard tasks so that by rotating men the crew could handle their responsibilities around the clock. Bỉnh's group mostly helped with hoisting and lowering the sails but also assisted with keeping lights burning for the nighttime sailing, watching the compass, and keeping a lookout for land. Occasionally the Vietnamese passengers would be asked to help with hoisting and dropping anchor, though Bỉnh noted that this was infrequent because they had little cause to stop during their passage across the open ocean. Sometimes, the men were also called upon to help measure distances. In commenting on their measurement of the voyage, Bỉnh noted that the distance from Macao to Europe was more than six thousand *dặm*, which meant that when it was daytime in Annam it was nighttime in Europe, and vice versa, a circumstance he attributed to the fact that "the world is round like a grapefruit."[82] Additional chores included untangling the ship's large hemp ropes and hauling up seawater every morning with which to clean the open decks. Brother Nhân demonstrated a talent for sewing and so was excused from other shipboard chores while he produced Western-style attire for those on board using material that the captain had brought along. Bỉnh passed the time by talking with the seven or eight Portuguese sailors on board. Among other things, Bỉnh could not resist describing the reason for his journey, telling them of his earlier unsuccessful efforts to send letters to Portugal and chatting with them about the situation of missionaries in Siam.

Bỉnh commented on this leg of their journey in a poem that discussed their contributions to these shipboard labors, ones he suggests the men were eager to provide as a concrete way of supporting the journey bringing them closer to completing their mission.

> *Helping to Hoist the Ropes on the Boat*
> From the time that we were able to find this merchant ship
> We resolved to help repair the tangled ropes.
> We assembled the necessary sail ropes, though covered with snow
> And each time we unraveled them, our heads would be covered with frost.
> Only once did we stand on land as we crossed the endless waters.
> For many months we traveled everywhere in the four directions.
> We insignificant ones obeyed the orders we had committed to accepting.
> Thank you, Lord, for your many mercies.[83]

When Bình was not occupied with shipboard tasks, he spent his spare time pacing the ship's decks, unable to sit still. At one point during those uneasy walks, the captain learned of his passenger's restlessness and ordered a crew member to find Bình and bring him up to the wheelhouse. When the captain saw Bình unsteadily ascending a ladder from a lower deck, he climbed down to examine him, and on looking at Bình's face asked him if he was ill. Bình replied that he was feeling dizzy, at which point the captain suggested that staying out on the decks in the fresh air might help. The captain also arranged for him to take some medicine and insisted that he drink a lot of water to reduce the sensation of dizziness. Taking this advice, Bình moved his bedding from below decks to the open deck and tried to sleep there when the wind and waves did not make it too difficult. The shipboard diet did nothing to improve Bình's physical or mental state, and as their journey dragged on the Vietnamese grew increasingly unhappy with the food they were given, which consisted chiefly of dry biscuits dipped in soup to make them more palatable. Bình complained that there was little variation in their diet and that the food was often prepared in unsatisfactory ways. He commented that there were times when he wanted to run down to the kitchen and cook the meat himself. They also often ate below deck in the dark, without candles or oil lamps, so that they could never really tell what they were eating.[84] Surprisingly, Bình noted, the sailors on board made no effort to catch fresh fish, even when the waters around the vessel were full of them.[85]

ST. HELENA AND ON TO LISBON

A Poem on Reaching the City of St. Helena
Suddenly there appeared from nowhere in the distant sea
The unexpected sight of the mountains of St. Helena.
These green mountains lay in the path of the coming and going
    ships;
fresh water ran forth from springs in the city.
Moving freely, we saw many people of note,
A mixture of every race of our people.
Thanks to kindness and fortune, water flowed freely
The mountains offered water in abundance, so there was no need for
    concern.[86]

The *St. Anne* sailed without further incident southwestward toward and then around the Horn of Africa sped by the prevailing winter-season monsoon winds. In such journeys timing was everything, and between their night sailing and their effective use of the monsoon winds Bình's boat made remarkably good time, arriving at the remote island of St. Helena on May 8.[87] This meant that the vessel had

FIGURE 8. Early nineteenth-century view of Jamestown Harbor on the remote South Atlantic island of St. Helena. It was here that Bỉnh broke his journey from Macao to Europe and where he transferred from an English ship to a Portuguese one for the last leg of his journey to Lisbon. Wellcome Library, London.

traveled more than 7,500 nautical miles in only forty days, averaging more than 180 miles per day.[88] It had been a much more rapid passage than their journey from Macao to the Malay Peninsula, in which a trip of roughly 1,300 nautical miles had taken a full five weeks. At more than a thousand miles from the African coast, St. Helena is one of the most remote places on earth. It is a tiny speck of land of only forty-seven square miles and is dominated by sheer cliffs and mountains rising more than 2,600 feet from the ocean's surface. It was discovered by the Portuguese admiral João de Nova Castella in 1502 and became an important stopping-off point for Portuguese vessels making their way along the coast of Africa as they traveled to and from Asia. Its existence remained a Portuguese secret until 1588, when the English also came upon it. Over time the Portuguese gradually lost interest in the island, while the British continued to make use of it. In 1658, an English captain, John Dutton, became the first British governor of St. Helena and built its first fortification. Fort James was erected in the northwestern corner of the island in a narrow defile in the cliffs near one of the island's few usable anchorages. This site gradually developed into a settlement known as Jamestown, which was staffed by members of the British East India Company.

When Bînh arrived at the port in Jamestown, his boat anchored at a wharf constructed less than a decade earlier, in 1787. He must also have seen the island's sole religious edifice, the Anglican St. James Church, which had been built in 1772, and to which a clock tower had been recently added.[89] Once their vessel anchored, Bînh and his friends went ashore for the first time since they had left the Malay Peninsula. This provided a welcome opportunity to recover from the hardships of shipboard life. The stopover presented the men with a different sort of opportunity as well when they noticed a Portuguese vessel anchored in the Jamestown harbor. They had planned to remain aboard the *St. Anne* to its destination in England, where they would then have had to find another boat to Lisbon. Now, however, the possibility presented itself that they might skip the journey to England and travel directly to Lisbon. With the help of one of their Portuguese shipmates by the name of João, the men approached the vessel, which had just arrived after a lengthy journey from Bengal. With João's assistance, the men were able to communicate their wishes to the boat's captain, who readily agreed to provide passage. They then said their farewells and thank-yous to the captain of the *St. Anne,* who to their great surprise tried to pay them for their shipboard work during the long voyage. The Vietnamese, however, refused to accept this payment, considering their free passage compensation enough.

The only downside to transferring to the Portuguese vessel was that it meant an expensive delay in waiting for their new vessel to take on water and give its crew a much-needed rest before completing the last leg of its journey, for Bînh and his companions had to hire boats for the frequent journeys between their vessel and the shore and had to pay for their own food while in Jamestown.[90] During the stay in St. Helena, the men took the opportunity to sew Vietnamese-style outfits for themselves that they planned to wear for their meeting with the Portuguese ruler to enhance their exotic appearance.[91] While Brother Nhân had done some sewing on the St. Anne, rough seas had often made this very difficult, and the calm of the harbor made his task easier.

After spending more than three weeks on St. Helena, Bînh and his companions finally departed on June 1. Their ship—the *Grão Pará* under the command of Captain Caetano Martinho—hoisted anchor and set sail for Portugal in a convoy of twenty-five English trading ships escorted by a three-decked English warship outfitted with between seven hundred and eight hundred cannons.[92] The military escort was necessary to provide protection against seaborne marauders, including Barbary pirates, who preyed on vessels sailing along the northwestern coast of Africa, and mercenary vessels belonging to the new revolutionary regime in France, which was aggressively targeting commercial traffic along the Atlantic coast of Europe.[93] To counter these threats the British government had instituted a policy for its vessels to travel in convoys starting in 1793, and in the year of Bînh's journey this had been made mandatory for British merchant vessels.[94]

Life on the Portuguese boat was substantially more comfortable than it had been on the English vessel. The majority of the crew was Catholic, and the boat featured an altar at which regular worship services were held. Also, there was a doctor aboard to handle shipboard ailments, and Bỉnh wrote that his friend Trung received treatment for an unspecified illness, possibly a recurrence of the rheumatism that had already troubled him before his departure from Tonkin. Finally, the Portuguese vessel offered a significant improvement in terms of food, both its variety and its quality. There was a baker on board, who regularly provided them with fresh bread, a welcome change from the dry biscuits available on the *St. Anne*. There were even live animals on the ship, which provided fresh meat for their meals. Sometimes animals would be killed specifically for meals, while at other times their unexpected death would prompt the kitchen to use them for the next meal. Bỉnh noted that when a pig died its meat was prepared for him and for his companions, it being understood that Vietnamese had a preference for pork. Similarly, when a goat died, it was given to the "cuan Mouro" (i.e., Muslim crewmen) because, as Bỉnh observes, their religion forbade their eating pork.[95] Moreover, the kitchen was responsive to fast days affecting its mostly Catholic crew and provided alternatives to meat, including dishes of beans or fish when requested. Bỉnh noted that they frequently ate fish because the crew caught a large number during their voyage. The kitchen workers tossed food waste overboard, causing fish to follow and sometimes even surround the boat, so that they were easy to catch with small nets.[96]

The *Grão Para*'s journey around the western coast of Africa was uneventful but comparatively slow. It took their convoy fifty-three days to cover the approximately 2,800 nautical miles that brought them within striking distance of the Portuguese coast.[97] At this point, on July 13, Bỉnh's vessel parted ways with its escort as the British ships continued northward toward their English destinations. The departure of their escort provoked considerable concern among those on Bỉnh's vessel about their new vulnerability, and Bỉnh reported that even the boat's captain was frightened. In response to this fear, the captain read from the Bible and sponsored masses for the sailors. Some offered prayers of supplication to the Virgin Mary, with promises of masses to be said in her honor if they reached their destination safely.[98] Men pledged different amounts toward these masses, and once the ship neared shore a crewman went around the boat collecting the promised donations that would be pooled to arrange for the saying of masses.

The Portuguese vessel was fortunate to have good winds and clear skies, and freed of the confines of traveling in a convoy their boat made rapid progress toward the Portuguese coast. The men finally spotted land on July 24, 1796, ten days after having left the safety of the British convoy.[99] Bỉnh was elated that he and his companions had made the long and dangerous journey unscathed. He was also delighted that passage for the entire journey had cost him and his friends virtually nothing, allowing him to preserve the meager funds with which they travelled for anticipated expenses in Europe. On both legs of their journey, the captains of each vessel had provided free passage for the Vietnamese and had given them food and drink.[100] In later recounting this good fortune, Binh would boast of the free passage he had managed to procure, directly contrasting it with the experience of some young Chinese Christian students who later traveled from China to Italy and whom he met during their transit through Lisbon. He wrote that these young men had had to pay more than 1,200 *dong pataca* for their own journey to Europe.[101]

4

Arrival in Lisbon and First Encounters

As Bình sailed up the Tagus on the *Grão Pará* on July 24, 1796, his gaze would have taken in the green hills that line both sides of the river on the approach to Lisbon. He must also have seen the Torre de Belem, a fifteenth-century Manueline architectural gem that stands as a tribute to seafarers. The monument's platform, shaped like the prow of a ship, juts into the river from its northern bank, serving as a landmark for sailors that signals their impending arrival at Lisbon's docks.[1] After months or possibly years away from home, the Torre must have been a tremendously welcome sight to the boat's sea-weary crewmen. Bình reported that when the *Grão Pará* finally reached the docks in the heart of the city it was greeted by a large number of men, women, and even children, who lined the river banks near the Praça do Comércio. He was initially under the impression that the crowds had all come to meet his boat, but soon learned these were simply Lisbon residents out for a typical Sunday afternoon stroll.[2]

Bình commemorated his arrival in Lisbon with a poem, the first he composed on European soil.[3]

> *Poem on Entering the Capital of the Country of Portugal*
> Now at last I have entered the Western world.
> As for the road into the future, no one knows how long it will be.
> We covered ten thousand miles, pushed by the currents of the four winds.
> We have suffered one tragedy, but already completed three stars.
> The eastern sky continues to the court of the silver clouds;

FIGURE 9. Late eighteenth-century depiction of the Torre de Belem, an imposing Manueline architectural monument to returning sailors, which greets vessels as they sail up the Tagus to approach the docks in the heart of Lisbon, just beyond. Portuguese National Digital Library.

> From the northern seas we have already crossed over the layers of waves.
> Now I have slaked a portion of that thirst,
> For the great drought we've experienced has been followed by a downpour.

The poem was a reflection on the hardships of the journey and the great uncertainties that it had entailed. He spoke of the seas and winds, the rivers and islands that he and his companions had traveled through, on, or past. He concluded his verse by invoking the metaphor of sustenance, the need for water and the spiritual thirst that they had endured through times of parching drought. From his perspective, their arrival in Portugal was no mere spring shower but rather an overflowing deluge. It represented the embarrassment of riches that came with finally setting foot on land again, a land of potential rejuvenation not merely for the four men but for the community that they represented. The poem was both a reflection on the hardships the men and their larger community had endured and an expression of hope about what Lisbon might offer.

ARRIVAL IN LISBON AND FIRST ENCOUNTERS

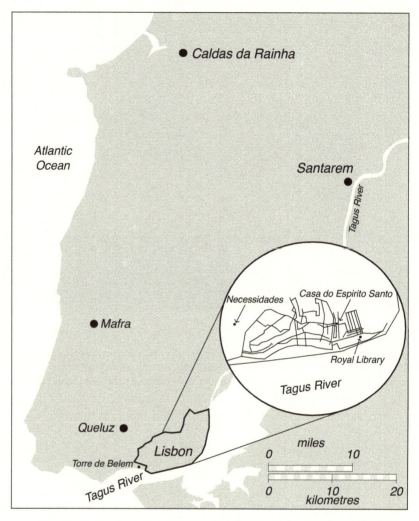

MAP 5. Map showing key sites in Portugal where Bình lived or that he visited after his 1796 arrival.

LISBON

When Bình arrived in Lisbon in the summer of 1796, he was entering an ancient city but one very recently and substantially transformed. Once the Phoenician port city of Olissipo, Lisbon had subsequently served as one of the westernmost outposts of the Roman Empire. Later still, during the fourteenth and fifteenth centuries, it had been transformed into the epicenter of European oceangoing exploration, particularly influenced by Henry, Duke of Viseu (better known as Henry the Navigator; 1394–1460), who actively promoted Portuguese global ventures. In the centuries that followed, Portugal's importance as a center of exploration declined along with its fortunes as a seagoing empire, though its location in the southwestern corner of Europe meant that Lisbon continued to serve as a major port of departure for many vessels leaving the continent for Asia. Several decades before Bỉnh's arrival, the Lisbon cityscape had been drastically reshaped by one of the most powerful earthquakes ever to strike Europe. The *terramoto* of November 1, 1755 (All Saints' Day), killed more than twenty thousand and destroyed the heart of Lisbon's urban core, including the Ribeira palace, waterfront home of the Portuguese royal family.[4] The royal family itself was spared only because its members had been away from their palace attending a religious festival. In addition to its physical destruction, the quake had psychological reverberations that extended across Europe, sparking theological debates about the relationship between God and humanity and raising questions about the event's religious implications.[5]

While an event of enormous destruction, the quake had a silver lining for the Marquis de Pombal, prime minister under King João V (r. 1750–77). The earth tremor's destruction afforded Pombal an opportunity to remake the city and to modernize it according to the principles of the Enlightenment. The haphazard and narrow streets of the ruined old city were replaced by a grid in the very heart of the urban area, which was also reconfigured through the creation of a series of impressive *praças* (open-air plazas).[6] Consequently, the Lisbon that Bỉnh sailed into on that July day in 1796 was one on which Pombal had left a substantial mark. Despite the earthquake's destruction, a rapidly rebuilding Lisbon remained one of Europe's major cities. Although not on the scale of the largest urban centers like London or Paris, at the turn of the nineteenth century Lisbon was still the fifth most populous city on the Continent, with around 200,000 residents.[7] This figure grew steadily during the first decades of the nineteenth century and by the early 1820s stood at more than 260,000.[8]

After the *Grão Pará* finally docked near the Praça do Commercio, news of Bỉnh's delegation was related to the officials and priests who had come to meet the boat. The next day, Bỉnh and his companions revealed their religious affiliation for the first time when they donned the long formal robes of Vietnamese priests that they had sewn during their journey in preparation for going ashore. This was part of a carefully calibrated strategy to make a dramatic first impression upon their Portuguese hosts. Bỉnh had calculated that such garb would enhance their exotic appearance and serve to distinguish them and their mission in the eyes of the Portuguese ruler and his court. As he wrote of this later:

> We had already sewn [these outfits] while crossing the ocean because we had the intention of presenting an unusual appearance, one different from Western customs,

to make it easier to gain entrance to the palace of the king, because he would wish to know about unusual things. If we were simply to dress ourselves in the manner of people in the West, we would be unable to get any financial support or assistance with arrangements for the four of us, and if we were to be attired in a very ordinary manner, then we would simply be regarded as impoverished people, and no one would even look at us, and it would be very difficult to complete our task, for impoverished people do not carry out important tasks. It's as the saying goes: "First you fear the palanquin, then you fear the outfit." Because no one here knew who we were, we had to go ahead and give the appearance of being officials.[9]

To further set them apart, Bình and his companions even eschewed European-style hats, choosing instead to cover their heads with what he calls "Đàng Trong style" bound kerchiefs (khăn cuấn).

The spectacle the men now presented had the desired effect, for they soon attracted the attention they had sought. When they first went to thank the captain of their boat for providing them passage, he was startled at their transformation and asked them why they had not made their identities clear earlier. Had they done so, he told them, he would have made arrangements for their food and lodging upon arrival. Later that morning several Portuguese officials boarded the ship to meet with the now impressively attired men, after which they reported the Vietnamese delegation's arrival to the Portuguese ruler, Crown Prince Dom João.[10] Two days later, on July 27, the prince sent his own delegation led by the Marques de Ponte de Lima (Tomás Xavier de Lima Teles da Silva, 1727–1800) to meet with the Vietnamese men and to bring them ashore to witness the festivities surrounding the feast day of Saint Anne and the anniversary of the canonization of St. Ignatius of Loyola, the founder of the Jesuit order. At the end of the day, however, Bình's party returned to the boat, where they still had free accommodation and meals, until housing arrangements could be made.

Even as his representatives were showing the Vietnamese around the city, the crown prince was consulting with officials about where to house the Vietnamese during their time in Lisbon. He sent his representatives a letter of instruction to give the Vietnamese arrivals and a man he referred to as an "accompanying Brazilian native convert" some local currency and to make arrangements for their temporary residence with the Oratorian religious community. The choice was likely deliberate, as the Oratorian congregation had been active in overseas mission work in Asia (notably on the Indian subcontinent and in Sri Lanka), and as such would likely have represented a welcoming community for the men.[11] The Oratorians had several residences in Lisbon, and the prince had to determine which would make the best temporary home for the Vietnamese visitors. This proved a complicated task. Initially, Bình wrote, the prince was going to send them to the congregation's Necessidades convent, also known as the House of the Virtuous Mary (Nhà Đức Bà).[12] But before this order could even be conveyed to Bình, the ruler changed his mind. When the crown prince's representative returned to the boat to update the men regarding the court's discussions, he told them that they would be housed at the Benedictine monastery of Saõ Bento, a massive structure in the Estrella district of Lisbon.[13] The men had not yet begun the preparations for moving to the São Bento monastery, however, when the prince changed his mind yet again. Upon further reflection, Dom João concluded that this residence was too far from the city center and ordered that the Vietnamese arrivals be housed instead at the Casa do Espirito Santo (House of the Holy Spirit), the Oratorians' primary residence, situated in the heart of the capital.

The matter appeared finally to have been settled, and the Vietnamese delegation, along with the "Brazilian native convert" mentioned in the royal order, made its way to the Casa do Espirito Santo. This Oratorian house stood at the eastern terminus of Rua do Chiado in the heart of the Chiado District, directly overlooking the newly built Pombaline city core. When the group presented itself at the house, however, its father superior told them that it would not be possible to accommodate them there after all: "[Sometimes] when priests come from boats and have duties in Lisbon and wish to stay at the house of the Virtuous Lord and Holy Spirit for one or two days they can do so, because that would be only one person. Your group, however, has five members and we do not have enough room here for you." The lack of space at the Casa do Espirito Santo was caused by ongoing repairs to the substantial damage it had suffered during the 1755 earthquake. The father superior suggested that the men go, instead, to the city's other major Oratorian residence: "I ask you please to go to the house of the very sainted Virtuous Mother of the Necessidades, which is a very large property and also has beautiful gardens in which you can go for walks."[14] Consequently, despite the prince regent's wishes that the men be situated near the heart of the city, Binh's delegation was reassigned to the remote Necessidades residence.

Before the men could finally be settled into their residence, a curious incident arose that required the intervention of the Oratorian leadership. This concerned the "Brazilian native convert," a priest whom the Vietnamese had apparently gotten to know during their journey from St. Helena to Lisbon. On coming ashore, this priest had done his best to remain in the company of the Vietnamese, taking them around and involving himself in their early meetings with local officials. At some point in these discussions, the man sought to convince these officials that he too was a member of this newly arrived party, to the point of suggesting that he was himself Vietnamese. Most likely, the man observed that these exotic visitors were being generously taken care of and saw a golden opportunity. In any event, his persistent but unsubstantiated claims were turned over to the Oratorians, who held a meeting to discuss the matter. After some discussion, the congregation's leadership determined that the man was an imposter and wrote to the crown prince of their conclusion: "This man does not know the Vietnamese language as these others do, because this man is only the on-board priest, whom the Vietnamese met for the first time during their trip from St. Helena to Lisbon, and thus we recommend that you look out for these four men who are the delegation from the Annamese Christians and reject this imposter priest who is trying to dip into the royal funds."[15] On the basis of this report, the ruler ordered the man expelled from the congregation house and barred him from any further association with the Vietnamese. Bính was relieved that this matter had been settled and their bogus companion had been sent on his way.

In addition to arranging housing, the prince regent promised financial support for the men during their stay in Lisbon. Bính quoted him as stating: "As for the matter of expenditures regarding the four men who are envoys of the Annamese Christians, however much they need shall be given to them, and funds shall be disbursed from the royal treasury as necessary. Whether this is once a month or three times a month does not matter."[16] Bính reported that this order opened the royal coffers and that the men had no problems with any expenses, either for their own needs or for those of the men assisting them in their early rounds to meet officials. Their primary expenses were for lodging and food while staying at the congregation house and local transportation, mostly in the form of carriage travel. Bính noted that every time they went out they would need to hire at least three horse-drawn carriages, for a single carriage could carry only two passengers, and though there were only four of them they always needed a third carriage for the local Oratorian priest who served as their escort.[17]

With their housing arrangements finally settled, Bính and his companions moved into the Necessidades residence on July 28. This large monastic compound had not been damaged in the 1755 earthquake (indeed, it had served as a refuge for the royal family in the quake's aftermath), so it was temporarily functioning as the primary Oratorian residence in Lisbon while the Casa do Espirito Santo was being rebuilt. The Necessidades house, or rather parts of it, had been built specifically to house priests, and King João V had given it to the Oratorians upon its completion in 1745.[18] In exchange for being given such a prominent residence with its close proximity to the royal family, the congregation was expected not only to staff the chapel of Nossa Señora das Necessidades, around which the larger compound had been built, but also to provide classes in a wide range of secular and religious subjects. To support its teaching mission, the monastery amassed one of the largest libraries in Portugal, containing more than twenty-five thousand volumes, and open to the public.[19]

Although Bính does not offer any detail, the new arrivals' rooms would have been on either the fourth or the fifth floor of the monastery building, with convenient access to the fourth-floor library. Their rooms would have looked out over the river or into the interior courtyard and toward the gardens. The men likely admired the richly decorated interior hallways and staircases, which were covered

FIGURE 10. The Necessidades palace (now home to the Portuguese Foreign Ministry) was Binh's residence in Lisbon from his arrival in July of 1796 until June of 1807. Author's photo.

in blue azulejo tiles, some depicting nature scenes, others merely floral and geometric decorations.[20] Bỉnh did not describe either their rooms or the interior of the building, but he did comment on the compound's hilltop location with its commanding views of the Tagus River and a vista that extended as far as the ocean. The men must have enjoyed the Necessidades's famous high-walled gardens, which continue to be maintained to the present day. Bỉnh wrote about the gardens in his journals, noting that people came from all over to admire and stroll around in them. He described the garden's flowers and trees, its many statues, and the seven stone wells found within its walls. He also noted its numerous fruit trees, such as lemons, which were sometimes harvested by the resident priests.[21] Finally, Bỉnh observed that a portion of the compound remained in the hands of the royal family, who frequently used it as a residence for foreign dignitaries, particularly those visiting from England.[22]

The Vietnamese envoys seem to have been well received by the Oratorian community upon their arrival at the Necessidades compound. Any reluctance its leadership might have had about hosting the visitors was dispelled by the ruler's assurances that he would fully cover all costs associated with housing, feeding, and otherwise accommodating them. The appearance of the Vietnamese contingent sparked considerable interest among the priests in the Oratorian residence. The men were asked many questions about themselves and their homeland, and the congregation's priests visited the Necessidades's library to look for books about the situation in Annam. As the local Oratorian priests were looking for insights about their new residents, Bỉnh was likely trying to understand the nature of the community in which he and his friends were now being housed. He was, in any case, extremely grateful to the congregation for sheltering his group, a sentiment he expressed in a brief poem of gratitude.

> *Poem of Thanks to the Order*
> We give thanks to the priests in this house
> Because of your compassion for these lost sheep who arrived here,
> Advising us in all matters with great clarity,
> Nurturing us to satiation in both body and soul.
> Every day there are offerings to the three saints
> And for weekend fasts you provide fasting meals.
> May the saints shower even more favors upon all your priests
> For extending your hands to rescue this group of men.[23]

THE ORATORIANS AND RELIGION IN LATE EIGHTEENTH-CENTURY PORTUGAL

The Oratorian congregation in Lisbon to which the men had been entrusted belonged to a network of religious communities established by the Florentine Philip Neri in the later sixteenth century. Originally a businessman, Neri had gradually moved in a more spiritual direction, making his way to Rome, where he held informal prayer and song meetings with like-minded Catholics. As these gatherings grew in popularity, the group began to meet in a larger hall, which became known as an "oratory," a place for prayer. In 1575, the group formalized its practice and community as a new type of religious community, which became known for its meeting place as the Oratorians. The Oratorian movement spread across Europe, including to Portugal, where a community was established in the late seventeenth century by Bartolomeu do Quental (1626–98), confessor to the Portuguese ruler in the 1650s. Along with the Oratorian congregation in Porto, its Lisbon community had become a distinguished and wealthy religious establishment by the time that Bỉnh joined it. Oratorians in Portugal, as elsewhere, established schools and became known in particular for their teaching of science. They also tended to become less involved in the kinds of politics that had often made the Jesuits lightning rods for criticism from secular authorities.[24] Since the middle of the eighteenth century and the reign of João V, the court had relied on the Oratorian clergy as teachers and their order houses as sites of education and scientific and philosophical inquiry. Also, since their establishment in Portugal, Oratorian priests had served as royal confessors. Throughout the second half of the eighteenth century, Oratorian clerics served as the queen's confessors, first Bishop Inácio de São Caetano beginning in 1759, followed in 1788 by José Maria de Melo, the bishop of the Algarve and brother of the patriarch of Lisbon.[25] The ongoing royal patronage of the Oratorian community meant that there were already well-established financial linkages between the court and the congregation, which presumably facilitated the transfer of funds on behalf of the Vietnamese visitors.

There were significant commonalities between the Oratorians and Bỉnh's beloved Jesuits, the most notable being that, like the Jesuits, the Oratorians, and particularly their Lisbon community, were very active in education, and some of their communal houses maintained significant libraries.[26] The Necessidades house even had its own printing press, allowing it to challenge the Jesuits in the realm of print culture.[27] The Lisbon Oratory was a prominent center of education in the late eighteenth century, in large measure because of the efforts of Teodoro Almeida (1722–1804), the head of the congregation at the time of Bỉnh's arrival. Almeida, who was noted for his scientific research and writings, arranged large-scale scientific conferences that were open to the public and were extremely well attended.[28] While the Oratorians shared the Jesuits' commitment to education and scientific inquiry, the two groups were nonetheless quite distinct and in rivalry with one another, engaged in what has been called a "contentious war over learning."[29] Royal patronage of the Oratorians in the 1750s and 1760s had been partially an attempt to establish a counterweight to the Jesuits, who had come to be seen in some circles as politically subversive.[30] Indeed, the symmetry between the two groups had led Pombal, hostile to both, to compare them to a married couple, the Oratorians being the wife and the Jesuits the husband.[31] Thus, while there was a considerable degree of similarity between the two religious communities, in residing with the Oratorians Bỉnh was living among local rivals of his Jesuits.

As he settled in with the Oratorians, Bỉnh was also coming to terms with the larger Catholic landscape that he encountered in Lisbon. The situation represented a virtual mirror image of that found in his homeland. At the end of the eighteenth century Portugal remained one of the most Catholic countries in Europe. Bỉnh found himself in a city where religion was the centerpiece of society and where Roman Catholicism lay at the very heart of state power. It was a place in which everyone was expected to be a good Catholic and where failure to participate in services would have marked one as an outlier. With his connections to the Oratorian house, Bỉnh found himself within these power structures—a far cry from the essentially powerless situation of the Catholic Church in Vietnam, where strength was measured merely in terms of the tolerance of the Vietnamese state rather than its blessings. He had left a land in which Catholics lived at the social and political margins, always under threat of attack, whether from the central state or from avaricious local officials. Catholics represented a small and fragmented percentage of the larger Vietnamese populations and lived a spiritual existence too often lacking key elements of church life, most importantly sufficient numbers of ordained priests. Once a refugee from state suppression, and a victim of internecine fighting among the various missionary communities, Binh now found himself able to flaunt his religion publicly both in his profession of it and in his garb and appearance.

Yet there were already clear signs of the erosion of the church and its power. Indeed, the overall trajectory of the religious orders in Portugal over the eighteenth century had been one of slow decline. By the second half of the eighteenth century many religious institutions faced financial crises. No new religious orders were being permitted to be established in the country, and starting in 1791 recruitment to religious institutions was suspended.[32] The decline in the influence and prestige of the religious orders was partly a function of Pombal's efforts, but it can also be linked to the impact of the Enlightenment more generally. Religious callings had become less attractive for many as new vocational possibilities had emerged. Pombal had worked sedulously to reduce the institutional power of the church, and particularly the religious orders, since he viewed these as the primary challenge to the absolutist power of the monarchy. His most notable triumph, as we have already seen, was his campaign to eradicate the Jesuit order in the Portuguese realm, but beyond that he had also succeeded in substantially reducing the autonomy of the church and diminishing its political influence. European Christianity in general had suffered from the rising skepticism of European philosophy, and the power and influence of the institutional church had waned significantly from its peak. The French Revolution's assault on all forms of institutionalized religion had been only the most direct manifestation of this trend.

Despite Pombal's many Enlightenment projects in the middle of the eighteenth century and the general erosion of church influence, a relatively conservative Catholicism still dominated society, culture, and many aspects of daily life when Binh reached Lisbon in 1796. With Pombal's fall from power after the death of Joseph I in 1777, the aggressive campaign to reduce the religious orders abated. Exiled churchmen and intellectuals began to return to Lisbon in the late 1770s, and religious institutions emerged once again as central to the power structures of the Portuguese state. While the Jesuits were not permitted to reconstruct themselves, communities like the Oratorians were allowed to resume their active schedules of teaching and religious involvement. An early nineteenth-century survey showed that as of 1810 the country had more than four thousand Catholic parishes for a population estimated at just over two million and that this was overseen by three archbishops and fourteen bishops, as well as a variety of other religious leaders.[33] In addition, the country still hosted 417 monasteries and 110 nunneries. Indeed, estimates place the number of clergy and those associated with religious institutions at fully 10 percent of the national population. Lisbon itself was home to 180 monasteries by the end of the eighteenth century.[34]

THE PORTUGUESE ROYAL FAMILY

While the Oratorian house and the larger religious landscape were significant to Bỉnh and his companions for both spiritual and material reasons, the Portuguese court itself was far more important to their project, as Crown Prince Dom João ultimately held the fate of the Vietnamese mission in his hands. Unfortunately for Bỉnh, his arrival in Lisbon coincided with a period of substantial turmoil and uncertainty within the Portuguese royal house, a situation that greatly affected the course of his mission. When Bỉnh landed in Lisbon in the summer of 1796, the nominal ruler of the kingdom of Portugal was Queen Maria I. She had ascended the throne on the death of her father José I in 1777. The new queen had demonstrated considerable talents during the early years of her reign and had become quite popular among the Portuguese people. Unfortunately for Maria I and her realm, a sequence of personal tragedies befell her over a seven-week period in the late summer and early fall of 1788 that set her life on a downward spiral from which she would never recover.

The first blow came in early September with the unexpected death, from smallpox, of her eldest son, the crown prince José. The young prince had been groomed to rule by Pombal, who had seen in him enormous promise, and who had, on José I's death, even contemplated finding a way to bypass Maria and install Prince José as ruler instead.[35] Although this had not proved possible, Pombal ensured that José would be given the kind of Enlightenment education he hoped would continue to guide Portuguese leaders. Prince José's death at the age of twenty-six was particularly devastating to his mother, who saw herself as culpable for having rejected the advice of doctors that she inoculate him for the disease that had taken his life.[36] The death of her beloved eldest son was soon followed by the death of her daughter in childbirth, and then of her newborn grandson followed by her son-in-law. These tragedies were followed by the sudden death of her longtime personal confessor and confidant Bishop Inácio de São Caetano.[37] The only surprise is that this sequence of heartbreaks did not immediately destroy the queen's mind; that would take several more years.

In the aftermath of these setbacks, Queen Maria's mental health was fragile, and many feared she would succumb to the same madness that had beset a maternal grandfather (King Philip V of Spain) as well as an uncle.[38] The outbreak of the revolution in France less than a year later and the subsequent overthrow of the Bourbon house and imprisonment of the French royal family was another huge blow to the Portuguese queen. The Bourbon monarchy had been a model for the Portuguese rulers, whose own Enlightenment efforts and cultural forms were closely patterned on those of their French counterparts. The cumulative effect of personal tragedy, expanding European political instability, and a growing religious mania became too much for her. On February 1, 1792, while attending the theater, the queen suffered a public breakdown, after which her mental health declined rapidly. Doctors, both domestic and foreign, were brought in to relieve her condition, but without success. Her days as a ruler were now at an end. The queen would spend the next fifteen years largely confined to one wing of her beloved Queluz palace.

The queen's madness thrust her younger son João into the center of the Portuguese political stage. This was a role for which the young man, who had grown up in the shadow of his older brother José, was clearly ill-suited and largely unprepared. His mother's descent into madness meant that João, a mere four years after becoming crown prince, was pushed into the political crucible as the de facto ruler of Portugal. By all accounts, the future João VI was not a man of vision or purpose or even physical strength, though he had somehow managed to survive childhood bouts of both smallpox and measles. As Jenifer Roberts notes of the crown prince and the challenge he now faced: "An indecisive young man at the best of times, [João] had no idea what to do in such an unprecedented situation."[39] A few contemporary accounts were favorable to the young prince, including a 1794 assessment by the visiting English novelist William Beckford, who saw him as a man of some talent and promise. Most, however, were much more critical.[40] Typical was a 1798 report by another visitor to the court, who observed that the prince regent was still young, politically inexperienced, and on the whole rather timid, dominated by his ministers, and, lacking the formal authority of the throne, unwilling to challenge those around him.[41] While he had stepped into the breach to serve as the de facto head of the royal family in 1792, João was not yet formally the monarch of the realm. When his mother's condition had first dramatically deteriorated in 1792, her ministers urged João immediately to assume the position of prince regent, which would have given him legal standing to act on his mother's behalf. The prince was intimidated at the prospect, however, and rejected their appeal. For the next seven years he continued to resist these entreaties, hoping that her doctors would somehow find a solution to his mother's condition.[42] Indeed, while he would eventually accept the position as regent, Dom João then nominally co-ruled with his mother, who remained the official monarch of Portugal until her death in 1816.

The crown prince's shortcomings were only amplified by those around him. The memory of his mother's popularity was constantly with him, as were her shrieks during his visits to the Queluz palace where she was confined. While his mother's mental state unsettled him, the crown prince was also intimidated by his young wife, whose character (if not her morality) was far stronger than his own. Princess Carlota Joaquina was an offspring of the Spanish royal family, and had been betrothed and then, at the age of ten, had been married to João in a 1785 ceremony.[43] The couple was incompatible from the outset. While João preferred hunting and contemplative pursuits at Mafra, Carlota actively sought to wield authority, spending more time near Lisbon in the palace at Queluz. Carlota's frequent dalliances with other men only deepened the couple's estrangement, and her numerous pregnancies by her paramours further alienated the princess from her husband.

FIGURE 11. The Portuguese ruler, Crown Prince Dom João, Bình's patron and the man he hoped would provide Tonkin with a new bishop. Engraving, 1799. Portuguese National Digital Library.

In short, Bình found himself in a position rich with irony. On the one hand, the Portuguese ruler, via the Padroado Real, had the legal authority and power to assign a bishop to Bình's community in Tonkin. This gave him, as far as Bình was concerned, an enormous authority, one that was unmatched among the rulers of Europe.[44] Indeed, it was the primary reason that Bình had made his way to Portugal. On the other hand, in a larger sense Dom João was arguably the weakest monarch of any major state in Europe. Through a series of unfortunate events, Dom João had gone from being the junior prince in a stable royal family of considerable wealth and some clout to being the de facto leader of a nation nominally headed by a madwoman and facing the increasing threat of war brewing in France. It was a situation that would have tested even the most able and intellectually gifted monarch, and for Dom João, who was neither, it proved too much. Although his circle of ministers allowed him to weather the early challenges posed by the Spanish and French, and an alliance with Great Britain provided some breathing space, the reality was that Dom João could not give his attention to Bînh's problem in any sustained fashion. Moreover, his tendency toward vacillating indecision, his ready capitulation to more forceful personalities, and his reluctance to move with any sense of urgency all further crippled Bînh's efforts.

Another significant challenge to Bînh's project was the prince's peripatetic habits: he moved regularly between several royal residences, most of which lay at some distance from Bînh's home. The prince rotated between his palaces in Lisbon, including the Palacio de Bélem and the Palacio da Ajuda, and those further away from the city, notably Queluz, on the outskirts of town, and his favorite retreat, the great country palace at Mafra. When in Lisbon the court typically stayed at the Palacio de Belem, which was near Bînh's Necessidades residence. At regular intervals, however, the prince opted to reside at one of his more distant palaces. Queluz was ten kilometers from the Necessidades Palace in a straight line, longer by road, and could take several hours to reach by horse carriage. The massive country palace of Mafra lay more than forty kilometers from Lisbon and could be reached only by an expensive two-day carriage journey.[45] Ironically, the Mafra palace was emblematic of the one element of the crown prince's character that particularly benefited Bînh: the ruler's strong personal piety and support for the institutions of the church. Dom João had reconfigured the Mafra compound to serve not only his passion for hunting but even more importantly his interest in religious pursuits. When he stayed at this palace, the crown prince was surrounded by clergy, mostly from the Augustinian and Franciscan orders, who conducted regular masses and communion services. The crown prince also took part in frequent religious processions and even sang in the choir.[46] Consequently, it was precisely when the crown prince went to stay at Mafra to be surrounded by institutions of the church that he placed himself largely beyond Bînh's reach.

BÎNH MEETS HIS PATRON: THE FIRST ROYAL ENCOUNTER

With his single-minded commitment to completing their mission, Bînh wasted little time in submitting his first formal request for an audience with the ruler. Just one day after moving to the Necessidades house, on July 29 Bînh presented his request to the court's representative, who duly passed it on to the crown prince. The prince agreed to receive the men, and a date was set for the following week. As it happened, however, Bình's first meeting with the Portuguese ruler was an impromptu one several days before the formal audience. One afternoon later that week, some local priests were giving Bình and his companions a tour of the royal treasuries and the nearby royal chapel. As they were walking through the grounds, the four Vietnamese and their escorts unexpectedly came upon the ruler and his party out for a similar excursion. Informed that these were the newly arrived Vietnamese, the crown prince began speaking with the men. He inquired whether they had traveled to the chapel by carriage or by horseback. Bình, suddenly and unexpectedly face to face with the man upon whom his future depended, was tongue-tied. He was too frightened to respond in part because he and his men had in fact walked to the chapel, despite having been given explicit instructions to travel by carriage wherever they went. One of the accompanying priests came to Bình's rescue by answering that the men had walked but had done so on their doctors' recommendation that it was healthier for them to do this.[47] The prince then asked which bishop had ordained Bình, to which he replied, "The Spanish bishop." At this juncture, at least according to Bình's account, the prince's party moved on, leaving Bình to puzzle over whether this first encounter with the ruler had left a favorable impression.

A few days after this informal meeting, on Sunday, August 7, Bình traveled to the Queluz palace on the outskirts of Lisbon for his first official audience with the ruler.[48] The Queluz palace had been built in the seventeenth century as a hunting lodge and had been substantially expanded and ornamented beginning in the middle of the eighteenth. Particular effort had gone into creating parklike grounds, which were highlighted by hanging gardens, a small network of canals lined with blue-tiled walls, and a large number of fountains.[49] The overall effect was of a modest Portuguese attempt to emulate the gardens at Versailles. While the scale was far smaller and the topography considerably less impressive than its inspiration, Queluz was still a distinctive and striking site.[50]

In preparing for their visit to Queluz, Bình and his companions once again donned their formal attire before stepping into the carriages that would take them to the palace. The men arrived at Queluz in the afternoon and were forced to wait for some time outside its gates before being admitted. The four Vietnamese were then led to the crown prince, who was strolling in the garden with his young wife. As Bình and his companions approached the royal couple the Vietnamese bowed, and Bình himself got down on his knees. The men then presented the modest gifts they had brought for the ruler: fifteen bolts of flower-patterned silk cloth, some hand fans, several combs, and an ivory betel nut box.[51] The crown prince took the gifts directly from their hands before passing them to an attendant. Bình, attempting to decipher the nuances of this encounter, noted that the prince did not tell the official

FIGURE 12. The Queluz palace on the outskirts of Lisbon was the site of Bỉnh's first formal audience with the Portuguese ruler. He and his companions were shown around the gardens and had an opportunity to present gifts to the royal couple. Author's photo.

to put away the gifts, and Bỉnh took this to be a sign of his esteem. Bỉnh and his men then kissed the crown prince's hand in the Western fashion as they had been previously instructed. The crown prince asked after the "king of Annam" and others, and Bỉnh replied, though in what words he does not say. It was only after these greetings were completed that the presents from the Vietnamese were finally set aside.

The crown prince then invited his guests to explore the garden at their leisure, which they did, periodically encountering the royal party. During one of these meetings the two groups stopped to converse, and someone commented to the Vietnamese visitors on the sultry early August weather and wondered aloud why the men were apparently not as hot and sweaty as the Portuguese. At the mention of the heat, and no doubt to Bỉnh's great pleasure, the prince regent and his wife took out their new Vietnamese fans and cooled themselves as the conversation continued. One of the ladies in the company asked after some of the missionaries in Asia, including a man named Bảo Lộc (Paul), and was told by Bỉnh that the man was in good health. Another woman startled Bỉnh by asking after his two friends in Tonkin, the previous Vietnamese envoys to Europe, Fathers Thiểu and Cuyền. Bỉnh was astonished that the men were known to her, and she explained that she had been in Rome during part of their residence and that the two had spent a month in her home during that time.[52]

At this point the conversation naturally turned to the state of Christianity in Tonkin and the impact of the dissolution of the Jesuit order upon the Vietnamese

Christian community. This offered Binh the opening he needed to make his first oral presentation of their plight and to describe the nature of his mission:

> We used this opportunity to express things quite clearly [explaining] that "because the Jesuit order has been lost, and has also died, we have only two [remaining European] priests, one is Father Agostinho Carneiro, a Portuguese, and the second is Father Nuncio Horta, a Neopolitan, and both are already quite old. There are also five [others]: three of these priests are of our country and are also quite elderly, and the other two are apostolic vicars of the Holy See—one is French, a cleric of the Paris Seminary, and the second is a Spanish Dominican from the Philippines, a Bishop Inpartibus. These men wished to take over the Jesuit Christians who belonged to the Portuguese, and we could not bear to [submit] to these priests, and so we have come here to appeal to the Virtuous King to request that he select a legitimate bishop, because the King of Portugal holds the Padroado of the Orient, and thus has this authority."[53]

In this short statement Binh put forth the core issues driving his mission in abbreviated but very clear form. While Binh did not record the ruler's reaction to his statement, he did later comment of the visit that "we were very happy, because we perceived that the Virtuous King had already accepted and taken up our matter. He had arranged for the house in which we were residing, had disbursed funds for our food, clothing, and [other] necessities, and also expressed various kindnesses before all under heaven."[54]

After this brief conversation, the crown prince led the men to a small fountain in the garden and ordered one of his attendants to turn it on. Binh later described it as having thirty-six sprays and a base decorated with stone statues of animals including frogs and toads. Binh was very impressed by this fountain (likely the first of its kind he had seen) and particularly by its main spout, which shot water up to "the height of a ship's mast." He also described the garden's numerous other fountains, its many broad lanes, and the fortress-like walls that surrounded it. The men continued to stroll around the garden until the sun set, at which point they bade their hosts farewell and began the lengthy return journey to their residence. Binh noted that although his group would return to the Queluz palace many times to meet with officials and to witness the baptisms of royal offspring, this was the only time they were ever taken through the gardens.[55]

The Vietnamese men's first visit to the court produced one unanticipated consequence, which grew out of their modest but distinctive gifts for the prince and his wife. After receiving the flower-patterned silk cloth the men had brought (probably from Macao), Princess Carlota ordered it made into outfits for herself. Seeing the princess wearing dresses sewn from this exotic fabric, the other ladies in her entourage were eager to acquire some of their own to emulate the new royal fashion. Several of them subsequently made their way to the Necessidades house and requested that Binh sell them some of this cloth. He explained to them that he was not a merchant who bought and sold goods, that he no longer had any of this fabric, and that even if he had he would not provide it, for he did not wish them to be imitating the styles being worn by the queen.[56]

BỈNH'S RECOGNITION AS A PRIEST

As the men slowly settled into their new surroundings and developed the beginnings of a relationship with the royal court, Bỉnh began to wonder about his own status as priest. Although he had been ordained in Tonkin, whether this would be recognized by the Portuguese church was unclear. Bỉnh raised the question of his clerical status with the ecclesiastical authorities, possibly because he hoped that local validation of his status might boost his standing in the eyes of the court. It is also possible that he wanted to be able to minister to his fellow Vietnamese until they were comfortable in the new religious environment. He is not clear on this point. As Bỉnh described it in his writings, the standard European practice for priests who changed locations involved providing church authorities with a formal permit affirming their status as ordained priests. Once this had been approved, the priest would be permitted to begin carrying out clerical duties in his new locale. For Bỉnh this presented some difficulties because there had been no need for such documentation when he had been in Vietnam. The community there was small enough that everyone knew who had been ordained as a priest, and any paperwork would have been superfluous. Bỉnh had not bothered to secure written acknowledgment of his ordination prior to his departure for Lisbon. His case was further complicated by his excommunication at the orders of Bishop Alonso for saying masses without permission and trading in goods for profit. The fact of his and his companions' excommunication had been circulated in letters, and Bỉnh feared that this information might have made its way to Europe. He wrote that he had been able to secure a letter in Macao certifying that the excommunication had been revoked but that this letter had not yet been delivered to the relevant authorities.[57]

Despite these obstacles, Bỉnh reported that on September 10, 1796, the archbishop of Lisbon, José (II) Francisco Miguel António de Mendonça (1786–1818), formally granted him permission to serve as a priest. Mendonça was not merely an archbishop; he also carried the title of patriarch of Lisbon, a position of even greater authority, whose trappings of power resembled those of the pope himself and included a college of priests, garbed, like Roman cardinals, in red finery.[58] The patriarch, in short, had the religious authority to act on Bỉnh's behalf, in this case formally approving his appointment as a priest, regardless of any obstacles or objections that might have been raised elsewhere within the church administration. Having been formally recognized by the Portuguese church as an ordained priest, Bỉnh reported that the other residents of the Necessidades house now fully accepted him as a fellow priest. They also told Bỉnh that he would have to shave his hair in a tonsure as a public and formal mark of his status as a member of the clergy. Bỉnh had earlier cut off his queue during his journeys back and forth to Macao and now took a further tonsorial step by shaving his hair in the European clerical style. As a result, while we do not have any images of Bỉnh or his companions, this at least hints at his appearance. The act of taking the tonsure would also have physically distanced Bỉnh from those he had traveled with, who were not priests and could not adopt this hairstyle.[59]

After altering his hairstyle to conform to local custom, Bỉnh petitioned the ruler for permission to dress in Western-style clothing. Although he had earlier ordered the Vietnamese to retain their native garb, the ruler now relented, but with a proviso. He told Bỉnh that any time the Vietnamese came to visit him or to attend a royal event, they would have to don their Vietnamese clothing, because, as Bỉnh writes, "He regarded this as important and wished to show everyone that he had foreigners from Annam in his capital."[60] Bỉnh and his men would have added some spice to the crown prince's royal audience halls and official receptions. The ruler further exploited Bỉnh's exoticism by sometimes requesting Bỉnh and his companions not merely to attend the audiences in their native attire but also to perform the ritual greetings to the ruler in the Vietnamese style. While Bỉnh does not describe what is meant by this, it presumably involved the Vietnamese prostrating themselves before their sovereign, a spectacle that drew a large audience including not only the ruler and his consort but other visitors who happened to be in the palace at the time.[61] It is clear that Bỉnh understood the ruler's motivation in requiring the men to retain their Vietnamese garb for such court events, and he certainly understood that the ruler was exploiting their appearance. It is equally clear, however, that Bỉnh himself had strategically emphasized his group's "foreignness" in their own sartorial strategies upon arriving in Lisbon. That the ruler had recognized their exotic nature and now sought to exploit it was only confirmation of the effectiveness of Bỉnh's strategy, and as long as it provided the access he desired he was more than happy to oblige the ruler's requests.

The last significant change that Bỉnh undertook at this time was to adopt the surname "do Rosario" (of the Rosary). It is not entirely clear when this occurred, though he wrote of it to his community in Tonkin in a letter of early 1800.[62] As a result, he was most likely known in Lisbon and among his fellow priests and Oratorians by the fully Europeanized Catholic name of Felippe do Rosario.[63] The change appears to have been undertaken for professional reasons and in keeping with Western convention.[64] This, like the tonsure, would allow him to fit into Lisbon clerical society much more easily. It also meant that when his name appeared on a roster of priests available to be hired for saying mass it would not confuse or scare off those who might consider hiring him. In his letters, at least through 1804, and certainly in his writings from later years, he continued to refer to himself by his earlier Vietnamese given name, Bỉnh. This name seems to have continued in use even among Europeans with whom he engaged, and in early nineteenth-century letters by church leaders he is commonly referred to as "Bỉnh" and sometimes erroneously as "Bink" or even "Chinh." On the other hand, he also routinely combined the Western, Catholic, and Vietnamese names to produce a hybrid name: Philiphê do Rosario Bỉnh, in which his Vietnamese given name was attached as a kind of curious appendage. Indeed, since Bỉnh was his given Vietnamese name, its juxtaposition with his Catholic name of Philiphê was always something of a naming anomaly.

Thus the stage was set for what was to follow. While Bỉnh never gave any indication of what he anticipated to be the timetable for his mission, the alacrity with which the men assimilated themselves to local culture and religious convention and settled into the Necessidades house suggests that they were preparing for a project that would take at least months, if not years. Indeed, at one point in his *Sách sổ*, Bỉnh reports that the leadership of the Oratorian house had agreed to host the men on the assumption that their mission would take at most one or two years.[65] The only precedent, such as it was, to which Bỉnh could look was the earlier mission of Fathers John Thiều and Paul Cuyên. That delegation's journey to Europe, with all of the complicated machinations surrounding it, had lasted a full seven years between a 1780 departure from Tonkin and an ultimate return in 1787. The prolonged nature of that mission had been caused by the Vatican's manipulation of their travel and restrictions placed upon their movement. Learning from their experiences, Bỉnh had made his way directly to Lisbon, where he was beyond the reach of the Vatican and ostensibly in the right location to carry out his task in an expeditious fashion. Thus he likely believed—or at least hoped—that he could move forward much more quickly than had Thiều and Cuyên. In the next chapter I examine Bỉnh's concerted efforts to accomplish his mission and the numerous challenges and obstacles he faced. While Lisbon may have been the right place to be, it was also a landscape dotted with hazards and, as he discovered, not entirely beyond the reach of the Propaganda in Rome.

5

Invoking the Padroado

Bỉnh and Prince Dom João

With the preliminaries of settling into his residence and meeting the prince behind him, Bỉnh could at last turn his attention to a systematic campaign to convince the Portuguese ruler to fulfill their request to appoint a bishop to Tonkin. The visit to Queluz in early August, during which Bỉnh presented a précis of his mission, had been merely a prelude to his larger project. The prince's initial sympathetic treatment of the delegation and indications of his regard for the Vietnamese visitors must have raised Bỉnh's hopes that his project might, after all, be quickly accomplished. It soon became clear, however, that this was not to be. After the initial glow of their arrival had faded, Bỉnh was acutely aware that time was one of his chief enemies. It was this awareness, as much as his desire to quickly return to his homeland, that drove Bỉnh's relentless campaign during his first decade in Lisbon. Over the years that would follow, Bỉnh came to learn the precise contours of the complicated ecclesiastical and political landscape in Europe. While his project hinged to some degree on the crown prince's willingness to pay attention to the Vietnamese requests, numerous other factors were also at work. These included both direct challenges to his project from the Vatican, through its papal representative in Lisbon, and indirect ones, such as the political situation in turn-of-the-nineteenth-century Europe. The growing tension between Spain and Portugal frequently distracted the Portuguese ruler, and the looming threat of continental war driven by Napoleon's ambitions also became a force that could not be ignored.

THE FIRST PETITIONS

Most of what we know about Bỉnh's relationship with the crown prince is contained in a series of fifteen petitions he submitted to the Portuguese ruler beginning shortly after his arrival in the summer of 1796 and continuing until the crown prince's abrupt departure for Brazil in November 1807. While Bỉnh's written appeals were certainly the most numerous and direct Vietnamese petitions to the Portuguese court, they were not the first such contacts between the two nations. Vietnamese Christians had sent similar petitions to the Portuguese court in 1727 and then again in 1787, both of which had gone unanswered. Then, as recently as 1791, a different kind of message had been sent from Đại Việt to Maria I. This letter had been sent by the leader of the Nguyễn military forces via a Portuguese merchant who had stopped in Sài Gòn on his way back to Lisbon, and the note requested permission to purchase armaments and ammunition. Nothing came of this request and the military supplies were never purchased. The letter suggests, however, that the Portuguese rulers were not entirely unacquainted with the Vietnamese realm and some of its concerns by the time that Bỉnh himself arrived in the summer of 1796.[1]

The first petition that Bỉnh presented to the Portuguese ruler had been drafted by the community and its European priests and subsequently rewritten with the assistance of a sympathetic Macanese during Bỉnh's brief transit through the Portuguese enclave.[2] Bỉnh wrote that this first *bản tấu* (petition) had been composed in the "Macao language" and consequently was not very decorous and also rather difficult to understand.[3] The people in Macao, many of whom had been there for years or decades, had lost the refinements of continental Portuguese, which would have been more suitable for a royal petition. Fortunately for Bỉnh, after hearing his description of how the Vietnamese had been received at court and the details of their petition, half a dozen Oratorian priests volunteered to help the visitors revise their document. The final version was rendered into "very courteous Portuguese" by José Pegado de Azevedo, who would later go on to become the bishop of Angra.[4] These revisions brought the Vietnamese petition into the form then presented to the Portuguese ruler.

Bỉnh's first petition, likely presented to the crown prince sometime in early August, articulated the rationale for and context of the Vietnamese delegation's mission to Europe.[5] The text opened by emphasizing the long-standing Vietnamese connection to the Portuguese world. The visitors referred to themselves as "Tonkinese Christians, of the Portuguese lineage" (Các bổn đạo nước Tunkim chúng tôi thuộc về Dòng Vutughê). This underscored the idea that their community considered itself part of this heritage, which had been established for and sustained by their ancestors, and which in their minds was still affiliated with Portugal. The petition spoke of three distinct religious orders in Tonkin: two smaller ones, the French and Spanish, representing relatively recent arrivals, and then the largest one belonging to the Portuguese, who had been spreading Christianity in Tonkin for two hundred years. The petition reminded Dom João that an earlier Portuguese king, João III (r. 1521–57), had been the key figure in first promoting

Catholicism in Tonkin and giving it a distinctively Portuguese imprint. The French and Spanish had been latecomers to the Vietnamese mission field, forced to rely upon the support of the Portuguese to start their own missions. It is clear that for the members of Binh's community the national affiliation of these European missionaries was very much part of their consciousness.[6]

The petition informed the ruler that despite this long and illustrious history of Portuguese involvement in Vietnamese Christianity, there were now virtually no Portuguese priests left to serve this mission field, even as it still boasted eighty large churches, numerous religious houses, and more than two hundred thousand adherents. Their own community of Padroado loyalists had twelve priests, but only one of them was a Portuguese, the octogenarian Father Tulano Carneiro, while the other eleven were native clerics, many of whom were old, blind, or ill. The petition then noted that the community had tried to resolve its shortage of priests by requesting the French and Spanish bishops to ordain five seminarians to serve as priests for their Portuguese lineage. The bishops had instead ordained two each into their respective orders (MEP and Dominicans), and only the fifth (Binh himself) had balked at this, insisting on remaining with the Portuguese community.[7] The result was a critical shortage of ordained priests, forcing nonordained lay people to step in to perform certain functions. The petition consequently urged the crown prince to follow in his ancestors' footsteps by supporting these Christians and sending them a Portuguese bishop. Indeed, it implied that the Portuguese ruler had a moral obligation to look out for those with a particular affiliation with his country. It also reminded the crown prince of the 1787 petition to which no response had been received. This was clearly a mild reproach and perhaps a further goad to the crown prince's conscience.

In addition to its moral entreaty, Binh's petition appealed to the Portuguese ruler's sense of nationalism by discussing the ways in which the Spanish and French apostolic vicars had been dividing up the country, forcing the people of the Portuguese community to choose between them. The petition described the vicars belittling Portugal as an insignificant country with great difficulties, few people, and few possessions, even as Binh assured Dom João that the community's members "did not listen to these lies." This argument must have carried some weight, though it probably lacked the impact it might have had earlier in the seventeenth century, when fierce nationalism had been a strong force motivating Portuguese rulers to defend their Padroado rights.[8] The petition mentioned that the elevation of Feliciano Alonso to the position of apostolic vicar had briefly raised the community's hopes, only to be shattered as the situation for the Padroado Christians had instead become worse.[9] Indeed, it was Alonso who had insisted on a departure from the Portuguese way of pronouncing "grace." Binh described Bishop Alonso's insistence that the community give up customs and practices taught them by Portuguese priests, routines with which they were acquainted and which Binh described as "easy."

In presenting this and subsequent petitions, Binh was largely counting on the Portuguese ruler's benevolence and compassion for suffering fellow Catholics, even as he also appealed to the crown prince's sense of nationalism. The Vietnamese envoy had almost nothing to offer in return for the Portuguese ruler's assistance, though he was not entirely without leverage. Binh's community still preserved some material assets of the former Jesuit priests that might be used as an inducement. As in Europe, the demise of the Jesuits in Asia had seen the widespread seizure of their churches, residences, and religious items, including books and artifacts. Binh noted that Bishop Alonso, along with his fellow apostolic vicar Jacques-Benjamin Longer, claimed that the pope had authorized them to seize Jesuit (i.e., Portuguese in the context of Tonkin) properties and churches and that they had quickly set about trying to take control of these assets. Binh reported, however, that he and his followers had refused to surrender these properties to the Dominican or MEP apostolic vicars. They would, however, require assistance from the Portuguese ruler if they were to continue this effort. Binh in essence told the ruler that these properties should be regarded as belonging not merely to the Jesuit tradition but to the Portuguese lineage, which had been supported and sustained by earlier Portuguese monarchs. Clearly he hoped that these assets might constitute at least a modest incentive for the Portuguese ruler to fulfill his request.[10]

The petition culminated with a formal request that the Portuguese ruler resolve all of these problems by appointing a primary bishop for Tonkin. This could bring an end to their schism and excommunication, allowing the community's members to be restored to the church and its sacraments. The petition assured the crown prince that if such a man were sent the community would look out for all of his needs and properties and would protect him from the French and Spanish clerics. It concluded by reiterating the plea for help, noting that the community had sent four men—one priest (Binh) and three traveling companions—to make their case. It expressed hope that God and the Virgin Mary would open the Portuguese ruler's heart to this appeal and noted in closing that the men had come to bring this petition on behalf of the Vietnamese community of Christians in the Portuguese lineage because there was no one else to whom they could now turn.

Drafted by the Jesuit loyalist Christian community of Tonkin and presented by Binh, this petition reveals how these Vietnamese Christians thought about themselves and their place in the global Catholic community and also how they sought to present themselves to the Portuguese crown. It speaks to the global flows of Roman Catholicism and the ways in which these flows had created, sustained, and shaped their experience of the new faith. At the same time, it expressed another way of thinking geographically and genealogically. While Vietnamese Christians viewed themselves as part of a genealogy that stretched back through the Bible, and as part of a geography that represented the world of the Old Testament figures, they also saw themselves as connected to more recent spiritual genealogies and political geographies that were more relevant to their immediate situation. As they sought to resolve the numerous challenges their community faced with the dissolution of the Jesuits and the growing pressure to submit to the apostolic vicars, the Padroado Catholics articulated a particular vision of their ancestry. This was a vision in which they understood themselves as belonging not only to a biblical genealogy but also to a distinct Portuguese Catholic lineage, one initially established and subsequently nurtured by Portuguese missionaries and priests. This was important not merely for abstract historical reasons but also for the fact that the Portuguese Jesuit tradition was bound up in distinctive elements of language and ritual. It was this tradition that these Vietnamese Catholics understood to be theirs and that they sought to protect.

Bỉnh reported that although this petition was formally directed to the Portuguese ruler, he also made its contents generally known among people in Lisbon who might be able to assist in some fashion. In fact, he appears to have distributed it as widely as he possibly could, more in the manner of a broadsheet than a royal petition. Bỉnh presented copies of the petition to four senior Portuguese officials, to the patriarch of Lisbon, and even to the papal nuncio, Archbishop Bartolomeo Pacca, who had arrived in Lisbon just two years previously in 1794. In addition to giving written copies of the petition to these senior clerical and secular officials, Bỉnh writes that he showed copies of it to many priests and other people "too numerous to count."[11] Bỉnh's strategy was to spread his message to as many people as possible. He wanted *everyone* to know about the plight of his community. It was a gamble in some respects, as he could not be certain which among these people might prove enemies rather than allies. For instance, giving a copy to the papal nuncio was, in retrospect, a miscalculation. Archbishop Pacca would prove to be an intractable opponent, deeply committed to resisting an expansion of Portugal's authority in such religious matters and repeatedly insisting that there were already enough bishops in Tonkin.[12]

VIETNAMESE CATHOLIC CONCEPTIONS OF "EAST" AND "WEST"

While the first petition established the Vietnamese delegation's ostensible Portuguese ecclesiastical roots, a second one soon followed on August 22, and in it the Vietnamese suggested another type of geographical orientation, one that conceptualized a globe divided between East and West. The petition, which was essentially a précis of their journey from Tonkin to Lisbon, begins with the words: "We are people of the East, natives of the country of Tonkin" (Chúng tôi là người Phương đông, sinh ra ở nước Tunkim). The phrase "people of the East" suggests that Vietnamese Catholics, now increasingly aware of a larger world that encompassed Europe, were undergoing a reorientation of that world and the relationship between its elements. Concrete ecclesiastical boundaries, represented in parishes, vicariates, archbishoprics, and so forth, had significant practical consequences for Vietnamese Catholics. At the same time, however, a different kind of geographical distinction, more conceptual than concrete, but with its own set of implications, was also emerging.

The distinction concerned two newly conceptualized spaces, bearing the labels "East" and "West" (*phương đông* and *phương tây*). European priests had brought this vocabulary with them to Tonkin, a reflection of their own understanding of the world, and it slowly began to make inroads among Vietnamese Catholics, particularly as they sought to situate themselves within a new global order. The introduction of the notion of "East" and "West" as spaces inhabited by particular peoples led some Vietnamese Catholics to begin to understand themselves as residents of a larger realm known as "the East," one whose other was "the West." That this way of thinking had taken root among Vietnamese Catholics is suggested in the opening words of Bỉnh's petition, as well as in the many other places in his writings where he uses the term *the West* to make broader generalizations about Europe, its people and institutions. But other educated Vietnamese Catholics were also becoming aware of the terminology, as suggested by a letter of June 1793 written by three Tonkinese Christians, Paulus Tĩnh, Augustinus Trân, and Jacobus Nhượng, to an MEP missionary who had returned to Paris, in which they spoke of this priest having "returned to the West" (trẩy về phương tây).[13]

This new "East"/"West" dichotomy represented a profoundly important reorientation of the Vietnamese view of the world. Prior to their encounter with Europeans, Vietnamese had, for historical and topographical reasons, rarely juxtaposed "East" and "West."[14] Instead, for them the geographical binary that mattered most was that of "North" and "South." The referents of these cardinal points varied over time and could include both transnational and domestic conceptions of space. At times this opposition had distinguished "Đại Việt" from its northern neighbor "China." In that context "North" (*bắc*; 北) had commonly served as a metonym for the Chinese realm, in contradistinction to the Vietnamese "South" (*nam*; 南). The geographical concreteness of this conception is captured in the titles of some of the earliest Vietnamese atlases, such as the *Atlas of the Boundaries to the North and South* (Nam bắc phiên dới địa đồ), dating from the later twelfth century.[15]

Although the use of "North" and "South" as references to the Vietnamese realm and its Chinese counterpart was historically the most significant, at times the Vietnamese also used these labels internally. At a purely topographical level a north-south orientation was hardly surprising. Vietnamese lowlanders tended to move north or south along the coast because of the long chain of mountains that often press against the sea and make traveling west impractical. In this context north and south were the primary directions of movement and settlement. Then, over the seventeenth and eighteenth centuries, "North" and "South" came to take on more distinctly political overtones in Vietnamese internal discourse.

In this context they referred to the two halves of a Vietnamese realm divided, since the middle of the sixteenth century, between the Trịnh and Nguyễn lords. Specifically, the cardinal reference spoke of a region that lay "north of the river" (Bắc Hà) to distinguish it from that which lay "south of the river," the river in question being the Linh Giang (Spirit River), which had emerged as the de facto boundary between the two realms after their inconclusive wars in the seventeenth century ended in 1672. Texts such as the later eighteenth-century Bình Nam Thực Lục (Veritable records of the pacification of the South), which described the Trịnh campaigns to defeat the Nguyễn, are emblematic of this internal use of such labels as political referents.

The most important exception to the historical emphasis on thinking in terms of "North" and "South" was found among Vietnamese Buddhists, for whom "West" was already an important geographical referent. For them "West" referred to the Indian subcontinent from which Buddhism had arrived.[16] Thus, like the later Catholic understanding of the "West," it referred to the place where their religion had its origins and from which it had arrived in Annam. An early example of this conceptualization of a Buddhist "West" is found in a fourteenth-century Buddhist treatise, the Thiền uyển tập anh (Outstanding figures in the Zen community), in which the Buddha (大師, lit. "great teacher") is said to have "come from the West" (自西).[17] This is clearly a reference to the subcontinent and a useful indication that Vietnamese had a distinct notion of "the West" as a remote source of religion that predated the arrival of European Catholicism.

In any case, the arrival and continuing presence of European missionaries began to transform Vietnamese geographical conceptions, suggesting new ways to think about cardinal directions, and with them new forms of self-conceptualization. Where once *East* had meant the ocean that hugged the Vietnamese landmass, and *West* had designated either the largely inaccessible upland region or the Indian subcontinent from which the Buddha had come, the two terms were now understood in entirely new ways. The meaning of *West* had been transformed, still representing a remote realm associated with a new religion and its popularizers, but now a reference to Europe and its Christianity. From this grew its opposite, *East*: no longer the sea, now a vast expanse of territory that included those living in Tonkin but many others as well. This radically reconceptualized East/West binary marked an important reorientation for Vietnamese Catholics. Although they had not, and could not, abandon the existing North/South binary that was a core element of Vietnamese geographical and historical conceptions, Tonkinese Christians now had another way to think about the world. Moreover, for important reasons this East/West dichotomy mattered a great deal, whether they knew it or not. The "West," however conceptualized, and however amorphous it might be, represented the source not only of their faith but also of those who brought it and of those who ultimately guided the evolution of their religious practice.

The "West"—represented by religious orders, biblical tales, the stories of saints, or the seat of the papacy—was now a part of the geography that mattered to them. In any event, Binh and his delegation were now representatives of this "East" on a mission to the "West," which was both the origin of their religion and the potential source of their ecclesiastical salvation.

CONTINUING AUDIENCES AND PETITIONS

The two petitions in August of 1796 marked the beginning of Binh's dogged efforts to complete his mission, which he pursued through additional petitions, direct appeals during audiences with the ruler, and regular meetings with an array of Portuguese officials. Binh's personal audiences with the crown prince were frequent in his first year: he enjoyed four royal audiences in 1796 alone, when he was still regarded as an exotic visitor from a distant land. This was clearly Binh's best opportunity to persuade the Portuguese ruler to act. Unfortunately for Binh, the crown prince's tendency toward indecision and unwillingness to act with any sort of alacrity was a significant challenge. As time dragged on without the appointment of a bishop, the sense of urgency that Binh had brought with him would dissipate. Binh knew only too well that one of his key assets had been the sheer novelty of his arrival and general appearance, both of which gave him a particular status at the court that was to his advantage in the early months after his arrival. His exotic flavor, however, wore off as time passed, and the crown prince understandably became absorbed with other matters. It took all of Binh's efforts to keep his own concerns before the Portuguese court.

Binh's initial pressure and advocacy bore fruit, though perhaps not as quickly as he would have liked. It wasn't until February of 1797 that the court began preliminary discussions about the possibility of appointing a bishop for Tonkin. In these deliberations it became clear that numerous permutations of the appointment of a bishop to the Vietnamese territories were available to the crown prince, not all of which were equally attractive to Binh. Some voices at the court raised the possibility of fulfilling Binh's request by appointing a Spanish Dominican as a new Padroado bishop for Tonkin. Hearing of this, Binh became alarmed and acted quickly to make his requirements more explicit. He argued that there were already Dominicans in Tonkin (administering the Vicariate of Eastern Tonkin) and that his community wanted someone from a different order (by which he clearly meant a *Portuguese*).[18] It is hardly surprising that Binh would have rejected a Spanish Dominican appointment, as it was precisely the policies of the existing Spanish Dominican bishop, Feliciano Alonso, regarding liturgical and linguistic matters that had spurred Binh's mission in the first place. Perhaps because of Binh's objections, this initial exploration of possible appointments did not come to fruition, and other matters soon came to dominate the court.

In particular the crown prince became preoccupied with the rising threat of conflict with Spain, and Bỉnh had to suspend his campaign for the rest of 1797. As he noted in his brief journal entry: "In this year there was an enemy, and though I went to the palace of the Virtuous King many times, I did not dare to say anything about our mission."[19] Prospects for Bỉnh's mission then brightened in the summer of 1798 as the Spanish threat ebbed and the court once again had time to address other matters. Taking advantage of this lull in the diplomatic crisis, Bỉnh presented his fifth petition in June of that year, reminding the crown prince that he was still determined to pursue his mission, and probably hoping it would be regarded with some favor in recognition of his patience during the previous eighteen months. However, Bỉnh found himself unable to regain the privileged access he had briefly enjoyed in 1796, and opportunities to present petitions directly to the ruler became increasingly rare. He was granted a single formal audience to present petitions in each of the years 1798 and 1799, and two audiences in 1800. Then, after a two-year gap, he gained audiences only in alternating years from 1803 to 1807.[20]

ILLNESSES AND TREATMENT

The problem of keeping the crown prince's attention was significant, but the Vietnamese soon found themselves plagued by another challenge, as they began to suffer from a variety of illnesses. This forced the men to use some of their time and financial resources to try to resolve them. While minor ailments had been common among the newcomers during their first several years in Lisbon, toward the end of 1799 Brother Nhân fell seriously ill. The Oratorian priests called for doctors to attend him, and two physicians responded, each prescribing different kinds of medications. Such consultation by multiple doctors was apparently the norm in late eighteenth-century Lisbon, with sometimes three or more being called to the bedside of the patient.[21] Brother Nhân's illness was determined to be beriberi (bệnh phù) and was attributed to dietary problems: partly the substantially different foods the men consumed in the West and partly the lingering effects of a shipboard diet, which had consisted predominantly of salted foods. The doctors instructed Brother Nhân to consume large quantities of chicken, and the men found themselves obliged to buy and attempt to consume an entire chicken every day, though they were often unable to finish it. Another doctor recommended eating tortoise meat, and yet another urged them to consume jalea, a mixture of deep-fried seafoods served with salsa, which Bỉnh, ever the penny-pincher, noted was more expensive than either the chicken or the tortoise.[22] Finally, one physician insisted that the only way to cure Brother Nhân was for him to drink two bottles of dry Madeira wine daily. Unaccustomed to the taste of alcohol, Nhân was initially unable to swallow the prescribed wine. Despite his reluctance, Bỉnh writes that his friend "had to drink it," and finally, after consuming ninety bottles, Nhân recovered, though whether because of the wine or in spite of it is unclear.[23]

While the Madeira wine treatment had seemingly relieved Brother Nhân's first serious illness, he continued to be plagued by a variety of other (unspecified) ailments. At the onset of his next malady, which struck in the summer of 1800, physicians suggested a new approach. They recommended he travel to a nearby hot springs resort.[24] As Bỉnh wrote, "The doctor advised us that we should go to the sulfurous hot springs to bath in and drink the waters, even though it was two days distant from the capital. We had to go there six or seven times, and each time we had to stay for more than one month."[25] Their destination was Caldas da Rainha (the Queen's Hot Springs), a small spa town eighty kilometers to the north of Lisbon and only a few miles from the Atlantic coast. The town's therapeutic waters had come to the attention of a royal visitor, Queen Leonor (1458–1525), the wife of João II, and after her visit in the late fifteenth century she donated funds to erect a hospital at the site of the springs. The hospital and an adjacent bathhouse complex became a popular destination for Lisbonites and foreign visitors, especially from Great Britain, seeking a cure for rheumatism and other ailments.[26] Later royalty, among them King João V (r. 1706–50), also came to the springs to take the cure.

The journey to Caldas took two days, including an overnight stop en route, and typically required the rental of two carriages and horses, as a single conveyance could not accommodate all four men. Thus, Bỉnh reports, the effective cost of round-trip transportation alone was that of eight days' worth of horse and carriage rental.[27] The difficulty of the trip was eased somewhat by the fact that the men could break their journey at the home of an acquaintance. They had developed a friendship with a wealthy Lisbon merchant whose sister owned a large home with extensive gardens along the route to Caldas. The woman had urged the men to stop off at her home any time they passed on their way to or from the hot springs, and she arranged for them to be fed while they rested there.[28]

Given the distance from Lisbon and the need for extended treatments in the sulfurous waters, the men would typically reside in Caldas anywhere between a month and a month and a half. This was, as Bỉnh repeatedly emphasized in his notebooks, a costly undertaking, beginning with the rental of rooms for their stay. Further expenses included food for their meals, which consisted chiefly of duck or chicken, since fish and beef were discouraged during the treatment. Then there was the cost of hiring domestic staff: a cook for their meals, a maid to clean their apartments, and a third servant to handle their grocery shopping. In addition, the men had to pay for transport within Caldas and then for the attendants at the springs, who helped with the bathing and the drawing of spring water to drink. Indeed, Bỉnh devoted an entire page of his journal to a detailed accounting of these expenditures, even though all of these costs continued to be covered from the royal treasury.[29]

FIGURE 13. A bathing hall of the baths at Caldas da Rainha, as depicted in an early nineteenth-century engraving. Bình and his companions made several trips to this spa town in 1799 and 1800 in an effort to relieve a variety of ailments. Wellcome Library, London.

Much of the treatment involved soaking in the waters of the hot springs' bathhouses located in the center of town. To supplement this primary treatment, however, the men also explored other therapies. For example, their doctors had recommended alternating bathing in the hot springs with intermittent immersion in the cold ocean waters.[30] Consequently, the men would periodically make the short trip to the coast for its bracing salt water. A third form of treatment involved bathing in pools of crushed grapes being fermented for the production of local wines. This treatment was available only during the beginning of the harvest season, when grapes were stored in enormous vats and patients would enter the vats and immerse themselves in the sticky mixture of fermenting grapes. Bính reported that people were known to drown in the deep vats, unable to swim or not strong enough to pull themselves up the rope ladders used to enter and exit the giant containers.

Bính commemorated their visit to Caldas with a poem, one suggesting the respite this spa town offered to the men, an opportunity to escape the city and to set aside the frequently exhausting pursuit of their mission:

A Chanted Poem to the Delights of Caldas
There is no delight such as that of Caldas,
Where we arrived in the fall season, as carefree guests.
After traveling many miles along a wide and bustling road,
We found the streams of fresh water that emit rising steam.
Day after day we met together in happy coziness.
In taking meals, we wrapped our hands around our bowls in a carefree manner.
Enjoying its leisure, the gull takes flight, recalling the good fortunes of the water.
Praise and thanks to heaven for creating such a place.[31]

Neither soaking in the hot springs nor swimming, whether in grape fermentation vats or the ocean, improved Brother Nhân's condition. Upon returning to Lisbon after his first visit to Caldas, Brother Nhân only became more violently ill, the ailment so severe that at one point he was presumed to be on death's door. Last rites had already been administered in anticipation of his imminent demise when a new treatment brought about a near-miraculous recovery.[32] While this pulled him from the brink of death, it could not resolve his lingering ailments. Brother Nhân was ultimately forced to spend most of the next three years in bed. Among other symptoms, he suffered from oozing pustules on his hands, which required his companions to change his dressings every day to keep them clean.[33] Despite being bedridden most of this time, Brother Nhân remained connected to the religious community because the Oratorians held services of Communion and arranged confession for those residents unable to attend mass at nearby churches. On days when he was strong enough, Nhân would walk to the Necessidades chapel, and when he wasn't capable of getting up, the sacraments were brought to him in his bed.

BRIEF TRIUMPH AND BITTER FAILURE (THE BISHOP WHO ALMOST WAS)

While Bỉnh and his friends tended to their health, several important developments increased the likelihood of the crown prince's finally fulfilling their request. The first had come when in 1799 the team of doctors caring for Queen Maria I definitively concluded that her mental incapacity was irreversible.[34] Dom João's advisers decided he could no longer defer the formalization of his political authority as the official prince regent. With his position enhanced, Dom João could now act in his own name instead of serving as a mere caretaker for his mother, though she continued to hold the formal designation as monarch of Portugal. The newly designated prince regent might now be more inclined to pursue political initiatives such as that being prodded by Bỉnh. The second critical event in that same year was the death in captivity of Pope Pius VI, a prisoner of Napoleon since 1797. Pius VI's death after twenty-four years as pontiff cleared the way for the possibility of a new and hopefully more activist papacy, one less burdened by the stigma of years of political chaos and temporizing on religious issues. Because the papacy, or perhaps more specifically those controlling it, had been one of the major obstacles to Bỉnh's mission, the prospect of a new pope must have been tantalizing for him. The Curia met for more than three months beginning in late November 1799, and in March 1800 it finally announced the selection of a new pope, Pius VII, who was installed to the papacy on March 14.

When word of the newly annointed pope reached Bỉnh in May, the first thing he did was commemorate the news by composing a poem expressing hope that this might constitute a new beginning, not only for the Catholic Church, but also for the Vietnamese mission.[35] He then wasted no time in drafting a seventh petition to the Portuguese ruler, in which he first thanked Dom João for his generosity in taking care of him and his companions and then conveyed sadness at the plight of his community, whose members continued to die without access to the holy sacraments. During the audience in which he presented this petition Bỉnh also pointedly noted that his party was missing two of its members, both of whom were too ill to attend. He speculated aloud that conditions in Portugal had induced their illnesses. He then went a step further, obliquely suggesting that the ruler himself might bear some responsibility for their poor health, which Bỉnh attributed in part to their worries about those they had left behind in such a perilous state. Bỉnh's appeal seemed to have the desired effect upon the prince regent, who promised he would now concern himself directly with Bỉnh's request for a bishop.[36]

Bình was encouraged by these developments, which seemed to bode well for his project, even as there were now some storm clouds on the horizon, a serious threat represented by the apostolic nuncio to Portugal, the papal ambassador to the Lisbon court. Although the Portuguese had substantially distanced themselves from Rome during the Pombal years, papal influence had slowly been restored over the 1780s and 1790s, and the authority of the papal nuncio at the court was once again considerable. The resident nuncio during the last years of the eighteenth century was Archbishop Bartolomeo Pacca (subsequently consecrated as a cardinal in 1801), who served as the papal envoy until his resignation in June 1801.[37] Archbishop Pacca was a staunch defender of the Vatican's position and acted vigorously to block the Vietnamese project.[38] The Vatican's objections to Bình's appeal for a new bishop for Tonkin were relatively straightforward. The system of apostolic vicars in Tonkin had been devised by the pope in conjunction with the Propaganda Fide to create a network of bishops who could be relied upon to implement Vatican policies. Bình's mission to invoke the Padroado powers of the Portuguese ruler was a direct challenge to the system of apostolic vicars. The Vatican feared that were the Portuguese leader to use his power to appoint a bishop to Tonkin it would muddy a mission field already neatly divided between the apostolic vicars. Such an appointment would produce a bishop seen as serving the interests of Portugal and answering to its monarch, and thus would erode the influence of the papacy. But equally significant, the appointment of a bishop for Tonkin would revive a contest among mission organizations for the allegiance of Vietnamese Catholics, one that had been significantly curtailed with the demise of the Jesuits in 1773.

Having heard that the prince was planning to name a Padroado bishop for Tonkin, the papal nuncio stepped in to derail his efforts.[39] In February 1801, Bishop Pacca wrote to Dom João strongly criticizing Bình and his mission, reiterating that there were already two perfectly good bishops in place in Tonkin and insisting once again that Bình and his community should finally accede to their authority. In his view, there simply was no need for any additional bishops. Bình reports that the nuncio referred to their actions as "disruptive of the faith" (rối đạo). Bình was shown a copy of Pacca's letter and given the opportunity to write a response, suggesting that sympathy for his efforts persisted in Lisbon, even in the absence of his longtime protector, the Marques de Lima, who had died the previous December. On February 26 Bình presented a written response to the nuncio's objections.[40]

In itself, Bình's retort to the nuncio would likely have been insufficient to sustain the momentum his request had gained. It was bolstered, however, by the arrival of a fortuitously timed letter from an unexpected quarter. The surprise missive was from Bình's old friends in Macao, Simon Liễn and Thomas Nhân, the two men who had made the first attempt to reach Europe in 1795, only to be turned back by the archbishop of Goa. Before leaving Goa to return to Macao, the men had received

BARTOLOMEO CARDINAL PACCA

FIGURE 14. Engraving of Cardinal Pacca, the papal nuncio in Lisbon and Bỉnh's chief opponent. Portuguese National Digital Library.

the archbishop's assurance that he would forward the petition they had been carrying to the Portuguese ruler. Even though Bỉnh had subsequently been sent to pursue the mission directly, the two men who remained behind in Macao continued to wonder what had become of their petition and whether it had, in fact, been sent on to the Portuguese ruler. At some point in 1799, still uncertain about Bỉnh's fate because they had not yet received any of his letters, Liễn and Nhân sent a follow-up letter and petition to the archbishop, describing their community's continuing plight. This letter must have tugged at the archbishop's conscience, reminding him of his unfulfilled promises, so he forwarded their petition, which reached Lisbon in February 1801. Since it was in Vietnamese, the petition was brought to Bỉnh, who translated it into Portuguese. The petition's arrival helped strengthen Bỉnh's case with the court by underscoring the urgent needs of a larger community of Catholics. The prince regent now had in hand both Bỉnh's response to the nuncio's objections and this new appeal forwarded by no less a figure than the archbishop of Goa. The combination of the two documents at this particular moment at last pushed the Portuguese ruler to do more than merely pay lip service to Bỉnh's petitions. Bỉnh reported that on March 12 the ruler issued a decree in which he formally directed his attaché (*tham tụng*) to select a primary bishop for Tonkin.[41]

Just when it appeared that momentum had once again swung in Bỉnh's favor, however, the smoldering conflict between Portugal and its Spanish neighbor flared up yet again. Spanish forces crossed the border and seized several Portuguese frontier areas, causing a diplomatic crisis requiring the attaché's intervention. The prince regent ordered his attaché to put Bỉnh's project on hold and to travel to Spain instead to negotiate an end to the hostilities.[42] The crisis dragged on through the summer, and the attaché was unable to return to Lisbon until the beginning of September. The moment he did, Bỉnh sent him a letter renewing his request for the man's promised assistance. Meanwhile, on September 28 Bỉnh received a letter from his two friends in Macao with an update on their perilous situation. He immediately translated this letter and presented it to the prince regent as yet another piece of evidence in support of his crusade. Two days later, peace on the Continent was temporarily restored when the French reached a preliminary agreement on an armistice with the British, almost at the same time that the Portuguese successfully concluded their own negotiations with the Spanish. While the final details of the Treaty of Amiens would be resolved over the next several months, the late September accord was widely seen as marking the official beginning of peace. With the Spanish crisis settled and the French revolutionary threat seemingly resolved, circumstances had given the Portuguese prince regent some breathing space to deal with Bỉnh and his relentless petitions.

Finally yielding to Bỉnh's pressure and the added weight of the letters from desperate Vietnamese Catholics in Asia, on October 22, 1801, the prince regent formally appointed a Padroado bishop to Tonkin. The bishop-designate was a thirty-two-year-old Franciscan by the name of Manuel Galdino (1769–1831). Galdino was a native of Lisbon who held a doctoral degree and had extensive training as an astronomer. He also had a reputation as a strong orator, and it was this skill that had initially caught the attention of the Portuguese ruler. Galdino had apparently been sent to the palace at Mafra for a celebration sponsored by the prince, at which the young priest delivered a sermon that deeply impressed Dom João. A contemporary account of their first meeting after Galdino's sermon suggested the dynamic between the two men: "After receiving a hearty applause, D. Fr. Manuel descended the steps of the pulpit, at which D. John VI, wanting to express his approval, extended his right hand to help Manuel down. 'My lord,' replied the friar, 'I want your hand

FIGURE 15. Portrait of Bishop Manuel Galdino, the Franciscan priest briefly appointed to act as the bishop of Tonkin. Reproduced in Manuel Teixeira, *Bispos e governadores do bispado de Macau*, vol. 2 of Macau e a sua diocese (Macau: Imprensa Nacional, 1940).

to go up, not down.' The prince regent, who understood the nature of the response, smiled and elevated him to the prelature, electing him as the bishop of Tonkin."[43] This episode clearly revealed Galdino as a man of ambition, one who seized opportunities when they presented themselves.[44]

The seeming triumph of their mission, after more than five years of waiting in Lisbon, elated Bỉnh and his companions, who celebrated their great success. Bỉnh recorded parts of this celebration in his *Nhật trình:* "At this time, all of the order houses lit candles and sounded their bells for three days to express joy as is the custom in the West, and our happiness at this time was so strong that it was inexpressible."[45] Also, as he had with other momentous occurrences in the course of his difficult journey, Bỉnh commemorated the event with a pair of short poems. The first, "Poem of Thanks to the Virtuous King of Portugal," was written on the day of the appointment, October 22. It was an expression of gratitude to the prince regent for finally answering their prayers and petitions. It is both an encomium lauding the Portuguese ruler's virtues and a reflection upon the actions of his predecessors and prayers for his bright future. The second, "Poem of Welcome to an Official Bishop," was written on October 27, five days after Galdino's appointment, and was a celebration of the appointment after Bỉnh's five long years of struggle in Lisbon.

Poem of Thanks to the Virtuous King of Portugal
We memorialize to the King that he might live a myriad years and preside over an era of harmony,
And might govern the country in this era through a time of great peace.
In earlier times [kings] selected priests to be sent to the country of Viet,
Now the king is sending a primary bishop to Tonkin.
There is affection above in the bright and shining ranks of the three saints,
While below there is love, both near and far, and together they are but a single soul.
We offer profound gratitude, an abundance exceeding both mountains and seas,
And pray the saints send further grace upon the family of our King.[46]

Poem of Welcome to an Official Bishop
How long have we been overseen by temporary bishops
that now we welcome having an official one in the official mold.
The rotten poplar wood chosen to represent the Holy See,
[Has been replaced] so that our overseer is now a man of great talent, holder of a doctorate
Adding to this, our dawn, is the renown of the Ruler
Who followed the example of the earlier powers of his blessed ancestors

So we now naturally lean upon and hold a firm hand
That will suppress the wolf and pacify and drive away our enemies.[47]

These expressions of profound joy and gratitude to the ruler and his designated bishop marked the high point of Bình's mission: he had succeeded against so many odds.

APPOINTMENT IN JEOPARDY

Several days after Dom João announced the appointment of Galdino, Bình and his companions made the long journey to the remote royal palace at Mafra to visit the prince regent and bishop-elect Galdino. They first met with the prince regent to offer their thanks for having finally fulfilled their long-standing request, and after paying their respects to the Portuguese ruler, the Vietnamese met with their new bishop, Father Galdino. The men congratulated him on his appointment to the newly created bishopric and also took the opportunity to show him copies of their prolific correspondence and petitions, detailing the enormous efforts they had made to gain his appointment. Bình claims that when he showed all of his documents to Galdino, the bishop-elect's happiness at the appointment to Tonkin became even greater. After seeing these many documents, Galdino (according to Bình) sent a note to the prince regent imploring the ruler "not [to] change my appointment to another city or to a different country, as I ask that you make me the bishop only of the country of Tonkin, because earlier there were those officials who wished to establish me as a bishop to Angola, and others who wished to appoint me as bishop to Nam King in China, because they knew that I was an astronomer."[48]

Galdino's note hinted that his appointment to Tonkin had not been as straightforward as Bình may have believed. In fact, Galdino's nomination as bishop to Tonkin was only the opening act in what quickly became a complicated drama. A few days after Galdino's appointment was announced, the Portuguese official for Far East affairs arrived at Mafra to argue that it would make more sense to appoint Galdino to the Portuguese colony at Macao. He reasoned that this was an established position under unequivocal Portuguese authority and that posting Galdino there would do the least to raise questions about the prince regent's authority to appoint bishops to Asia. In any case, the argument ran, from a position in Macao Bishop Galdino could easily manage religious affairs in Tonkin. According to Bình's later account of the events, Galdino himself rejected this suggestion and firmly stated that he was committed to becoming the bishop for Tonkin. At this juncture, Bình appears to have regarded the decision as final, for he wrote of its apparent culmination:

> Then [the official who had petitioned for the Macao posting] did not raise that issue again, and the entire matter was settled. For this reason we prostrated ourselves to

thank the King and the Virtuous Teacher and returned to the capital. Then the Virtuous Teacher instructed us to compose a letter to send news of this to all the clergy and Christians that they might know it and those in Macao could then concern themselves with preparations on these two issues, because the day of his departure was not far distant. We immediately began to occupy ourselves with this task.[49]

Bình's optimism proved premature. Far from being settled, the appointment quickly unraveled, and what had been Bình's great excitement at the apparently successful conclusion of his mission turned into unimaginable disappointment. The agent of this decisive blow to Bình's hopes was, not unexpectedly, Nuncio Pacca, who had recently been elevated to the rank of cardinal. Having already tried earlier in the year to throw up roadblocks to Bình's efforts, the cardinal intervened again, now with a greater sense of urgency as the appointment had already been made. The nuncio submitted a letter to the prince regent pointing out yet again that there were already two bishops in Tonkin and that a third would only complicate the ecclesiastical hierarchy. According to Bình's memoirs, Pacca reiterated this message in a subsequent personal encounter with the ruler at his Mafra palace on November 4. During this meeting, the nuncio argued that the religious problems in Tonkin stemmed not from a shortage of bishops but rather from the intransigence of the local Jesuit loyalist Christians, who were stubbornly refusing the authority of the existing bishops.[50] Moreover, according to Galdino's later memoirs, the nuncio underscored his argument with a threat, namely that Rome would refuse to confirm Galdino as bishop to Tonkin, thus annulling Dom João's effort.[51]

The prince regent clearly felt the pressure of the Vatican envoy's words and warning. Bình later reported Galdino's evocative description of the dynamic between the Portuguese ruler and the nuncio: "The King stood up, at which the nuncio prostrated himself at his feet. This caused the ruler to hang his head [in shame], whereupon the nuncio proceeded to dance upon the ruler's neck."[52] Unwilling to defend his decision in the face of Cardinal Pacca's concerted efforts, the feckless prince regent surrendered to the nuncio's threats. Shortly after meeting with the cardinal, on November 11 Dom João agreed to change Galdino's appointment. In a small measure of defiance, however, he announced that Galdino would not be appointed to the proposed destination of Macao but rather would be installed as the bishop of Cochin in India, which had once been part of the Portuguese empire's holdings on the Asian subcontinent.

Bình's dream of a Padroado-appointed Portuguese bishop to Tonkin had lasted precisely twenty days.

FURTHER COMPLICATIONS

The redirection of the appointment to the subcontinent, however, was not the end of the episode, for this new destination had its own complications. The chief of these was that there was already a bishop in Cochin, a man with no intention of leaving his post. The appointment of Galdino to Cochin was clearly not going to be possible, and this raised at least the small possibility that the original posting to Tonkin might be restored. After the devastating news of the Tonkin appointment's collapse, this glimmer of hope energized Bình, who raced around for the next several weeks trying to figure out where to make appeals and which officials would be most likely to support the restoration of the Tonkin appointment. But every official to whom he presented his petition sent Bình to someone else. No one was willing to intervene directly on his behalf, prompting Bình to write in despair, "We no longer had any idea with whom we should speak."[53]

While Bình lobbied hard to restore the appointment to Tonkin, the prince regent was apparently unwilling to return to that possibility, even as Cochin clearly was not an option. At this juncture an unexpected message made possible a reasonable compromise. A letter fortuitously arrived from the incumbent bishop of Macao, Marcelino José da Silva, announcing his intention to resign his position and return to his native Portugal.[54] This made the ruler's choice a simple one, and on December 16 the court issued a new order appointing Galdino as the bishop of Macao. The debates had come full circle, returning to the original suggestion about appointing Galdino to that Portuguese outpost. Galdino apparently accepted the new position with little hesitation, even as he reiterated his continuing commitment to the cause of the Tonkinese.[55] This resolution of the predicament likely pleased the prince regent, for it spared him the further wrath of the nuncio. It represented simply the replacement of an existing Portuguese bishop in a Portuguese colony, rather than the more radical step of establishing a new bishopric in a territory with little meaning for Portugal. Moreover, the nuncio's arguments, presented as the official view of the papacy, provided the prince regent with a legitimate excuse to cease his efforts to seat a bishop in Tonkin. So ended a year of ups and downs, one of raised expectations followed by dashed hopes for Bình and his companions. They had briefly rejoiced in the successful culmination of a project with its origins in the first Vietnamese envoys to Europe in the 1780s, only to see their triumph snatched away by political machinations that they could not overcome.

It is interesting to compare Bình's report of these events with that of Galdino himself, who described the situation and the background to it in his memoirs. Galdino's account, with the advantage of hindsight, offers a critical perspective on the role of the Vietnamese delegation in Lisbon and suggests that the redirection of his appointment from Tonkin to Macao was entirely appropriate:

> The deluded Tonkinese did not wish to give obedience to the apostolic vicars. Horta and Carneiro had failed because they were already very old and the delegation that they had sent to Lisbon in order to bring them this Portuguese bishop had already spent ten years (sic) in Lisbon, where they obtained nothing but promises. Meanwhile, the Christians of the Portuguese mission, having placed their hopes in those

at the court, did not wish to obey the vicars, and a schism was declared and they were perishing without the sacraments. A mistake was made when they named me bishop of Tonkin because in the letter they wrote Tonkin in place of Nanking, the place to which they had actually wished to nominate me.

The papal apostolic nuncio to Portugal, Cardinal Pacha (sic), stated in an official declaration that Rome would not confirm me [to the position in Tonkin], as it did not wish to compromise with Spain and France. As it happens, at the same time with the retirement of Snr. D. Marcelino, they forgot about Nanking and nominated me for Macao, but because of these doubts it took more than a month and a half, during which I treated the Tonkinese in Lisbon like my children, and learned that it was their spirit of division rather than zeal that motivated them, and that the priest among them had been educated since his childhood in the home of the Spanish apostolic vicar, and had been ordained by him, but as soon as this ordination had taken place he had become the leader of Carneiro's treacherous party, rejecting obedience to the vicars despite having his ordination suspended, and they continued to exercise the orders and to hold to the ideas of the Portuguese priests in seeking Jesuit fathers and Portuguese bishops.[56]

This account of the sequence of events between late 1801 and early 1802 offers a new perspective and a far more negative assessment of the Vietnamese delegation's project. Galdino argues that it was simply not realistic for the Portuguese ruler to appoint a bishop for Tonkin in the face of the papal nuncio's vehement resistance. Galdino also suggests that the appointment to Tonkin was actually a mistake, that the intention had been to write "Nanking." This seems implausible, given how long discussion of Tonkin had been in the works and how low the odds of such a scribal error were. Galdino later attributed his initial misappointment to Tonkin to divine intervention: "God wanted me to be appointed bishop of Tonkin so I could learn all [their] secrets and take advantage of them once I had become undeceived regarding their bad faith."[57]

This account, like Bỉnh's, makes it clear that, while Galdino might initially have been sympathetic to the Vietnamese delegation's wish for a bishop, the more he learned about their precise circumstances, the less he found himself in agreement with their stance. Once Galdino became aware of the situation in Tonkin, he came to share the MEP and Dominican view of the Jesuit loyalist community as troublemaking schismatics whose resistance was misguided and hopeless. Indeed, he saw Bỉnh's mission to Lisbon as having been orchestrated by the community's aging Jesuit loyalist priests, whom he referred to as "Carneiro's treacherous party." While it is quite likely that these clergy had been closely involved in planning the mission, and had certainly provided part of its impetus, it is clear that Bỉnh embraced what the mission represented: namely, the only chance his community had to retain their Portuguese-inflected Jesuit identity and to continue their particular approach to ritual and liturgy.

One can only imagine the impact of Bỉnh's bombarding the bishop-designate with documents on their first meeting, all designed to underscore his sense of vindication in Galdino's appointment. If anything, the papers did more to undermine than to reinforce the Tonkinese delegation's position. In them, Galdino would have seen the nature of the arguments for their persistent rejection of the authority of the apostolic vicars, which hinged, ultimately, on what must have seemed rather flimsy pretexts. Galdino himself said as much in a subsequent letter to the Spanish apostolic vicar for Eastern Tonkin:

> I was appointed bishop of Tonkin, and the ardor with which I took up the cause of these people, the love that I showed them, convinced that your procurers in Lisbon spoke the truth, [and] the confidence I created in them, all led them to confide in me and [by which they] made known to me their bad faith. As soon as I suspected [this], I went to inquire with more care and found that the repugnance of Rome in confirming me [for this post] was justified, and His Highness the Prince Regent of Portugal saw fit not to insist that Rome confirm [me, but rather] promoted me to the [post of] bishop of Macao.[58]

In short, he managed to convince the men to "confide in me," and it was as a result of this that he learned of their "bad faith." Galdino clearly regarded himself as a representative of the Portuguese state and its ecclesiastical powers in conjunction with those of the Vatican. His mission was straightforward: to enforce these powers, not to serve as an advocate for the underdog Tonkinese in their chimerical pursuit. Bishop Galdino fully understood where power lay and he respected that power, for it represented the potential for his own advancement. Consequently, from Bỉnh's perspective Galdino was more than unsympathetic; he represented a serious threat to their project.

THE AFTERMATH

Whatever the desires of the Portuguese prince-regent, the papal nuncio, or even Galdino himself, the appointment proceeded at a glacial pace. There were two major obstacles to the new bishop's departure and one important logistical consideration. The first was that Bishop Marcellino's letter had announced, not his immediate resignation, but rather his intention to depart once a suitable replacement had been found. Indeed, his formal resignation would not take effect until September 16, 1802. The second obstacle was that Galdino's appointment required confirmation by the Vatican, and until this was secured he could not depart for Macao. The logistical issue determining Galdino's departure was the sailing schedule of vessels departing Lisbon for Asia. Such ships left only once a year in accordance with the prevailing winds, which meant that the earliest Galdino might have left after his initial appointment to Macao would have been the spring of 1802.

These factors dictating Galdino's departure timetable must have been part of the calculus of all concerned, meaning that there was no great sense of urgency once the first window of opportunity had passed. And as long as Galdino remained in Portugal, Bính continued to hold out hope that he might somehow restore the appointment to Tonkin.

Meanwhile, Galdino's growing hostility to the Vietnamese delegation was creating other problems, for he apparently mounted a campaign to have its members deported back to Tonkin. The bishop-elect likely felt a certain unease about leaving Portugal while Bính remained behind to continue his advocacy for a new bishopric for Tonkin, fearing that Bính might yet create problems in Lisbon. Bính wrote that he and his friends continued to be protected by the ruler who still held them in affection, but Galdino declared that "if I were the king I would chase you out."[59] Galdino also criticized the priests of the Oratory for maintaining their assistance to the Vietnamese and chastised a cleric in Macao for continuing to send them letters.[60]

With Galdino's departure stalled by circumstances, Bính found that he still had some time to salvage the situation and immediately renewed his petitions and requests for a bishop for Tonkin. In this effort, Bính had the sympathy and support of at least some of his fellow Oratorians, among them Father Antonio Alvares (1753–1807), who went so far as to write a petition in support of Bính's efforts in January of 1802.[61] Published that same year under the title *Memoria sobre o Real Padroado da Corte de Portugal nas missoes do reino de Tunkin* (Memorial concerning the royal Padroado of the Portuguese Court with respect to the missions to the kingdom of Tonkin), the petition to the throne was a summary of the Portuguese missions to Tonkin and the gradual, and illicit (according to the author), MEP intrusion into this mission field.[62] It was a vigorous and detailed defense of the Padroado rights, one that precisely echoed the arguments that Bính had been making to the Portuguese ruler. This was hardly a coincidence, for Alvares clearly knew Bính and had heard his stories. Indeed, the text describes the efforts by Vietnamese envoys, including those of Bính and his colleagues, to persuade the Portuguese ruler to appoint a bishop to Tonkin. There is little doubt that this petition was inspired by Bính's mission, and while Bính does not mention Father Alvares in his notebooks, the men must have been at least collaborators if not friends. The petition's account of the trials and tribulations experienced by Bính and his companions could have come only from Bính himself.[63] The timing of the petition to the court in early 1802 suggests that Alvares must have been infected by Bính's outrage at the collapse of Galdino's appointment to Tonkin. Moreover, its systematic critique of the papal nuncio's position and its forceful articulation of the ruler's historical rights and responsibilities toward the Tonkinese mission field suggest that it was inspired by Bính's attempt to fight a rearguard action somehow to restore the appointment. While Alvares's petition did not persuade the

Portuguese ruler, it serves as a reminder that Bỉnh had managed to secure some local allies for his project while in Lisbon.

BỈNH'S ONGOING EFFORTS

The aftermath of the failed appointment prompted Bỉnh to recalibrate his overall strategy. The complex machinations surrounding the Galdino appointment had given Bỉnh a clear sense that the prince regent had doubts about his authority to enact such appointments and feared alienating the pope. Bỉnh thus decided on yet another approach: appealing directly to the newly installed Pope Pius VII himself, in the hope that this would defuse the source of the prince's unease. Bỉnh hoped that Pius VII might both be more independent-minded than his predecessor and evince greater sympathy for Bỉnh's point of view. In pursuit of this new strategy, Bỉnh arranged a meeting with the prince regent's envoy to Rome, Dom Alexandre de Sousa Holstein (1751–1803), a prominent nobleman.[64] Bỉnh described the meeting as very positive, with Dom Alexandre expressing sympathy for their cause and promising to deliver their message to the pope personally.[65]

Bỉnh's appeal to the pope on the basis of the Padroado was a gambit that placed him squarely in the centuries-old debate about the proper scope of that papally granted authority and the limitations the papacy chose to place upon it. More specifically, it involved him in the fraught relationship between Lisbon and Rome that dated at least from the early seventeenth century. The two parties had frequently been at odds about their relative degrees of authority in religious matters, whether ecclesiastical hierarchies or doctrine.[66] There was also a tension about where exactly the loyalties of Portuguese missionaries lay. During Bỉnh's time in Lisbon, Portuguese missionaries departing for overseas posts still took an oath reminding them of their ongoing status as subjects of the Portuguese crown, whatever their obligations to the Roman church. In it, they swore "to be loyal to Her Most Faithful Majesty in all places of her dominion through which I pass or where I exercise the ministry of a missionary, and not to prejudice in any respect her royal rights."[67] As this oath suggests, the Iberian rulers continued to inspire their missionaries with a nationalism that appears to have rubbed off on their flock in Tonkin, as suggested by Bỉnh's mission.

Dom Alexandre surely had some of this in mind when he departed Lisbon for Italy not long after his meeting with Bỉnh in April of 1802. He carried with him a note from the Portuguese ruler, Bỉnh's petition, and various other documents given him by Bỉnh describing his delegation's continuing efforts in Portugal. Unfortunately for Bỉnh, Dom Alexandre's journey to the Vatican was interrupted when he found himself delayed in Genoa for several months while his wife gave birth.[68] Consequently, the Portuguese envoy did not arrive at the Vatican until late November of 1802. There, as promised, he presented Bỉnh's petition to Pope Pius VII.

FIGURE 16. Engraving of Dom Alexandre de Sousa Holstein, who served as the Portuguese court's ambassador to the Vatican and carried an 1802 message to the pope on Bỉnh's behalf. Portuguese National Digital Library.

According to Bỉnh's later account of this meeting, the envoy made a strong case to the pope, underscoring the fact that this prerogative (to assign bishops) was one granted long ago to the Portuguese rulers under the terms of the Padroado Real. While acknowledging the truth of this argument, Pius VII did not dare (or wish) to reaffirm the Portuguese ruler's authority to make such appointments. The pope's final message to Dom Alexandre deflected responsibility to his representative: "I already have a papal envoy in Portugal, and he will handle things there for me because this is what the Holy See wishes."[69]

Given the enormous challenges facing the new pope, as well as the Papal States in general at this time, it is hardly surprising that such a relatively minor matter would have been delegated in this fashion. The pope had only recently (July 1801) hammered out the terms of the Concordat with Napoleon regarding the restoration of Catholicism in France. He was also actively involved in restoring the political authority of the Papal States after the long period of warfare that had swept his predecessor out of Rome and into imprisonment. Furthermore, the pope had just completed a comprehensive housecleaning of the French bishops, thus asserting a powerful degree of papal authority.[70] While Pius VII would later be remembered as an accomplished and activist pope, and indeed would eventually be responsible for restoring Bỉnh's beloved Jesuit order, in these earlier years of his papacy he was occupied with a complex array of pressing administrative concerns that likely crowded out remote issues of the type Bỉnh was trying to raise. Whatever political or practical considerations underlay the pope's decision to defer to the nuncio's recommendations, it was clearly a significant setback to Bỉnh's project. His new strategy to involve the pope in his campaign had only backfired by further strengthening the nuncio's hand and probably reinforcing the prince regent's inclination to adhere to the nuncio's advice.

Meanwhile, shortly after Dom Alexandre had set out on his mission to the Vatican, the Holy See sent a new nuncio to Portugal. Bishop Lorenzo Caleppi (1741–1817) had been appointed as nuncio to Lisbon one week after Galdino was reassigned to the Macao bishopric, and he arrived in Lisbon in May of 1802, just as his predecessor was leaving.[71] Bỉnh reports that when word of the new envoy's arrival reached them, "We went out to greet him, because we thought that here was a different face and a different name." Whatever hopes Bỉnh might have harbored for the new nuncio were soon dashed. It turned out that Caleppi "had the same heart, which was no different [from that of Bishop Pacca], and even though he was the envoy of the virtuous sainted Pope Pius, he was still doing the work of the Holy See and exerting himself to create obstacles to the task of our Christians."[72] Indeed, Bỉnh came to believe that Caleppi was not just representing the Holy See's continuing determination to block the appointment of a formal bishop for Tonkin but also working as a sinister agent to ensure that Galdino would accept the Macao appointment, rather than insisting on the restoration of the Tonkin post. Bỉnh reports that Caleppi met with Galdino and told him: "If, when you arrive in Macao, you can create obstacles in the matter of the Annamese Christians pursuing a Portuguese bishop, then I will be able to promise you that posting."[73] Galdino allegedly agreed to this scheme to solidify his assignment to the Macao

FIGURE 17. Engraving of Bishop Caleppi, the second papal nuncio to Lisbon during Bỉnh's residence. Bildarchiv, Österreichische Nationalbibliothek.

position. Bỉnh also writes that "it was not long thereafter that Nuncio Galepi [sic] sent a letter back to Rome in which he requested that the virtuous saintly pope order Bishop Marcelino give up his post in Macao so he could send Bishop Manuel to take his place."[74]

The confluence of circumstances and pressures meant that formal papal approval of Galdino's appointment became inevitable. Less than three weeks after his meeting with the Portuguese envoy, on December 20, 1802, Pius VII finally gave his approval for Galdino to replace Bishop Marcelino in Macao. Given the timing of these events, it is conceivable that in raising the issue of the Tonkin appointment Dom Alexandre had only spurred the Vatican to take action on the stalled Galdino appointment. Having rejected Bỉnh's appeal (as delivered by Dom Alexandre), the logical next step for the pope was to authorize Galdino's assignment to Macao, particularly now that the bishop-elect had made clear his willingness to support Vatican priorities in Tonkin. Bỉnh's efforts to bolster his project appear to have backfired. Galdino's departure for Macao was now only a matter of the sailing schedules for Asia, as Bỉnh's final hope for a change in the appointment had evaporated.

CONTINUING SETBACKS

The disappointment that resulted from the envoy's protracted and ultimately unsuccessful trip to the Vatican was soon overshadowed by more immediate misery. On the day after the envoy's meeting with the pope (November 22, 1802), Bỉnh watched as Brother Nhân finally succumbed to dropsy/edema (*thủy thũng*), with which he had been struggling for several years. The disease had left Brother Nhân bedridden and prone to frequent outbreaks of oozing pustules on his hands, which required his companions to change his dressings every day in order to keep them clean.[75] With his death at the age of forty-two, Brother Nhân became only the second Vietnamese person to die on European soil.[76] More significantly from Bỉnh's perspective, this was the first member of their little group to die, a sobering reminder of his own mortality and of the distinct possibility that he too might be fated to die in Europe rather than to return to his native land.

Upon Brother Nhân's death, ritual commemorations began almost at once. Since he had died in the middle of the night, the priests first lit candles before starting to say prayers for his soul. Then they prepared his body for the funeral and laid it in state at the Necessidades house. Bỉnh reports that a large number of priests, both from the Oratorian residences and from other religious houses, said masses for Brother Nhân's soul, the cost of which was borne by the royal treasury. Bỉnh commented on how much easier it was to arrange for such masses for the dead in Portugal than in his native land, where there were few priests to say masses and the process was not so straightforward. In addition, once word got out that one of the Vietnamese priests had died, public interest was stirred, and a large number of Lisbonites came to the Necessidades house to pay their last respects and to see the Vietnamese priest laid out in his exotic robes for the commemoration of the dead.[77]

Not long after Brother Nhân's death, Dom Alexandre returned from the Vatican with news of his disappointing meeting with the pope. Bỉnh now understood that his efforts at wooing the Vatican had been in vain and that he would have to find some other means to persuade the prince regent. For his part, when the prince regent received the report in which the pope indicated that the matter lay with his envoy to Lisbon, he appointed a senior cleric to act as the new liaison between Bỉnh and the papal nuncio. This new intermediary was the septuagenarian archbishop of Evora, Manuel do Cenáculo Vilas Boas (1724–1814), and Bỉnh had a preliminary meeting with him on February 20, 1803. Bỉnh brought all of his paperwork and presented it to the archbishop, explaining his project to yet another Portuguese official.[78]

As if his situation were not complicated enough, Bỉnh now reported what he regarded as a sinister plot on the part of Nuncio Caleppi to derail their mission. Caleppi was clearly as hostile to the Vietnamese envoys as his predecessor, which he revealed in a letter of early February 1803 (probably written to Rome) where he described what he regarded as Bỉnh's (he calls him "Bink") numerous transgressions. The nuncio accused him of causing grave disorder in Tonkin, of rejecting the authority of the apostolic vicars, of celebrating mass despite having had his privilege suspended, of being insubordinate, and of fomenting a schism. The litany of violations suggests the depth of antipathy felt by the Vatican toward Bỉnh and his project.[79] According to Bỉnh, the nuncio began efforts to coax the remaining three Vietnamese to come with him to Rome, where, he assured them, it would be far more convenient to discuss the arrangements for appointing a bishop to Tonkin. Bỉnh recorded his understanding of the situation and its implications in a journal entry of 1803:

> The nuncio tried three times to lure us to Rome, saying that he would assist us with finances. [But in reality] he had the intention of plotting with the Holy See to throw us in jail, because as long as we remained in Portugal he had to worry about us. If we were to go to Rome he would denounce us by stating that we were not firmly with the Pope, that this was contrary to the faith and a betrayal of the Holy Church.... So at that time we took these as warnings and saw that this man's objective was to make things so difficult that we could not succeed.... Although the Virtuous Pope is compassionate towards us, he is still more respectful toward the Holy See, and this is something that is true.[80]

Bỉnh understood that as long as he and his friends remained in Portugal they retained their autonomy and some leverage. Were they to accept the bishop's invitation to travel to Rome, they would be trapped or worse. Indeed, Bỉnh surely recalled the fate of the last Vietnamese delegation to Rome, whose members had been detained there, then detoured to Paris, and finally unwillingly repatriated to Tonkin, or the scheme enacted by the bishop of Macao, who had permitted brothers Liễn and Nhân to make the long journey to Goa, only to use his letter to the archbishop to force their return.

THE END GAME OF THE GALDINO APPOINTMENT (APRIL 1803)

Once Vatican approval for Galdino's posting to Macao had been granted, the only thing left was to wait for the April 1803 sailing season. Galdino's impending departure injected a new sense of urgency into Bỉnh's efforts to salvage something from the situation. A glimmer of hope appeared on April 22, when Galdino brought Bỉnh news of some softening of the papal nuncio's position regarding their desire for a bishop for Tonkin. The nuncio indicated that if the Vietnamese Christians in Bỉnh's community would accept the authority of the existing bishops, then the Vatican would permit the Portuguese ruler to appoint a Padroado bishop after first sending Bishop Galdino to Tonkin to investigate the situation and report his findings to the ruler.[81] Unconvinced, Bỉnh argued with Galdino about what he saw as an unacceptable compromise, but his reproaches fell on deaf ears, and Bỉnh recognized that he would probably have to accept the nuncio's proposal. But he was not going to allow Galdino to travel on such a mission without some way to keep an eye on him and to defend the community's interests. Bỉnh asked permission from the Portuguese ruler to accompany Galdino on his trip to Macao, but the request was turned aside, likely at the behest of Galdino himself.

On April 28, Bỉnh met yet again with Archbishop Vilas Boas and was told that permission had finally been granted for *one* of the men to accompany the bishop. Although the official permit was not yet ready, the men would now have to make hurried preparations for one of them to travel with Galdino. Confusion now beset the Vietnamese delegation, and Bỉnh was unsure whether there was enough time to organize someone to accompany the bishop-elect. In the event that it would not be possible to send someone to monitor Galdino's actions in Macao, on April 29 Bỉnh hastily drafted a letter to his colleagues in Macao detailing the circumstances of the new bishop's appointment. The letter was a warning about Galdino's true intentions vis-à-vis the Tonkinese Padroado Christians, cautioning his friends not to trust the new bishop and "not to listen to him when he says that he will help us with respect to the two bishops of the Holy See."[82] This letter was added to a packet of eighteen additional letters (the contents of which Bỉnh does not detail) and a Portuguese-Vietnamese dictionary (almost certainly de Rhodes's lexicon).

The day after he wrote this letter of warning, Bỉnh suddenly received word that Galdino's boat was preparing to depart. He and his friends hurried to the docks to say their good-byes and to deliver the letters and dictionary for their friends. When they arrived, Galdino surprised the Vietnamese by announcing that he had finally received the paperwork for one of them to accompany him. But, he hastened to add, he had informed the messenger that it was now too late and that he no longer wished to permit the Vietnamese to travel with him. This undoubtedly reinforced Bỉnh's feeling that Bishop Galdino had once again betrayed the men who had trusted and put their hopes in him. But at this point there was nothing the Vietnamese could do as they watched Galdino's vessel slowly pulling away from the Praça do Comercio's docks. They could but pray that he would not prove to be the final blow to their effort to resist the apostolic vicars.

THE NEWS FROM TONKIN

While he waited for letters to update him on the impact of Galdino's arrival in Macao, Bỉnh tried to glean what information he could from other sources, notably newspapers published in Lisbon. Although newspaper culture was not nearly as developed in Portugal as in other parts of continental Europe, such as Germany or the Netherlands, Lisbon did have its own thrice-weekly journal, the *Gazeta de Lisboa.* The *Gazeta* had first appeared in the 1710s and was published regularly throughout the eighteenth century and into the first several decades of the nineteenth. Despite its name, the *Gazeta* did not focus on events in Lisbon but rather provided news from London, Paris, Rome, and other major cities on the Continent, as well as offering some reports from the rest of the world. Bỉnh makes several references to it in his writings, and it must have been the primary source of his information about events in both Europe and Asia. As Bỉnh noted, "The custom in the West is to publish information and distribute it so that all under heaven might know about it because people are passionate about seeing [this information] and these sheets [of information] are called 'Gazeta.'"

Reading this newspaper, with its modest four to eight pages per issue, would have been an important experience for Bỉnh and an unprecedented one, for the first newspaper would not appear in Vietnam until 1865. The *Gazeta* allowed him to discuss Europe-wide events throughout his writings, including both the French military campaigns and the developments that surrounded the reemergence of the Jesuits, first in Russia and then gradually in Spain after their formal restoration in 1815. The *Gazeta* and other newspapers also enabled Bỉnh to keep up with some of the general developments in Annam to the extent that they touched on church matters.[83] These newspapers provided not only statistical information—the numbers of baptisms, conversions, European priests—but also reports of persecutions and changes in the clerical hierarchy, and even such events as a meeting between the apostolic vicars and the newly enthroned Nguyễn rulers. While such reports were irregular at best, they allowed Bỉnh to maintain a measure of contact with his homeland, even when letters were no longer arriving. As late as 1818, and drawing on news reports, he knew the names of both apostolic vicars then serving in Tonkin as well as the numbers of local priests and the total population of Christians in its two vicariates, which he gives at 190,000 in Western Tonkin and 180,000 in Eastern Tonkin.[84]

It was news gleaned from the *Gazeta* that in 1804 spurred Bỉnh to consider a wild new strategy for securing a bishop.[85] This scheme grew out of reports that the Nguyễn had finally defeated their Tây Sơn rivals. Bỉnh read that both of the apostolic vicars had gone to pay their respects to the new emperor and, more significantly, that the Nguyễn ruler had given permission for the free propagation of the faith.[86] Bỉnh expressed some skepticism about the accuracy of this news but clearly hoped it was true.[87] If it was, he regarded it as an opportunity that might fruitfully be exploited. Specifically, he sketched out a scenario that might take advantage of these circumstances to approach his project from a different direction. Bỉnh's new plan would involve a member of the community drafting a petition in the name of the Nguyễn emperor to request a Portuguese bishop. The petition would emphasize the Catholic community's Portuguese heritage and its dearth of priests and would suggest that if a Portuguese bishop were not sent the displeased Nguyễn emperor would expel all of the missionaries currently in his country. In effect, Bỉnh's plan was nothing less than a crude form of blackmail: give us our Portuguese bishop, or we will make sure not only that the recent advances of Catholicism in Tonkin are rolled back but that the entire venture is put into jeopardy.[88] While he never set this scheme in motion, it is evidence of the creativity, and perhaps desperation, to which Bỉnh's various earlier failed gambits had driven him.

ONE LAST EFFORT: BỈNH AND DOM JOÃO IN 1807

Unbeknownst to Bỉnh, 1807 was the last year in which he would have any realistic chance of completing his mission. The previous year had seen virtually no movement on his project, chiefly because Dom João had begun spending most of his time at his Mafra palace, nearly forty miles from Lisbon. This put him out of Bỉnh's reach both geographically and financially. While the distance was certainly a factor, the main obstacle was the cost of transport to the remote palace. Bỉnh wrote that the father superior of the Necessidades house was "stingy" (*hà tiện*) and unwilling to spend money for their needs. In particular, he was reluctant to authorize funds to rent the carriages required to transport Bỉnh and his two companions to Mafra and the additional money needed to cover their living expenses while they stayed near the palace.[89]

With his mission stalled, and increasingly frustrated by the father superior's refusal to pay for trips to visit the ruler, in early May of 1807 Bỉnh took matters into his own hands. Bỉnh knew that the ruler would be celebrating his fortieth birthday on May 13 and, by tradition, would have a royal audience at which he would receive birthday congratulations from his officials and others in attendance. Such an audience might present at least a brief opportunity to speak with the prince. Bỉnh's two companions were once again ill, which further heightened Bỉnh's sense of urgency but also meant that he would have to travel alone. Without authorization or any guarantee of reimbursement for the expense, Bỉnh hired a carriage for the two-day journey to Mafra and soon set off from Lisbon. He arrived at the ruler's remote palace on May 12.

Upon reaching the massive royal compound, Bỉnh opted not to wait for the next day's birthday audience but instead sought to manufacture an earlier meeting with the prince. He heard that the ruler was off on a daylong hunting expedition in the extensive forests that surrounded the Mafra complex, and he hoped to catch him upon his return. Thus Bỉnh donned the long traditional Vietnamese robe that he kept for royal audiences and took up a position outside the palace's side gates. There he waited throughout the day, then into the early evening, and Bỉnh began to wonder whether the ruler would in fact be returning that day. Just as Bỉnh had begun to lose hope entirely, the prince's hunting party finally came into view. As the ruler approached the palace, Bỉnh ran forward to meet him, bent down on one

FIGURE 18. A mid-nineteenth-century engraving of the massive Mafra palace compound in the countryside north of Lisbon. This palace and its extensive hunting grounds were a favorite retreat for the prince regent, and it was here that Bỉnh made his final plea to the ruler to help with his mission. Portuguese National Digital Library.

knee, and seized and kissed the prince's hand. Disconcerted, Dom João responded to this unexpected welcome only with a query: "Have you come here alone?" To this Bỉnh barely managed to reply, "Yes, I have come alone, because my friends are ill," before the ruler, apparently not deigning to reply, resumed his progress and entered the palace compound, leaving the Vietnamese priest standing alone outside Mafra's imposing walls.

The next day was May 13 and the prince regent's birthday. Bỉnh woke early and joined the ranks of officials who entered the palace's audience chamber to offer their congratulations to the ruler. In this manner, Bỉnh was again able to approach the prince, but only briefly: long enough to kiss the royal hand but not to convey a message of any sort. In the course of his visit to the audience chamber Bỉnh learned that Dom João's birthday plans included another hunting expedition. Seeing the possibility of orchestrating a further encounter with the ruler, Bỉnh once again stationed himself near the rear gate of the compound where he knew the horses were kept and where the hunting party would exit. Before long, the ruler and his party arrived, and as Dom João climbed up on his horse, Bỉnh ran over to kiss his hand yet again. The ruler, apparently impatient at once again being accosted by the priest, spat out the words "If there is something you want, please tell me." It was little more than an idle invitation, however, for even as he said this the prince regent was swinging his leg over the horse's back, and before Bỉnh could open his mouth Dom João had galloped away.

Bỉnh was forced to swallow his disappointment as he returned to his local residence to plan his next move. Since he had come without an official invitation, Bỉnh scrambled to find a place to stay. There were few if any nearby homes, much less inns offering short-term residence. When parties, sometimes as large as ten thousand people, would come to visit the crown prince, they would simply reside in the enormous Mafra palace itself, having no need for outside accommodation. Fortunately for him, Bỉnh came to the attention of a priest closely connected with the court who took him in and provided him with room and board in his spacious residence.[90] Not only did this man give Bỉnh food and shelter, but also, and more importantly, he agreed to approach the prince on Bỉnh's behalf. Meeting with the ruler, the priest reported that Bỉnh hoped to arrange a meeting. Unwilling to grant Bỉnh such access, Dom João told the priest to inform Bỉnh that if there was something he wanted he should submit it in a written petition.

By the time the priest returned to his residence it was already midnight, but when he told Bỉnh that such petitions were presented to the monarch during morning sessions, Bỉnh wasted no time. Despite the late hour, he immediately grabbed pen and paper and returned to his room to work on his petition. Bỉnh already knew what he wanted to say and was able to produce the document without difficulty. The completed version contained three elements. The first was an apology for not having attended an audience with the crown prince for more than a year, something he and his companions had deeply desired but had not been able to carry out. The prince's extended residence at Mafra over the past year and the financial obstacles to traveling there had made such visits impossible. The second component of the petition was simply a reminder that their mission continued to languish. Bỉnh brought up the fact that an envoy had been sent to Rome in 1805 but that no word of his mission had yet reached them. Then Bỉnh had the temerity to remind the ruler yet again of his rights under the Padroado Real regarding the appointing of bishops to Asia, "imploring and begging the Virtuous King that he think about the souls of our brothers in Annam."[91]

The last part of the petition was more mundane, namely permission for Bỉnh and his companions to relocate from the Necessidades house to the Casa do Espirit Santo, the Oratorian residence in the center of Lisbon. In making his case, Bỉnh cited the declining population of the Necessidades house as well as his need to take care of his frequently ill companions. Living at the Casa do Espirito Santo would be far more convenient for the men in terms of both its location and its larger population of priests who could assist Bỉnh in tending to his friends. Furthermore, it would provide easier access to the services and churches of the city core. Another unstated factor driving this request must have been Bỉnh's obvious unhappiness at the reluctance of the Necessidades's father superior to authorize expenditures for the Vietnamese.

The petition was ready by the next morning, and the priest presented it to the ruler on Bỉnh's behalf. He later reported to Bỉnh that upon receiving the petition Dom João immediately read it aloud and to a very attentive audience, confident that it would contain nothing that could not be publicly aired.[92] The manner in which Bỉnh recorded this episode in his notebooks shows how gratified he was at what he took to be an act of royal approbation. Despite the petition's favorable reception, no response was immediately forthcoming. In fact, Bỉnh had to wait in Mafra for more than a month before the king finally presented his answer. When the royal response arrived on June 19 it was, like Bỉnh's petition, in three parts, issued as three separate decrees. The first granted formal approval for the men to leave their current residence at the Necessidades convent. The second gave the three men permission to take up residence at the Espirito Santo house as Bỉnh had requested. To an extent, this marked the fulfillment of the ruler's initial intention in 1796 to house the men there, a plan that had been derailed by the ongoing earthquake repairs. Now, more than a decade later, the men would finally be able to move to this more central location. The third decree was directed to the head of the royal treasury, informing him to communicate directly with the head of the Casa do Espirito Santo to make arrangements to cover their financial needs.

Several things are noteworthy about the ruler's response to Bỉnh's petition. The first was its delay. While it may have been necessitated by more pressing court business or a need to coordinate the logistics of the desired move, it may also have been a way for the ruler to remind Bỉnh of his place and of the relatively low priority being accorded to him and his requests. The second is that the prince regent addressed only one of the three points in Bỉnh's petition, while completely ignoring the other two. Clearly the ruler did not wish to dredge up the issue of the envoy to the pope again, and almost certainly he did not appreciate yet another lecture by Bỉnh about his prerogatives and duties under the moribund Padroado. But beyond this, he did not even give Bỉnh and his companions permission for a royal audience. Clearly, after more than a decade in Portugal, the exotic Vietnamese had lost their luster. While their garb and distant homeland had initially beguiled the ruler and some of the ladies in the court, the intervening years had reduced the men to the ranks of marginal petitioners. While they could not entirely be ignored—something Bỉnh made sure of—they were no longer accorded the respect and access that had defined the early years of their residence in Lisbon. Indeed, when Bỉnh expressed a desire simply to visit the prince regent to offer his thanks for the ruler's response, he was told by the court's liaison official that the timing was not

FIGURE 19. The Mafra palace, its exterior largely unchanged, in 2006. Author's photo.

right.[93] The prince regent had his hands full meeting with a visiting envoy from India, after which an opportunity might present itself for an audience, and perhaps even the possibility of seeing to their remaining requests. As it turned out, the prince regent's agenda became more complicated with the looming threat of a joint Franco-Spanish invasion.[94]

Despite these snubs, Bỉnh was delighted that his request to change residences had been approved, as he clearly hoped it would improve the material aspects of their lives. At the same time, he understood that this transfer was politically delicate, as it affected the relationship between the two Oratorian houses. He decided that it would be best to feign ignorance regarding the reasons for their reassignment to the Espírito Santo house. When the king's decree was brought to Bỉnh, he pretended that the order to move had taken him by surprise and did not let on that he himself had made the request. When priests at the Necessidades house asked him about their impending move, he simply replied: "The Virtuous King has ordered that we change our residence to another house, and so I must obey." The head of the Espírito Santo house was happy to welcome the three men, particularly as he was feuding with the head of the Necessidades house and probably saw this as a chance to gain not only more clerics but also the court-guaranteed income that came with the Vietnamese delegation.⁹⁵

BÌNH LOSES HIS PATRON: THE PORTUGUESE COURT FLEES INTO EXILE

The pleasant hunting expeditions at Mafra soon became a distant memory for the crown prince. Over the summer and early fall of 1807 the clouds of war gathered and grew, and it became clear that Portugal was the eventual target of Napoleon's Franco-Spanish forces. Efforts to deflect the armies through negotiation went nowhere, and there was little chance that the undermanned and underequipped Portuguese forces could ever hope to hold off the combined Napoleonic armies. Faced with a looming invasion, and having exhausted its limited diplomatic options, the Portuguese court concluded that the only way to ensure its survival was retreat. With the Atlantic at its back, the logical destination for the court was its Brazilian colony, which was both sufficiently remote and wealthy enough to support the royal family and its extended entourage.⁹⁶ As the French armies closed in on Lisbon, the ruler gathered his family and close supporters and on November 27, 1807, boarded a waiting English vessel.

The impending departure of the one man who could fulfill Bình's mission came as a staggering blow to the Vietnamese priest. He had just submitted his fifteenth and final petition to the ruler, once again begging him to send a bishop to his homeland. On hearing the news that the royal family was making preparations to weigh anchor and set sail for the New World, Bình acted immediately. As he had done eleven years earlier in Macao, when searching for a Europe-bound vessel, Bình hired a small boat to take him out into the harbor. This time his objective was clear: the sailing ship on which the imperial family would shortly depart. In his desire to join the royal exodus, Bình had an enormous amount of company. Many of Lisbon's upper classes as well as assorted others were trying to join the court in its flight to Brazil, fearful of life under French occupation. Patrick Wilcken captured the situation in Lisbon at this moment:

> We may never know how many people managed to board the fleet, but it seems that around 10,000 people would travel out to Brazil in the first wave—a huge number considering that the population of Lisbon was at the time no more than 200,000. A vast retinue of courtiers—royal surgeons, confessors, ladies-in-waiting, keepers of the king's wardrobe, cooks and pages—was joined by the great and good of Lisbon society—counselors of state, military advisors, priests, judges and lawyers along with their extended families. From the original nucleus of the court and government functionaries, bribes and the calling in of favours had widened

FIGURE 20. A contemporary engraving depicting the prince regent's departure for Brazil in November of 1807 as Napoleonic armies stood at the gates of Lisbon. Portuguese National Digital Library.

the group to include petty bureaucrats, businessmen, distant relations and assorted hangers-on.[97]

As Wilcken's description suggests, Bính's attempt to join the royal fleet paralleled that being made by much of Lisbon society at that moment. When his small rowboat finally reached the royal barge, Bính formally requested permission to travel with the ruler to Brazil. Unsurprisingly, his request was turned down. As he wrote, "At this time the winds were very weak, no one was permitted to board the vessel, and so we were unable to see the King's face, and the vessel was impatient to depart."[98] Bính's failure, like that of so many others, was partly due to his belated effort but primarily reflected his lack of political capital. Bính was forced to turn his boat back to the shore of the Tagus, left to ponder a future of enormous uncertainty.

The winds that slowed Bính's effort to approach the prince regent's ship also stalled the departure of the royal flotilla itself. The British were eager to begin the journey to Brazil, but as long as the winds were blowing toward shore they could not depart, even as the invading armies got ever closer to Lisbon. It was not until November 29, a single day before the arrival of General Junot's French armies, that a favorable wind finally began to blow down the Tagus and out into the

Atlantic, at last permitting the royal entourage to set sail.[99] The flotilla ultimately consisted of fifteen Portuguese and English vessels, joined by more than thirty Brazilian merchant ships, which collectively transported somewhere between sixteen thousand and eighteen thousand people.[100] Escorted by a convoy of British naval vessels, the royal party made its way to the Brazilian port at Rio de Janeiro, which would become the home of the Portuguese court for the next fifteen years. Portugal had been left to the mercy of the French and Spanish armies and to the governance of a hastily assembled regency, whose chief task was to surrender to the arriving forces.

6

Waiting for Bình in Tonkin and Macao

While Bình assiduously pursued his mission in Lisbon, he was acutely aware that many people in Tonkin and Macao were eagerly awaiting the outcome of his project. They had placed their faith and their hopes in him, and with his departure they were forced to wait and pray that he would somehow overcome the enormous obstacles that stood between him and success. Whether those who awaited him truly comprehended the long odds Bình faced is not certain. Most probably placed their faith in God with Bình as his agent, trusting that the mission would turn out as it was meant to. At least a few in the community, however, must have understood the true nature of the challenges that lay before him. In any event, for those left behind in either Tonkin or Macao, Bình's departure for Lisbon in 1796 began an agonizing wait. It was measured against a ticking clock as the two elderly European priests who served the community became more feeble and their mortality a source of growing anxiety.

But it was not only the grim reality that the last of their aging Padroado clergy would soon be gone that provoked this unease. The members of the community also continued to face relentless pressure from the apostolic vicars to accept their episcopal authority and to give up lingering hopes that somehow another bishop would be appointed to serve their needs. These vicars used a combination of suasion and threats of prolonged excommunication in their efforts to compel the community to surrender. Bình's extended absence would have been part of the calculus for each side in this drama, for while it gave hope to the community that he might rescue them from their plight, it also created an opportunity for its opponents. With Bình out of the way, the community was missing one its core defenders and strongest advocates. The apostolic vicars used Bình's absence—during which they saw the Jesuit loyalists as particularly vulnerable—to redouble their efforts to win over the community. The more time passed without Bỉnh's return, of course, the more the odds tipped in favor of the apostolic vicars, and the stronger their arguments became that Bỉnh would not succeed and in all likelihood would never return.

PARALLEL GEOGRAPHIES

With Bỉnh's departure for Europe in 1796, the stories of the three groups of resistant Vietnamese Jesuit loyalists—in Lisbon, in Macao, and in Tonkin—began to follow very different trajectories. Each group faced its own difficulties and challenges: spiritual, material, and political. Though separated by enormous distances, each set of Vietnamese actors was closely tied to the others. Their histories simultaneously played out on geographically separated stages, but even the simultaneity was complex, for knowledge of their counterparts' situations and actions arrived only intermittently and long after the fact. Thus they acted in a context of great uncertainty, guided at times as much by hope and prayer as by actual information.

For their part, Bỉnh and his fellow travelers in Lisbon, as we have seen, found most of their material and spiritual needs being met. They were in one of the centers of global Roman Catholicism, with churches seemingly on every street corner, religious processions a regular occurrence, and no shortage of services to attend, or at which Bỉnh could officiate. The Portuguese royal treasury was providing a generous annual stipend that covered the cost of their residence and food, as well as expenses related to travel and the purchase of religious items and clothing. On the other hand, the men also faced challenges, both political and personal. Over the first decade of his time in Lisbon, Bỉnh maintained an exhausting schedule of meetings, visits, and appeals across the palaces and state offices in the Portuguese capital as he tried somehow to advance his cause. Throughout this period he constantly struggled with the formidable obstacles of European church politics, which repeatedly derailed or at least detoured his efforts. On a personal level, as we have seen, recurrent illness was a significant concern, one that necessitated medical attention and therapeutic treatments and had by 1802 already killed one of their number. The men also faced the immediate challenges of European secular politics and some of the hardships this entailed. The Napoleonic Wars at the turn of the nineteenth century often dominated the attention of their Portuguese patron, forcing their own requests to be set aside until calm could return. As Napoleon's armies drew closer this only intensified, and with the Franco-Spanish invasion of Portugal in late 1807 the three remaining envoys found themselves struggling with the food shortages and general hardships of the French occupation and its aftermath.

Meanwhile, back in Macao, Brothers Liên and Thuyên faced far more challenging circumstances. These stemmed chiefly from acute penury, as most of the group's financial reserves had naturally been sent along with Bỉnh and his companions in anticipation of the presumably substantial expenses for the journey and subsequent residence in Portugal, where, ironically, they had little need of them. The second enormous challenge the men in Macao faced was finding ways to avoid drawing attention to themselves, particularly from the ecclesiastical authorities, including the bishop, the MEP procurator, and the papal envoy. Any of these men might challenge the Jesuit loyalists' right to remain in the city or might seek to bar them from access to religious facilities. Third, the men were confronted with enormous uncertainty, both about their own prospects in Macao and about what had become of Bỉnh, from whom they heard nothing for several years after his departure. The only aspect of their lives from which Liễn and Thuyên would have derived some comfort was in the spiritual realm. Like Lisbon, Macao had no shortage of churches where they could attend mass and have their confessions heard, a substantial improvement on the often perilous religious circumstances they had left behind in Tonkin.

The last of the three parallel stories is that of the resolute Padroado Christians still waiting in Tonkin. Their peril was by far the most acute. While Bỉnh doggedly pursued his mission, those who had dispatched him from Tonkin suffered from material shortages, from the political vicissitudes of a Tây Sơn regime in its waning years, and from unpredictable shifts in state policies toward their Catholic faith. Sending Bỉnh had represented a huge gamble for the community. In dispatching him, they had sent one of the only native priests loyal to and directly serving the Padroado community, and one of the few priests sympathetic to their defiance of the authority of the apostolic vicars. While Bỉnh had regularly performed the sacraments for members of his community, virtually no other priests in the region were willing to do so, and indeed, most had been formally prohibited from serving the defiant Padroado Catholics. As far as these priests were concerned, the community's members were schismatics and stood outside the circle of the church. Given these circumstances, the community had pinned its hopes on Bỉnh successfully and rapidly completing his mission and then returning to take up his priestly duties once again. Even if he failed in the mission and was ultimately forced to return to Tonkin, at least Bỉnh would then be able to resume supporting their spiritual and ritual needs.

In some respects these narrow inter-religious problems were the least of the Padroado community's worries, as Roman Catholicism itself came under growing pressure from the state. The Tonkinese regime was sometimes tolerant toward the Christian minority and at other times very hostile toward it. At the time of Bỉnh's departure in late 1795, Tonkin was enjoying a respite from the drawn-out civil war between the Tây Sơn regime and the Nguyễn, and Catholics were benefiting from a degree of state tolerance. It was, however, an extremely fragile calm. The first two Tây Sơn emperors, who had ruled separately over Tonkin and Cochinchina, had died in 1792 and 1793 respectively, and the regime was now headed by a single young emperor and his regents. The core of Confucianist scholars who had committed themselves to supporting the fledgling regime was starting to drift away as the once bright prospects of a new dynasty rapidly dimmed. Thus, already by 1795, the calm that prevailed in the North was troubled by fears of the regime's political weakening. This manifested itself in a devolution of power in which regional figures became increasingly autonomous, corruption grew, and localized crackdowns on Christians intensified.[1]

Meanwhile, the Nguyễn military had been gathering momentum in its southern stronghold and was beginning to encroach on Tây Sơn–held territory. As the Tây Sơn regime in Tonkin found itself under growing military pressure from its Nguyễn rivals there was a corresponding increase in hostility toward Christians. This antipathy grew from two factors. The first was the Tây Sơn court's awareness of European missionaries among the Nguyễn regime's supporters, which brought with it a general fear that Christians more broadly might be in alliance against it. The second factor was the regime's commitment to restoring orthodoxy as part of a generalized social revival calculated to revive the dynasty's flagging fortunes, and Christianity was seen as a substantial deviation from cultural norms.[2] This renewed persecution was punctuated by the 1798 capture and subsequent execution of a pair of Vietnamese Christians, Emmanuel Triệu and Jean Đạt, the first state killings of Christians in decades and an indication of the newly perilous situation for Vietnamese Catholics.[3]

The year 1802 brought the end of the Tây Sơn regime, and with it a halt to the harsh crackdown against Catholicism that had marked the regime's waning years. The new Nguyễn regime was much more lenient toward the faith, in part because of its ruler's long-standing alliance with the MEP's apostolic vicar for Cochinchina, Bishop Pigneaux de Béhaine.[4] Although the bishop had died in 1799, the new Gia Long emperor (Nguyễn Anh) continued to evince general tolerance toward the Catholics in his realm. But while the spiritual situation in Tonkin improved during the early years of the Nguyễn dynasty, this period brought growing difficulties in the material realm. In particular, because the regime had come to power by force, it needed to find a way to secure authority and consolidate its victory by gaining political recognition from the Chinese. Such recognition was understood to be a critical element of the legitimation efforts of any new Vietnamese dynastic house. It was particularly vital for the Nguyễn, since they had overthrown an existing dynasty (the Tây Sơn) that had been formally acknowledged by the Chinese court.

The Nguyễn, however, ran into difficulties securing Chinese affirmation of their status, which had direct consequences for all who lived in Tonkin, Catholic and non-Catholic alike. Writing from their perch in Macao, Thuyên and Trạch reported the circumstances in their homeland to Bỉnh in a letter dated September 17, 1803:

As for life, it is even more miserable than before, because the Nguyễn are building citadels and ramparts in the Western style everywhere and are forcing the people, both men and women, to work on them, causing people to cry out and lament these hardships, which are worse than in the Cảnh Thịnh [i.e., Tây Sơn] era. We are once again suffering from drought, which has caused hunger and thirst. In Đàng Ngoài [Tonkin] we still have chaos, because before the Nguyễn were able to enter [this region] they took the name of the Lê house so that all under heaven would venerate and assist them, up until the time that they became the kings. Thus nothing in the country is at peace, and this has brought about continuous chaos. Moreover, the Nguyễn house has sent an envoy to ask for enfeoffment, but the Supreme King [the Chinese emperor] has not given this enfeoffment but has seized and jailed the Nguyễn envoy for the past two years, and they have not been able to return home, and for this reason the Nguyễn have been erecting citadels and building ramparts as well as preparing their soldiers to fight with the Chinese [Nhà Minh]. Consequently, the people suffer hardships many times greater than before, and this is how things are in our country.[5]

In short, the failure of the Nguyễn to secure immediate Chinese recognition of their new regime was taken as an ominous sign. It suggested that the Chinese court, which had formally recognized the short-lived Tây Sơn dynasty, might choose to maintain its support for that regime's surviving members. Alternatively, it could even opt to side with the many surviving supporters and members of the ousted Lê dynasty. Unsure of Chinese intentions, the Nguyễn felt that they had little choice but to prepare for possible war with the Qing, preparations that included compelling the Tonkinese populations to build defensive fortifications. Populations who had been awaiting rescue from the hardships of the Tây Sơn regime found their hopes dashed by the even more onerous impositions of the new regime.[6]

BỈNH'S LETTERS: MAIL AND THE TENUOUS LINK TO HOME

Separated by enormous distances and living in radically different circumstances, these three groups of Vietnamese Catholics were physically linked by the most tenuous of threads—sporadic communication in the form of letters traversing the oceans between them. From his notebooks it is clear that Bỉnh kept up a fairly active correspondence in Tonkin before his departure and then in Portugal, at least during his early years in Lisbon. His collected letters constitute a small but significant part of his written output and place him within an important Vietnamese Catholic epistolary tradition. A small body of letters written by Vietnamese Catholics has survived in European missionary archives, notably that of the MEP in Paris. These letters were typically sent to the MEP leadership or to priests who had once served in Tonkin but had later returned to Paris. In any case, most of them were petitions seeking additional missionaries to support their communities. Such letters typically described the hardships caused by years of neglect or the absence of ordained priests permitted to carry out the sacraments. While belonging to this tradition, what sets Bỉnh's letters apart is that they actually created and sustained lines of communication linking Tonkin and Europe. Although Vietnamese had sent letters to Europe before, as far as can be determined none of those missives was ever answered, so they cannot be said to have established communication between the two places. This time the situation was different. Letters sent to Europe received a reply, and these replies were themselves answered. The exchange of letters between Bỉnh and those he had left behind linked these distant places in a new way, and in a manner that did not involve Europeans, except as couriers. A channel had been created, however tenuous, for the exchange of news. Vietnamese Christians now had direct access to Europe through their envoy in Bỉnh, and while the network lasted a mere eight years, it was crucial while it survived.

The letters these men exchanged provided updates of ever-changing circumstances; they offered glimpses of hope, despair, resolve, and growing desperation. At a very basic level the letters indicated that those from whom they were separated had been alive when their letter had been dispatched. They sketch for us the experiences of these three groups and provide some sense of both their separate lives and of their continuing interactions across great distances. Bỉnh used his letters as a way to keep the community apprised of his progress or lack thereof. His letters were dispatched from Lisbon to Macao, from where some were sent on to Tonkin. We do not have the original letters, but Bỉnh carefully recorded copies of at least some of those he sent and received in a notebook he entitled *Nhật trình kim thư khất chính chúa giáo* (Golden book recording a journey to seek an official religious leader). That notebook contains copies of twenty-three letters that Bỉnh sent between the years 1798 and 1804 and also records sixteen letters that he in turn received between 1795 and 1803. He recorded no letters in that notebook after 1803, possibly because the Napoleonic Wars interrupted shipping, preventing vessels from sailing to Asia, or, just as likely, because by then his contacts in Macao had already returned to Tonkin. It is also conceivable that additional letters were preserved in Bỉnh's other three notebooks of collected documents, which are apparently no longer extant.[7]

The letters that have survived indicate the degree to which their timing was dictated by the departure schedules of ships traveling between Lisbon and Asia. Virtually all of Bỉnh's letters were written in the springtime, usually between February and April, when boats began to set sail for Asia. After writing the letters, which he typically sent in batches, Bỉnh entrusted them to missionaries whom he knew to be on their way to Macao. Unfortunately for him, Bỉnh discovered that this method was far from foolproof; it was subject to the same church politics with which he struggled in Europe. He reported, for instance, writing letters in 1802 and entrusting them to a pair of Macao-bound Vincentian missionaries, Fathers Nicholas and Fernando. He later learned these letters were never delivered to their intended recipients. Bình viewed this as a deliberate effort to derail his project rather than as an oversight or some other innocent error, and the episode led to a vow not to send any future letters via priests from the Order of St. Vincent. Accordingly, the following year he gave his letters to an Italian priest of the Franciscan order who was going to pass through Macao on his way to China. This priest also did not fulfill his promise to deliver the letters, and this second betrayal caused Bình to observe, in a rare flash of cynicism, that "such is the custom in the West."[8]

The distance and logistical complexity of sending mail from Lisbon to Macao, as well as the many things that could and did go wrong, meant that those whom Bình left behind in Macao, as well as the Jesuit loyalist community in Tonkin, had little guarantee that they would ever hear from him again, much less receive updates in anything like a timely fashion. We know that the trip from Lisbon to Macao could be done in as little as eighteen weeks. Galdino, for instance, departed Lisbon on April 30 and arrived in Macao on September 7.[9] While the journey itself could be completed relatively quickly, the primary obstacle to more frequent and timely communication was not so much the time needed for the journey as the schedule of departures. Since Asia-bound vessels left Lisbon only once a year, this meant there would always be a gap of roughly one year between letters arriving in Macao from Lisbon. Once packets of letters were received in Macao, those addressed to the community in Tonkin were forwarded, a step representing an additional delay before the letters reached their final destination. Commenting on the reverse transmission of such letters, Bình noted that in several cases it had taken ten months from the date on which letters were written in Tonkin before he finally received them.[10] Clearly those at both ends of this long and tenuous link understood the time involved and were aware of at least some of the many things that could go wrong: shipwrecks, the deaths of the letter carriers, or carriers' willful or neglectful failure to deliver the messages that had been entrusted to them. Given the numerous obstacles, it is not surprising that it took several years before the two sides were finally able to exchange letters with any consistency.

Bình understood the critical importance of updating those who had dispatched him, for they were both eagerly awaiting news from him and looking for guidance in their continuing struggle with the apostolic vicars. The significance of the letters is revealed in an 1804 report by an MEP missionary, Jean Jacques Guérard, based in central Tonkin, who wrote of the situation: "Nothing remains but to comment on the aftermath of the revolt that the letters of Father Bình have assured. On his departure from Tonkin for Macao, he left behind a stamp for the chief of the schismatics, which is like a seal by which to judge and to assure the veracity of his letters. All the others that do not carry this said vile mark must be rejected as false."[11] From this account and from some of the replies recorded in his notebooks, we know that at least some of Bỉnh's letters reached their destination. Father Guérard's letter further makes it clear that Bỉnh had taken safeguards to ensure that the members of his community would recognize these letters as being from him, and not forgeries intended to mislead them and perhaps cause them to give up their defiance toward the apostolic vicars.

Knowing how eagerly the community was awaiting word of his arrival, Bỉnh began writing as soon as he could after reaching Lisbon, and while he did not record the earliest letters he sent, the later ones, beginning in 1799, give a sense of their content. Most of these letters featured updates on his situation as well as continued reassurances about the status of his mission to the Portuguese court. Equally important, they expressed his understanding of the tremendous difficulties the community continued to face. In a letter dated April 25, 1800, Bỉnh wrote of his group's safe arrival and of their being housed with the Oratorians, noting that all of their needs were being taken care of. He described the European political situation, in particular the ongoing warfare that impeded both his mission and any possibility of leaving Europe as shipping lanes were blocked by naval conflict between the French and the British.[12] The letter also reported that he had yet to receive a reply to any of his earlier letters, suggesting that he had no real information of the community. This explains why a letter dated nearly four years after his arrival in Lisbon would still discuss the particulars of their group's first reaching the Portuguese capital: he had no way of knowing if any of his earlier missives had reached their destinations. This letter also included special reassurance for Brother Liên, noting specifically, "I have already memorialized to the Virtuous King that there is a person by the name of Simão [Liên] whom I left behind in Macao, and that he is waiting for us."[13] Bỉnh wrote too, that although physically distant, he still considered himself spiritually close to those he had left behind, and he urged the men in Macao to send news of the community in Tonkin and its happenings. He concluded by writing that he and his companions were able to receive Communion two or three times every week and that he himself faced no obstacles at all to saying mass. This news must have engendered some envy among those left behind in Tonkin, who faced so many barriers in their own practice of the Christian faith.[14]

Bỉnh's letters provided news to his friends but also enabled him to sustain his involvement in the affairs of the community, even from afar. In addition to updates, his letters contained instructions from a man who continued to regard himself as a leader of the community and was still viewed as such by those he had left behind. His letters frequently contained specific directives to members of the community, for example guidelines on how to mourn and pray for those who had died.[15] Bỉnh also used his letters to provide reminders about the need to preserve the Jesuits' former property and buildings, which he had continued to promise the

Portuguese ruler would be protected in the event that a Portuguese bishop might be sent.[16] In another letter of May 1800, he urged the community to find someone to send to Macao to help Brother Liễn, whom they had left by himself.[17] In short, Bỉnh's letters enabled him to serve as a remote but engaged spiritual and community leader for the Padroado Christians, for whom his letters represented a lifeline.

Finally, Bỉnh used the letters to offer exhortations and encouragement to those whom he had left behind. Most notably, he urged them to remain steadfast in the face of unrelenting pressure from the apostolic bishops. He implored them not to worry or become discouraged, but rather to "carry the cross of the Lord a bit higher still" and to rely on it for stability and strength. Bỉnh also urged them to put their faith in Jesus, quoting a Bible passage about Jesus telling people to place their troubles and burdens on him. When Bỉnh learned of Father Nuncio Horta's 1801 death, which had left only a single priest to serve the community, he wrote urging its members to remain true to their tradition, which he noted had roots in the efforts of Alexandre de Rhodes and Geronimo Maiorica, "the first Portuguese people [người Vutughê] to preach to our ancestors that they might know the Way."[18] While this was patently untrue—de Rhodes was a Frenchman from Avignon and Maiorica an Italian from Naples—Bỉnh was clearly seeking to reinforce the importance of the Portuguese in their worldview. To underscore his message, Bỉnh reminded his followers that even when Jesus ascended to heaven he left behind his Holy Spirit, as well as the message that whenever two or three people were gathered in his name he would be there among them. In short, Bỉnh sought to reassure the community that as long as they clung to the faith and to each other they could survive even without any priests.[19]

In his missives urging patience upon the community, Bỉnh turned to the Bible for an instructive parallel to their situation. He conjured up the image of Moses (Bỉnh) ascending Mount Sinai (Lisbon) to receive the Ten Commandments (a bishop), while the Israelites (the Tonkinese Catholic community) waited at the foot of the mountain for their leader's return.[20] In another (undated) letter he took the analogy one step further, again comparing his community to the Israelites but this time reminding its members that in Moses's absence the Israelites had begun to worship in unacceptable ways. When Moses returned from the mountain peak with the Commandments, he found that his followers, despairing of his return, had begun to worship idols and false gods (the golden calf). In using this story, Bỉnh was cautioning his followers to remain steadfast in their allegiance to the Jesuit church and not to begin to follow the false gods of the Dominican or the MEP apostolic vicars.[21] He was all too aware of the difficulty that such waiting entailed, for he knew the history of what happened the first time the Jesuits were removed from Vietnamese territory in the 1680s. During that period there had been large-scale defections from the Jesuit fold and substantial growth among the flocks of the other religious communities. It was precisely this that he sought to avoid.

The idea of Bỉnh as a kind of Vietnamese Moses clearly took root in the minds of the community, and it is likely that its members invoked it when encountering clergy associated with the apostolic vicars. That local missionaries had become aware of his self-characterizations is evidenced in an 1801 letter by Bishop Longer, the apostolic vicar for Western Tonkin. In it, Longer wrote in scathing terms about the arrival and impact of one of Bỉnh's letters:

> He is encouraging the Christians not to imitate the Israelites, who, seeing Moses very much delayed in descending from the mountain, began adoring the golden calf (he is no doubt Moses, and we are the vile animal which he is prohibiting them from worshipping). As for the rest, we are a long way from compelling the Christians to carry out any sort of act of adoration for our consideration, and at the same time are not without doubts about the intentions of exhorting the Christians to hold good during the schism, but there are still those who are seduced by these letters, true or false, and await his return somewhat as the Jews await the Messiah, but there is also a great number who are sent into great shillyshallying [*tergiversation*]. I believe that the Holy Seat would do well to send him back to his Apostolic Vicariate, or confine him in a monastery for the rest of his days.[22]

This report suggests the degree of animosity that existed between the two groups and the sway that Bỉnh continued to exercise over his community, even at a great distance.

Three long years later, as Bỉnh's return, much less any success in securing a bishop, seemed unlikely, the Padroado community continued to cling to hope. They were still defying efforts by the apostolic vicars to bring them into their fold, as attested in an 1804 follow-up letter by Bishop Longer, in which he described the Jesuit loyalist community's ongoing defiance: "Ever since Father Binh and his followers left Tonkin in 1795, many Christians of the ex-Society have come to me [saying] that they wanted [to wait] only three years in order to receive news of the said Father Bỉnh. I replied to them that if they were to wait thirty years I would not have the strength to force them to submit to legitimate authority, and that the kingdom is full of pagans among whom I deplore this blindness."[23] As the writer concluded, commenting on Bỉnh: "He is their master so that they do not dare to contradict him." This all suggests the enormous influence that Bỉnh wielded over the Vietnamese Jesuit loyalist community and the ability he had to persuade them to hold fast in their resistance against the apostolic vicars, even from a great distance.

WAITING IN MACAO

While Bỉnh was being awaited by a dwindling community of Catholics in Tonkin, a tiny cohort in Macao was also anxiously anticipating his return. Simão Liễn had been left behind because of his illness and had later been joined by Paolo Maria

Thuyên. The two men had remained in Macao to look out for the Padroado community's interests on the island and to serve as a communications link to Bỉnh in Europe. It was a difficult assignment at the outset, given their loyalty to a defunct religious order and the latent hostility demonstrated by ecclesiastical figures in Macao. The men had very little protection, legal or ecclesiastical, and at best could rely on a very small circle of sympathetic European residents. They were also extremely short of funds.

The men faced numerous challenges, but the biggest, at least initially, must have been the anxiety and uncertainty that came from waiting for the first reports from their friends who had departed for Europe. The men certainly understood the distinct possibility that Bỉnh and his fellow travelers might perish on their long voyage. And, as first one year passed, and then a second, and even a third, without any word from Lisbon, the possibility that the Catholic envoys had not reached their destination grew. It is easy to imagine Brothers Liển and Thuyên clinging to hope in Macao, anxiously querying each arriving European cleric as to any news or, better still, letters, that they might be carrying from the delegation in Lisbon. As even more time passed, this growing anxiety must have given way to despair and eventually resignation.

Then, more than four years after his delegation had set sail for Europe, Bỉnh's first letters finally reached Macao in March of 1800.[24] A communications link had at last been established between the delegation in Lisbon and those waiting in the remote Portuguese outpost. One can only imagine the jubilation that must have greeted the arrival of these letters with their confirmation that Bỉnh and his three compatriots had safely reached Lisbon, had been well received by the Portuguese court, and were making progress in their mission. While Liển and Thuyên had been waiting, they had been sending reports to Bỉnh, updating him as best they could on their own circumstances and those of the community in Tonkin. It is unclear when these reports were first sent or how many of them failed to reach their intended recipient. The first to reach Bỉnh arrived on November 26, 1800, and included news dating back to 1798, indicating uncertainty about whether Bỉnh had received any letters before that date.

The letters written by Brothers Liển and Thuyên describe an increasingly desperate situation as they tried to find ways to remain in Macao despite dwindling funds and increasing pressure from hostile ecclesiastical authorities. Among their biggest challenges was finding a place to stay. For some time after Bỉnh's departure the men had been able to maintain a low profile in Macao, essentially waiting for developments in the form of news or even Bỉnh's return. But as time passed this became more difficult and their housing situation more precarious. Forced to move from their apartments in the summer of 1800, perhaps for financial reasons, they looked around for another place to live before eventually finding refuge at the St. Paul order house in July. The head of the house, Father Rodrigo da

Madre de Dios, was sympathetic to their plight, possibly because his residence had been established by the Jesuits. When news of their new accommodations reached the ears of Bishop Marcelino in March 1801, he went to visit Father Rodrigo and asked him point-blank: "Why have you permitted these two Tonkinese people to stay here?" Rodrigo replied that he was under the impression that whom he gave rooms to was his own affair, requiring no one's prior approval. He apparently went on to note that if the bishop wanted to have someone else run the order house that was his prerogative but that as long as he (Father Rodrigo) was in charge he would offer residence to people at his own discretion.[25]

Despite his initial defiance of the bishop's demands, Father Rodrigo continued to feel the prelate's pressure, which became increasingly difficult to resist. After holding out for another five months, he finally succumbed to the bishop's authority and informed the Vietnamese they would have to make alternative housing arrangements. At this juncture, September 25, 1801, the men wrote to Bỉnh of their hopelessness, saying they had no idea where they would be going next or where any subsequent correspondence should be sent.[26] The letter containing this news, along with others carried by the same boat, reached Bỉnh on July 5, 1802. As these missives carried nothing but miserable news—an unmitigated litany of hardships, both material and spiritual—this must have been one of the most difficult days of Bỉnh's sojourn in Lisbon.

While his companions in Macao were struggling to find a new place to live and scraping together enough money to sustain themselves, the community in Tonkin was suffering even greater hardships. The Tây Sơn regime had issued anti-Christian edicts in 1797–98, and the regime remained suspicious of Christians whom it feared might be in collusion with their Nguyễn enemies to the south. Although the religious situation eased somewhat by 1800, the looming final confrontation between the Tây Sơn regime and the Nguyễn forces increasingly absorbed people's energies as they struggled to survive. Even beyond this, the letter reported that the Jesuit loyalists continued to feel the ferocious pressure to yield to the apostolic vicars. The timing of this campaign was probably tied in part to the death in 1801 of Father Nuncio Horta, one of the community's two surviving European priests. In any case, the men in Macao reported news from Tonkin of a systematic campaign of preaching and political pressure to lure the holdouts to the side of the apostolic vicars. They told of a rumor that "[the vicars] use a [special] tonic causing Christians who eat it to follow them [the vicars]." They also reported that "anyone who follows that teacher and permits him to enter their church [will be left alone], but those who do not permit this, or who do not follow them, will lose their right of confession [phép Kỉ Bỉnh]." There was even a rumor suggesting threats of arson against church communities that continued to defy the apostolic vicars: "Priests and people from [that] house say that 'this is a church that is contrary to the faith [rối đạo], and this being so, the Holy Spirit will use flames from the heavens and send them down to burn that church,' and some of the community [members] believed this and followed the [vicars]."[27]

Given the tremendous difficulties now facing both the community in Tonkin and its representatives in Macao, it is not surprising that Liễn and Thuyên urged Bỉnh and his companions to return home, regardless of whether their mission was completed. They wrote that if Bỉnh and his friends could not all return, then at least some of them had to if the community was to continue its resistance against the apostolic vicars: "Thus I appeal to you and the teachers with you to find a means by which all of you might return this year, for if this is not possible the community will face great hardship and will find it difficult to continue to preserve the properties in our country any longer."[28] In short, they were urging Bỉnh to give up on a mission whose likelihood of success now seemed minuscule. They were forced to weigh their own dire circumstances and the grave hardships facing the community in Tonkin against a growing sense that Bỉnh's petitions to the Portuguese ruler would ultimately fail. They had obviously concluded that their community was doomed without Bỉnh's presence, as its members would, through coercion or enticement, gradually be drawn into the fold of the apostolic vicars.

The growing skepticism about Bỉnh's prospects was not restricted to the men in Macao but had also begun to infect the community waiting in Tonkin. In June of 1801 Bishop Longer wrote to his superior that the group of "schismatics" was becoming weaker by the day, suggesting that they posed less and less of a threat to the authority of the apostolic vicars.[29] The community's growing doubt about Bỉnh's prospects is confirmed in a letter Bỉnh received in July 1802 from an old friend, Wenceslao Đậu, writing from Tonkin. Đậu's letter expressed considerable skepticism about Bỉnh's likely success in his mission. After reading one of Bỉnh's letters describing the Portuguese king's kindness toward the Vietnamese delegation, Đậu had gone to speak with "Cố Định" (Father Augustin Carneiro) to ask him how to interpret this information. Carneiro apparently answered that an earlier Portuguese king (João V) had once done a great favor for the Jesuit order by asking for a particular bishop for their country and that the Holy See had approved the request. But, Father Carneiro argued, the present situation was very different, and no matter how many promises a great many people might make, these did not amount to much. Đậu reported Carneiro as saying: "I reflect that the Virtuous Ruler of earlier times worked very hard but was unable to succeed [in appointing the bishop to Tonkin]; how then is it possible that our present matter, in which we dare to ask for these men, will succeed?" Indeed, Carneiro described the Vietnamese delegates as pawns in a game of chess being played by the Portuguese ruler.[30]

In short, it is clear that by July of 1802 Bỉnh was fully aware of the grave hardships facing those whom he had left behind. Moreover, he was now confronted with direct pleas from Liễn and Thuyên that he and his companions return home as quickly as possible to preserve what remained of their community. He had also heard from the community itself that there was increasing doubt about the likelihood of his success. By now, had he been honest with himself, he probably would have reached the same conclusion. This presented Bỉnh with an enormous dilemma. He continued to hope that he might find a way to salvage the Galdino appointment, perhaps optimistic that Dom Alexandre would be able to persuade the new pope to see things from Bỉnh's vantage point. Thus it is easy to understand why Bỉnh felt that he could not yet leave Lisbon, the only place he could secure the bishop who might save his imperiled community. At the same time, these reports from home were making it clear that what had been a situation of great difficulty when he left in late 1795 had now become virtually unsustainable. There remained only one very elderly priest (Father Carneiro) still willing to serve the community, there was still a ban on Catholicism at the state level enacted by the failing Tây Sơn court, and the apostolic vicars were relentlessly pressuring the community's members to end their intransigence. There was, moreover, little reason to believe that any of these circumstances would change.

Bỉnh thus faced a stark choice, a variant of that with which the community had wrestled in 1795: either to continue trying to complete the mission, even with its success looking extremely doubtful, and thus risk the distinct possibility that the community would in the meantime dissolve under the pressure of circumstances and the apostolic vicars; or to admit failure after six years and return home as quickly as possible to salvage what remained of the community. Both choices were unpleasant, and each carried risks. Staying on in Lisbon offered only the remotest likelihood of success. Even if an appointment could somehow be secured, Bỉnh now understood how slowly the ecclesiastical bureaucracy moved. The successful appointment of another bishop to Tonkin might again be endangered by delays, during which the nuncio could once again take measures to undermine or reverse it. The second option, returning to Tonkin, was also rife with dangers and uncertainties. There was the long ocean journey, the perils of which Bỉnh had seen on his first trip. Then there was the danger of being ensnared by the bishop in Macao, which Bỉnh would have to negotiate on his way to Tonkin. Finally, there was the grave uncertainty of the political and ecclesiastical situation in Tonkin, where Bỉnh's arrival might not be sufficient to save the community. It was a dilemma that must have tested Bỉnh, yet it is one about which he did not write in his journals or even in his letters. If anything, his letters continued to keep up a facade of optimism: Bỉnh acknowledged the setbacks and challenges he had encountered, yet continued to hold out hope based on the Portuguese ruler's ongoing expression of goodwill toward his Vietnamese guests.

DESPERATION IN MACAO

As Bỉnh contemplated his unpalatable options, the situation in Macao was becoming even more dire. Brother Liễn fell violently ill in September of 1801, apparently confirming Bỉnh's presentiments about his general fragility. Thuyên took Liễn to the Santa Casa da Miseracórdia's hospital, which, along with the Senate, was one of the most prominent and powerful institutions in Macao. That religious institution oversaw not only a hospital but also a charitable agency and an orphanage and was well funded through bequests and donations presented by transgressing Catholics as a form of penance.[31] It soon became clear that Liễn's illness could not easily be remedied, and his hospitalization dragged on, with no positive results from the ministrations of either Portuguese or Chinese doctors. As it did so, the costs of his treatment ate into the men's paltry financial reserves. In the end, the doctors could do nothing for him, and Brother Liễn succumbed to his illness on March, 26, 1802, at the age of fifty. He was interred at the Franciscan order house in Macao, and Bỉnh reports that its priests said a large number of masses for his soul.[32] With Brother Liễn's death the group had lost one of its more senior members, and the considerable expenses for his unsuccessful treatment and subsequent funeral (the latter cost more than 200 pesos) represented a significant financial setback.[33] When word of Brother Liễn's death reached Lisbon in August of 1803, Bỉnh remarked upon the contrast between the deaths of Brother Liễn in Macao and Brother Nhân in Lisbon: "[Brother Liễn] was bedridden for many years, and while over here there was a great deal of assistance [for Brother Nhân], on your side there was only Brother Thuyên all by himself who had to look after the invalid, and this was a great hardship."[34]

Brother Liễn's death left Brother Thuyên entirely alone, now even more vulnerable to pressure from the religious authorities. To address this, the community arranged to send another man, Brother Trạch, to join him.[35] Trạch arrived in Macao sometime in the summer of 1802, bringing with him news of the community and of the dramatic changes in Đại Việt, where the Nguyễn armies had finally invaded the North in early 1802. By July of that year, southern troops had entered Thăng Long and overthrown the Tây Sơn regime. The implications of this change of regimes for Vietnamese Christians were still far from clear at that juncture, though all expressed hope that it might bring an end to the persecution the Tây Sơn had instituted in their final years. Having a new companion must have been of great comfort to Brother Thuyên, who had been living alone and exhausted from his efforts in caring for a dying Liễn. At the same time, Trạch's arrival forced Brother Thuyên to look for housing that could accommodate two men. An extensive search for such a residence was in vain, and in the end Thuyên had to rent separate apartments for each of the two men, which proved more expensive than a single, larger accommodation.[36]

GALDINO ARRIVES IN MACAO

Meanwhile, as letters flowed back and forth between Lisbon, Macao, and Tonkin, and as Bỉnh contemplated his unappealing options, the situation in Macao changed dramatically with Bishop Galdino's arrival on September 7, 1803, more than eighteen months after his appointment to the bishopric. Despite his abrupt refusal to allow Bỉnh or one of the other Vietnamese to accompany him on the trip to Macao, the new bishop did follow through on his promise to deliver a packet of their letters to Trạch and Thuyên, who were eagerly awaiting his arrival in Macao. One can only imagine their disappointment when they read Bỉnh's note informing them that this man was not, as they had hoped, the answer to their prayers but rather a replacement bishop for Macao as well as a likely threat to their already tenuous residence there.[37]

Galdino's arrival in Macao portended the end of the line for Bỉnh's companions still holding on in the Portuguese enclave. The new bishop's efforts to end the religious schism must have been guided by his now thorough understanding of the issues and politics of the matter. Not only had he been in close contact with Bỉnh and heard his side of the story, but he had also met regularly with the papal nuncio who had explained the Holy See's position. Over the fifteen months between his appointment and his departure for Macao, Galdino had immersed himself in the politics of Bỉnh's project and had had time to consider and determine a course of action. This would have put him into a considerably stronger position than the man he was replacing, Bishop Marcelino. Bishop Marcelino had asserted his authority in Macao by preventing Bỉnh's trip to Goa in 1794 and then nearly derailing his 1796 departure for Lisbon. Marcelino, however, had been content to limit his involvement in the feud between the Jesuit loyalists in the Padroado community and the apostolic vicars to such maneuvers and had not embroiled himself in their conflicts further afield in Tonkin. Galdino, however, was a man of action and a climber in the Catholic church hierarchy and was fully prepared to engage with the Tonkinese holdouts. He would brook no resistance, and his aggressive crackdown on the recalcitrant Vietnamese Jesuit loyalist community clearly reflected his character.

The reality of Bỉnh's warning about Galdino soon sank in for Thuyên and Trạch. When the new bishop first arrived in Macao, the two Vietnamese went to welcome him and to present their concerns and to discuss the problems of their community in Tonkin. Rather than addressing any of the matters the two men raised, Galdino bluntly questioned their very presence in the Portuguese enclave, asking, "Why are you staying here in Macao?" The men responded that they were waiting for their friends to return from Portugal. Galdino replied that he already understood that and went on to criticize Bỉnh and his followers for resisting the authority of the existing bishops in Tonkin. He informed Thuyên and Trạch in unequivocal terms that they had no choice but to obey the apostolic bishops already in place in Tonkin. Moreover, he insisted that the two men not only return to Tonkin but also formally apologize to the two bishops and ask forgiveness for having lost their hearts (mất lòng). Galdino then played his spiritual trump card, formally banning the men from going to confession until they had complied with his demands.[38]

Thuyên and Trạch looked around for a way to deflect or sidestep this draconian edict from the bishop but found none. They tried arguing and reasoning with Galdino to persuade him to change his mind. When this failed, they sought to delay their departure by telling the bishop that there were no boats going to Tonkin at that time. He suggested that they take a boat to Gia Định or the central Vietnamese city of Phú Xuân, but they replied that it would be very difficult to procure transport from either of those ports to their homes in Tonkin. To some degree they were probably exaggerating the difficulties, but with the Nguyễn–Tây Sơn wars only recently concluded, transport to Tonkin likely remained problematic as captains waited for the situation to settle down before risking a return. The men then asked whether it might be possible for just one of them return to Tonkin while the other remained behind. Galdino rejected their proposed compromise, repeating that both of them had to leave and to do so at once.

Galdino believed, or wished to believe, that his efforts had been successful. In a letter to the Dominican apostolic vicar in Eastern Tonkin not long after his arrival in Macao, Galdino described his actions and their apparent result: "I arrived in Macao on September 7 [1803], and the first thing I did on that very same day was to deal with the sponsor of the schism, the father who had brought it about and sent them here [to Macao]. [I ordered the two men] to write to the Christians of Tonkin to undeceive them. They obeyed for fear of one thing and another, and so I remit from them two copies written in Chinese so that the Christians of Tonkin might read them and be undeceived."[39] This letter suggests that Galdino had succeeded in cornering the men and had effectively dealt with the matter of the schism. Yet subsequent events made it clear that the schism was far from resolved and that the men in Macao were more resilient than the bishop had expected. Furthermore, Bishop Galdino's power to control them was more limited than he had believed, and the community in Tonkin more tenacious than he could have imagined.

Indeed, despite Galdino's efforts, the two Vietnamese clerics continued to resist his ultimatums. They were unwilling to accept the fact that their efforts had reached a dead end and that they would be unable to stay on to greet Bình upon what they hoped would be his eventual return. Moreover, they feared the certain humiliation they would face if they returned on Galdino's terms. They wrote to Bình about this, describing their apprehensions, even as they continued to cast around for options.[40] They appealed to their former ally, Father Rodrigo, but he informed them that there was nothing more he could do. They would have to accept the bishop's commands.[41] When this failed, the two men tried to comply with Galdino's instructions by drafting the letter of contrition that he had insisted they send to the two bishops in Tonkin. After writing the letter they took it to Galdino to see whether it was acceptable, but it did not meet his requirements. Moreover, he instructed them that (if they were to remain in Macao) he would require them to submit written petitions for any requests and that these would then be passed on to the bishops in Tonkin for their reply.[42] Galdino likely proposed this convoluted process as a means to paralyze the two men and thus further persuade them to return to Tonkin.

In addition to using his office to press the men to submit to the MEP and Dominican authority, Galdino acted to take control of the remaining Jesuit assets in his jurisdiction in Macao. Determining that these funds lay under his authority and could not belong to a religious order formally dissolved by the pope, Galdino moved to seize the money that Thuyên and Trạch were still safeguarding. Galdino likely saw this as a concrete way to enforce his order for the Tonkinese to return to their homeland. As long as they had some financial resources, the men could continue to remain in Macao, whatever his spiritual pressures upon them. By confiscating their funds, Galdino would make this nearly impossible. The money was being held for the men by their old friend Father Rodrigo. Initially, Father Rodrigo refused to surrender the Jesuit assets that the Vietnamese had entrusted to him. When Galdino threatened him with excommunication, however, he relented, and in mid-January of 1804 he reluctantly turned over the sum of 5,890.5 bronze *reals* to the papal nuncio in Macao, Giovanni Baptista Marchini.[43] Bình was furious when he learned of this, well after the fact, though he could do nothing except once again denounce Galdino's actions in his writings, observing that "there were two occasions on which we were beset by pirates, once at sea and once on land."[44]

The loss of the money they had long protected plunged Thuyên and Trạch into despondency. They wrote to Bình describing these events and expressing great despair at the unlikelihood of receiving any further word from him. Confiscating the remaining Jesuit assets had been only the first act in Galdino's more aggressive campaign to dislodge the Vietnamese in Macao. Increasingly frustrated with Thuyên and Trạch's foot-dragging in the face of his repeated demands that they give up their perch in Macao and return home, the bishop finally resorted to force. Sometime in March of 1804, Galdino sent a contingent of soldiers to the house where the men were residing. The troops marched the two Vietnamese to a waiting boat, where the soldiers watched to ensure that they boarded it. Their time was finally up, and Thuyên and Trạch helplessly watched Macao recede into the distance as the boat slowly carried them toward their homeland.[45] Their eventual arrival in Tonkin was noted in passing by an MEP cleric, Father Guérard, who reported in a letter dated August 3, 1804, that "finally the two young men returned from Macao." At least, he noted, they did not return empty-handed, for they "[served] as the bearers of letters from the said Father Bình to some in particular: to a former blind preacher who is in the district where I am at present, and to a catechist in chief in that house where earlier lived a Portuguese preacher named Augustin Carneiro, who died two years and some months ago, at the age of ninety."[46]

GALDINO PURSUES THE JESUIT LOYALIST COMMUNITY IN TONKIN

Bishop Galdino must have taken some satisfaction in the progress he had made in Macao. After some difficulties, he had now succeeded both in expelling the two Jesuit loyalists and in securing the remaining Jesuit funds. He had also looked into the matter further and sent a report to the Portuguese ruler in which he pointed out that Bình's community were schismatics for rejecting proper authority and that the Vietnamese whom the prince regent was assisting were renegades.[47] But he still hoped to put a definitive end to the schism in Tonkin itself.[48] He wrote numerous letters to the community during his short term in office, repeatedly urging its members to end their defiance of his and the apostolic vicars' leadership and to accept their ecclesiastical authority. Several of these letters survive and testify to his efforts to bring the community under control.

In writing to the community, Galdino repeatedly emphasized his understanding of their situation but also argued that their intransigence was misguided, that they had been deceived by their elderly Jesuit loyalist clerics and the younger Vietnamese priest and catechists who supported them. The letters were unyielding in their insistence that the community had no option but to accept the apostolic leadership of the bishops already in place in the Vicariates of Eastern and Western Tonkin. Galdino's letters were particularly critical of Bình for his role in the entire affair, accusing him of substantially misrepresenting their situation to the Portuguese ruler. Even toward Bình, however, Galdino extended something of an olive branch, for he wrote in one of his first letters, "I know that the pope has forgiven the priest Filippe and his companions with the condition that they return to Tonkin to remedy the evil they have done. Our bishops are also ready to forgive you if indeed you have sincerity of heart and subject yourselves to [their authority]."[49]

During his letter-writing campaign, Bishop Galdino received a note from the new apostolic vicar of Eastern Tonkin, Bishop Ignacio Delgado (1761–1838), with an update on the situation in his vicariate. Bishop Delgado had replaced Bishop Alonso upon the latter's death in late 1799 and had taken an aggressive approach to the schismatic community. Whereas Alonso had been quite accommodating toward Bình and the other Padroado loyalists, seeking to win them over through patience and suasion, his successor was considerably more forceful and uncompromising. In his letter to Galdino, Delgado offered a scathing assessment of his precursor's failures:

> My predecessor, the illustrious Snr. D. Fr. Feliciano Alonço . . . filling the duties of a vigilant pastor and loving father sought to dissuade them and remove them from their false ideas and the bad seed they planted in this field, punishing a few for disobedience [while] elevating others for seeming to him, in terms of the culture of

letters in our seminary, better able to serve this church with prospects for the future and to undeceive their brothers. Not only did Snr. Feliciano fail to be useful, despite his good intentions, but those whom he provided with greater benefits were the ones that caused him the most suffering, disrespecting, with regard to the new priesthood's character, all ecclesiastical laws, speaking falsehoods and calumnies against the apostolic vicars, refusing to obey them, and putting their question in the hands of His Highness the Prince Regent of Portugal, in whom they placed all their hopes, as if the Most Serene and Faithful Prince did not know how to distinguish between truth and falsehood.[50]

Bishop Delgado hoped that he would have a strong ally in Bishop Galdino to assist with his ongoing effort to stamp out the schism brought about by the adherents to the Portuguese Padroado mission.

No doubt buoyed by having a like-minded bishop in Tonkin, Bishop Galdino continued his campaign to bring the Padroado community into line. In early April of 1804, the bishop wrote a fourth letter in which he referred to his previous three letters, whose essential message he reiterated for any who might not have grasped it:

> First, the Company of Fathers known as the Jesuits was extinguished by the pope more than thirty years ago, and the Lord King of Portugal was the first who asked this of the pope, therefore, you were deceived by all those who told you that you had to have Jesuit fathers; second, it does not fall to you or me to ask the reasons as to why your bishops have forbidden the ancient books, because it is only the bishops themselves who regulate which books are most useful; third, as a result you should deliver everything that belonged to the churches to the bishops.[51]

Like his earlier letters, this one again denounced Bình and reiterated the bishop's insistence that they surrender to the apostolic vicars. Galdino also wrote that he had received word that the Portuguese ruler had expelled the remaining three Vietnamese clerics from his capital, suggesting both that their mission had ended in failure and that Bình was on his way back.[52] This information must have been a crushing blow, though it offered some small consolation that with his return Bình could minister to the community. The news, however, was false. No such thing had happened, and the men were still firmly rooted in Lisbon, where Bình was continuing his efforts. Whether Bishop Galdino had deliberately lied or had himself been misled cannot be ascertained, though we know that he had been (at least indirectly) involved in efforts to have the Vietnamese envoys removed from Portugal prior to his departure for Macao and had written a letter in which he expressed surprise that the men had not yet returned to Asia.[53]

Even as Galdino mounted an aggressive letter-writing campaign to sway the remaining Padroado holdouts, the community in Tonkin was dealing with pressures both real and imagined. Rumors began to circulate in Tonkin about steps being taken to end the Jesuit loyalists' defiance. Word of one reached Macao, and Thuyên and Trạch reported it in their final letter to Bỉnh in September 1803: "We have heard that there was a bull from the Holy See about our country in the year 1802, which had already been spread everywhere by March of 1803, and which said that if any person in our community did not accept the authority of the two bishops, they would not be regarded as a person of the faith, though it is not clear whether this is true or not, because I cannot believe that people of our house would go over."[54] Although the men made clear that they were uncertain about the accuracy of this report, one can imagine that rumors of such a decree would have had considerably more impact on the Jesuit loyalists than the letters of the Macanese bishop. In fact, there had been no such bull. Even so, life continued to be particularly difficult for Catholics attempting to cling to their faith. In the same letter, the men write that "as for religion and daily life in our country, these past few years have been very difficult. With regard to religion they [Tây Sơn officials] have taken all of the churches and all of the religious houses and have taken much of the money of the Christians, and from Xứ Nghệ southward they have forced many people to abandon the faith. They have killed two priests, one was our Cụ Triệu, and the second was Cụ Đạt of the bổn cuốc [MEP]. After that they also arrested two or three other men; we do not know when this will end, nor in what fashion, and as for our lives, there is chaos everywhere."[55]

The community in Tonkin was even feeling pressure from their former allies. Notably, Father Rodrigo, the man who had previously housed Thuyên and Trạch in Macao, joined the chorus of voices calling on the community to end its defiance of the apostolic vicars. On October 20, 1803, he wrote a message to the community in which he informed them that appointing a Portuguese bishop to Tonkin was impossible. Moreover, the letter claimed that the Portuguese ruler now understood Bỉnh and his delegation to have been deceptive in their representation of their situation when they said that they had neither a bishop nor any priests in Tonkin. He closed by exhorting them to accept the authority of the vicars. The content of the message, as well as its tone, which parallels Galdino's own missives to the Tonkin community, and the fact that he wrote it only six weeks after the new bishop's arrival, suggests that Father Rodrigo wrote it under pressure from the bishop, who may even have dictated its contents.[56]

Meanwhile, Galdino's tenure in Macao proved brief. He had barely had a chance to wade into local and regional church politics before his ambition drove him to higher positions. Less than a year after arriving in Macao, in August of 1804, Galdino was appointed to serve as the coadjutor archbishop of Goa, a considerably more prominent and influential posting than the relatively remote Macao bishopric. Before leaving for Goa, however, and aware that his impending departure might allow hope to flare up again among the Tonkinese Jesuit loyalists, Galdino sent a final letter to the community: "I will be leaving for a post as the archbishop of Goa, and another bishop, a fellow [Franciscan], will [replace me] in Macao.

Understand that this new bishop is informed of everything; that he will give you no assistance in your errors, and that in addition to this he will do what I tell him. I ask you again in the name of the Wounds of Our Lord Jesus Christ that you immediately obey the Spanish and French bishops and that you deliver to them everything that belonged to the Jesuits."[57] Shortly after Galdino's appointment to Goa, another Portuguese cleric, Father Francisco Chacim, was named to succeed him as bishop of Macao.[58] Galdino sailed off to Goa, where he would serve alongside the incumbent archbishop, Emmanuel Felix Soares (de Santa Catarina), until the archbishop's death in 1812, after which Galdino held the post in his own right.

CONCLUSION: THE END OF THE COMMUNITY

The array of pressures on the community continued to build. The combination of the rumors of a papal bull and of the deliberate destruction of churches, the letters from Galdino, and the complete absence of priests supporting the community all took their toll. The little news that did arrive from abroad was almost always dispiriting, offering little hope of success or any indication that such might be achieved in a reasonable time frame. Moreover, with the return of Brothers Trạch and Thuyên at some point in the summer of 1804 after their expulsion from Macao, the community's spirit must have plummeted. Without this toehold in Macao there was no way to represent their interests at the level of higher ecclesiastical authority in the Portuguese outpost and almost no way to receive news from Bỉnh in Portugal. Even with the men in place, getting news had been a slow, difficult, and uncertain process. Moreover, the community was at the mercy of such news that did trickle in and had to determine whether or not to believe what they heard. While they no doubt trusted the letters they knew to be from Bỉnh, these came sporadically and at lengthy intervals, and there was no way to know when or even if the next might arrive. There were probably occasional letters from those serving their interests in Macao, though we have no record of these. And there were the letters from Galdino, forceful injunctions to give up their resistance and accede to the authority of the apostolic vicars.

For his part, all that Bỉnh could do was to fulminate against these actions from afar, criticizing the pressures being brought upon the community by the Spanish and French apostolic vicars under the direction of Galdino. As he wrote in his *History of Annam*: "These actions were inhumane and they caused senseless things to happen, and they were not only immoral with respect to us, and all of the Christians of the Jesuit order in the country of Annam, but they were also disobedient toward his king because [the ruler] was still working on our behalf and he had not instructed him to do these things, but rather he had followed his own ideas and done the work of the Holy See in order to respond to the promises of the nuncio of Rome."[59]

What, then, became of Bình's community of Padroado Catholics in Tonkin? Although there is very little direct evidence of the community's fate, all indications are that by 1805 there was no longer a viable, if any, community of Christians in Tonkin who openly retained an allegiance to the Portuguese Jesuit tradition. By this point Bình had been gone for a decade, the last two remaining European priests supporting the community had died, the two Padroado representatives had been forced to return from Macao, and Bishop Galdino had sent letter after letter exhorting them to give up their intransigence. The combination of ecclesiastical and material pressures, the depressing reports from Macao, and the growing sense that Bình would not be returning made it virtually impossible for the Padroado community to continue its defiance of the apostolic vicars. They had tried, through their emissary Bình, to find a way to maintain their autonomy, and this effort had failed. They could not minister to themselves without an ordained priest to carry out the sacraments, and their refusal to accept the apostolic vicars had denied them access to the services of the priests who served under those vicars. They faced a stark choice: they could continue to resist the vicars but would effectively become lapsed believers, since Roman Catholicism required the ongoing performance of the sacraments if they were to remain Catholics in good standing. Or they could end their more than three decades of resistance and enter the fold of the apostolic vicars. For some this must have been particularly humiliating: a defeat of considerable magnitude after their long-term defiance in the face of long odds. For all it would mean at least minor alterations in the performance of their services, the pronunciations of certain words, and an acceptance of the strictures of their new clerical superiors.

Consequently, letters from the ecclesiastical leadership in Tonkin and Macao written between 1804 and 1806 all suggested that the schism was nearing its end and that the remaining holdouts were finally surrendering. Already in 1804 Bishop Delgado wrote from Tonkin to Nuncio Marchini in Macao that the schism had ended and that he hoped Bình could be kept at a safe distance in Europe. Galdino wrote to the nuncio in the following year, similarly asserting that the schism had been suppressed.[60] Then, in a May 1805 letter, Bishop Delgado observed: "In all of their tours of all of the parishes [*giáo phận*], the bishops have been received with hospitality by all of the seedlings [*giáo hạt*] who previously belonged to the Jesuit order; they have now recognized their previous errors and are ready to follow the words of truth."[61] Finally, a letter dated Janury 2, 1806, from the new bishop in Macao, Father Francisco Chacim, similarly reported that the schism had at last come to an end.[62]

7

Life in Lisbon and the Casa do Espirito Santo, 1807–33

As the Padroado community in Tonkin was at last surrendering to its longtime foes, Philiphê Bỉnh, likely unaware of their fate, was struggling with his own transformed circumstances. The prince regent's departure for the New World in November 1807 had left Bỉnh in a difficult position. The one man who could fulfill his request for a bishop was now five thousand miles away. No one, least of all Bỉnh, had any idea when, or indeed if, Dom João would be able to return. Bỉnh was faced with two choices. He could continue his efforts to join the ruler in Brazil, something made extremely difficult by the warfare that swirled around Lisbon for years after the prince regent's departure. Or he could simply await Dom João's return, hoping that the prince regent's exile would be short-lived. Bỉnh opted for the path of action, continuing to look for a way to join his royal patron in Rio de Janeiro. However, circumstances made this impossible for years after the ruler's departure, and Bỉnh was forced instead to wait.

The departure of the Anglo-Portuguese fleet transporting Dom João and his court to their Brazilian exile marked the beginning of a new phase in Bỉnh's life. It began with hardship but also presented Bỉnh with new opportunities. The hardship was caused by the French invasion and subsequent occupation of Lisbon. Looting by French troops and their forced quartering throughout the city greatly disrupted life for Lisbonites. Bỉnh and his remaining companions also experienced an interruption of their long-standing subsidy from the royal coffers. Not only was the monarch no longer present to ensure continuation of these payments, but the officials who had stayed behind to mitigate the impacts of the occupation had more pressing matters on their hands than maintaining Bỉnh's stipend. With his primary source of revenue gone, Bỉnh had little choice but to increase his work as a priest to bring in money to support himself and his remaining two companions. This is reflected in the number of masses that Bỉnh recorded in his notebooks, which more than doubled compared to the 1805–7 period. Consequently, Bỉnh found himself engaging with Lisbon's wider Catholic community much more directly, traveling between its many churches and immersing himself in its urban culture. At the same time, however, with more time on his hands Bỉnh also began to write extensively about and for the Vietnamese Catholics he had left behind. And it is no accident that the vast majority of Bỉnh's written output dates from after 1807.

This chapter will focus on the quotidian elements of Bỉnh's life beginning in the second half of 1807. In part it examines specific aspects of his experiences of the French occupation, but more generally it sketches the broad outlines of Bỉnh's material life in his new Oratorian residence, the Casa do Espirito Santo. Bỉnh's writings provide a substantial amount of detail on aspects of this material life, from foodways to medical care, which I will explore here. While Bỉnh wrote with often exacting detail about his pursuit of the mission to secure a bishop, providing concrete dates and details, his accounts of daily life in Lisbon were not, for the most part, temporally specific. Instead, they consisted of general observations of particular phenomena that he witnessed, or habits or patterns associated with life in Lisbon generally and the Oratorian house more specifically. It seems likely that his accounts of material life were broadly representative of his experience across the more than three decades during which he resided in Portugal. Again, this reflects the manner in which he documented his time in Lisbon.

But this was more than a period in which Bỉnh had time to look around and begin to describe life in Portugal; it was also the beginnings of a different type of personal geography. The landscape in which he operated had now changed, both metaphorically and literally. He found himself in a new relationship to his place of residence. What he had viewed as a temporary home, of however extended a duration, was now increasingly looking like a permanent residence. This changed Bỉnh's view of his surroundings, of the life that lay before him, and, I would argue, of himself. While he continued to refer to himself as an "envoy" of the Tonkinese Christians, it is very clear that his position was more that of an exile, and one with little likelihood of returning to his homeland.

Furthermore, Bỉnh faced new geographical circumstances more literally as a result of his and his companions' relocation to their new residence, the Casa do Espirito Santo. The location of this religious house in the heart of Lisbon transformed the ways in which the men interacted with their adoptive city. Their view of the city changed significantly, for they now found themselves in its cultural and religious center, surrounded by churches but also secular attractions like the bookstores and coffee shops lining the street that led to their new home. This new urban geography altered how the men experienced Lisbon and presented a new set of possibilities for their participation in its community. It seems clear that their relocation to the Casa and the prince's relocation to Brazil shortly thereafter together had dramatic impacts upon the Vietnamese delegation, shifting their mental and personal geographies in ways that would shape the trajectory of Bình's life to its very end.

THE CASA DO ESPIRITO SANTO

Having received permission from the ruler on June 19, 1807, to move from the Necessidades convent, Bình and his two surviving compatriots wasted no time in relocating the several short miles to the Casa do Espirito Santo. This new residence would remain their home throughout the remainder of their respective lives.[1] The move from the Necessidades house to the Casa do Espirito Santo was in some ways analogous to their earlier departure from Tonkin for Lisbon, as the men were moving from a peripheral location to the heart of Lisbon. For the three Vietnamese, this geographical transition changed their relationship to their adopted city in significant ways. Overlooking the heart of Pombal's newly rebuilt city, the Casa was an elegant four-story structure built into a hillside with entrances providing access to both the upper and lower parts of the city. It was ideally situated within easy walking distance of most of the major churches in the center of Lisbon. It directly overlooked the small church Nossa Senora da Victoria and was only one block north of the Nossa Senora da Conceição, for which the district's parish was named. Although the residence had been damaged by the 1755 earthquake, and its inhabitants forced to relocate to other sites around the city, steady progress in repairs had allowed a slow expansion in the number of priests it could accommodate. And while it had had no space for the Vietnamese on their arrival in 1796, a decade later this was no longer the case.

The Chiado district, in which the Casa occupied a prominent location, had emerged over the eighteenth century as an elegant part of Lisbon where the city's spiritual and secular worlds mingled.[2] The district contained several religious order houses and a number of prominent churches but was also home to numerous cafés and bookstores. The latter half of the eighteenth century had seen the emergence of a Lisbon café culture modeled to some degree on that in Paris and London. Numerous establishments serving both coffee and tea had appeared in the heart of the city, many of them found in the Chiado district.[3] Bình wrote of frequenting these coffee shops, where he learned Portuguese coffee- and tea-drinking rituals and enjoyed the pastries accompanying them.[4] From the Casa, Bình would also have had an easy stroll down the hill into the commercial heart of the city, which Pombal had rebuilt in highly regulated fashion in the aftermath of the 1755 earthquake. Its construction was subject to strict building codes that stipulated the number of stories, the kinds of windows that might be installed, and the width of

FIGURE 21. The building that once housed the Oratorian residence, the Casa do Espirito Santo—Bỉnh's home from 1807 until his death in 1833. In 1834 the building was taken over by the state and served various functions before being transformed into a commercial retail center in the late nineteenth century, a function it still serves today. Author's photo.

the new streets, which were partly designed to provide easy egress in the event of a future large-scale earthquake.

While Bỉnh occasionally visited the local coffee shops, far more important for him would have been the nearby houses of worship. From his new residence, Bỉnh could walk to some of the most important churches in Lisbon in less than fifteen minutes. Whereas there had been only one church within a kilometer of the Necessidades convent, there were ten churches within half a kilometer of the Casa do Espirito Santo at which Bỉnh could now perform masses. This eliminated the need to hire carriages to move around the city, which had in any case become impossible without the prince's financial support. Just up the street from the entrance to the Casa were three churches that could easily be reached by foot. The closest of these, and also the newest, was the Basilica of Our Lady of the Martyrs (Basilica Nossa Senhora dos Mártires), built in the 1770s and early 1780s to commemorate the English and other crusaders who had driven Muslims out of the city during the twelfth century. Located a bit further west on Rua do Chiado was Our Lady of the Incarnation (Nossa Senhora da Encarnação), another new construction,

FIGURE 22. Close-up view of an 1833 map of Lisbon, showing the location of the Casa do Espirito Santo and numerous nearby churches. Author's collection. 1) Casa do Espirito Santo, 2) National Library, 3) Bertrand Bookstore.

completed just as Bỉnh arrived in Lisbon. Facing it across the narrow street was yet a third church, Our Lady of Loreto (Nossa Senhora da Loreto), which served as the primary church of the Italian community in Lisbon.

Slightly further away and just up a hill north of the Rua do Chiado was the Igreja do São Roque. This late sixteenth-century structure would have had particular significance for Bỉnh, as it had been established by the Jesuit order and had remained Lisbon's primary Jesuit church until the order's dissolution in 1759. Bỉnh provides a detailed description of the church in one of his notebooks, commenting in particular on its impressive mid-eighteenth-century Chapel of St. John the Baptist, which had been constructed in Rome, blessed by the pope, and then dismantled for shipment and installation in Lisbon.[5] Further afield to the west but still an easy walk was the Paulist Church of Santa Caterina, which had been established in the mid-seventeenth century and then rebuilt after the earthquake. A longer walk, of perhaps fifteen minutes, would have taken Bỉnh to two other important churches, São Domingo and the city's cathedral. São Domingo lay to the northeast of the Casa, while a walk to the southeast and through the heart of the old city would have taken Bỉnh to the cathedral, the Sé, located near the waterfront in the Alfama district. This imposing edifice had been constructed in the middle of the twelfth century and, like most others, had been damaged by the Great Earthquake and then restored. Indeed, Bỉnh's new home was just a short walk to one of the most dramatic reminders of the earthquake's force. The ruins of the Igreja do Carmo lay just a few hundred yards north of the entrance to the Casa, and its surviving Gothic arches and walls served as testament to what had once been one of Lisbon's most visually striking religious structures.

THE FRENCH OCCUPATION

But before Bỉnh and his friends could take advantage of their new location, or get properly settled into their new home, their lives were upended by the arrival of Napoleon's army, just one day after the Portuguese royal family set sail on November 29, 1807. Before leaving, the prince regent had ordered his officials not to resist the French advance but to welcome the arriving forces. Resistance would have been futile in any event, and this strategy of capitulation was calculated to spare the city's residents the hardships of armed conflict. The initial French entry in late November was, consequently, relatively peaceful, and not entirely unwelcomed by Portuguese elites.[6] As W. F. P. Napier noted in his classic history of the Peninsular Wars, "Although great discontent and misery prevailed, the tranquility of Lisbon during the first month after the arrival of the French, was remarkable; no disturbance took place, and the populace were completely controlled by the activity of a police, first established under the Prince Regent's government by the Count de Novion."[7]

While the French entry had been achieved without fighting, and their takeover of the city had been relatively smooth, their military occupation soon became onerous, and the rapacity of their forces quickly turned popular opinion against them. As José Hermano Saraiva has noted, after the entry into Lisbon, "The French general installed himself there in his general quarters, imposed heavy war indemnities, seized all of the goods of those who had exited for Brazil, and did the same with all of the silver in the churches, to be brought back to France."[8] Before long this unhappiness was transformed into action, and there were outbreaks of armed resistance against the occupiers in the countryside.

Bỉnh was an eyewitness to these events and wrote about them in some detail in his summary of life in the post-1807 period. Two things in particular stand out from Bỉnh's description of this period: extensive looting and severe food shortages.

Almost immediately upon their arrival, French troops set about stealing or requisitioning as much wealth and food as they could. The targets of their avarice included the royal treasuries as well as local institutions whose wealth caught their eye, notably the many well-endowed religious houses scattered throughout the city.[9] The French commander issued an order in February of 1808 requiring religious institutions to surrender their valuables, and Bình described the staggering amount of wealth that was then brought forth. After collecting these items, the French set about systematically melting down the objects of silver and gold to mint coins to pay their troops.[10]

Numerous eyewitnesses attested to the avarice of the French army, whose reputation for looting and harsh impositions on subject populations had preceded it. A typical comment is that of an Englishman accompanying the British army in its subsequent counterinvasion of Portugal:

> That they have plundered in the most atrocious manner, it is impossible to doubt. The French came into the country unincumbered [sic] by baggage, as is their custom; indeed, they were even destitute of necessaries; and they are carrying off more of every description than should properly belong to an army of three times their number. Since the armistice, they have had the audacity to strip the museum and library of all that was valuable; to take from the Deposito Publico, where litigated property is lodged, 25,000 [reals]; and subsequently to the ratification, from the public magazines, for the equipment of their troops, and the discharge of debts, articles to the amount of 16,000 [reals].[11]

The French plundering of the royal treasury must have been particularly painful to Bình, for this was the source of his and his companions' stipends during their residence in Lisbon. The court's departure and subsequent French looting cut off this heretofore reliable source of funding. Under these circumstances, Bình was forced to throw himself upon the mercy of the leadership of the Casa do Espirito Santo. This must have been particularly awkward, as the Vietnamese had been living there for less than six months. They were not as well known and had not yet put down deep roots within this community as they had during their decade-long residence at the Necessidades palace. Bình was hopeful that the royal funding might eventually be resumed but was uncertain when, or if, this might take place. Thus, as he wrote, "We begged the people to look out for us until the Virtuous King returned to the country, or such a time as there was an opportunity for us to find a way to travel to the New World to be with him."[12] Bình promised that this money would somehow be repaid, either from the treasury, once the king returned, or by some other means. In any event, the congregation's leaders finally agreed to continue to house the men and to provide them with meals.[13]

The French occupation, however, meant that conditions were difficult for the men even with the continued support from the congregation. Food shortages, in particular, became acute. Upon their entry into the country, French soldiers had seized most of the provisions held in local storehouses. This reduced an already limited food supply, for Portugal had long been a net importer of staple foods. As Bỉnh writes, the country had certain crops, such as olives and grapes, in great abundance and routinely exported these to other parts of Europe, which yielded significant profits. On the other hand, staple foods like rice were grown only in limited quantities in Portugal's rocky soil, and Bỉnh noted that the country produced each year only enough for three or four months' consumption. The other eight to nine months' worth of rice had to be imported. But with the tight embargo on shipping brought about by the French invasion, commercial vessels were neither arriving nor departing Portugal, halting the exports necessary for cash and the imports needed for food.[14] Overland trade had also been severely curtailed by the French army and the hostile government in next-door Spain, both of which blocked key transportation routes. The shortages caused by the combination of French looting and these disruptions of commerce resulted in widespread hunger during 1807 and 1808.

In addition to seizing foodstuffs, the French also imposed themselves upon the local population in other ways. For instance, Bỉnh wrote that the Napoleonic troops were quartered in the religious houses throughout the city, "and we had to prepare lamps and beds and mats, as well as everything else they needed, and also had to bear all of the costs of this."[15] General Junot placed restrictions on local populations, including a nighttime curfew curtailing movement after dark. Consequently, Bỉnh noted that there were no celebrations on Christmas Day that year. It was a time of considerable gloom and uncertainty as people wondered how long they would have to endure these hardships and when their ruler might return. One glimmer of hope came in the form of news that the prince regent had safely arrived in Rio de Janeiro after a thirty-nine-day crossing of the north Atlantic. Bỉnh reported that the people in Brazil lit lanterns and celebrated for nine days, elated at seeing their king in person more than three centuries after the colony had been established.[16]

The French invasion and occupation brought back vivid memories for Bỉnh of events he had experienced a little more than twenty years earlier. In 1786 he had been traveling about Tonkin in the company of Father Castiglioni when the Tây Sơn armies had invaded and then occupied that region. Like the rest of Tonkin's inhabitants, Bỉnh had watched the arrival of the rebel armies with great uncertainty about their long-term intentions. Consequently, it is not surprising that his descriptions of the Napoleonic attacks on Portugal feature repeated comparisons to the Vietnamese case. He noted, for instance, that the French troops had banned the Portuguese from ringing their bells, a common element of religious services, for fear that this might be used as a signal to insurrection. This was, Bỉnh noted, like the Tây Sơn ruler's order to Tonkinese villages that they not sound their gongs, which, might similarly have been used to call for an uprising against the rebel armies.[17] He also wrote that the French practice of co-opting Spanish troops to fight in the Portuguese campaigns was "similar to [Emperor] Quang Trung ordering the troops of Quảng [Nam] to go into Đàng Ngoài—and then [ordering] the troops of Đàng Ngoài . . . to go into Quảng [Nam]"[18] (that is, taking troops from one region to fight against those of another). Clearly, what he was seeing in Lisbon looked all too familiar to Bỉnh, even if some of the particulars were different.

While he did not comment on it directly, it is also easy to imagine that Bỉnh would have seen parallels between the Franco-Spanish army's comprehensive looting in Lisbon and the pillaging carried out by the Tây Sơn forces in the Tonkin territories they had occupied. The French seizure of food supplies from government storehouses was certainly reminiscent of the Tây Sơn seizure of the large state-controlled granaries on the coast at Vị Hoàng when they first entered Tonkin in 1786.[19] In any case, as he reported the city's many hardships and the countless distressed people he saw in the streets, Bỉnh reflected that "it looked as it did in our country of Annam in the year *mậu tuất* [1778]," a reference to a severe drought that had struck Tonkin several years before the Tây Sơn invasion, during which rice prices had climbed to astronomical levels and later chronicles had spoken of people dying along public roads.[20]

Bỉnh's description of these events conveys a strong sense of déjà vu, the echoes of the not-too-remote Vietnamese past reverberating in his Portuguese present. That he saw the parallels and commented on them suggests that despite their many obvious differences Bỉnh regarded these widely separated countries as not all that dissimilar. He does not seem to have viewed "the West" as a place of superiority and advancement, for all its technological and institutional innovations, but rather as one that also suffered warfare, hunger, marauding armies, and the challenges presented by ambitious military-political figures. The most telling indication of the similarities Bỉnh observed was his comment in *Nhật Trình* regarding the rise to power of Napoleon. Writing of Napoleon's self-coronation as emperor, Bỉnh commented: "In 1804, on the second day of January, a person like Quang Trung by the name of Bonaparte, who had been born in Corfu in the country of Italy, elevated [himself] to become emperor of the countries of France and Italy."[21] The comparison of Napoleon with the slightly earlier Vietnamese general and then emperor Quang Trung suggests the degree to which Bỉnh saw parallels between the two cases he had now witnessed in the span of only twenty years. Once again he saw a powerful military figure leading large armies across vast territories, turning existing political structures upside down, and cementing his military successes by naming himself emperor. It is another reminder of the ways in which Bỉnh engaged in cross-cultural comparisons, looking for language and images to render his narrative comprehensible to an audience with a particular frame of reference.

THE EXPULSION OF THE FRENCH

The hardships of the French occupation and the emergence of organized resistance in rural areas caught the eye of the British, who not only had long-standing interests in Portugal but were particularly concerned with blunting the aggression of their continental nemesis, Napoleon. In early August of 1808, the British decided to intervene, sending Arthur Wellesley to head an expeditionary force to assist the Portuguese in driving out the French "to restore their 'lawful Prince' to the throne, and guaranteeing the independence of their kingdom and the preservation of their 'holy religion.'"[22] Cognizant of Portuguese reverence for their brand of Roman Catholicism, and also seeking to make a good impression on the bishop of Porto (D. Francisco de Noronha), who headed the Portuguese interim governing body, Wellesley issued explicit orders to his troops to respect religious institutions and images.[23] His force landed along the central coast and established its first encampment near the old university town of Coimbra.[24] The British engaged the French military almost immediately, dealing General Junot's army a resounding defeat and prompting the general to agree to talks. The two sides quickly reached an agreement—the Convention of Sintra—signed on August 30, 1808, which called for the repatriation of French forces on British naval vessels and allowed Napoleon's forces to retain the profits of their extensive pillaging.[25]

Binh reported the arrival of the British after their defeat of the French with considerable enthusiasm. He wrote of seeing the French flag being lowered and then being replaced by the Portuguese banner. He noted that the British fired their cannons in celebration and set off fireworks. The local religious houses lit candles and rang their bells. It was, he wrote, "as though we had died and then been brought back to life."[26] Yet even after the expulsion of the French by Wellington, the situation in Lisbon was grim and life remained on a wartime footing. As an English soldier wrote from his station in Lisbon in September of 1808: "Society in Lisbon, or amusements, there are none. The opera is closed for want of funds, and in private families, that is the few that are in Lisbon, people meet of an evening, sometimes with great formality, but the change, and distrust of difference of opinion, while the French were here, and petty intrigues, evidently cast a gloom over every Portuguese."[27] He also reported an atmosphere of lingering suspicion of potential traitors and anger with those who had served the French, which poisoned relations among many urbanites.

The French retreat proved temporary. Only a few months after the evacuation of their troops, and indeed before the year was out, Napoleon's armies mounted a second assault on Portuguese soil. This time the invaders were better prepared. The Portuguese army, now commanded by Arthur Wellesley, Lord Wellington, and amply supported by British troops, needed two years to expel them, which it did in the fall of 1810 at the battle of Bussaco, north of Coimbra. A third French attack by General Massena soon followed and was directed southward toward Lisbon. The British and Portuguese armies built an extensive rampart known as the Lines of Torres Vedras sixty kilometers north of the Portuguese capital and succeeded in stalling the French drive. Facing severe supply shortages, by April 1811 the Napoleonic army was forced to retreat, shifting the battle to Spanish soil, where it would continue, involving many Portuguese taken captive by the French, for the next four years.[28]

By the spring of 1811, Portugal had seen the last of the French military force. The aftermath of the final French defeat seems to have improved the situation in Lisbon considerably. By 1812 reports from foreign soldiers posted there spoke of a population that had been restored to the rhythms of antebellum life and the resumption of public activities and artistic performances.[29] Yet despite the French departure the situation in Portugal remained uncertain, and as long as it did the Portuguese court opted to remain in Brazil. For his part, the British commander Lord Wellington was unwilling to leave the country at the mercy of any further French or Spanish military designs, so the British army and its commanders remained in place, ostensibly protecting Portugal in the absence of its ruler but for all practical purposes running the country as a kind of extension of the British empire.[30]

BECOMING A DIASPORIC PERSON

While some degree of normalcy had been restored for the average Lisbonite after the French departure, for Philiphê Bỉnh there could be no return to normal. For him, life in Portugal had changed drastically with the prince regent's departure. Most obviously his benefactor's absence forced Bỉnh to suspend indefinitely his project to secure a new bishop. The ruler's departure also came not long after a second important change in Bỉnh's situation, namely an end to his correspondence with those he had left behind in Macao and Tonkin. While the departure of his patron and the arrival of the French armies obviously had profound material and political implications for Bỉnh's situation in Portugal, the conjuncture of these two events also had, I believe, a significant psychological impact on Bỉnh, substantially altering his relationship to his residence in Portugal. During the first decade of his residence in Portugal, Bỉnh's active engagement with his mission and his certainty that its successful conclusion would mark the end of his task meant that he continued to regard his sojourn in Europe as temporary. This was not a form of exile, merely a condition of his particular employment. Although the duration of his mission had clearly extended well beyond what he had initially anticipated, requiring some logistical adjustments, Bỉnh's frame of mind was still very much shaped by a certainty that he would be returning home. This likelihood was further underscored by the letters he was receiving, which were fiercely tugging at him to return to Tonkin. The combination of these factors substantially shaped the way in which Bỉnh regarded his position in Lisbon. He remained very much "an envoy"—an employment that has inherent in it the notion of temporariness. Such a person is sent to perform a task of varying duration and upon completion of that task returns to his homeland.

The end of Bỉnh's correspondence with his coreligionists in Asia severed one important thread that constantly tugged at him, while the king's departure for Brazil abruptly suspended any practical likelihood that he could sustain his efforts to complete the mission. Indeed, the prince regent's departure had the effect of now pulling Bỉnh in a new direction. Although his effort to join Dom João's armada as it sailed for South America had failed, Bỉnh continued to harbor a strong desire to travel to Brazil to resume his supplications, as he had intimated to the head of his new Oratorian residence. Bỉnh now found himself being pulled to the west and across the Atlantic, rather than back to the east from where he had come. As long as such a trip to the west remained impossible, Bỉnh was forced to reorient himself to life in Portugal.

I would argue that Bỉnh's condition took on a new aspect: he was now a diasporic individual. By this I mean that Bỉnh's relationship to Portugal had shifted in ways that altered how he understood his status there. The rhythms of his life changed as he could no longer make the rounds of the Portuguese bureaucracy, much less invest time in trying to gain royal audiences. His daily interactions and vocation were conducted in Portuguese and among the populations of Lisbon. He ate meals, shared religious ceremonies, and conversed with his fellow Portuguese clerics in the Oratorian residence. He left the residence in clerical garb and sporting a priest's tonsure to say masses at churches around the city of Lisbon. In this respect he had a publicly Portuguese persona, one developed through a decade of constant engagement with Portuguese society from the court to the streets of Lisbon. Although he had participated in each of these activities to some extent before the prince's departure, they now became much more prominent parts of his daily life. In short, he was becoming somewhat more "Portuguese" and a bit less "Vietnamese."

His writings in this period served to reinforce the ways in which he rethought his identity, his role, and his relationship to the geographies that bound him. This is particularly evident in the introductions that he wrote for each of his many notebooks. In virtually every one, he situated himself both geographically and temporally in ways that illustrated how he straddled the lines between past and present, his homeland and his place of exile. A sample taken from his *Tales of St. Francis Xavier* suggests these dynamics: "Tôi là Thầy cả Philiphê Bỉnh đi Sứ bổn đạo Dòng Đ.C.J. nước Anam năm 1794, làm sách này ở Kẻ chợ nước Portugal năm 1818" (I am Father Philiphê Bỉnh, who traveled as the envoy of the Christians of the Jesuit order of the country of Annam in the year 1794, and have made/written this book in the capital of the country of Portugal in the year 1818). This brief introductory note nicely summarizes Bỉnh's personal geographies and his understanding of how his life and mission had stitched these geographies together: he was a priest who had traveled as the emissary of a particular community of Christians, those of the Jesuit order; he had traveled from Annam at a specific moment in time, 1794; and he had now written (or perhaps, more accurately, "made") this book in the Portuguese capital in 1818. By identifying himself in this fashion Bỉnh reinforced the linkages between his Vietnamese homeland and his current residence and reminded himself, and the reader, that he was both a priest and an envoy. Moreover, he was not merely a Catholic but of a particular Catholic heritage—the Jesuit order. This preface, like the rest, offers some notable juxtapositions reflecting Bỉnh's awareness of the changes he had encountered. Geographically it contrasts his point of departure, Anam, with his current place of residence, the capitol of Portugal. Temporally it contrasts his date of departure, 1794 (his first trip to Macao), with the time in which he wrote this book. Each of these pairings would serve to remind Bỉnh of where he had started and where he now found himself, linking his present with his past.

Like many exiles, Bỉnh retained important psychological links with his home in Tonkin. Indeed, he maintained a very distinct Vietnamese persona, as well as a strong consciousness of the community and society back in Tonkin. His writings make it very clear that he continued to occupy a mental world in which he was at home among the Vietnamese Catholics whom he had left behind. By continuing to think and express himself in his mother tongue, Bỉnh preserved an important link to his homeland. Moreover, Bỉnh's connection to his homeland and his compatriots endured as the years progressed, and there are scattered comments in his later writings about the manner in which these psychological links were maintained. As he wrote in 1822 at the end of the narrative portion of his *Sách sổ*: "This year, in which I am composing the present book, I am already sixty-three years old, and I do not know how much longer I will live, but I ask that my brothers remember my soul, for as long as I remain alive I cannot forget them. Amen."[31]

This conclusion to Bỉnh's *Sách sổ*, like the beginning where he wrote, "Tôi là thầy cả Philiphê Bỉnh" (I am the priest Philiphê Bỉnh), is emblematic of another element of Bỉnh's personal transformation, namely his now constant use of the Vietnamese first-person singular *tôi* as a term of self-reference. Its use here is significant, for Vietnamese rarely used the autonomous "I" form in speaking of themselves before the twentieth century. Self-reference had, historically, been situtational and relational. What one called oneself depended upon whom one was addressing and the relationship between the two people. The term used to refer to oneself marked hierarchy, respect, and a sense that the speaker understood the relationship with his or her counterpart. The use of a neutral term, such as *tôi*, was virtually inconceivable, yet Bỉnh uses it here, and in most of his prefaces, anticipating by more than a century its first common though hardly ubiquitous use. Indeed, many Vietnamese continue to use a range of situationally specific forms in everyday conversation.[32]

The fact that Bỉnh used the first-person term *tôi* in this way is striking and speaks to his shifting sense of identity. While one can only speculate as to his adoption of this term, there are a number of likely reasons for his choice. The first, of course, is that in writing the prefaces to these works, Bỉnh was addressing a mixed and largely unknown audience. When he wrote his books he could not be certain that anyone he had known personally would read them. Thus the use of a situationally bound form of the first person would be nearly impossible. Perhaps just as important, it seems likely that after more than a decade in Portugal Bỉnh would have begun to recognize that in his new home the autonomous "I" (in Portuguese *eu*) was the standard form of self-reference in a place where modern conceptions of the individual had already emerged.[33] In conversation it would have been the common form, and one that Bỉnh would have used routinely in his encounters with fellow priests and Lisbonites as he traveled the city. Perhaps, then, his use of the term was un-self-reflective, his way of rendering his spoken Portuguese into his Vietnamese writings. Yet because *tôi*, as the autonomous "I," was a significant departure in the Vietnamese language both from earlier self-referential forms and from the term's previous incarnation as "servant" or "subject" of the ruler, it seems more likely that Bỉnh was aware of the distinctive nature of his usage and that it was deliberate. In any event, whether conscious or subconscious, the term was a marker of a personal autonomy, a reflection of a man who had struck out in new directions and undertaken tasks never before attempted by a Vietnamese. At the same time, it is worth considering that his use of *tôi* was also an indication of personal anomie—a sense of aloneness and disconnectedness from his surroundings that he could not dispel despite the company of his fellow Vietnamese and the many Oratorian brothers with whom he lived.

BỈNH AS AN ORATORIAN PRIEST

The most visible manifestation of Bỉnh's self-transformation would have been his now regular service as a Catholic priest. Although his ordination had been formally recognized by the patriarch of Lisbon in 1796, and Bỉnh had periodically been hired to say masses during the first decade of his residence, such work had been irregular at best. Bỉnh had been preoccupied with his primary mission to petition the ruler and relevant officials to secure the bishop for Tonkin, leaving little time for other activities, Furthermore, the remote Necessidades location without any nearby churches or chapels at which Bỉnh could perform services was also a significant factor. In any case, facing grave financial uncertainty, it now became necessary for Bỉnh to begin a more regular routine as a local clergyman operating alongside the many others of his Oratorian house. In short, the combination of the suspension of his primary mission, the location of the new residence, and his need for income all pushed Bỉnh to work more frequently as a priest. As a result, in the years between 1807 and 1811 the number of masses Bỉnh was saying annually doubled, and then between 1814 and 1817 increased by another 50 percent. In looking at his meticulous register of the public masses he was saying, one sees a dramatic increase with the prince regent's departure, and while the numbers fluctuated over the next decades, they continued to be far higher than prior to 1807. In fact, Bỉnh conducted an average of 135 masses per year over the two decades after the prince regent's flight.[34]

Unlike parish priests assigned to particular churches, Bỉnh and the other Oratorian clergymen were essentially itinerant priests for hire who would say masses, hear confessions, perform baptisms, and conduct the other sacraments at churches throughout the city. Given the overwhelmingly Catholic population in Portugal, as well as the centrality of the church calendar in the lives of the people, there was enormous demand for priests' services in all of these capacities. Bỉnh wrote that there were a great many priests in the city and that parishioners might sometimes approach them personally to request the saying of a mass. It was a common practice for people to contact priests to say masses on behalf of themselves, friends, or relatives, and often these priests would be summoned to perform masses at the supplicant's home, as many local residences had private altars and all of the necessary ritual material for conducting masses. The other way to engage a priest was to visit a local church, where priests had placed their names on a roster of available clergy and people could select them from this list. In addition to being hired for such private masses, priests were needed to conduct virtually hourly masses throughout the day at many houses of worship. Bỉnh noted that there were more than eighty feast days every year, and each such occasion also required that masses be said at every church in Lisbon. On these holy days, each religious house would assign five priests to conduct hourly masses at their chapel for members of the general public, while others were available to conduct services in private homes. Also, as some churches did not have enough priests to hold their hourly masses on feast days, they would employ priests to fill in their gaps, with the cost being borne by the parishioners.[35]

Bỉnh provides a fairly detailed picture of the general procedures involved in conducting masses in Lisbon. He compared this to his own experiences as a clergyman in Tonkin, noting how much easier things were for priests in Europe:

> Now I will talk again about the local priests in the West, who do not have it as difficult as the local priests in Annam, because the priests in Annam have a very wide territory, and they are by themselves, while the local priests in the West have very narrow [territories], and they have people to help them. Here these are called curate priests. For example, in the village of Santarem in the country of Portugal, there are thirteen local priests, and fourteen order houses, and in the capital there are forty local priests and many order houses, and as for the local priests in the village of Santarem, each is assigned to one hamlet, and as for the local priests in the capital each has

one district [phô], and not only can all of the order houses of this saint or that saint hear confessions that provide assistance for their flock, as well as some priests from the outside that have humaneness and virtue, but in each locality there are between five and eight of these curate priests, and every locality has at least one curate priest, and they take turns performing the mass between them.[36]

Binh reported that people called for priests to perform a variety of religious functions. Priests noted for their singing (i.e., in the sung parts of the mass) or preaching were in particularly high demand and would command commensurately higher donations. Binh noted that people would go to different religious houses to engage the most noted preachers to perform these various duties. Sometimes religious houses themselves would have to employ priests to supplement their own ranks or if regulations prevented their performing certain kinds of services, particularly on feast days. And Binh wrote that there was great demand for priests to ring the bells and perform the different services, in some places four or five times per day. Priests were also hired to perform services in smaller villages that lacked their own priests, or at least enough of them, while female orders and religious houses would also have had a constant need for priests to perform the masses and other sacraments for their residents.[37]

For priests, including Bình, saying masses at various churches was their primary source of income. While priests could not formally require payment for saying masses in parish churches or for private services, they were always remunerated for their services via donations. These contributions would generally follow local custom and to a degree reflected the overall cost of living, with priests in more expensive locales receiving correspondingly higher contributions. Bình noted that because living expenses were very high in Lisbon, Christians there tended to donate fairly generously for masses, the customary donation being two *tiền* for each mass, though even as the cost of living rose people rarely adjusted their contributions to account for this.[38] In any case, the contributions given for the saying of a mass were not fixed, so some people gave even more, sometimes up to four or, on rare occasions, even five *tiền* for a mass. He noted that during the reign of King Manoel (r. 1495–1521) the ruler stipulated a fixed amount that he would contribute for the masses that he regularly requested. The priests who said these masses could choose to be compensated either in money or in kind in the form of rice or noodles. Those who preferred cash received twenty *đồng*, while those who chose to be paid in kind were given one *thăng* (roughly two dry liters) of rice or noodles. The value of the two forms of compensation was equivalent at the time the regulation was issued, though the worth of the food would fluctuate, so there were times when one or the other would be preferred.

Although saying regular daily masses was the primary source of income for priests, they could also supplement these earnings by officiating at other types of religious services. These included, most notably, baptisms and funerals, for which families would make contributions to the officiating priest according to their own wealth. Also, at Easter all Christians made donations to the priests to ensure that their names would be recorded in the annual registers of confessions.[39] The Lenten season and its emphasis on penitence meant that there was typically a dramatic increase in the number of people going to confession. Although Catholics could go to any priest to hear their confession, they would then have to bring proof of this to their own parish priests. The Oratorians developed a form for this purpose that they printed by the thousands and distributed among all of the congregation's priests. Thus during the Lenten season priests were constantly filling out these forms, as people would go to the order churches or other places to say their confessions, and the priest would then have to complete the form with his own name and the name of the person who had had his or her sins absolved, a time-consuming and onerous task.[40]

LIFE AT THE ORDER HOUSE

When he wasn't out serving as an itinerant priest, Bỉnh, like his companions, spent much of his time at the Oratorian house to which the men had moved in 1807. It was home to a large community of priests, all members of a common congregation. They ate, slept, and worshipped in common but during the day carried out religious duties not only at the Casa but throughout the city where their services were required. Indeed, Bỉnh's experience of living with the Oratorians revealed the distinctive nature of the religious houses in Lisbon of this time. In the first place, most of these residences were remarkably porous vis-à-vis the community in which they were located. They typically did not sequester their residents, who moved freely through the city and country and interacted with the laity. Those who lived in religious houses, such as the Oratorian residence, were often quite autonomous from its workings. There were common meals when residents chose to partake of them. There were collective religious gatherings as well. Some would have worked together to provide instruction in the congregation's school.[41] The men also shared facilities such as the congregation libraries that Bỉnh frequently visited. But aside from this, the men who lived in these residences came and went freely. Moreover, the priests in the congregations such as the Oratorians did not share their possessions or hold items in common. Rather, each had his or her own source of income and private possessions. Consequently, Bỉnh wrote, upon their deaths the residents' goods could be willed to relatives or others and would not simply be claimed by the religious house in which they lived.[42]

Unfortunately, Bỉnh provided little description of his residence or his interactions with the other priests. However, thanks to his careful record keeping in his *Sách sổ*, we have some glimpses of his material life as reflected in the lists of items that he purchased for his own use over the years. Not surprisingly, the material elements that Bỉnh records were chiefly items of religious paraphernalia, some more durable and others more ephemeral. His records of expenditures included items such as candles, sticks for casting holy water, rosary beads, and sacred wax. In addition, he seems frequently to have purchased printed images of saints, and in large quantities (two entries alone record five hundred and six hundred purchased at one time). These were likely distributed in the course of religious duties.

Drawing from these and other reported purchases, one can picture Bỉnh and his companions living in their apartments at the Casa do Espirito Santo in rooms heavily decked out in religious items.[43] There would have been an altar (perhaps a small iron table) draped in an altar cloth and topped by a standing cross with three small saint statues at its base. The altar likely also featured bronze or silver candlesticks flanking the crucifix. In addition to these central devotional items, there would have been a few related accessories: scissors to trim the candles and a small basket for the discarded wax and trimmed wicks. Against one wall would have been a bed with mosquito netting for the hot summer months during which open windows provided some relief but also exposed the room's inhabitants to insects. There would have been a reading table on which the men could have stored the saint images they needed for their services. The pair of eyeglasses might also have sat on this table. There would have been numerous earthenware containers with the rice, tobacco, and tea that they used for private consumption.[44] They also had their own utensils for eating and drinking, and Bỉnh lists among these knives, skewers, spoons, cups, and bottles.[45] This suggests, as do later expenditures, that the men occasionally consumed food and drink in their own quarters. Bỉnh lists periodic purchases of tea and rice, so they must have had access to a kitchen, or perhaps a fireplace in their apartments where they could prepare hot water for tea or to boil rice. While the men routinely ate their meals in the common dining room of the congregation house, they would occasionally have visitors or temporary guests and would have to feed them separately.[46] Consequently, they would have additional food purchases, including rice and chicken. The men also purchased tea and tobacco for their own consumption.

In addition to the many items they purchased, Bỉnh and his companions also paid for the services of local craftspeople. Bỉnh has records of hiring an artist and a carpenter to craft the three statues of saints placed at the foot of the cross on their private altar. His account of expenses details the regular purchase of numerous religious goods, from crosses, to images of saints, to candlesticks. These were apparently commissioned from local craftspeople, as his records speak of payments to a "craftsperson" or to a "printer." The Vietnamese also had to hire seamstresses to sew them Western-style outfits and, periodically, to repair their clothing or the hats that they wore when walking about the city. Bỉnh would have to pay for the raw materials for producing these items as well, everything from wood to metal, from wax to cloth, depending on what the craftspeople needed. At other times, however, the men may have carried out certain domestic tasks themselves, for Binh's list of expenditures also records the purchase of sewing materials including silk thread and scissors, as well as cleaning supplies, though whether the men cleaned their own quarters or hired others to do so using these supplies is unclear.

FOOD AND DINING EXPERIENCES

Although it is difficult to get a precise sense of Binh's life in his quarters, his notebooks provide a detailed account of at least one aspect of life at the Casa do Espirito Santo, namely the preparation and consumption of daily meals. As communal meals were a central feature of life in the religious house, it is perhaps not surprising that this would be the case. These meals gave Binh the opportunity to taste a wide range of foods and witness many different food preparation styles, which he reported on in great detail. Binh was extremely interested in comparing the Portuguese diet and food habits more generally to those he had grown up with in Tonkin. Thus in his *Notebook That Transmits and Records All Matters* Binh recorded extensive details about the types of foods that were served, how they were prepared, and how they contrasted with Vietnamese foodways. Binh's decision to write in such detail about food reflects his awareness of how people's relationships to food were shaped by their experiences and local customs: "This is a matter that I know very clearly because [when I first arrived] I did not wish to eat or drink things in the manner of the West no matter how they were made, and as for the people of the West they also do not wish to eat things prepared in the manner of Annam regardless of how they are cooked. [This is] because people in this country or that country are acquainted with the customs and manners of eating and drinking in their own country from the time that they are young."[47] Binh was able to overcome his initial resistance to local cuisine, and his subsequent descriptions show the experience of many years of dining in the Oratorian houses where he made his home.

Binh provided detailed descriptions of his daily meals, beginning with the simple morning meal, which usually consisted of tea and buttered bread or toast.[48] Lunch and dinner were more extensive repasts, with an assortment of food set out in the dining hall, where those who sat around the tables would serve themselves. Lunch typically featured meat of some kind, often beef, as well as some variety of soup accompanied by crackers. There would also be a dipping sauce for the bread, a mixture of mustard seeds and vinegar. In addition to the food that was presented communally, each diner was given one piece of bread, a bottle of water, a smaller bottle of wine, and a plate of seasonal fruit. Those who preferred not to eat the meat served as the main course received instead three chicken eggs.[49] Binh reported that these were sold by the dozen, and not in units of ten as in Vietnam. He also listed the price for a dozen, noted the variations on that price, and even provided instructions for making egg breads.[50]

Fruits were an important part of the diet, and Portugal's southerly climate meant that these were often available. Among the most common local fruits were oranges and grapes, both of which were readily grown in and around Lisbon. Bỉnh noted that people typically ate two or three oranges at any given meal and that grapes were also frequently served. Grapes were often cultivated on the grounds of the monasteries around the city and were either consumed by the monks or sold in the streets of the city, with the income being earmarked for the saying of masses. As an early nineteenth-century visitor reported of this practice: "They are cried about the streets as *uvas pelas almas* [grapes for the souls]; and when the price is asked, the answer is generally considerable."[51] Grapes were also frequently used to produce local wines, which, Bỉnh reports, residents of the Oratorian houses drank as freely as water.[52] Although the assortment and availability of fruits would have paled in comparison to what he remembered in Tonkin, for Bỉnh these represented an important element of his meals.

Dinner was the largest meal of the day, usually featuring some form of beef as the main dish, though occasionally this was replaced by roast pork. Bỉnh wrote that leg of beef was a nearly daily offering and that beef tongue was also fairly common. Other meat entrees included boar's head, tripe, leg of pork, pork thigh, and pork sausage. The Portuguese consumed significant amounts of red meat, particularly in contrast to the Tonkin Bỉnh had left behind, where it was likely a rarity reserved for only the wealthiest Vietnamese. He reported that there were forty butcher's shops in Lisbon and that every day as many as three hundred cows and 150 calves were slaughtered in the fields outside the city. His discussion of meat dishes led him to compare Portuguese and Vietnamese attitudes toward the consumption of different kinds of animals. Each society regarded animals as either edible or inedible, depending on either religious or cultural convictions. Thus Bỉnh reported that people in the West refrained from eating a variety of animals—among them horse, donkey, dog, cat, and rat—all of which they regarded as disgusting.[53] Other animals were not eaten because of religious taboos, among them snakes because of their connection with the serpent who tempted Eve in the Genesis story in the Old Testament.

Although meat was a regular part of their diet, the priests, as Catholics, avoided meat on Fridays and during the Lenten season leading to Easter. To accommodate these restrictions, the Oratorian kitchens shifted their offerings on Fridays and during Lent toward seafood of all sorts. Bỉnh reported that this meant lunches that would consist first of a plate of bread cooked in fish or shrimp broth, occasionally a variety of bean, chopped greens with peas, or even dried hazelnuts. The second plate would then feature a portion of fresh or dried fish or eel, or sometimes squid. These would be served with condiment trays consisting of vinegar and oil and salt and pepper. The fish would sometimes be boiled or grilled, but Bỉnh was particularly interested in the local process of frying the fish, noting that "the methods of frying and those for grilling among the people of this country are better than ours." He reported on the procedure by which the fish were first dried, then dredged in flour, and finally fried in olive oil. The fish served at these meals would typically be accompanied by other dishes alternating between rice, noodles, and seasonal vegetables.

Binh's record of food at the Casa suggests that it was a topic of particular fascination for him, but he did not write of it merely because of his own interest or because of the potential curiosity of his Vietnamese-reading audience. Rather, he was mindful that these details might be useful information for any who might follow him on trips to Europe. He understood the considerable difficulties that travelers to distant lands often found in adapting to local foods and customs. He observed that this period of adjustment had constituted a real hardship for the early Jesuits who had come to Annam. Some had fallen ill and had had to be recalled to Macao to recover.[54] Thus Binh's detailed account of Portuguese foods might help ease the cultural transition for any future Vietnamese visitors. As such, Binh could be said to be anticipating some of the future geographies of Vietnamese Catholicism, ones in which additional Vietnamese would be making the long journey to Europe either for the sake of the community or for their own spiritual needs.

At another practical level, Binh used these notebooks to record recipes for preparing some of the foods that he was learning to consume. He devoted several pages to discussing the preparation of different dishes, commenting on how easy and tasty they were and how readily they would feed large groups of people. He focused on dishes involving rice garnished with chicken or pork meat. He also discussed methods for preparing both dried and fresh pork dishes, noting that "the method for making dried pork is not difficult at all, as I will set forth here," at which point he went into a detailed description of the steps involved in preparing dried pork. It seems clear from his careful descriptions that Binh must have watched this process numerous times, and one can imagine him wandering into the kitchens at the congregation residences, observing the cooks in action. Certainly, the details he provides on adding spices and placing the meat into pots of boiling water just so are ones only a careful observer could have known.[55]

Binh was also quite interested in how the Portuguese made bread, which he noted was the staple food in Europe, unlike in his native Tonkin, where rice played this role. He mentioned that when he was in Tonkin he had tried to make breads using wheat and corn flour by watching the European missionaries make them, but without success. Then he wrote: "But now I know how, because I have watched the priests and it is not very difficult, and so I am recording it here, as in the manner of the world in which all matters are contained in books, so that when anyone wishes to carry out any kind of task, he can open a book and see how it is done."[56] He then provided a detailed recipe and explanation for how to bake bread. This recipe was followed by further and lengthy discussion of bread, its various forms, and the difference in bread consumption between Asia and Europe. He noted that the wheat needed to make good bread flour grew much more readily in Europe than in Asia, so that finding the ingredients to make proper bread was extremely easy. This was particularly relevant for those making the communion wafers required for Catholic mass, and he described the difficulty that Christian communities in Tonkin faced when they tried to manufacture their own wafers.

Although much of what he saw in Portuguese foodways was alien to Bỉnh, one habit was already very familiar to him, namely tea drinking. In Tonkin, as in Portugal, tea was commonly imported from China and was consumed as a regular part of meals or other social interactions. The one major cultural difference between Vietnamese and Portuguese tea consumption was how the tea was prepared:

> The tea that the merchants brought back to the West was truly good tea, but they put sugar into both the good and the bad [teas], and then it would always smell and taste very sweet.... For this reason [the first few times] when I went to out to visit people and they invited me to drink the tea I did not say anything but remained silent and drank the tea in the same way that they did. [Eventually] there came a time when I had to say something, and I asked them not to put sugar into my tea, which they regarded as very odd. Then I told them that in my country of Annam, and in the country of China, when one drinks tea one does not put sugar into it so that one might know the scent of the tea. But in the West when merchants come back from the East, and people buy the tea... they [first] look at it and smell it, but immediately thereafter they put sugar into it to make it sweet.... From that time forward, when I would go to visit people, they would know not to put sugar into my teacup, because they now understood my preference.[57]

In this regard, Bỉnh was able to compare directly two very different tea-drinking practices. He laid out detailed descriptions of the European methods for preparing and serving tea, not merely as a point of information for his imagined audience, but also as a primer in what to expect were anyone to follow him from Tonkin.

CIVIC INSTITUTIONS IN LISBON

In addition to his commentary on life as a priest and life in the Oratorian house, Bỉnh wrote at length about other elements of Portuguese urban life that intrigued him. The Tonkin that Bỉnh had left behind had little in the way of an urban tradition or the types of infrastructure often associated with it. The country had several small seaports, a growing market town at Sài Gòn, and a somewhat more elaborated imperial capital at Thăng Long (Hà Nội). Even Thăng Long, however, was primarily a royal center to which had been attached an artisanal community and market area to support the court and its populations.[58] In writing about civic institutions and customs in Lisbon, Bỉnh became the first Vietnamese to offer a detailed description of the many day-to-day practicalities of life in a European city.

Unlike other European travelers, who typically offered only sketchy descriptions of urban institutions, usually comparing them unfavorably with the counterparts found in their own countries, Bỉnh offered detailed and very matter-of-fact explanations of urban structures and their function. In doing so he brought an almost ethnographic eye to his project, providing detailed descriptions in dispassionate language. As one of his earlier biographers, Thang Lãng noted, Bỉnh was a scholar across a range of disciplines: historian, linguist, theologian, literary scholar, and, to this we might also add, ethnographer.[59] His detailed writings on early nineteenth-century Portuguese urban life provide valuable comparative perspectives on its various social and cultural elements, with particular attention to a number of major institutions, ranging from libraries and the postal system to the daily lottery games and public safety apparatus.

Libraries and Bookstores

Among the most important civic institutions for Bỉnh's life after 1807 was Lisbon's network of libraries and bookstores, which made possible his later writing project. Bỉnh was the first Vietnamese with access to the European print world in the form of large, readily available libraries and to a lesser extent the bookstores that had begun to crop up in the eighteenth century. Like so many things in Europe, publicly accessible libraries would have been a complete revelation to Bỉnh. The Tonkin Bỉnh had left behind featured an extremely narrow tradition of book collecting, and access to written materials was severely circumscribed. The only institutional book collections were those held by the Vietnamese court and by a handful of Buddhist monasteries.[60] Both would have offered highly circumscribed access, with the court collection limited to members of the royal family, officials serving the court, and sometimes scholars invited to carry out research projects such as writing histories, geographies, or other kinds of texts for state use. Moreover, the Vietnamese publishing industry was virtually nonexistent, with tight state controls on wood-block printing, meaning that aside from some Buddhist printing there was little printed material available in any case. In short, access to written, much less printed, materials in Tonkin remained restricted by law or custom, meaning that people like Bỉnh would rarely have had access to books, either printed or handwritten. The only time he might have had such access would have been in the course of his seminary studies.

In Lisbon, by contrast, Bỉnh found a world awash in books in a Europe where printing had been accelerating over the centuries since Gutenberg's development of movable type. The publishing circumstances in Portugal were radically different from those with which Bỉnh was familiar in his homeland. Here enormous numbers of books were being printed, sold, and circulated. Books were also regularly imported from other parts of Europe and were offered for sale in the numerous bookshops of the Portuguese capital. The de facto Portuguese national newspaper, the *Gazeta de Lisboa,* regularly featured advertisements announcing the publication of new books. Most importantly, book collections in libraries, both private and public, represented a wealth of knowledge that made possible the large-scale writing project that Bỉnh undertook after the departure of the Portuguese ruler.

During the earlier years of his residence Bỉnh had ready access to the Necessidades convent library, one of the larger book repositories in Lisbon. When it opened in 1750 it already held more than twenty-five thousand volumes. Although he was quite busy during his years in residence at the Necessidades house, the library's primary value likely lay in giving Bỉnh access to texts he could copy out in his spare time for subsequent use, including de Rhodes's *Dictionarium* as well as his *Cathechismus.* But it is also possible, and indeed likely (though Bỉnh does not say as much), that the holdings of this library opened his eyes to the possibilities for his future literary project. Once Bỉnh moved to the Casa do Espirito Santo in the center of the city in 1807, he traded ready access to the Necessidades library for a five-minute walk to the newly opened Real Biblioteca Pública da Corte (the Royal Public Library of the Court), the largest library in Lisbon. Established by royal charter in 1796, the year Bỉnh arrived in Lisbon, the library was housed on the second floor of the massive edifice Pombal had built encircling the Praça do Comércio on the Tagus.[61] This library contained more than eighty thousand volumes, was open to the public six days a week, was staffed by accommodating librarians, and offered a fine reading space. During his 1800–1801 visit to Lisbon, the British traveler Robert Southey remarked on the accessibility and quality of the library: "The Public library here is magnificently established—the books well arranged, with ample catalogues, a librarian to every department and free access to all—with a cloak. The ruin of the Jesuits gave rise to this foundation. The libraries were all brought to Lisbon and the books remained as shoveled out of the carts for many years. They are not yet wholly arranged."[62] Bỉnh commented on his own experience at the Royal Library:

> The king of the country of Portugal . . . built twelve libraries [rooms] in order that those under heaven might see it, and these contained every book that had been written by priests of the Jesuit order in the West. Thus, if anyone wished to see any kind of book, they had [only] to cite the name of the book and its author to the person responsible for [such] matters, who would then look at a catalog of books that had the names of the authors and then would know where the book was kept, and as for these twelve libraries, any of the books or reports were there for anyone who wished to copy it or to copy any paragraph from it.[63]

In addition to the public library and the Necessidades collection, three other monastic repositories in the city provided public access to their materials, and Bỉnh may have used them as well.[64] Bỉnh's clerical status likely also opened doors to some of the city's private monastic libraries and their specialized collections, such as that

FIGURE 23. The west wing of the government ministry buildings surrounding the Praça do Comércio. It was built by Pombal and housed the Royal Library, opened in 1796, which Bỉnh used during the course of his research. Author's photo.

of the Saint-Vincent de Fora monastery, which reportedly had between twelve thousand and fourteen thousand volumes at the turn of the nineteenth century.[65]

In addition to libraries, Bỉnh had access to bookstores, another novelty to him. At the Casa do Espirito Santo Bỉnh lived one block from the most prominent bookstore in nineteenth-century Lisbon, Bertrand & Sons. As Henry Frederick Link wrote of this shop in 1801: "There are many booksellers' shops in Lisbon, the masters of which, however, have no foreign business. I shall only name the widow Bertrand and Son, near the church of Nossa Senhora dos Martyres acima do Xiado. New Portuguese works are easily procured there, and at the prices marked in the printed catalogue. Each book has a price prefixed, and the bookseller is contented with a moderate profit."[66] The bookstore, the oldest continuously operating bookseller in Europe, moved to its location on what is today rua Garrett in 1773, having been rebuilt after its destruction in the 1755 earthquake. It can still be found there today in the Chiado district, a European literary institution Bỉnh must have passed regularly on his way to and from his residence.[67]

Over the years, partly because of the availability of these bookstores and partly through the generosity of friends, Bỉnh built up a modest personal library, whose contents he listed in his *Sách sổ*. The list includes a description of the books as well as their prices if he had purchased them and remembered how much he had paid. It is entirely possible that he purchased some of these books at Bertrand, given its proximity, though he does not mention this. He also notes that some titles for which prices were not listed were ones that had been given to him by friends. The collection

FIGURE 24. The Livraria Bertrand, which opened in 1732, is the oldest operating bookstore in the world. It is only two blocks from the entrance of the Casa do Espírito Santo, and it is likely that Bỉnh would have shopped here when purchasing books for his collection. Author's photo.

eventually totaled forty books and was a combination of liturgical and historical texts. The titles suggest that some of these books must have been the primary sources for his own later writing projects, as they include several volumes of tales about the Jesuit forefathers, including four on Francis Xavier, two on Ignatius Loyola, and one of tales from his homeland. Bỉnh also came to own three volumes of tales about Japan, which would have appealed to him as the site of the first Jesuit project in Asia.[68]

The Postal System

Another prominent Portuguese institution that impressed Bỉnh was the postal system, which loomed so large in his own life. This had no real counterpart in Đại Việt, for while messages could be carried between government offices, this was strictly a royal institution with an extremely circumscribed purpose. In Portugal, Bỉnh encountered a system with far broader public application, one that linked Lisbon to the rest of the country and Europe beyond. He noted that every residence had a house number on its door so that postal carriers could always find a particular residence to deliver its mail. Mail was delivered and picked up twice a week all around the country by letter carriers on horseback. He discussed the enormously busy central post office in Lisbon (*nhà chứa thư ở Kẻ chợ*) sorting all the mail for its many different destinations and putting it into leather sacks, then on the back of a horse. Postal carriers would ride day and night, regardless of the weather, in order to deliver letters to their destinations, all the while collecting mail destined for Lisbon. He spoke of the varying costs of postage, depending on whether mail was light or heavy, going near or far, and reported that the postal system brought in considerable revenue and represented an important royal monopoly. Bỉnh observed that the number of letters of important business (*thư có việc*) was very small, while the vast majority of the letters were simply conversational (*thư nói truyện*), "as was the custom of the West."

Bỉnh even provided a sense of his own direct experience of this system, describing how it functioned at his residence. His house would send a servant to collect their mail at a central location, where payment would be made for any applicable postage, after which the letters were brought back to the house and there sorted alphabetically by letter, a process Bỉnh described in detail: "For example, if my name were Antao [Anthony], then I would look for the letter 'A,' and if my name were Bảo Lộc [Paul], then I would look under the letter 'B,' etc. And if you saw your name then you could go to get the letter, otherwise not. And if you did not get your letter on the day it came, then you could go back to check the next day to see if it was there."[69] This system applied to overseas mail as well, and Bỉnh's letters from Macao and from the New World arrived in this fashion. One can only begin to imagine, then, Bỉnh's eager anticipation of the daily mail delivery, particularly when vessels returning from Asia docked on the Tagus, something that would have been common news in the city.

At one level Bỉnh's description of the postal service seems remarkably mundane. Modern postal systems rarely attract the attention of foreign visitors. None of the European travel accounts of Lisbon in the eighteenth or nineteenth centuries bothered to talk about it. But Bỉnh's commentary allows us to look at this institution with fresh eyes and consider it from the perspective of a man who had come from a society in which something of this type did not exist. Vietnamese were certainly able to communicate with one another in the early modern period, but their worlds were, in some regards, much smaller. Long-distance communication was irrelevant for most, and extremely limited literacy would have made a postal system largely unnecessary. But here was a system that worked, and worked very logically, and perhaps just as importantly, was a system linking Bỉnh to his homeland.

The Lottery System, Public Safety, and Health

Another institution that fascinated Bỉnh was the Portuguese lottery system, which also had no equivalent in Tonkin. As he described it, the system was run as a concession from the king to private entities who had been granted the right to conduct the contest by printing and then selling tickets, paper chits with numbers on them. Bỉnh reported that princesses of the royal court would sometimes purchase as many as twenty tickets, wealthier commoners might buy between five and ten tickets, and the poor would pool their resources to purchase and share a single ticket. In such cases, the ticket was apparently torn into parts and distributed among the people who had contributed to its purchase. When the numbers were announced, these people would come together and compare their ticket sections to see if they had won and would then go together to collect the prize. He noted that some people would even buy tickets every day to increase their chances of winning and that once all tickets were sold the drawing would be held. In case his reader was still unclear about how the system worked, Bỉnh wrote that when the drawing was held if your number was drawn you would win, and if not then you would have lost the money you spent to buy the ticket. Prizes for the contest were as high as 50,000 silver *crusados* for first place, 40,000 for second, and then a graduated series of lesser prizes.[70]

The remainder of Bỉnh's description involved the mechanisms for distributing the prizes, including printed announcements regarding the winning numbers. He noted that an army of young children was involved in the lottery system, first selling tickets and later tracking down winners, for which they often collected a modest finder's fee. While Bỉnh had clearly never seen anything like the lottery in his homeland, he tried to provide a usable frame of reference for his readers and came up with the Vietnamese civil service examination system, or rather its later eighteenth-century incarnation. At this time the system had become subject to certain abuses, among which was the opportunity to bypass the initial round of screening exams by paying three coins of cash (*các kẻ đi thi sinh đỗ ba quan*) as a type of administrative fee. Then, as with the lottery in Portugal, the vast majority would fail and thus lose their investment, while only a very few would succeed.[71] While there are clear limits to the usefulness of this analogy, it again revealed the distinct perspective that Bỉnh provided for thinking about this particular Portuguese institution.

A third civic institution that caught Bỉnh's attention was the organized system of public safety, represented by both police and fire departments. His lengthy description of the fire suppression service is worth quoting:

> In the capital houses burn very quickly, especially in the summertime when there are sometimes two or three fires every day. Even though the streets are so crowded, it is still easy to determine quickly where the fire is burning so no harm is caused.

The first task is to protect individuals by ringing the bell to wake the sleeping so they can immediately flee the house, while the second is to call the troops who bring the water, because they will come out both night and day. They sleep in places near water sources, and [when there is a fire] they immediately bring several water carriages, together with a vehicle carrying ladders in order to reach the upper windows, and travel quickly to the location of the fire.

After this he described the city's water sources from which bucket brigades could be set up to battle fires. He concluded by observing: "Any time there is a fire in a house, all of the churches ring their bells as a signal for people to come out to try to save the house; there were times when the fire would be on the upper story, and times when the fire would be on the lower story. [This is because] in these apartment houses there were kitchens on every floor. Often the fires began not in the kitchen but outside, caused by the [oil] lamps that had to be lighted throughout the night while one slept."[72] As a long-term resident living in the middle of the dense urban core, Bình obviously had a vested interest in the functionings of this system, which he must have witnessed firsthand over the many years of his residence.

The final institution that Bình came to know quite well during his time in Lisbon was the medical establishment and its manifestations in the form of physicians, pharmacists, and the treatment regimens they prescribed. Bình and his companions had frequent encounters with the world of medicine, as the men suffered from numerous ailments during their earlier years in Lisbon, with some of these conditions becoming severe. The priests at their residence regularly called in doctors, whose visits and prescriptions Bình described in considerable detail. If the initial treatment did not resolve the illness, further doctors were brought in to discuss the case and to prescribe other medicines. Bình noted that during the early years of their residence the substantial costs associated with their illnesses were covered by the head of the Necessidades house, who assumed that the men would be staying at most a year or two.[73] As it turned out, the Vietnamese delegation's stay extended into years and then decades, and their illnesses and the costs associated with them also continued for years. Brother Ngân, for example, was in poor health and in frequent need of doctors from the early part of the nineteenth century until his eventual death in 1817.

Bình directly compared the Portuguese doctors that he observed to those in Annam. He noted that the Western doctors seemed to be less compassionate and less attentive but far more persistent than their Vietnamese counterparts. He wrote that if Vietnamese doctors could not effect a cure they would simply leave for fear of being embarrassed by their failure. The doctors in the West, however would not leave if things did not go well. Instead, they would advise their patients to call additional doctors to consult on the matter, while the original doctor would remain as well. When illnesses became too severe, patients were referred to hospitals, a concept with no equivalent in Vietnam, where all medical care would have taken place at the patient's home. Bình was greatly impressed by the concept of the hospital, which he translated as "Houses of Compassion" (*nhà thương xót*) to which seriously ill patients could be brought and where they would be given not only medical care but also meals and beds.[74] He observed that in the West such institutions were found not merely in the largest cities but also in smaller towns, and he reported that Lisbon itself had many such entities. He wrote about the fees associated with hospitalization, noting that it was sometimes more economical to send a patient to the hospital than to call specialists to a private home. Indeed, as Bình writes, part of his motivation for offering a detailed description of Western-style hospitals and their services and costs was to deflect possible criticism of those who might complain about the substantial expenditures for Brother Liễn's lengthy hospitalization in Macao.[75] In short, he regarded hospitals as a significant public service, but because it was an institution unknown in his homeland, he explained its functioning and logic to an audience who might need a context for understanding their envoy's use of their funds to pay for hospital expenses.

RESTORATION OF THE JESUITS

During the years after the French occupation ended, Bình's life consisted primarily of the routine work as a priest and the daily life at the congregation's residence. However, this routine was broken at several junctures, each of which prompted Bình to write of it in his notebooks. The first of these events occurred in the later summer of 1814. This event was profoundly important for Bình, as it was the restoration of his beloved Jesuits. On August 7, 1814, Pope Pius VII made the short journey from his seat in the Vatican to Il Gesù, the home church and spiritual heart of the Jesuit order. There, from its lofty pulpit, he formally declared that the Company of Jesus was restored and could once again admit priests to its ranks. Bình was, understandably, tremendously excited at the news that the Jesuits had been restored.[76] As he recorded shortly thereafter, the restoration soon bore fruit as the order once again admitted members and began to send them out as missionaries.[77] He also commemorated the event with the first poem that he had written (or at least recorded) since the summer of 1802, and though it is not dated it seems clear that Bình must have written it directly upon learning the news.

> *Poem Giving Thanks That the Order Lives Again*
> From the time the news reached my ears
> I felt a great sense of relief, being able to shake off my feeling of sadness. I rejoice that [the order] has now already clearly been restored
> For I had earlier feared this was still but a dream of fortunate words.
> These flames conceal the image of the morning wind.

Truly this is a firm cornerstone with a solid support.
Jesus's representatives now flourish more than ever.
The words spoken in past times were truly not false.[78]

Bình hoped, of course, that the restoration meant that Jesuits would soon be sent back to his homeland. He apparently wrote another letter imploring the Portuguese religious hierarchy to send a group of Jesuits to Tonkin, assuring them that "the Jesuits are awaited by the people like Christ himself."[79] As he soon discovered, however, it was not such a simple matter. While the Jesuits had been restored with great pomp in Rome, they were not so readily welcomed in the public eye, and most made their way back onto the scene very quietly—"on tip-toe," as Jean Lacouture put it. And indeed, even with the pope's blessing, the Jesuits' presence in Europe remained uncertain: the order saw its advances frequently turned back because of continental politics. The Jesuits were expelled from France no less than three times in the period from their restoration to the end of the nineteenth century.[80] They were also expelled from Holland in 1818, from Russia and Spain in 1820, and from Mexico in 1821. In fact, they were not permitted to return to Bình's Portugal until 1829, only a few years before his death.[81] Their return to Vietnam would also have to wait until well into the twentieth century.

THE DEATH OF FATHER NGÂN (1817) AND RENEWED THOUGHTS OF BRAZIL

Three years after the restoration of the Jesuits, and a decade after the Portuguese ruler's departure, a second major event shook the routine of Bình's life. This was the death of another of his companions, Brother Ngân, who had been ill for the previous fifteen years.[82] Ngân had been the youngest member of their group and was only forty-seven years old upon his death. It had been sixteen years since Brother Nhân's death in 1801, and the intervening years had changed the dynamics surrounding the demise of one of the Vietnamese residents. Bình wrote that unlike Brother Nhân, who was interred in his Vietnamese garb, Brother Ngân was buried in the robes of the Oratorian house. Whereas Nhân had still been a Vietnamese temporarily resident in Lisbon and anticipating a return to Tonkin, by 1817 Ngân had become an Oratorian brother and fully integrated member of its community.[83] Viewing their friend's body being prepared for burial in Western robes underscored the extent to which their lives had changed. In fact, in his *Notebook,* Bình specifically commented on the differences between the two funerals, suggesting the degree to which he was conscious of the changes that had transpired.[84]

Father Ngân's death in mid-May did not merely inspire reflections on the men's changed relationship to the religious community in Lisbon. It also caused Bình and Brother Trung to contemplate once again the possibility of joining the exiled

Portuguese court in Rio de Janeiro. The two men had apparently been considering this since at least 1810, according to a letter written by Nuncio Caleppi to the apostolic vicar of Eastern Tonkin in July of that year.[85] Father Ngân's death would have served as a reminder to Bỉnh that he was not getting any younger, perhaps also causing him to reflect that he had now been in Portugal for more than two decades and that the king's return looked as distant as ever. As long as the Portuguese ruler even nominally retained the Padroado authority, it was possible that he might once again consider Bỉnh's request, but only if Bỉnh could present another petition and make his case in person. From Bỉnh's perspective, the restoration of the Jesuit order three years previously had also brightened his prospects, for the king could now theoretically dispatch a Jesuit to serve as bishop of Tonkin. In any case, with this confluence of circumstances—easier travel options, advancing age (he was now fifty-eight), and the restoration of the Jesuits—Bỉnh must have felt an increasing sense of urgency.

Preliminary overtures to the king apparently led nowhere, though Bỉnh writes that he understood that the ruler was not entirely averse to the possibility of the Vietnamese joining him.[86] In November of 1817, Bỉnh revived the matter in a petition to the local official handling the king's affairs in Lisbon. This time he was told that travel on a private vessel would be difficult and extremely expensive but that if he was willing to wait for a public boat (one conducting state business) the journey would be far easier and more affordable. Bỉnh apparently acceded to this compromise and so began to wait for such a boat and for formal permission. Finally, in April of 1818, Bỉnh received official permission to make the journey to Brazil and immediately began to prepare for departure. He purchased two tickets, one for Father Trung and one for himself, at a total price of 496 *quan*. Everything was in readiness, and Bỉnh must have been eager to embark upon this next stage of his long project. Just as the two Vietnamese were on the verge of departure, however, their plans were dealt a major setback when Father Trung suddenly fell ill. The trip had to be put off. This must have come as a tremendous disappointment to Bỉnh, just when his fortunes seemed to have changed. His hopes were soon raised again, when renewed inquiries yielded a promise that he would be allowed to travel on a warship carrying the English envoy to the court in exile. Once again, Bỉnh made preparations, but before this ship could sail, circumstances yet again intervened to overturn his plans. The onset of the constitutionalist fever that spread across Europe in the late 1810s and early 1820s resulted in growing political chaos, with numerous uprisings in Spain against the Catholic orders, and the instability was threatening to spread to Portugal. In these uncertain circumstances, the trip was postponed once more, and Bỉnh's final opportunity to become the first Vietnamese to travel to the New World slipped away.[87]

Even as Bỉnh was contemplating the trip to the New World, he was beginning to grow rather cynical about the king's religious attitudes. In particular, Bỉnh noted that the restoration of the Jesuits, which opened the door for Jesuit appointments to bishoprics, had not budged the Portuguese ruler's latent anti-Jesuit sentiments. Thus, while he continued to hope that the ruler might offer support to his mission, Bỉnh had come to recognize the odds against it. As he noted in his *Nhật trình* notebook, the king was reluctant "because the ruler and the Portuguese officials were covetous of the properties of the Jesuit order and were not providing any assistance to the souls of our people, as their ancestors before them had, and because they did not wish to accept the Jesuit order, whose [priests] are teachers, not only in foreign countries, but also in their own country."[88] Clearly Bỉnh was frustrated by King João VI's continuing hostility toward the Jesuits, as this precluded what the Vietnamese priest viewed as an ideal resolution to his long-standing problem: namely appointing a Jesuit to serve as the official bishop to Tonkin.

More immediate problems in Lisbon were also attracting Bỉnh's attention, in particular the series of revolts and popular protests that had broken out in the late 1810s and that continued episodically into the next decade. One episode especially caught his attention, the 1820 seizure by rebel forces of Bỉnh's former home, the Necessidades compound. He noted that the troops had established an encampment in the monastery-palace and evicted all of its residents, including the remaining clergy, who were forced to find other accommodations.[89] This episode may have shaken Bỉnh's confidence in the security of his own housing arrangements, which now seemed vulnerable to precisely these kinds of vicissitudes of worldly affairs. Where once the church had reigned supreme in close coordination with the authority of the throne, new forces were at work disrupting traditional power structures and casting into doubt older arrangements. Indeed, while Bỉnh's Casa do Espírito Santo was never claimed by rebel forces during his lifetime, it would eventually succumb to the sweeping and swift dissolution of the religious orders that happened just a year after Bỉnh's own death. In short, the takeover of the Necessidades palace foreshadowed events that would change the balance of religious and secular power in Portugal forever.

THE RETURN OF THE KING AND POLITICAL TURMOIL IN PORTUGAL

Eventually, the need to travel to Brazil evaporated with the return of the Portuguese court from its Brazilian exile in the summer of 1821. Bỉnh reported the ruler's homecoming in his *Nhật trình* notebook: "In 1821, on July 3, King João VI returned from the New World to the capital of Portugal, and on the fourth day he went ashore, first going to the church of the archbishop and giving thanks to the Virtuous Lord of Heaven for permitting him to cross the seas safely, and then going to the offices where the Cortes met and there stating that he would accept their constitution, and after that he finally returned to his palace in the middle of the night." Bỉnh then writes, "Our king having returned, we also went along to offer our congratulations [on his return]."⁹⁰ It is likely that this was the final time that the two men met, for Bỉnh does not report any other meetings, and by this time the ruler would surely have had no time for dealing with Bỉnh's petitions, for he was struggling to deal with the convulsions that were sweeping through his realm.

During the time of the royal family's exile in Brazil, the European world had changed, and Portugal along with it. The Portugal of 1821 was a radically different place from that in which Bỉnh had landed in the summer of 1796. Just a year before the court's return, and indeed precipitating this event, was the Revolution of 1820, a coordinated effort by elites and soldiers in Porto and Lisbon to seize power, partly in response to growing frustrations with the lingering authority of the British, who had continued to maintain a relatively oppressive protection status in the ruler's absence. The leaders of the revolution wrote a progressive constitution, one that limited the power of the monarchy, established a legislature, and created a surprisingly wide electorate.⁹¹ Bỉnh devoted several pages of his *Nhật trình* chronology to this sequence of events and the efforts of the reformers to impose their new law codes upon the Portuguese elites. He described the patriarch of Lisbon's resistance to the new leadership and his subsequent imprisonment. He also detailed a test of wills in which he reported that the secular reformers sought to force Portuguese to eat meat during Lent as a mechanism for breaking the power of the church, while elements of the church leadership aggressively resisted this.⁹² Bỉnh must have watched these events play out in Lisbon with great dismay as the church, which was at the center of his life, saw its influence under concerted attack.

It was to such a transformed Portugal that the royal family finally returned. And while Dom João had left Lisbon as a prince and returned as a king, he did so more in name than in substance. The lengthy exile had dramatically weakened the power of the royal family, whose absence had clearly demonstrated that Portugal could function without it. Second, the concerns of the court, which at times in the 1790s and early 1800s had been taken up with the threats of warfare from beyond its borders, were now focused on the internal threat represented by reformist and at times revolutionary voices that had come to dominate Portuguese political discourse. The court was thus not only less capable of acting on Bỉnh's behalf but also far less interested in doing so. By the 1820s, Bỉnh's novelty had long worn off. Moreover, the king was now fifty-three years of age, no longer the young and modestly energetic figure he had been at turn of the nineteenth century. He was weaker, both physically and politically, as a result of his extended exile and more than a little world-weary. The esoterica of the Padroado Real upon which Bỉnh had pinned his hopes probably held little interest for the ruler. Consequently, while Bỉnh rejoiced at the king's return, it did little to change his situation, something that he no doubt quickly came to realize.

THE DEATH OF BROTHER TRUNG IN 1824

Even as political events and eventually war swirled around him once again, Bỉnh continued to be occupied by the more mundane aspects of his day-to-day life. With the passage of time and particularly the deaths of his companions, mortality began to nag at Bỉnh. He became more aware that his years were limited. He no doubt understood that his mission no longer had a chance of success, and his perspective shifted to the routines of daily life that he had sustained now for many years. The reality of his waning years became more concrete with the death of his last surviving Vietnamese companion, Brother Trung, in the summer of 1824. Bỉnh wrote that Trung had long suffered from rheumatism (*bệnh thấp*), an illness he had already experienced before leaving Annam.[93] Brother Trung's passing left Bỉnh no one to speak Vietnamese with, and no companions with direct experience of his homeland. Curiously, Bỉnh's writings offer few comments on Trung's death or reflections on his background like the ones he had offered for his earlier companions. Regarding Brother Trung's passing he wrote only briefly in his *Tales of Annam*: "As I finish this book, it is the twenty-sixth day of September, 1824. Teacher Trung has just passed away, as he had not only been ill, but had also become white-haired with age. As for tales regarding Teacher Trung, these I have already recorded in chapter 31, on page 378, and as for the death of Teacher Liên, this I recorded in chapter 48, page 704, and as for the death of Teacher Nhân, this I recorded in chapter 50, on page 719."[94] The brief, almost emotionless comment comes as a kind of epilogue to the volume, penned over two pages that follow the volume's initial conclusion, originally written in 1822. Bỉnh offers no detail about Trung's death or any summary of his life. The reader is simply referred to earlier pages in the volume. Their relationship remains a mystery, but it would seem that Bỉnh was not very close to Trung, for whatever reason.

But Trung's death, while it spurred no recorded outward sense of grief for the loss of his last surviving Vietnamese companion, did give Bỉnh something to reflect on, namely his own mortality. He followed the brief note of Trung's death with some thoughts about his situation as the last survivor of his group and his own eventual death: "Now only I remain, and when I die my brother Christians will not know the time, because there will be no one to record it in this book, nor to inform them of the news that they might know the day and month [of my death]." This in turn led to further reflections, including speculation as to how word of his own death might be treated. Here Bỉnh once again raised a voice of defiance against his enemies, for he reflected with some certainty that his death would spur a round of celebration among his enemies.

> For, as we already know: when we have all died, no one will mourn us, and some might simply laugh and remark: "How is it that those cruel bullies have lived such a long time?" But one must remember that from the time that we went abroad until

the present more than thirty years have passed, and in our country of Annam many others have already died, and among them would have been many who were younger than we are, because death is the tax that we pay to the Virtuous Lord Jesus, the one that none can escape.[95]

He then conjured up an imagined dialogue with his critics in the aftermath of his eventual death, offering him a chance to rebut them from beyond the grave:

> There might also be others who would say: "It was because those men refused to accept the bishops that they have died in this manner." To them I would respond with my own question: "Is it the case that those who *did* accept the bishops of the Holy See have not died, and that none of them has been lost?" Then I must, myself, be lost, because many people have died who followed the bishop, and in these [past] many years more than seventy cardinals at the Holy See have also died, as have many others, such as six bishops, fifty priests, fourteen deacons, and these seventy Cardinals. And as for popes, two generations of them, Pius VI and Pius VII, have also both died, and Pope Leo XII just ascended the holy seat on the fifth of October in the year 1823.

Then he noted that it had been the same with kings and lords in all countries, "for in Dai Minh [China] there have already been two generations of emperors, Qianlong and Jiaqing, and now a third [Daoguang] has just mounted the throne." He concluded his comments by underscoring his point for those who might still not appreciate it: "Since it is like this, there is no one who can escape death, and yet they still belittle us in this fashion. It is interesting that Enoch and Elias still live, but on the Judgment Day it is the people who have spread the faith and who have suffered death who will be raised into heaven."

Trung's death was a reminder to Binh of his own mortality, further magnified by the fact that he was now quite alone. While he continued to remember his community back home and the fact that he was here on their mission, he was beginning to wonder whether they remembered him. As he very pragmatically pointed out, many had died in the intervening years since his departure, and many had since been born. The composition of that community was changing, and Binh and his companions were almost certainly increasingly being forgotten. He appeared to comfort himself in the knowledge that death was inevitable, coming not only to his friends and eventually to himself but also to the most powerful figures in the world. Moreover, Binh's aggressive reply to imagined critics upon his death was a reminder of the intensity of the struggle in which he had been engaged. Even now, seventeen years after his mission had essentially ended with the prince regent's departure for Brazil, Binh kept alive the animosity engendered by the struggle between those who had accepted and those who had refused the authority of the apostolic vicars.

8

The Tales of Philiphê Bỉnh

As became clear in the previous chapter, Bỉnh's life was radically altered by the Portuguese ruler's departure. No longer were his days spent drafting appeals to the prince and then traveling between innumerable state offices seeking supporters within the Portuguese bureaucracy. Bỉnh now experienced a measure of routine as he became increasingly absorbed in the rhythms of the Oratorian residence as well as those of the church calendar. At the same time, he began to redirect his considerable energies beyond the daily religious exercises demanded of his service as a priest. In particular, he used the opportunity presented by the prince regent's extended absence to dedicate himself to what became a massive literary project. Although Bỉnh had already done some writing and translating during the early years of his residence in Lisbon, the vast majority of his written output dates from between 1812 and 1830. Indeed, most of it was produced in the relatively brief span between 1815 and 1822. The project's start was delayed by the disruptions of the French occupation and its aftermath, so it was not until five years after the prince regent had departed that Bỉnh finally began to write in earnest. By this time it had become very clear that Dom João's exile would be lengthy and that Bỉnh himself was unlikely ever to see his native Tonkin again. This confluence of factors prompted Bỉnh to turn from trying to secure a bishop for Tonkin toward creating a written legacy that might serve future generations of Vietnamese Catholics.

To some degree, this chapter represents a departure from the earlier sections of this book, for in it we engage more with Bỉnh's mental world as expressed in his writings and ideas than with the material and mundane aspects that had defined the previous two decades of his life. For the next twenty years this literary project consumed much of Bỉnh's time and energy, and it would ultimately constitute his historical legacy. Only because of these writings do we know anything about Bỉnh as a person and as a Catholic envoy. Consequently, to fully understand Bỉnh we must examine them in some detail. Furthermore, his writings are of particular importance for understanding Vietnamese Catholic geographies, as his writings, like his travels, reveal multiple manifestations of these geographies—cultural, genealogical, temporal, and spatial—that appear both in the form and in the content of Bỉnh's many notebooks. In terms of form, we see Bỉnh using new ways of presenting information to his Vietnamese coreligionists. Bỉnh's exposure to the books he found in Lisbon's libraries transformed how he conceived of books and the ways in which they were organized, produced, and written. He adopted new apparatuses, such as chapter titles, indexes, source citations, and time lines, to serve his intended readership. In short, he was a significant innovator in the production of Vietnamese books.

More important than its new form, however, was the content of Bỉnh's literary output, which represented and reflected the new geographies of Vietnamese Catholics by articulating new genealogies, lineages, and global connections. It also described new temporal geographies, ones expressed in the flows of history, and, more mechanically, in different ways of recording and detailing the passage of time. His books about Catholic saints—both collected morality tales and lengthy hagiographies—suggest the new spiritual and physical landscapes that were significant to Vietnamese Catholics. Perhaps more than any other work, his two-volume history of Catholicism in his homeland stands out for the ways it links the histories and geographies of Vietnamese Catholics with those in Europe. These volumes, though substantially based on published books Bỉnh found in Lisbon, connect Vietnamese Christians to the flows of global Catholicism by validating their participation and presence in the expansion of the faith. In Bỉnh's account of Catholic history in the two halves of "Annam," the Vietnamese themselves are the central figures, active participants in their faith, many of them enduring martyrdom for their new beliefs. In focusing on his fellow Vietnamese, Bỉnh raises them as exemplars of faith, dedication, and devotion that will serve future generations of Vietnamese. Where once the exemplars were drawn from the history of European Catholicism, now they could be found among the Vietnamese and on their native soil.

BỈNH'S NOTEBOOKS

To understand Bỉnh's writings, we need first to consider the notebooks in which he collected and organized the material that he gathered and then transformed into longer stories and records. Bỉnh wrote in what appear to be hand-bound notebooks with slightly bluish paper and unadorned leather covers. These unassuming books slowly filled the shelves in his quarters as his project evolved, taking their place alongside the printed volumes he had purchased or received as gifts over the years.

TABLE 1

Title of Notebook	Date written	Type of Work	Number of Pages
Golden book recording a journey to seek an official religious leader	1793–1826	Original work	598
Vietnamese-Portuguese-Latin dictionary	1797	Copy	916
Catechism and baptism	1797	Copy	333
A method for explicating tales of the popes	1798–	Copy	453
(Various Liturgical Materials)	1802	Copy, trans.	285
Book of the daily sacred observances	1802–1810	Original work	557
Book explaining the conducting of the mass	1802–1810	Original work	172
Book of Instructions on Prayers for the Mass	1802–1810	Original work	106
Alma Instruida na Doutrina e vida christã	1811	Copy	643
Alma Instruida (2nd volume)	1811	Copy	547
Alma Instruida (3rd volume)	1812	Copy	525
(Materials on Mission History)	1813?	Copy	362
(Miscellaneous materials about Annam)	1814–1816	Original work	437
Book of exemplary tales (first volume)	1815	Original work	507
Book of exemplary tales (second volume)	1815	Original work	275
Tales of Fernando Mendes Pinto	1817	Translation, original work	202
Tales of Saint Francis Xavier	1818	Original work	612
Tales of Saint Ignatius of Loyola establishing the Order of the Virtuous Lord Jesus	1819	Original work	734
Tales of Saint Francis of Borgia	1820	Original work	643
(Materials related to the Jesuit Order)	1820	Translation, original work	79
Tales of Annam, the Outer Region	1822	Original work	775
Tales of Annam, the Inner Region	1822	Original work	721
Notebook that transmits and records all matters	1822–1832	Original work	646
Tales of Saint Anne	1830	Original work	626

There is little doubt that Bình was, by far, the most prolific Vietnamese writer in the newly developed romanized script of *quốc ngữ* prior to the twentieth century, and possibly the most productive Vietnamese author in any script before 1900. The full extent of his productivity is apparent from a list of his writings produced between 1793 and 1832, the year in which he laid down his pen for the last time.

As Table 1 indicates, Bình's manuscript notebooks include both original compositions and translations into Vietnamese of works originally in other languages. But even the ostensible translations are often significantly reworked adaptations of the original texts upon which they are based. His writings also include several works that Bình copied out in their original language (either Portuguese or Latin) but upon which he also left his own mark in the form of comments, updates, and selective editing.

There is a fairly clear trajectory to Bình's written output over the years of his residence in Lisbon, as an earlier literary output focused on his immediate spiritual and political needs eventually gave way to a writing project dedicated to a more long-term purpose. The earlier written works, composed or copied between 1793 and 1815, can be divided into four rough categories. The majority are liturgical or instructional. These were likely written to serve Bình's spiritual life and reflected his own needs and perhaps those of his community, which he assumed he would soon be rejoining. They range from commentaries on the mass to descriptions of devotional practices to methods for memorizing the lineage of popes. Bình also copied out by hand versions of two of Alexandre de Rhodes's published works. The second category consists of the numerous petitions that he presented to the Portuguese ruler between 1796 and 1807 in pursuit of his mission to secure a bishop for Tonkin. The third form of writing that Bình left from this period is his correspondence, the many letters he exchanged with his compatriots in both Macao and Tonkin, discussed in chapter 6. Finally, Bình also recorded at least forty-five poems during this period from 1793 to 1815; some, as we have seen, were "travel poems" written to commemorate key events of his and his companions' journeys, while others were reflections upon significant moments in his life in Lisbon.

In 1815 Bình's writings took a new direction. He produced no more liturgical work, left no more letters or poems, and, with the ruler now long absent from Lisbon, was no longer drafting petitions concerning his mission. Instead, Bình began to research and compose lengthy collections of what he labeled "tales." Bình's decision to redirect his literary energies toward producing such historical texts rather than writing additional liturgical volumes was driven by a determination to leave a useful legacy for future generations, whatever the outcome of his now seemingly hopeless mission. These writings might become the basis of an institutional memory for the Vietnamese Catholics he had left behind. He started with a two-volume set of exemplary tales, taken from the lives of saints and from popular accounts of ordinary people whose lives demonstrated admirable or deplorable actions. He followed this with three lengthy hagiographies of Jesuit forebears, written one per year between 1818 and 1820. He then turned to arguably his most important literary work, a two-volume history of Roman Catholicism in Vietnam, the first extended treatment of this topic in Vietnamese. After a long hiatus, between 1822 and 1830, Bình wrote one more long-format work, a collection of stories about St. Anne, the pseudohistorical mother of Mary.

WHY WRITE? THE PURPOSE OF BÌNH'S WRITINGS

Bình's massive written output during his years of exile in Portugal was motivated by several factors. The first of these was related to his acute awareness of the community he had left behind. Bình felt obligated and responsible toward those who had dispatched him on their behalf. Thus he felt compelled to preserve records of his own actions, his experiences, and even his expenditures. He was also driven by a strong desire to accumulate and record practical information for potential future envoys or travelers to a Europe with whom Vietnamese Catholics were now clearly bound. His detailed descriptions and commentary on elements of Lisbon's urban life, ranging from communications infrastructure to public safety, were calculated to ease the transition of any future visitors from Tonkin and also to bridge the gap between the two peoples in a more general sense. Finally, Bỉnh's elaborate Catholic histories, of both the Jesuit leaders and his homeland, were calculated to create resources for Vietnamese Christians who still lacked such materials. By preserving these records and accumulating knowledge to be shared with other Vietnamese, Bỉnh felt he could continue to serve as a productive member of the community even while absent over the years and miles.

Closely linked to this sense of obligation to Vietnamese of the present was a desire to communicate with generations of Vietnamese Catholics yet to come. Early in his history of Cochinchina (*Truyện Anam, Đàng Trong*) he connected the two by observing: "Now I will translate [the following] into the language of our country, not only so that future generations might know it, but also for those of the present time, for there are but few people who still remember the events of earlier generations."[1] Elsewhere in the volume on Tonkin (*Truyện Anam, Đàng Ngoài*), as he began the story of his complex project to reach Europe, Bỉnh emphasized the importance of clearly and carefully preserving memories for those who would follow:

> The customs and practices of all who have come before [me] are such that when one crafts any book of tales, or if one records any kind of history and sets forth tales, then one must speak of all matters from the earlier to the later in order to express [things] clearly, or else one would still be mistrustful, for it might then have one meaning when seen by a person of the present, and then [a different] meaning for those of future generations. Thus, if one does not speak clearly and there are people of future generations who wish to know something, they will not know whom to ask, because all of the people of the previous generations will already have died. Thus I am recording things in these tales in order to fully express my ideas, as will be told in what follows.[2]

It is not surprising that Bỉnh would be acutely conscious of these future generations. He understood himself to be part of a long Catholic lineage in Tonkin and an even longer series of lineages, represented first in the Jesuit order and then in the larger trajectory of the Catholic Church and its origins among the biblical patriarchs. Indeed, Bỉnh very self-consciously represented himself as lying within an important Christian literary tradition dating to the authors of the four Gospels of the New Testament and beyond, stretching into the earlier eras of the Old Testament. In the preface to his *Truyện Anam, Đàng Ngoài*, he notes that the four Evangelists "recorded the Gospels that all under heaven might know of the fact of Jesus's birth" and that "the blessed Moses recorded the Prophecies that we might know of the matter of the Virtuous Lord of Heaven creating the earth."[3] By invoking these biblical antecedents, Bỉnh was suggesting that his own writings belonged to this historical record keeping—that he, like Moses, and the Evangelists before him, was both a preserver of the traditions and stories and a kind of linchpin between past and present.

Although Bỉnh wrote with these very practical objectives in mind, his writing also served a spiritual purpose. Reading through his prefaces, one finds dedications to various figures, either the saints about whom he was writing, the Virgin Mary and other biblical figures, or God. At a religious level, these works were all dedicated to a higher purpose: to venerate and give gratitude to the spiritual figures who lay at the center of Bỉnh's life as a Catholic. As he wrote in the preface to the first volume of his *Tales of Annam*:

> I am the priest Bỉnh who has written this book to honor the Virtuous Lord Jesus, and also the very blessed Virtuous Mother Maria, and the Sainted Joseph, and Saint Joaquim, and Saint Anna, and Saint Ignatius, and Saint Francis Xavier, and all of the saints, because they are among those who helped me to write this work so that my brothers might be able to use it.
> —IN THE CAPITAL OF PORTUGAL IN THE YEAR 1822.

This dedication neatly captures the dual dynamic driving Bỉnh's writings. On the one hand, he was writing the volume "to honor the Virtuous Lord Jesus" as an act of spiritual devotion; on the other he was writing it "so that my brothers might be able to use it," a service to the members of the Padroado community.

Finally, even as Bỉnh created these works to preserve histories of Catholic missionaries and Vietnamese converts and to perform an act of personal devotion, writing them also served another, somewhat more mundane function for him. Namely, these notebooks must have constituted a form of companionship during lonely periods in his room, or more generally during his long stay in Lisbon. Although he had company in his Vietnamese companions until 1824, it seems clear that simply talking with them was not enough to satisfy Bỉnh's needs. Indeed, the degree to which these men remain absent in most of his writings except as the victims of illness and death suggests that their presence was not nearly sufficient company for him and that a significant part of him was still powerfully connected to those left behind. Writing these notebooks offered Bỉnh a creative outlet through the long years of unintended exile, and, like journals or diaries, they served as uncomplaining receptacles for the outpourings of his mind. They provided him with a way to articulate ideas, knowledge, or emotions that might not otherwise be expressed or expressible.

For Bỉnh, these writings represented a kind of ongoing dialogue with an absent, but not invented, audience. The community that Bỉnh had left behind was thus both a motivation for his writings and his imagined audience. He addressed its members directly in much that he wrote, and his literary style suggests a dynamic in which he placed himself in the midst of these people. His sense of the readers as an actively present audience becomes clear when Bỉnh steps out of his narrative to address them directly. In *Tales of St. Ignatius*, for example, he writes: "In the previous chapter *I spoke* [*nói*] of matters pertaining to devils being frightened of St. Ignatius, and in this chapter *I will speak* [*sẽ nói*] of people who were frightened of St. Ignatius."[4] And in his volume on St. Francis Xavier, this conversational style appears once again, in a passage where Bỉnh shifts from talking about Xavier to talking about Christianity and explains his logic in carrying out this shift: "But now I will not speak of the various things carried out by the Jesuit order in many other countries but will speak only of the countries of Dai Minh and Annam, because it is easy for you to know what you have heard and also easier to understand, and thus I will tell of it as follows."[5] Here, as in so many other moments in his storytelling, there is a palpable sense of the community as an always present audience for Bỉnh as he wrote, guiding both what he wrote and how he wrote it.

Indeed, Bỉnh's narrative voice is very much that of the traditional storyteller rather than the dispassionate researcher. He was speaking these tales as much as writing them, and clearly understood that those who might eventually receive the labors of his project would hear rather than read them. Bỉnh was acutely aware of the importance of oral tradition and the role that it played in Vietnamese society as a source of both entertainment and enlightenment. The number of people who learned by reading in eighteenth- and nineteenth-century Tonkin was tiny; the vast majority learned by listening. In the introduction to his two-volume *Book of Exemplary Tales* (*Sách gương truyện*), he commented on the ways in which orality functioned in the context of Vietnamese Catholicism: "I already know that when the Christians of our country go to hear a sermon or encounter the priests telling one or two stories, they will immediately remember them for a long time, and they will also retell them to others that they might also know them."[6] Thus he anticipates that his books will be read aloud to the members of the community. In this respect much of his literary output can be understood to straddle the line between the world of writing and the world of telling.

Even as Bỉnh wrote for an audience steeped in oral lore and the informal transmission of stories, he sought to ensure that his own writings were rigorously grounded in fact and their religious message suitably presented. Thus, in his *Notebook That Transmits and Records All Matters*, Bỉnh sought to reassure his future readers by declaring: "This matter and many others have already been printed in books so all under heaven might know about them, and these were not simply things that I heard someone say" (chẳng phải rằng tôi có nghe ai nói truyền khẩu).[7] These books were ones that Bỉnh had gathered as he explored Lisbon's many libraries and bookshops, reading and collecting volumes to form the foundation for his work. He conducted this search with a measure of confidence, instilled by his understanding of Portuguese publication practices and regulations, which ensured that books circulating in Lisbon had been carefully scrutinized for their content. In the introduction to his *Book of Exemplary Tales*, Bỉnh described the relationship between his anthologizing process and the Portuguese controls on the distribution of publications:

> As for the tales that I am translating here, these are some of the stories found in the printed books in the West, but I have selected them from many books, and I have written them in this volume to organize them, because in all of those books, when they speak of any particular thing, or comment on some particular matter, then they just speak of that story, and this is just like when they preach. Also, among all of the orders in the West, when they wish to produce any kind of book, they have to request permission from the king and all of the examining agencies, and only [once permission has been granted] can they begin to sell them . . . and if there is something that should not be there, then they will not be permitted to sell it, and the printer may not print that book. All of the published books carry the name of the person who wrote the book, as well as the name of the government official and the offices in the order and . . . so when people go to buy it they need not worry that there are any false things in the book. It is not the case that anyone who wishes to write anything can do so, or that anyone who wishes to publish can do this anywhere, because if they are caught this is [considered] a crime in this country. Thus all of the books from which I am copying the following stories are ones that the government has already examined and for which the court has already given permission to be published in limitless quantities and for sale to everyone.[8]

Here Bỉnh was explaining a screening and censorship process still common in early nineteenth-century Portugal, even as it had relaxed substantially in most other parts of Europe.[9] Another late eighteenth-century visitor to Lisbon similarly described the process for screening printed material being imported to Portugal from other parts of Europe: "Every book, every imprint that arrives in Lisbon is taken to the [censorship] bureau, and it is not delivered to its owner it until it has received the approval of this tribunal."[10] Bỉnh clearly admired this process in part because it ensured that the contents of his anthology project came from materials that had already been sanctioned by the state as both reliable and religiously acceptable.[11]

The reliability of these volumes rested not merely in their having been examined and authorized by state entities but also in the fact of their fixity in print and the clear identification of each author. Bỉnh strongly approved of this practice in which authors acknowledged and claimed their work; it stood in contrast to much of the Vietnamese literary tradition, whose collections of tales were often anonymous, reflecting their origins in oral traditions. Bỉnh looked askance at anonymous works, viewing them as a convenient cover for people writing falsehoods of various sorts or simply not taking responsibility for their writings. In *Truyện Anam* Bỉnh writes about the frequent copying and recopying of Geronimo Maiorica's works that has taken place in his homeland, noting that often Maiorica's name is left out in these recopyings, either deliberately or unintentionally. The problem, he notes, stems from the fact that Maiorica's works have never enjoyed the fixity afforded by being printed, a process that assures the preservation of the author's identity.[12] He contrasts this with the writings of Maiorica's contemporary and counterpart in the Asian mission Matteo Ricci, who was also writing books for Asian Christians. Ricci's books were printed in Europe, thus guaranteeing that future readers would know that he was their author. While his own books were never printed, Bỉnh was still determined to ensure that his own authorial responsibility would be preserved. He clearly identified himself as the author at the outset of each of his notebooks, and in the introduction to his *Nhật trình kim thư* he speaks directly to the importance of accepting accountability for one's writings: "It should be the custom that on this earth any time someone writes any sort of book, he puts his name in that book so that everyone will know who wrote it. If one produces a book and does not record one's name in it, then that person is a scoundrel, and for this reason I will write my name here in order that everyone will know who wrote this book." He then wrote with a flourish, and in exaggerated strokes of his pen, the words "I am the priest Philiphê Bỉnh."[13]

INNOVATIVE ELEMENTS OF BỈNH'S WRITINGS

Bỉnh's writings were inspired not merely by the contents of the many books he had access to in Lisbon but also by their form and technical elements. Consequently Bỉnh was both an innovator in his production of books in Vietnamese about Catholicism and a pioneer in his way of organizing and presenting them. These innovations included his extensive use of the romanized script, which he found all around him in the European books he consulted. They also included the creation of chapter titles, indexes, and chronologies to make his books more readily usable by the audience for whom he had written them. The chronologies in particular are an instance of Bỉnh's invocation, throughout his writings, of new geographies of time and new genealogies and frames of reference.

The Script and Structure

The Vietnamese adaptation of the Roman alphabet to represent their vernacular marked an important textual shift in the long evolution of the Vietnamese language. The Roman script was the third major writing system to be employed by literate Vietnamese. The first was that imported by the Chinese during their millennium of political suzerainty. Now commonly referred to as "classical Chinese" or by Vietnamese as *chữ Hán* (the Hán script) or *chữ Nho* (the Confucianist script), it was used for every literary endeavor from record keeping to poetry writing, and it continued to be employed into the early twentieth century. Its chief drawback was that it could not be used to render the Vietnamese vernacular. Thus there was a significant gap between spoken Vietnamese and the writing system being used by literati. At some point, no later than the thirteenth century, the Vietnamese began to develop a second writing system to overcome this gap, making it possible to represent the Vietnamese vernacular.[14] This new script, which became known as *chữ nôm* (the demotic script, lit. "southern characters"), or *quốc ngữ* (lit. "the national language"), adapted Chinese characters by combining them to represent Vietnamese words. These modified vernacular characters could reflect both sound and meaning by using local pronunciations of Chinese characters. The resulting system enabled scholars to write in the vernacular and to render Vietnamese names in written form. However, this system suffered from a complexity and lack of standardization that made learning it extremely difficult.[15]

Consequently, when the first European missionaries arrived, they found a complicated textual landscape that did not readily lend itself to the transmission of their religious texts. They first used both the Chinese and *nôm* scripts for creating and distributing texts, often reprinting books that had already been created for the Jesuit mission in China, such as Matteo Ricci's Chinese-language catechism.[16] Even as they used the existing writing systems, these missionaries were exploring ways to develop an entirely new script to serve their project. They understood that creating basic literacy in an alphabetic script would be far simpler than doing so using one of the prevailing ideographic writing systems, classical Chinese or the Vietnamese vernacular modification thereof. Furthermore, by employing a completely different form of writing, the missionaries could free themselves and their converts from the cultural associations bound up in the older script systems. Thus the newly developed romanized script would itself emerge as a kind of script of the faith. Missionaries began to experiment with ways to represent spoken Vietnamese using their Roman alphabet, employing diacritical marks to represent the six tones that are an integral part of spoken Vietnamese. The transliteration system that gradually evolved appropriated the label *quốc ngữ* (lit. "national language") earlier used to refer to the *nôm* script, and its written elements and conventions of sound reproduction came almost entirely from Portuguese with a few minor references to Italian.[17] The key innovators in developing the system and those who laid its foundations were the early Portuguese missionaries Francisco de Pina, Antonio Barbosa, and Gaspar do Amaral.[18] While the system was not his invention, Alexandre de Rhodes is usually credited with having subsequently done the most to standardize this script, chiefly through his production and publication of a large-scale Annamese-Portuguese-Latin dictionary. This was drafted as a pedagogical tool that would allow priests on the ground, many of them Portuguese, to carry out careful translations of religious tracts, or to assist

Vietnamese in producing their own texts, including confessions of faith or letters to the church hierarchy.[19] The creation of the romanized *quốc ngữ* script was an important development, but the new writing system did not immediately supplant the existing *nôm* script, which had been used in the early years of the Catholic mission. Indeed, as Jacques points out, extant Christian texts from the seventeenth century comprise more than four thousand pages of *nôm* versus only seven hundred or so in the romanized script.[20]

By the time Bỉnh was writing his journals and religious texts at the dawn of the nineteenth century, however, *quốc ngữ* had become more commonly used by literate Vietnamese Catholics. The fact that Bỉnh wrote so extensively in this script, particularly compared to his insignificant output in *nôm*, suggests that by this time, within his community at least, *quốc ngữ* had become the de facto preferred script.[21] Since Bỉnh's aim was to make his writing accessible to the community and to teach its members about a range of issues, it would be logical that he would write in the script most useful to them. The decision to write in *quốc ngữ* was likely also influenced by several other factors. Living in a country that used the romanized script, and indeed, the one from which the Vietnamese romanization itself was derived, meant that Bỉnh was surrounded by it and that all of his sources were written in the Roman alphabet. Using *quốc ngữ* would also have facilitated his transmission of information about aspects of Portuguese and Catholic life in Europe, as terms and names could much more easily be transliterated when necessary, with reference to his copy of de Rhodes's *Dictionarium* as needed. Finally, the script offered a flexibility, adaptability, and, especially, a degree of standardization that *nôm* could not match. While Bỉnh was not always able to come up with a Vietnamese term for the things he was seeing or hearing about—hospitals, the postal system, a national lottery—he was able to use *quốc ngữ* to describe them in ways that explained the concepts with a fair degree of precision. That these materials are largely readable by a modern audience is testament to the relatively advanced level to which the script had already developed by the early nineteenth century.[22]

Bỉnh wrote in *quốc ngữ* to make his works both legible and intelligible to his audience, but he took additional steps to make his notebooks more accessible to his readers. These included organizing them into discrete chapters, creating tables of contents, and compiling extensive and sometimes multiple topical or alphabetical indexes. Bỉnh's notebooks are almost all divided into chapters, each of which is given both a number and a (usually descriptive) title. This facilitated the creation of tables of contents, found at either the beginning or the end of each volume, listing chapter numbers, titles, and starting pages. In many of his notebooks he also included indexes, which at times were crucial for locating particular information. This was nowhere more true than in his notebook of miscellany, *Sách sổ sang chép các việc*, which lacked chapters, consisting instead of a haphazard mixture of running narrative, lists of expenditures, random notes, and various records. Finding particular bits of information in it would have been difficult without a more elaborated finding mechanism, so Bỉnh created a detailed index. As he commented in its preface: "[This book] does not have discrete chapters like other books, and for this reason I have provided three separate indexes [mục lục], in order to make it easy to find [things], and if anyone wishes to see a particular matter, then he can look for it in the index concerning that topic." Three indexes then follow, with each simply arranged in ascending page order, more like a table of contents. The first is an index Bỉnh labels "Speaking of Some Things Regarding the Jesuit Order." The second is an index titled "Speaking about Matters Concerning Father Bỉnh and His Friends," and the third bears the catchall heading "Speaking of All Other Matters."[23] Thus an interested reader can choose between these three paths for exploring the book's content. While indexes were particularly important for readers of *Sách sổ*, Bỉnh incorporated them in many of his notebooks, and his lists of keywords and concepts illustrate the kinds of information he regarded as important or interesting. Most of Bỉnh's volumes had a single index, but some, like the *Sách sổ*, had several, and his *Truyện Ông Thánh Phanchicô Xaviêr* (Tales of Saint Francis Xavier) featured no less than five.

The compelling need for indexes was partly to compensate for the somewhat haphazard manner in which Bỉnh compiled his notebooks, an approach he defended in the introduction to his *Sách gương truyện*, where he wrote: "As for all of the priests, if any of them wish to copy out any particular tale from a book, then they may do as they like, or if they wish to discard any tale they may do as they please, and they are not forced to copy any of these, because in preaching everyone has his own ideas, and no one has the same idea as others."[24] While some of the tales in his collections were organized chronologically, most featured a substantial degree of randomness, something that ties these volumes to the spontaneity of the oral tradition. In reading through his notebooks, one is struck by a sense of Bỉnh's having created a container, labeled, for example, "Tales of Saint Francis," which served as a repository for material that he happened across in his research. Sometimes chapters are clearly linked, but more often Bỉnh was simply jumping from one story to another, periodically interrupting himself in asides to his readers, such as instructions about where in his books to find related material. This suggests that one might read any given volume silently or aloud by dipping into it at random. In any case, it was precisely the spontaneous and somewhat haphazard way in which Bỉnh assembled his collections of tales that necessitated his elaborate indexing schemes. The indexes represented a kind of post hoc imposition of order upon what had been created as distinctly free-form volumes.

New Geographies of Time

Another transformative element in Bỉnh's writings is their reflection of changing Vietnamese Catholic conceptions of temporality. Just as European colonialism and semicolonialism would later introduce to Asia transformed ideas about time in the form of Western calendars, mechanical clocks, timetables, and opening hours for stores and offices, earlier Catholic missionaries had already introduced their converts to new ways of thinking about the passage of time, in both its cyclical and its linear manifestations.[25] This was another element of their lives that was geographically shaped, but it was a geography of time rather than space.[26] The new conceptions of time had profound implications for Vietnamese Catholics, changing how they thought about the rhythms of their lives. Like the new spatial geographies introduced by Catholicism in the form of congregations, parishes, and vicariates imposed upon existing geopolitical divisions of space, these new temporal structures were overlaid upon prevailing notions of time and constituted an important reminder of the socially and culturally constructed nature of time itself.[27] Consequently, Vietnamese Christians found themselves engaging simultaneously with both new and traditional temporal frames of reference. Although Bình's writings offer only glimpses into these transformed geographies of time, they are suggestive of the changes being experienced by the larger Catholic population.

The new temporalities introduced by European missionaries were manifest in a number of different ways. Perhaps the most immediately relevant for Vietnamese converts were notions of time centered on the rhythms of the year and the days marked out for commemorating Catholic saints. Historically, the Vietnamese state had carefully calculated and then distributed annual calendars to mark the shifting dates of ritual events, from the New Year's Festival to the commemoration of village deities to the time for cleaning one's ancestral gravesites.[28] This distribution of calendars was a public service, but even more importantly it was an assertion of state authority and of its control over the rhythms of the people's lives. The Catholic Church similarly issued new calendars every year to mark the dates on which saints were celebrated and to indicate shifting events on the liturgical calendar such as Lent, Holy Week, and Easter. Vietnamese Catholics found themselves simultaneously inhabiting new spatial and temporal worlds that coexisted with those imposed by the secular authorities. Furthermore, they found themselves caught within contending calendric visions of the competing Catholic mission organizations. The Jesuits and the MEP would each issue their own calendars, highlighting different saints, and the distribution of these calendars consequently became a point of contention and rivalry. Indeed, the religious organizations used these liturgical calendars as a way to stake claim to adherents.[29]

The calendars were calculated using the European solar-based method for determining the length of the year and its component months. This stood in contrast to the Vietnamese approach, a complicated luni-solar system that relied primarily on the phases of the moon but included periodic adjustments (using intercalary, or leap, months) to keep the calendar substantially in phase with the seasons. While he was still in Tonkin, Bình would have participated in the complex overlay of these two time-measuring systems, each of which had a particular contextual relevance for him, as for other Vietnamese Catholics. Once he arrived in Lisbon, however, Bỉnh used the European solar calendar exclusively, briefly summarizing its functioning in one of his notebooks:

> These days in the West, people follow the solar calendar, so that each year has twelve months, and they never have an intercalary month, because there are seven months that have thirty-one days, and four that have thirty days, and one that has twenty-eight days, and from one year to the next it is always like this. As for Lent, Advent, and the feast days, these change, but the celebration of Christmas is always on the twenty-fifth of December, and the Naming Day is always the first day of January, and the Virgin Mary's birthday is always on the eighth of September.[30]

While he had made the adjustment upon his arrival to Lisbon, where the dating of both spiritual and secular events would be dictated by the local solar calendar, Bỉnh continued to occupy a kind of hybrid and in-between temporal space. This is revealed in his writings, which routinely mix Western solar and Vietnamese lunar dates, particularly in discussions of his travels and then projects in Lisbon. Although Bỉnh uses the lunar calendar primarily when discussing events during his time in Tonkin and then switches to the solar calendar once his narrative reaches Lisbon, he is not consistent. Making sense of his dating is further complicated by the fact that the Vietnamese rendering of Western months, like that for lunar months, simply uses the convention of numbering the months sequentially from one to twelve (e.g., June is simply "the sixth month"). Consequently, it is impossible to determine from Bỉnh's notebooks whether a reference to "the fourth day of the sixth month" is to the lunar or the solar calendar. In any case, Bỉnh's shifting between the two calendar systems suggests the ways in which rhythms of time were changing for him, as for other Vietnamese Catholics. Moreover, the fact that he and other Vietnamese Catholics had to live with these two calendar systems simultaneously hints at the complex notions of time with which they engaged.

New concepts of time were found not only in the cyclical rhythms of the liturgical year, or the passage of time marked by the movement of celestial bodies, but also in linear chronologies that dated events in relation to the unfolding of history on a larger scale. Bỉnh's writings contain chronologies that emphasize the long-term unidirectional passage of time, spanning history from the creation of the earth to the events in which he himself participated in the early nineteenth century. Unlike the changing rhythms reflected in the shift from luni-solar to solar calendars, the changes in conceptualizing linear time are about both the particular events being recorded and the temporal framework being used to measure the flow of this time. These changes are strikingly illustrated in the chronological timetables that Bỉnh inserted into the prefatory material to four of his notebooks: his copy of de Rhodes's *Cathechismus* and his own *Truyện Anam, Đàng Ngoài; Truyện Ông*

Mendes Pinto; and *Sách gương truyện*. Bỉnh almost certainly adapted the idea of chronologies from books that he encountered in his library research, as it was not a feature of earlier Vietnamese books. In these chronologies we encounter elements of the changing temporal geographies inhabited by Bỉnh and other Vietnamese Catholics. Bỉnh combines and intermingles elements of Vietnamese history, biblical events, and Catholic missionary milestones in a common time frame. This amalgamation of temporalities suggests the new ways in which Bỉnh, and at least some other Vietnamese Catholics, conceptualized not only the new world in which they were living but the ways in which historical geographies were linked.

The first volume into which Bỉnh inserted a chronology was his handwritten copy of Alexandre de Rhodes's *Cathechismus,* produced in 1797. Like the chronologies that follow it, this one is not chronological. Rather, it consists of a list of events presented seemingly spontaneously, without an effort to arrange them in their historical order, thus prefiguring the often haphazard form of Bỉnh's later histories. A later chronology, included in the first volume of Bỉnh's 1815 collection of exemplary tales (*Sách gương truyện*), is nearly identical, if slightly more comprehensive, making it a good illustration of how Bỉnh crafted his timetables. This chronology, like all the rest, is presented on a single page with events appearing in the left-hand column and the corresponding years since the occurrence of the event on the right.

From the birth of Jesus	1802
From the creation of the earth	5805
From the Great Flood of Noah	4150
From the year that Saint Francis Xavier went to Asia	262
From the year that Ignatius established the Jesuits	262
From the year that Alexandre [de Rhodes] arrived in Annam	200
From the year that Bishop Xiem left the country of Annam	232
From the year that two missionaries and nine Jesuits died for the faith	80
From the year that four missionaries and two *thay gia* died for the faith	66
From the year that the Blessed Pope Clemente XIV disbanded the Jesuits	29
From the year that Đinh Thiên Hoàng governed the country of Annam	1002
From the year that the country of Annam escaped from the unfortunate temples of Liễu Thang	236
From the year that Thái Đức and Quang Trung emerged to govern the country of Annam	24
From the year that Brothers Thiều and Cuyên returned from Rome	23
From the establishment of the city of Rome	2558
From the year that King Constantine offered his respects to Pope Sylvester	2485
From the year that I came to the country of Portugal	20
From the year that King Henry governed the country of Portugal	664

From the year that King Nanoc, who governed the country of	
Portugal, opened India	320
And the same ruler opened the New World [gioi moi]	308
From the year when Cu Franco and Diogo introduced the faith in	
the era of the Founding Lord	194[31]

This timetable, tied to the European Gregorian calendar, begins with the number of years since the birth of Jesus, then jumps back to "the creation of the earth," which is precisely noted as having occurred 5,805 years previously.[32] This is followed by the "Great Flood of Noah," at 4,150 years. Bỉnh then shifts again from this biblical time frame to one defined by Catholic missionaries, giving dates for Francis Xavier's travel to Asia, Ignatius Loyola's founding of the Jesuit order, and Alexandre de Rhodes's arrival in Annam. There follows a miscellany of other religious events—80 years since several people were martyred in Annam, 29 years since the disbanding of the Jesuits, 23 years since Thiều and Cuyến returned from Rome. But the list also includes political events: 1,002 years since the first Vietnamese emperor, Đinh Thiên Hoàng; 24 years since the two Tây Sơn emperors, Quang Trung and Thái Đức, came to power; 2,558 years since the founding of Rome; 308 years since a Portuguese ruler opened up the "New World." Perhaps most tellingly, it includes an entry for Bỉnh himself, quietly slipped into this mishmash of events, reminding the reader that it has been twenty years since he arrived in the country of Portugal.

This timetable, for all its chaos, illuminates some significant dimensions both of new Vietnamese Catholic temporalities and of Bỉnh's particular view of global structures of time. Unsurprisingly, the list of events privileges the birth of Jesus not merely for its religious significance but also as the benchmark for European calendric systems. This reflects the fact that Catholicism, a profoundly historical religious tradition, simultaneously introduced new theological and temporal frameworks for Vietnamese Catholics. But after acknowledging this foundational event and the dating structure it suggests, Bỉnh begins to destabilize it by offering what seem to represent alternative ways of recording time. The rest of the dating benchmarks are a hodgepodge of religious, political, and secular events, mixing occurrences in the biblical world, in "Annam," and in Portugal. Clearly some of these events have great significance for Bỉnh's life: the founding and then the dissolution of the Jesuit order; the coming to power of the Tây Sơn rulers, under whom he lived for roughly a decade; and of course his own arrival in Portugal in 1796. However, the rest is an odd assemblage of religious and secular happenings.

In this dating schema Bỉnh has constructed a hybrid temporality, one incorporating elements of multiple historical trajectories and interlacing historical events in Europe, in the Catholic tradition, and in Vietnamese history. Indeed, it seems clear that he viewed himself in a self-conscious fashion as belonging to each of these

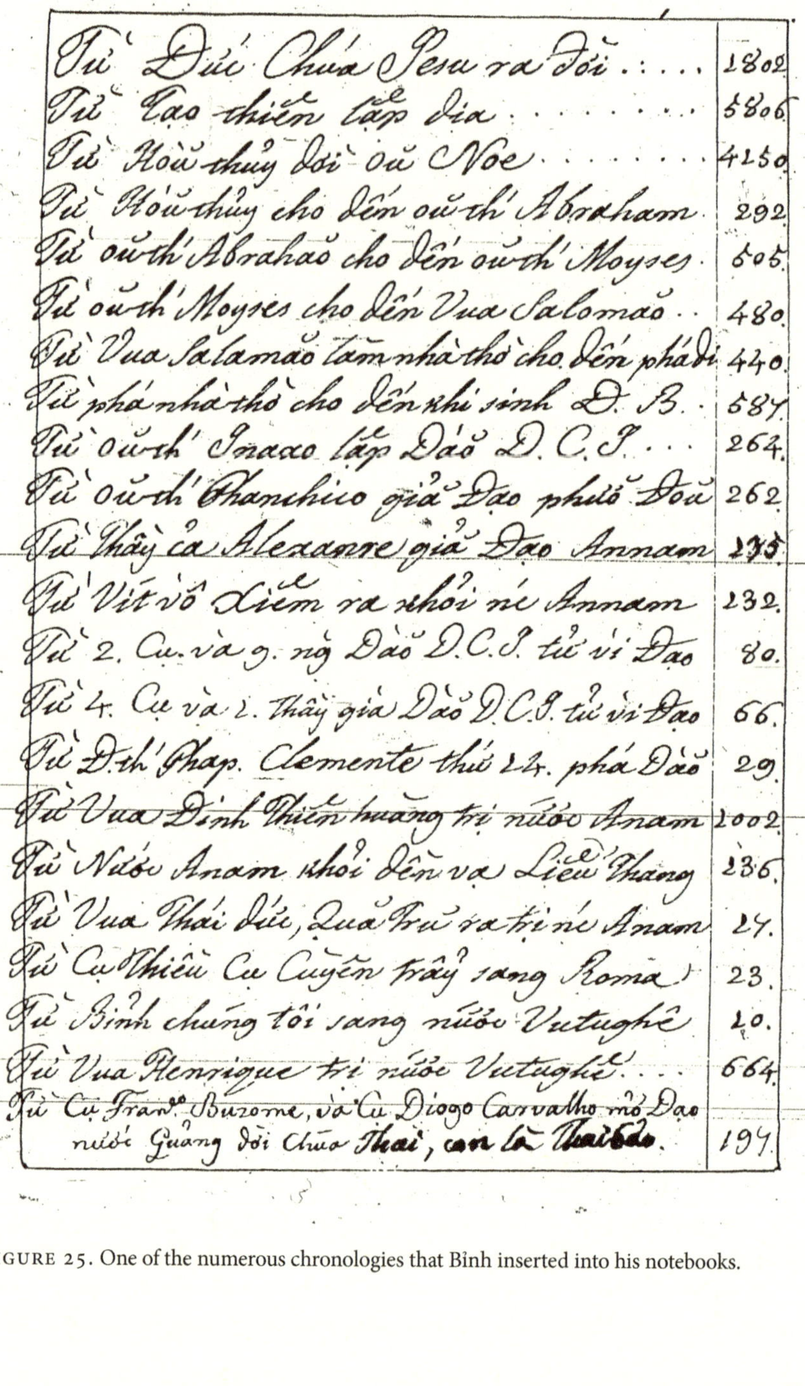

Từ Đức Chúa Jesu ra đời............	1802
Từ Tạo thiên lập địa...............	5806
Từ Hồu thủy đời ou Noe...........	4250
Từ Hồu thủy cho đến ou th' Abraham.	292
Từ ou th' Abrahao cho đến ou th' Moyses.	505
Từ ou th' Moyses cho đến Vua Salomão..	480
Từ Vua Salomão làm nhà thờ cho đến phá đi	440
Từ phá nhà thờ cho đến khi sinh Đ. B.	587
Từ ou th' Inacio lập Đạo D.C.J...	264
Từ ou th' Chanhico giả Đạo phuỉo Đou	262
Từ Thầy cả Alexandre giả Đạo Annam	175
Từ Vit vỏ Liêu ra khỏi nể Annam	132
Từ 2. Cu và 9. ng Đạo D.C.J. tử vì Đạo	80
Từ 4. Cu và 2. Thầy già Đạo D.C.J. tử vì Đạo	66
Từ Đ.th' Phap. Clemente thứ 24. phá Đạo	29
Từ Vua Đinh Thiên hoàng trị nước Annam	1002
Từ Nước Annam khởi đến vua Liêu Thăng	236
Từ Vua Thái đức, Qua Tru ra tri nể Annam	27
Từ Cu Thiều Cu Cuyển trảy sang Roma	23
Từ Binh chúng tôi sang nước Vutughé	20
Từ Vua Henrique trị nước Vutughé....	664
Từ Cu Fran.co Buzome, và Cu Diogo Carvalho mở Đạo nước Quảng đời Chúa Thai, con là Thai Bảo.	197

FIGURE 25. One of the numerous chronologies that Bình inserted into his notebooks.

historical flows, heir to all of these events, whether the reign of Đinh Thiên Hoàng, the creation of the earth, the birth of Jesus, or the establishment of the Jesuits. This list suggests a combination of knowledge and temporal structures learned in and brought from Tonkin and those gathered in the libraries of Lisbon. Bỉnh's innovation was to bring these elements together and in doing so to interlink these two worlds and worldviews for Vietnamese Catholics. The important thing here is that the timetable suggests, not a complete disruption of existing Vietnamese understandings of the flow of time, but new possibilities that placed Vietnamese and their history on a larger global stage. Bỉnh's altered worldview reflected in this chronological table did not entirely displace one frame of reference for another. Bỉnh had not abandoned Vietnamese historical touchstones in order to take up Christian/European ones.

Two years later, however, we see a rather different representation of the timetables of history. In his 1817 volume excerpting portions of *The Travels of Mendes Pinto*, Bỉnh sets forth the following table:

From the birth of Jesus to the present	1817
From the creation of the world	5822
From the Great Flood at the time of Noah	4166
From the time that Thang Cam erected the Tower of Babel	4256
From the time that the Lord gave Moses the Ten Commandments	3308
From the time that Saint Peter governed the blessed church to the time of Pope Pius VII, the 253 [sic] generation of popes[33]	
From the time that Pope Paul III gave the patent to Saint Ignatius to establish the Jesuit order	279
From the time that Saint Francis Xavier traveled to the East to spread the Gospel	278
From the time that Father Alexandre and Father Phero Marchesio traveled to spread the Way in Annam	190
From Father Francisco Busomi and Father Diogo's spreading the faith in Quang [Nam] in the time of the Founding Lord	202

Here we find a much more focused list, one that has removed all secular events and, even more importantly, has dropped references to Vietnamese history that do not have any bearing on Catholicism. Moreover, this time the list does not stand in isolation but immediately leads in seamless fashion to a dense summary of martyrdoms over the early eighteenth century in Vietnam.[34] Like the earlier list it links Bỉnh's homeland with the Europe that was the source of its new religion, but it concentrates on biblical and missiological events. It is not clear that this timetable represented a new direction for Bỉnh, for each of these timetables was an experiment with dates and events. This was just a different way of presenting information that was relevant to him at the moment of its creation.

What is abundantly clear in all of Bỉnh's chronologies is the way in which they illustrate the new temporal geographies that had come to matter for Vietnamese Catholics. Not only had Catholicism brought with it new ways of understanding Vietnamese genealogies, but it had linked these to new conceptions of space and time as well. These new conceptions displaced Sinic-influenced origin tales about the Vietnamese people stemming from the quasi-mythological sagely emperors of the Chinese past. Now the key chronological touchstones could be the birth of Jesus, and before that the founding of the world, the Flood, or the receiving of the Ten Commandments. These were all available to Vietnamese Christians as new ways of thinking about their origins and as the historical facts with the greatest resonance for their lives. For some, like Bỉnh, the history of the church and its missionary work also became a crucial part of this temporal framework, for it had led to the creation of the Jesuits, and in turn to the spread of the Christian message to the Vietnamese realms. While in a spiritual sense the Vietnamese might understand themselves to be part of the lineage that could be traced back to Abraham and the Israelite peoples, in a religious-political sense they were part of a different kind of lineage, one that for Bỉnh had been transmitted to his homeland by the Jesuits.

NEW GENEALOGIES AND FRAMES OF REFERENCE

Bỉnh's chronologies reveal the ways in which Vietnamese Catholics considered themselves a part of new genealogies, something that becomes even more evident in the body of his written tales, journals, and correspondence, where these new genealogies are a frequent touchstone. At numerous levels, Roman Catholicism represented a new and alternative worldview for the Vietnamese people. Among the most obvious manifestations of this shift was the way in which the stories of the Bible became a central part of Vietnamese Catholic identity. Bỉnh's community had come to view itself as descending from a genealogy laid out in the Old Testament. In this respect—foreshadowing the strained colonial articulation "nos ancêtres les Gaulois"—Vietnamese Catholics could speak of an Old Testament ancestry that ran through the lineage of Adam through Abraham and David. Indeed, Bỉnh makes this explicit in his *Sách sổ sang chép các việc*, where he writes: "Our first and foremost ancestor is Adam" (Trước hết tổ tông ta là ông Adam).[35] He follows this with a lengthy discussion of the lineage that issued from Adam, meticulously recording how long each of Adam's descendants lived (their ages calculated in centuries), beginning with Adam's own 930-year life span.

In Bỉnh's view, the Vietnamese integration into this biblical lineage was not merely theological but also biological and, consequently, genealogical. Bỉnh came to regard the Vietnamese people themselves as descended from the survivors of the Great Flood represented in the Old Testament as having destroyed all life on earth, save that which was preserved in the ark. Bỉnh's discussion of this event emerges in a text ostensibly recounting the voyages of Mendes Pinto, *The Travels of Mendes Pinto*, a book he must have encountered in one of the Lisbon libraries. Bình's notebook with the title *Tales of the Travels of Fernando Mendes Pinto* offers only a fragmentary translation of Pinto's *Travels*.[36] The majority of the volume deals with Bình's conceptions of global geographies, with a strong focus on Asia, including China, Japan, and the Vietnamese territories. He is particularly intrigued by the complex linguistic landscape of "Dai Minh": he writes that it has fifteen regions under the authority of the Chinese emperor and that each has its own language. To explain this, he looks to the Old Testament accounts in the book of Genesis that discuss the repopulation of the devastated earth after the Flood, but he also links it to the story of the Tower of Babel. As the biblical account goes, the tower was designed to reach the sky and serve as a monument to the greatness of its builders as they constructed the city of Babylon. Seeing this, and the dangerous hubris that drove their effort, God caused the people to begin to speak different and mutually incomprehensible languages. This foiled their attempts to work together, and as a result they could not complete the tower, and were instead scattered to populate the various corners of the earth.[37]

Drawing on this story, Bình writes that this dispersal of peoples now speaking different tongues accounted for China's regional linguistic diversity. Just as significantly, he writes that "one of these people was our ancestor who traveled over to the land of Annam." Following closely on the account in Genesis, he adds, "And for this reason there are many countries in the realms under heaven, and each country has a single [different] spoken language."[38] The idea that Vietnamese Catholics are not merely spiritual but also literally biological heirs to this biblical history is significant. It represents a radical shift in their worldview that displaced one long-standing genealogical and ideological heritage for another. In this altered context the stories of their biblical ancestors came to matter and became historical touchstones. This shifting worldview with its new genealogies brought with it new temporal geographies as well. Bình and other educated Catholics began to draw on the Bible, particularly the Old Testament and sometimes various apocryphal books, for precedents to articulate their own experiences. Where once Vietnamese had invoked tales of Confucian sages and rulers, Vietnamese Catholics now represented themselves and their traditions by looking to their new spiritual roots. This becomes clear in the course of Bình's numerous writings, and especially the tales, in which he draws on people, episodes, and historical dynamics in biblical events to explain his own experiences to his audience. As an ordained priest with a substantial degree of education, and now access to the libraries of Lisbon, Bình had significant knowledge of the Bible and the Apocrypha, suggesting that he was hardly representative of the typical Tonkinese Catholic. Yet because he wrote not to entertain himself but to reach a wider audience, it is likely that his readers would be expected to understand the biblical stories Bình was using. There is at least fragmentary evidence of such wider knowledge, as when Bỉnh reported that people in Tonkin were referring to the Dominican bishop Alonso as King Herod and to one of his associates as Pontius Pilate—or when Christians in the area of the Western Tonkin Vicariate wrote to the Paris Mission Society headquarters, comparing the Tây Sơn troops' attacks on Tonkin to the attacks launched by Romans against Judea, suggesting their idea of the Tonkinese collectively as the Israelites.[39]

Bỉnh drew on numerous Old Testament figures and episodes to illustrate his tales and to drive home his message, none more frequently than Moses and the stories surrounding him, as we saw in chapter 6. Bỉnh, for instance, compared each of the Jesuit founders, Saint Francis Xavier and Saint Ignatius Loyola, to Moses, writing in the preface to his *Tales of Annam* that they were men of great strength, for they had come to Annam carrying with them the two stone tablets of the Ten Commandments that "we might know the Sacred Law of the Lord of Heaven and preserve it." Their accomplishment in transmitting the faith to Asia was, he noted, "just like when the blessed Moses accepted the task of taking the two stone tablets of the Ten Commandments of the Way of the Lord of Heaven from the top of Mount Sinai and bringing them down to the people."[40]

More commonly, however, Bỉnh used Moses and the Israelites to refer to himself and the long-suffering Padroado community. Both in his tales and in his earlier letters home, Bỉnh repeatedly represented the members of his community as the Israelites in their Egyptian exile, while depicting himself as Moses, their leader and eventual savior. Portraying himself as his community's deliverer clearly resonated with its members, who also understood their own depiction as the struggling Israelites. They were living in the wilderness of excommunication and were suffering (as they understood it) the oppression of the clerical authorities. Bỉnh represented their only hope of rescue. As was described in chapter 6, Bỉnh expressed the idea of himself as Moses in reference to two distinct biblical episodes. The first drew upon the story of Moses's visit to the court of the pharaoh, where, as the representative of his people, he appealed to that ruler on their behalf—and, as Bỉnh acknowledged, enjoyed the benefits of residence in the ruler's palace and its many comforts. Bỉnh too, clearly felt more than a little guilty at the relative luxury he enjoyed—both spiritual and material—in Lisbon, even as the members of his community suffered in both of these respects. When he found himself under attack from the apostolic vicars, Bỉnh fought back in his *Sách sổ*, where he observed that "no one criticized Moses, when in the prophecies it said: Moses lived in the palace of the pharaoh for forty years but left it when he realized that the ruler was creating hardships for the Judean people, for he did not wish to be happy while his people were crying in despair, and so he entered the forest and spent those forty years tending sheep for his father-in-law, and then he brought his people back to the land of their ancestors, and this was because he had spent forty years in the forests."[41]

The second story, designed to comment on his absence from the community, was that of Moses ascending Mount Sinai to receive the Ten Commandments from God. As Moses's time on the mountain stretched on and the Israelites became increasingly uncertain of his return, they began to explore other spiritual options and to drift from their commitment to their God. Bỉnh used this tale to describe several historical episodes. First, he had used it to talk about the events surrounding the 1682 Jesuit recall to Rome, during which their Tonkinese followers had been left surrounded by the temptations of other religious orders and congregations. Many, he noted, had given up on the Jesuits and had turned to worshipping "the golden calf"—becoming adherents of the other orders.[42] But the more relevant historical analogue for Bỉnh was his own situation, in which he was the absent Moses, while the members of the Padroado community were the exiled Israelites. Like Moses before him, Bỉnh was away from his community for an extended period and with no timetable for his return. Moreover, the Padroado Catholics he had left behind were under enormous pressure from the apostolic vicars to give up their loyalty to their traditions and to accept the authority of the sanctioned religious leaders. Bỉnh was acutely aware of these pressures, and in representing himself as the absent Moses he was encouraging his people not to give in to these pressures and to remain steadfast in their spiritual affiliations. He explicitly invoked this analogy in an 1800 letter to the community, in which he wrote of his delay in returning to Annam, indicating he understood that they might begin to abandon hope just like the Israelites when faced with Moses's delay in returning from Mount Sinai.[43]

Elsewhere in his account of his adventures, Bỉnh shifted his frame of reference, representing *himself* as akin to the Israeli people in terms of the dangers that they had faced. He did so when he compared the Israelites facing the danger of an impending attack by the pharaoh (and fleeing with Moses into the Sinai desert) to the time when he had been in Macao and word had reached him that the bishop was going to summon him to the episcopal residence and demand that he return to Annam. Just as the Israelites were warned and then protected by God in their flight from the pharaoh, so too, Bỉnh, argued, God had rescued him from the impending danger represented by the Macanese bishop by making the bishop's intentions known to him.[44]

In addition to repeated references to the stories of Moses, Bỉnh found considerable value in stories of King David. To discuss the jealousy felt by the European latecomers to the Vietnamese mission field toward the Jesuits and their large flock, Bỉnh cited the envy of King Saul toward the young David. In the biblical story, Saul was jealous of David's prowess on the battlefield in defeating the giant Goliath and responded by trying to kill David.[45] Elsewhere, in discussing the relationship between his two companions in the project to secure a bishop, Brothers Trung and Nhân, Bỉnh described their close relationship as being like that between David and Jonathan, men who began as enemies but then became like brothers.[46] In yet another story of David, Bỉnh spoke of one of the missionaries in Tonkin feigning illness in order to avoid a meeting with the Dominican apostolic vicar and noted that this was very much like King David feigning madness so that King Achis would not kill him.[47] In short, whether speaking of jealousy, love, or deceit, Bỉnh used stories of David to connect with his readers.

Bỉnh also found other biblical figures useful for discussing the challenges that he and his community faced. As his time in Portugal dragged on, Bỉnh invoked the long-suffering Job, whose faith was tested by God.[48] Although Bỉnh was expressing his frustration at his drawn-out hardships, he also took hope from these biblical precedents, for while Job was forced to suffer extended hardships, in the end he was rescued by God and his sufferings were repaid.[49] Indeed, given the significant sufferings experienced by Vietnamese Christians through generations of persecution, martyrdom, and other challenges to the exercise of their faith, it is unsurprising that Bỉnh would regularly invoke the story of Job. Bỉnh also used it in his historics of Vietnamese Catholicism to comment on the wide range of challenges faced by Christians of Đàng Trong in the early years of the mission, representing them as a kind of collective Job.[50] Later, in a letter to the members of the waiting Padroado community, he discussed their hardships by referring to the tales of Job to indicate that he understood their sufferings but also to remind them that Job endured and by maintaining his faith in God was eventually rescued.[51] Elsewhere, in a letter of 1798, Bỉnh found another biblical analogue for suffering in the story of Tobias, contained in one of the apocryphal gospels. Now, it was the suffering but enduring Tobias who in his strong faith served as the exemplar Bỉnh hoped to emulate. At the same time, Bỉnh expressed the hope that he and his delegation, like Tobias, who was protected and eventually cured of his blindness by the Archangel Raphael, would be protected by God throughout their struggles.[52]

Bỉnh also invoked the Bible's villains as a way to criticize his enemies, both directly and indirectly. In an 1804 letter, Bỉnh compared Bishop Galdino to Judas, the man who betrayed Jesus to the Romans: "In the year 1803 we sent a bishop to Macao by the name of Manuel to bring to all of you a dictionary and eighteen letters, because he had already become our bishop. But then, once he reached Macao, he changed his heart like the traitor Judas, who received thirty pieces of silver and sold his Master, and [Galdino] no longer thought about his king who had nurtured him from the time that he was young until he became grown up and then made him a bishop."[53] It was a damning critique of a man who had gone from their savior to their destroyer. But Bỉnh also targeted others, comparing them to biblical villains that his readers might understand. Thus he compared Pope Clement XIV to Pontius Pilate, the Roman official who had condemned Jesus to death. Just like Pilate, Bỉnh argued, the pope had known that the Jesuits were innocent of the malicious charges that had been raised against them, but he had acted anyway out of cowardice.[54] Elsewhere, Bỉnh invoked other biblical villains in a more general sense. Thus he compared the struggles and persecution of the Christians in Đàng Trong to King Herod's killing of firstborn children to eliminate the threat posed by Jesus's birth. He also mentioned the Egyptian pharaohs who persecuted the Israelites, though this was a shifting reference—to the bishop in Macao, to the MEP and Dominican clerics in Tonkin for their persecution of the Padroado Christians, and even to the Portuguese ruler, at whose court Bình, as Moses, was living in luxury, while his compatriots suffered in their land of exile.

Bình's frequent references to what he regarded as biblical precedents, whether heroes or antiheroes, suffering believers or evil betrayers, suggest the degree to which the historical and conceptual framework of Vietnamese Christians had been transformed. His use of biblical antecedents as a way to speak about the present suggests that a completely new vocabulary had come into being for Vietnamese Catholics. This was a language that in the context of their homeland was unique to them—it marked them off as distinct from fellow villagers who had not been introduced to this new world and its historical references. Moreover, the references to figures from the Bible were not merely ways to communicate in a new idiom; they also represented links to a new set of spiritual ancestors. As a profoundly historical religion, one rooted in a core text that is as much historical as it is revelatory, Christianity necessarily brings with it its own temporal geographies. These take the form of particular historical figures populating a distinctive landscape, and while elements of this past reveal universal characteristics (evil rulers, oppressed peasants, hardships, family life, etc.), many are rooted in a particular place and time. Moses was a specific individual in a very specific set of circumstances, and no one would mistake him for an ancient Confucian minister in a generically "Chinese" setting. Just as importantly, by invoking the people, stories, and places of the Bible, Bình and other Vietnamese Catholics were laying claim to this past and suggesting that the events and experiences of these Old Testament figures were now appropriate for reflecting their own experiences.

BÌNH'S "TRUYỆN" AND THE VIETNAMESE AND CATHOLIC TRADITIONS OF TALES

These new geographies—temporal, spatial, and genealogical—are most prominently featured in Bình's post-1815 writings, which he labeled "tales" (*truyện*). This is a usefully elastic term Bình extended to cover a range of subjects that he writes about in a number of different forms. His "tales" are firmly situated within the longer trajectory of the *truyện* genre, one of the oldest recognized Vietnamese literary forms in prose. The earliest example of this genre is likely the *Báo cực truyện* (Tales of the sublime), a devotional text dedicated to the worship of a variety of spirits and composed during the first independent Vietnamese dynasty, the

Lý (1009–1225).⁵⁵ Subsequent works in this genre include the *Việt điện u linh tập* [越甸幽靈集] (Compilation [or compiled tales] of the potent spirits of the Việt realm), which dates to the fourteenth century, and the somewhat later (possibly fifteenth-century) *Lĩnh Nam chích quái* [嶺南摭怪] (Strange tales from the dusts of Linh Nam).⁵⁶ This genre of "strange" tales, which was inspired by a Chinese literary tradition, continued to develop among the Vietnamese, perhaps reaching its apogee with Nguyễn Dữ's early sixteenth-century *Truyện kỳ mạn lục* [傳奇漫錄] (Collection of strange tales; lit. "uninhibited records of strange tales"). This collection of tales became widely popularized, particularly in its subsequent vernacular rendering.⁵⁷

While Bỉnh's books shared the label of *truyện* with these earlier texts, in some respects an even more significant literary predecessor would have been Vietnamese emulations of the Chinese "transmission of the lamp" genre (傳燈錄), a literary form used by Buddhist monks to record the genealogies of their monastic communities in the form of biographies of eminent monks within their lineage. There are numerous exemplars in the Chinese tradition but only one noteworthy Vietnamese title, the *Thiền uyển tập anh* (禪苑集英, Collection of outstanding figures of the Zen garden), printed in woodblock form in the year 1337.⁵⁸ Like the tales of Catholic saints, this volume was designed to preserve the memories and examples of major spiritual figures within a particular religious tradition. While it is unlikely that Bỉnh would have been aware of this particular text, the existence of this genre, which probably continued in some form into the eighteenth century, provided a precedent for public appreciation of the later volumes of Catholic tales. These were not merely stories of the fantastical but also accounts of venerable religious forebears whose lives were considered worth remembering and emulating.

Against this backdrop of a rich tradition of tales, both oral and written, invented and historical, Catholicism was transmitted to the Vietnamese populations in the early seventeenth century. While tales served to entertain, they also played a didactic function, transmitting particular religious beliefs and values to largely preliterate populations. Thus it is not suprising that European Catholic missionaries would turn to tales as one element of their project to introduce Roman Catholicism in Vietnam. The first person fully to take advantage of the possibilities that didactic religious stories might represent in the Vietnamese mission field was the Italian Jesuit Geronimo Maiorica, active between 1630 and 1656. These were the early decades of the mission, and there was an intense need for written materials in the local language. Father Maiorica understood both the need for vernacular religious materials and the benefits that such texts might provide. He ultimately produced several dozen collections of edifying tales to popularize elements of the Catholic faith among the Vietnamese.⁵⁹ He was firmly committed to the idea that illustrating good behavior through stories was much more effective than simply instructing local Catholics. In a brief introduction to his collected tales, Maiorica quoted the Roman philosopher Seneca as distinguishing speaking from acting, noting that the former was the long, winding path, while the latter was the direct route. By analogy, Maiorica argued that one could teach by telling or by showing.[60] While this would seem to be a rather strained reading of Seneca's argument, Maiorica's intent was clearly to suggest that instruction by example was far more effective than instruction by injunction. By using the label *truyện* and by writing in the vernacular demotic script, Maiorica was able to reach a broader audience for whom both of these elements had a measure of familiarity. Furthermore, Maiorica's stories about the miracles of Catholic saints fit neatly into the existing *truyện kỳ* genre of "strange tales" that had gained such popularity in the sixteenth century.

By the time Bỉnh began to write his own collections of tales in the early nineteenth century, he was following in a dual tradition of tales: that of stories compiled and retold by earlier Vietnamese storytellers and that of the more recently introduced didactic Catholic tales popularized by Maiorica and others. It is clear that Bỉnh was particularly and profoundly influenced by Maiorica's writings and held their author in great esteem. In one of his rare writings substantially in Portuguese, a text labeled "Missionario de Tunkim," contained in an untitled volume of miscellanea—surveying the lives of the many European missionaries who had been active in Vietnam since the founding of the mission—Bỉnh devoted the very first entry to Maiorica; only after describing Maiorica's life and contributions did he do the same for Alexandre de Rhodes.[61] This reverses the conventional representation of de Rhodes as the de facto "father" of Vietnamese Catholic history, while also altering the chronology, since de Rhodes arrived in Annam before Maiorica.[62]

In producing his own volumes of *truyện*, Bỉnh was thus bridging two important literary traditions as well as several scriptural realms. His *truyện* represent a new phase in each of these lineages. Furthermore, Bỉnh's extensive writings in the *truyện* genre make him an important figure in the historical development of Vietnamese religious literature. Indeed, although clearly inspired by Maiorica's writings, Bỉnh's tales marked a significant departure from them. First, by using the alphabetic script rather than the character-based vernacular or even the older classical Chinese, Bỉnh was writing for a new generation of Vietnamese Catholics in a community whose scriptural traditions had evolved and changed in the century and a half after Maiorica. Bỉnh's second innovation was in his dramatic expansion of the genre's form. The majority of Maiorica's tales were brief, some no longer than a few hundred words. Maiorica did compose several tales that were contained in entire stand-alone volumes, but even these were not particularly long. Bỉnh extended the genre, at least in the Vietnamese context, to near-epic proportions. His four hagiographical volumes of "Tales," for example (of St. Francis Xavier, St. Ignatius Loyola, St. Francis Borgia, and St. Anne) average more than 650 pages.[63] Moreover, Bỉnh was aware of his work's innovation in this regard. He commented, in the introduction to his *Tales of Saint Francis de Borgia*, that the books of earlier chroniclers of the saint in Asian languages, including those of both Matteo Ricci and Geronimo Maiorica, "were compilations of the stories of many saints, [meaning that] they had to speak in summary form, while I have now written a whole book [about St. Francis de Borgia], and thus I am able to include many things."[64] Given the luxury of time, and access to vast libraries unavailable to Ricci and Maiorica writing in Asia, Bỉnh was able to produce lengthy, even comprehensive volumes about his spiritual subjects. Bỉnh's production of "tales" was a kind of forward migration of both this genre and the subjects popularized by Maiorica.

In many respects, Bỉnh's role in producing these tales—whether historical anecdotes to illustrate the Ten Commandments, or stories from the history of the Catholic Church in Vietnam—was as a linguistic mediator. He was making a vast array of European-produced religious literature accessible to a Vietnamese reading audience. In some cases, Bỉnh directly translated materials that he found in the European libraries, and he says as much. In most cases, however, he seems to have been *retelling* the stories he was discovering in the classic style of the storyteller. He was not merely *translating* these tales into a comprehensible language: he was also *transforming* them into a literary idiom comprehensible to a particular Vietnamese audience. Thus he was first a collector of tales and then a very self-conscious transmitter of these tales so that others might receive them and hopefully benefit from their didactic elements.

In writing his tales, Bỉnh understood himself to be situated within several literary genealogies. First, he recognized "tales" to be part of a long-standing biblical practice, as he suggested in sections of the *Tales of Annam* in which he inscribed parts of the early biblical genealogy by tracing briefly the descendants of Adam through Abraham and Levi.[65] He saw this as a type of "transmission" (*truyên*), and stated that all of these descendants of Abraham retained "the language of their ancestors." He also stated that Moses recorded "prophetic tales" (*sấm truyên* [chan zhuan; 讖傳]) in writing the first books of the Old Testament. At the same time, Bỉnh saw his tales as lying within a distinct literary genealogy of transmitted stories specifically about his Vietnamese homeland. He briefly discussed this genealogy in the preface to his *Tales of Annam*, in which he noted that such stories and histories had been written by Vietnamese court historians, by European missionaries such as Alexandre de Rhodes, and even by visiting English merchants.[66] These writings, he pointed out, either were not accessible to Vietnamese readers because they were written in European languages or were out of date because so much time had passed since their composition. Consequently, Bỉnh saw his task as "writing these tales in our language in order that everyone might know them."

SÁCH GƯƠNG TRUYỆN: MORAL EXEMPLARS

The newly framed world of Catholic saints as moral exemplars was reinforced in the first full-length works Bỉnh produced, his two-volume set of "exemplary tales" (*Sách gương truyện*). This pair of volumes contains a wide range of biblical, apocryphal, and historical anecdotes used to offer examples of both good and bad behaviors. Bỉnh's inspiration for these volumes lay in Geronimo Maiorica's mid-seventeenth-century writings, specifically his predecessor's *Sách gương phúc gương tội* (Book of exemplars of virtue and sin).[67] As Bỉnh wrote in his preface, "In our country of Annam in the past there was the Jesuit priest by the name of Jeronymo Maiorica who translated many kinds of books with examples of both positive and negative [behaviors] . . . and thus I will call this book the book of moral exemplars."[68] Although Bỉnh added the term *tales* to his own title, his *Sách gương truyện* closely emulated Maiorica's approach, namely using the lives of saints and other historical figures as exemplars of various types of behavior. While tales of saints are scattered throughout his works, Bỉnh's two-volume *Sách gương truyện* represented perhaps the most direct early nineteenth-century manifestation of this saintly lore. Bỉnh's exemplary tales included both stories about saints and miscellaneous anecdotes illustrating morality.

Bỉnh described his rationale and approach in the preface he composed for the first volume:

> [This book] has examples not only of bad [behavior] but also of good [behavior] because bad examples cause one to become fearful and to abstain from doing that, while good examples make one happy in spirit and desirous of imitating them, just as when one speaks of the hardships of hell and the delights of heaven, so that we may strive to avoid punishment and seek happiness, because happiness in the land of heaven is that which everyone desires and longs for, while the hardships of hell . . . who does not fear this?[69]

Bỉnh's exemplary tales are striking for their brevity. Unlike the longer historical accounts found in some of his later writings, such as his hagiographical volumes, most of these tales are anecdotes rather than fully formed stories. Their brevity becomes clear when one notes that the second of the two volumes contains 196 tales spread over a mere 217 pages.

The chapters in these volumes are structured around two sets of Catholic religious obligations. The first is the Decalogue (Ten Commandments), and Bỉnh provides brief anecdotes that illustrate elements of each commandment. In these chapters, the "tales" are typically presented in one undifferentiated paragraph followed by another, in no particular order. For some commandments he presents a large number of "tales," while he gives others much more cursory treatment. There are, for instance, thirty-two tales for the eighth commandment ("Thou shalt not steal"), while commandment numbers 3 and 10 ("Thou shalt not take the Lord's name in vain"; and "Thou shalt not covet thy neighbor's possessions") merit only two tales each. The second set of obligations for which Bỉnh provides guiding examples is the "Commandments of the Church," comprising five expectations of good Catholics as stipulated by church authority:

1. You shall attend mass.

2. You shall confess your sins at least once a year.
3. You shall receive the Eucharist at least during Easter season.
4. You shall observe the days of fasting and abstinence.
5. You shall help provide for the needs of the church.

As with Bỉnh's earlier tales concerning the Decalogue, there is no balance across the five commandments of the church. Some are illustrated with numerous tales, while others have no exemplars at all. Bỉnh includes forty-three "tales" pertaining to the second obligation—confession of sin—while he offers only one for the fifth—helping the church—and none for item 3 concerning receiving the Eucharist. One can speculate as to this spotty coverage, but it likely represents both Bỉnh's sense of the items most relevant to Vietnamese Catholics—confession being extremely significant—and perhaps the kinds of stories that Bỉnh was able to locate in his perusal of materials in the libraries in Lisbon.

While the format varies for each, an example of Bỉnh's style can be found in one of the tales regarding the requirement to observe fast days. He prefaces the anecdote by noting its local relevance: "In the records of the books of the Jesuit order there is a tale that took place in our country of Annam in the year 1652."[70] He then recounts an anecdote about how a Christian who ate meat during a fasting period was divinely punished and was then ultimately redeemed. He then offers a concluding gloss on the episode: "This miracle took place when our country had had the faith for only twenty-five years, and since that time our Christians have not dared to eat meat on fast days. I had known the idea behind [this practice], but now I have seen this tale, and thus I ask my brothers and sisters that they might look at the example of this tale from our country and hold it as important, otherwise the Virtuous Lord of Heaven might punish us again, and then it would be even worse."[71] The gloss neatly illustrates Bỉnh's specific model in presenting the exemplary tales and more generally his engagement with his imagined audience, in this case imploring his co-religionists to read this tale and heed its warning. In any case, this and the other exemplary tales nicely illustrate the logic articulated earlier by Maiorica, loosely following Seneca: namely, it is far more effective to teach people about behaviors to be pursued or avoided through concrete examples than through abstract lists of exhortations such as the Decalogue and the five commandments of the church.

These tale are also significant for having expanded the geographical imaginary being presented to Vietnamese Catholics. Maiorica had introduced Vietnamese Catholics to a bewildering range of places across the biblical lands and Europe. His tales of saints had populated these strange and strangely transliterated sites that must have puzzled more than a few Vietnamese Catholics. On the one hand, Maiorica's writings would have been familiar to Vietnamese audiences, in terms of their being "tales" and being replete with "strange" occurrences. On the other hand, however, they would also have been quite alien to Vietnamese readers in terms of their geographical dimension. His largest collection, *Các thánh truyện* (Tales of the saints), which surveyed the lives of thirty-nine saints ranging from Policarpe to Basil the Grand, told stories of events taking place across completely unfamiliar landscapes. These *truyện* played out in regions stretching from the Balkans to the Indian subcontinent and across various parts of the Middle East. Numerous European countries also became part of the saintly landscape: France, Spain, Italy, Germany, Poland, and Sweden, among others. The stories of saints also had as settings specific cities across these countries, including Seville, Alexandria, Antioch, Valencia, Rome, and Paris. Thus they introduced not only spiritual figures but new geographies that became part of the Catholic imaginary as people read or heard these tales.

Following in his predecessor's footsteps, Bình's tales also focused on a wide range of non-Vietnamese geographies. Drawing on materials available to him in the libraries of Lisbon, his tales added to the list of places found in Maiorica's works, from Flanders to the Canary Islands, and from Burgundy to Bamberg. These were new geographies too, but now also ones that carried a certain meaning, for they were the places in which these saints had attained the reputations that elevated them to positions as spiritual intercessors. Arguably, the important element of these stories was typically not where they took place—indeed, some of the brief tales of the saints make no mention of where they occur. Yet I would argue that these new and strange place-names became part of an imagined geography of Roman Catholicism that changed the Vietnamese Catholic worldview. The tales, along with those found in the Bible, presented new ways of thinking about the world, one peopled by historically important figures whose lives either contributed to the trajectory of Old Testament history or (in the case of saints) provided examples of suitable behavior. Like the new genealogies that Catholicism brought, which shifted some Vietnamese from a focus on Confucian and Sinic antecedents to Christian ones, the new geographies represented a kind of displacement of existing geographical imaginings.

THE HAGIOGRAPHIES

After completing the two volumes of moral exemplars, Bình turned to a much more substantial undertaking, namely crafting hagiographies of the three towering figures of the early Jesuit missionary project: Saint Francis Xavier, Saint Ignatius of Loyola, and St. Francis de Borgia. These are works in the traditional Catholic genre of hagiography, which Hippolyte Delehaye once described as "a new form of literature . . . part biography, part panegyric, part moral lesson."[72] In short, they are not merely accounts of saint's lives but devotional texts designed to edify and illuminate those who read or hear them. A detailed study of each of these lengthy texts is well beyond the scope of this book, but a description of the structure and approach Bỉnh used in his *Tales of Saint Francis Xavier* is indicative of his method. In the introduction to this 589-page volume, Bỉnh positions himself within the hagiographical tradition, using the self-deprecating language common to both Catholic scribes and Confucian scholars:

> This tale [referring to his primary source] was written by the priest and doctor Joao de Lucena of the Jesuit order, a person of humane virtue and broad intelligence, and was printed in the Portuguese language in the year 1600 in ten volumes. And as for the languages of the other countries, the priests of our order have already [translated them] so that all under heaven might know them, as in the country of Đại Minh, where [it was done] by the priest Mattheo Ricci, and in the country of Annam, where it was done by Father Jeronimo Maiorica, a person of broad intelligence. Although I, myself, am a person of limited talents, I have seen in the Prophecies where it speaks of the virtuous Lord of Heaven opening the mouth of Balaam, and also in the Gospels where it is written that the Virtuous Lord Jesus praised the woman for making a contribution of two *đồng* of cash, because the gift of cash was truly from her heart. For this reason, I dare to write this book in veneration of Saint Francis Xavier and ask that people pray for assistance and strength for me to be able to carry out this task.[73]

This introduction suggests that Bỉnh saw his own production of a hagiography of St. Francis Xavier as part of an existing Jesuit lineage that included not only the author of his primary source, Joao de Lucena, but also those who had rendered the story into Asian languages. In particular, he cites Matteo Ricci, who wrote of Xavier in Chinese, and Geronimo Maiorica, who wrote the saint's tales in vernacular Vietnamese. As with some of his other works, Bỉnh here saw his task as making stories of this towering figure of the Jesuit tradition accessible to another generation of Vietnamese whose literacy was in the alphabetic script of *quốc ngữ*. The volume itself begins as an adaptation of Lucena's *Vida do Padre Francisco Xavier*, which Bỉnh follows initially but from which he eventually diverges.[74] Bỉnh's work is also a substantial reduction of the original, which runs to more than seven hundred printed pages. What Bỉnh does is to distill the elements of the story that most interest him and render them accessible to a Vietnamese audience. As such, *Tales of Saint Francis Xavier* is as much Bỉnh's work as it is a translation of Lucena's, if it ever was that.

The tenuous link with Lucena's work is completely broken after fifty-five chapters and more than 440 pages, when Bỉnh suddenly announces that he is about to leave Xavier behind and turn his attention to the issues of the Jesuit spread of Catholicism to China and Vietnam. Although Xavier's connection to these later missions in Asia was quite limited (he had died in 1552), this does not appear to have bothered Bỉnh, for instead of creating a new notebook for this topic he elects to append it to the volume on Xavier. With chapter 56, Bỉnh shifts his attention to the Jesuit mission to China, using Francis Xavier's death on the small island of

Sanchao just southwest of Macao as a transition to discussing Matteo Ricci's mission to China ("Speaking of Matteo Ricci Being the First to Spread the Way in the Country of China").[75] But this story about Ricci is itself only a segue to the next chapter, which begins an extended discussion of the early history of the mission effort in Cochinchina and Tonkin, one initiated by Father Francisco Busomi, who arrived in what is today central Vietnam in 1615. The remaining 150 pages of the book trace the history of Catholicism in Tonkin, with commentary on martyrs for the faith, including a marginal note about the deaths of several MEP priests at the hands of Nguyễn authorities in 1820.[76] This pattern of appending seemingly unrelated material to his hagiographies was to be repeated. The volume on St. Francis Borgia, for instance, leaves behind its main subject on page 630 and for the next 92 pages addresses issues of early nineteenth-century European Catholic history.[77] But Bỉnh never forgets his titular characters, and he circles back to them at the end of the volumes, as he does in the one about St. Francis, which concludes: "Anyone who sees these tales will know that Saint Francis Xavier had many titles that describe his beatitude: Prophet, Scholar, Martyr, Confessor, and also founder of the Jesuit order with his friend St. Ignatius. Confessor was his primary role; and, as a Prophet he was a person who knew many things that were to come; as a Scholar he spread the faith, and he was a Martyr because he accepted death for the Virtuous Lord Jesus."[78] Bỉnh's hagiographies are substantial paeans to the heroes of his beloved Jesuit order, yet they were more than that. Like his other collections of tales, these volumes linked these European Catholic figures to the history of Vietnamese Christianity. The connection existed both because these volumes were written in Vietnamese, making them a part of the Vietnamese literary tradition of Catholicism, and, just as importantly, because of the ways in which Bỉnh told these stories and appended his own anecdotes and observations.

TALES OF ANNAM

Bỉnh's writings in the genres of exemplary tales and hagiographies are important dimensions of the shifting Vietnamese-language religious literature, but arguably his most significant contribution to that tradition, and the tradition of Vietnamese historical tales more generally, is his two-volume history of early Vietnamese Catholicism. The two volumes are entitled *Truyện Anam, Đàng Ngoài* and *Truyện Anam, Đàng Trong* ("Tales of Annam, the Outer Region," and "Tales of Annam, the Inner Region"). Their separation reflected the political divisions of the Vietnamese territories of the seventeenth and eighteenth centuries, between the Trịnh-dominated northern realm of Đàng Ngoài from which Bỉnh had come and the Nguyễn-ruled southern realm of Đàng Trong. While reflecting this political divide, the volumes also speak to an ecclesiastical separation, for the two regions were served by missionaries who had limited contact with one another. The regions had also been formally separated by church leaders for administrative purposes, with Tonkin and Cochinchina each governed by their own apostolic vicars. Consequently, Bỉnh's decision to present his history in two separate volumes was a logical extension of both of these realities, for the trajectories of early Vietnamese Catholicism in each region ran mostly in parallel and rarely intersected.

These two volumes are the first and most important Vietnamese-produced texts recounting the history of the Christian faith in what later became Vietnam. These two works, each over six hundred pages, trace, if somewhat episodically, the history of Vietnamese Catholicism from its beginnings in the late 1500s to the early nineteenth century. They are less anecdotal than Bỉnh's other collected tales, and each follows a more discernable chronological trajectory. The books contain his descriptions of the church's growth and expansion, the foreign missionaries who were its primary agents, and the Vietnamese converts who became its earliest adherents and later some of its first martyrs. Indeed, the volume on Đàng Trong deals primarily with the lives and deaths of seventeenth-century martyrs in the Nguyễn realm. It offers detailed accounts of the events leading to their conversion to Christianity, their subsequent persecution, and their eventual execution by the state for their religious beliefs. Thus this work is an important exploration of the processes by which Catholicism took root in the Vietnamese realms and the mechanisms by which it transformed the lives of at least some Vietnamese people. Indeed, in his preface to the two-volume collection Bỉnh makes a deliberate point of commending these tales to his readers, presumed to be in Tonkin, who might not be familiar with the history of these martyrs in the southern portion of the Vietnamese kingdom.[79]

Bỉnh lays out his rationale and approach on the title page of the first volume, that on Đàng Ngoài, in which he explains both his project's antecedents and what he hopes will be its own contribution: "I speak of events from the time that our ancestors knew of the blessed Jesus and worshipped him, and also of all the saints who suffered death for the faith, and all the people of humaneness and virtue, along with many other matters, and I have divided them into two books, of which *Đàng Ngoài* is book 1, and *Đàng Trong* is book 2, that they might be read, and if one wishes to know something then it can be [readily] found, as that which pertains to each region is placed into that region['s book]."[80] This brief preface is followed by a much lengthier introduction in which he expanded upon his motivations for this project. Here he contextualizes his work within the field of historical accounts by earlier generations of European missionaries and merchants:

> As for historical records of events in Anam, the king has already recorded numerous matters in our country, but when the teacher Alexandre went to spread the faith, he produced a book of tales which was printed in Rome in Latin, Italian, and French so that all the priests who traveled later would be aware of the matters in our country. Likewise, the English arrived to carry out commerce, and they also composed books of tales about our country, which they published in their own language, telling of

various other customs, along with the appearance [of the land], and [local] products, so all the merchants from their country would know these things and go there to carry out commerce. But we cannot see the history of the kings, and we cannot understand the tales of the teacher Alexandre because they are in a foreign language. Moreover, from then until now much has happened, because two hundred years have passed. For this reason, I am writing these tales in our language, so that every person might know them.[81]

In short, these are stories that Bỉnh considered important for Vietnamese Christians and worth preserving for future generations as well. Moreover, while some such stories were recorded earlier by "Teacher Alexandre" (du Rhodes), these were written in languages that the Vietnamese could not read. Bỉnh's book, however, records these tales in Vietnamese, and specifically in the romanized vernacular increasingly used by literate Vietnamese Catholics.

Ironically, a substantial portion of these volumes is based upon the writings and reporting of European missionaries, many of whom returned to Europe to write accounts of their experiences, which were then published and distributed. These included notably de Rhodes's *Histoire du Royaume de Tunquin, et des grands progrez que la prédication de l' Évangile y a faits en la conversion des infidelles* (1651) and Giovanni Marini's *Historia et relatione del Tunchino e del Giapponne* (1665) and *Relation nouvelle et curieuse des royaumes de Tunquin et de Lao* (1666), but many others began to appear in the second half of the seventeenth century as well. In the late eighteenth and early nineteenth centuries, a multivolume set of letters from the Vietnamese mission field began to be published as *Nouvelles lettres edifiantes des missions de la Chine et des Indes orientales,* and it is likely that Bỉnh had access to these in the Lisbon libraries. As he notes in the preface to the first of the *Truyện Anam* volumes, "Although I am a person of a later generation, I have already heard [tales] told by our elders, and I have also seen books written by later generations that have recorded events in our country, and thus I have come to know of them and have translated them to create these two books so that people of future generations might know of them [as well]."[82]

Although Bỉnh was writing stories of Vietnamese Catholics by drawing on European missionary accounts, these accounts were merely the raw materials for a final product that was distinctly his own. In the first place, Bỉnh was taking the European source materials and retelling their stories of Vietnamese Catholics in a language that they themselves could read and understand. Second, as he noted in the preface, portions of his knowledge came not from these books but from the community elders who told him stories of their past. In his twelve years of traveling around Tonkin as a catechist of Father Castiglioni, Bỉnh would have had many opportunities to speak with older members of the Catholic community, and over time he collected their stories, which constituted the folk memory of their religious lives and churches. He could thus draw upon both written European accounts and orally transmitted Vietnamese accounts in drafting his compendium of Catholic history in his homeland.

Combining these two distinct but complementary evidentiary streams was certainly a significant innovation, one that makes Bỉnh's two volumes more than simply a distillation of European histories of Vietnamese Catholics. But an even greater contribution of Bỉnh's approach was the way in which he recentered the Vietnamese as actors in the drama of the development of Catholicism in their homeland and relegated European missionaries to the margins of the stories. The primary actors were now Vietnamese, and the tales focused on their triumphs and tragedies, with their capacity to serve as role models for future generations of Vietnamese Catholics. This was extremely important, not only because it placed Vietnamese at the heart of their own history, but also because it reflected a shift in the geographical setting of Catholic exemplary tales. As we have seen, most previous volumes of Catholic tales written in Vietnamese, including all of Maiorica's and indeed many of Bỉnh's own, dealt with stories set in other parts of the world, featuring non-Vietnamese exemplars. These settings were typically European countries but also extended to the Middle East, and even parts of India and Africa. Bỉnh's tales in both *Truyện Anam* volumes are set in his homeland and deal primarily with the Vietnamese people themselves in their own language. In this respect, by writing about Vietnamese people in Vietnamese, Bỉnh was returning to the Vietnamese roots of the "tales" genre.

At the same time, Bỉnh's history of Catholicism in his homeland was profoundly important for giving Vietnamese Catholics a legitimate history of their own, one that recorded their stories, their struggles, and their sacrifices for the faith. It was a history that linked the trajectories of Vietnamese and Portuguese Catholicism in new ways—a tale not merely of the Portuguese missionaries who traveled to Annam to become spiritual guides to the Vietnamese but equally of a Vietnamese (Bỉnh) who journeyed to Portugal, where, in serving as a priest, he offered spiritual succor to the Portuguese. As such, his story establishes a kind of historical equivalency between the two peoples, validating the Vietnamese participation in the globalized community of Roman Catholicism. Indeed, in his own writings Bỉnh pointed to this historical equivalency and the symmetry between the two sides of the globe when he wrote of his impending journey to Europe: "This [my journey] is a matter that the Virtuous Lord of Heaven has already determined, and so I must accept this; just as Saint Francis Xavier traveled to the East [*Phương Đông*], so too I must travel to the West [*Phương Tây*]."[83] While Binh was no Xavier, his comment captures a degree of Vietnamese Catholics' agency that is fundamental for understanding their own engagement with this new world religion.

While important for offering a Vietnamese history that challenged the seeming monopoly of European church histories, Bỉnh's story of Vietnamese Catholics was also significant within the indigenous Vietnamese historical tradition. Unlike almost all previous Vietnamese histories, which were typically chronicles of political or military events, and were centered on the court as symbolic of the entire Vietnamese state, Bỉnh's collection of historical tales was, instead, the history of a particular group of believers in a common religious doctrine. Thus it demarcated the collectivity in a very different way, with the organizing principle being not a ruling dynasty but a community of religious adherents. In this regard, it was more similar to the genre of Buddhist Vietnamese genealogies discussed earlier, in which the core teachings of the tradition were transmitted from master to disciple and religiously structured genealogies were critical to preserving these lineages.[84]

The trajectory of the volume on Đàng Ngoài is also noteworthy for the manner in which it begins and ends. After what amounts to a brief statement of the core beliefs of Christianity, on the second page Bỉnh starts with the Genesis story, describing the creation of the earth, the formation of man and woman, and the temptation by the serpent that led to original sin and the expulsion of Adam and Eve from the Garden of Eden. Bỉnh continues the story through subsequent generations to Noah and the Flood, then reaches the critical story of the Tower of Babel.[85] For Bỉnh, the history of Christianity in Tonkin must be traced to the origins of the world itself, or rather these origins as understood by Vietnamese Catholics. To give a sense of the passage of time, Bỉnh summarizes using a logic seen earlier in his prefatory chronologies: "From the time that the Virtuous Lord of Heaven created heaven and earth, to the time that we had our own king and could call ourselves a country, 4,800 years passed, because there had been four thousand years from the founding of the world to the time that the Virtuous Lord Jesus was born, and it was then eight hundred years after his birth that King Đinh Thiên Hoàng first ruled our country, changing its name to Annam and dividing it into eleven regions."[86] In this short passage Bỉnh links the creation of the world to the birth of Jesus then to the rule of the founding emperor of the Vietnamese territory. For him, this is an important sequence reminding the reader that the Vietnamese are a legitimate part of the global history of the Catholic tradition.

Having begun with the Creation story, and then taken it through the birth of Jesus and the origins of the autonomous Vietnamese state, Bỉnh fast-forwards his account to the sixteenth century. Here he introduces the birth of the Jesuit order and then the arrival of de Rhodes in Annam. The second chapter of the volume, "Teachers of the Jesuit Order Arrive to Spread the Faith," and the twenty-eight chapters that follow trace the history of the growth and spread of Roman Catholicism in Tonkin. Much of this account details the numerous conversions and martyrdoms of the seventeenth and early eighteenth centuries. Overall, however, the volume is substantially focused on more recent history. Of its fifty chapters, the first thirty deal with events prior to Bỉnh's adulthood, covering the period 1627 to 1780. The remaining twenty chapters address a much narrower time period, that of Bỉnh's active career, between 1790 and 1824, the year in which he finished the volume. In fact, thirteen of these twenty chapters describe an even shorter period between 1794 and 1805.[87]

Thus, beginning with chapter 31, Bỉnh's history of Vietnamese Catholicism in Tonkin reaches the present and becomes a personal recollection of his own role in these histories rather than a research project. Consequently, Bỉnh is not only summarizing, excerpting, and translating many accounts pertaining to the development of Catholicism in Vietnam from the early decades of the seventeenth century but also bringing this record up to date, adding information he knew from personal experience or had learned from people with whom he had direct contact. In this telling, Bỉnh himself becomes the latest link in this long history of Vietnamese Catholicism, and *Tales of Annam* becomes *Tales of Philiphê Bỉnh*. In this section of the *Tales*, Bỉnh provides a detailed description of his own involvement with the church, and then of his and his companions' missions, first to Macao, then to Goa, and finally to Lisbon. Thus his own "tales" are very much, in his mind, part of this larger body of "tales" relating the history of the Catholic Church in Tonkin. This is a natural development in the context of the genealogical nature of these tales, which begin with God's creation of the earth, suggesting that Bỉnh regarded himself as part of this long biblical genealogy as well as heir to the earlier Catholic history he traced in the previous chapters.

Another distinctive feature of this first volume of *Tales of Annam* is its introduction of a new geographical dimension to the telling of Vietnamese history. These tales, like Bỉnh and his friends, cross the seas and find their continuation in Europe. Thus the stories are not bound by or restricted to the geographical space in which they are primarily set. Rather, in Bỉnh's telling of them, "Annam" goes with those who move to Europe, and their life stories as Vietnamese continue there. These men all hoped that their sojourn would be temporary and that they would be able to return and resume their lives in their homeland. That they were unable to do so does not make their tales any less those of "Annam." To a large degree this reflects Bỉnh's abiding sense of responsibility to the Padroado community he had left behind. The story remains about them and their history, even as the focus of the tales shifts to Europe. Moreover, the fact that Bỉnh was writing these volumes specifically for that audience back in Annam suggests the ways in which these remain very much tales of Annam and not "Tales of Portugal" or "Tales of Exile." Yet Bỉnh concludes this volume with three chapters recording the lives and deaths of his three companions, Brothers Trung, Nhân, and Ngân, so that his "Tales of Annam" does ultimately end in Portugal.

The second volume of this paired set, *Tales of Annam, Đàng Trong,* runs temporally parallel to the volume on Tonkin, covering roughly the same period from the early seventeenth century to the early nineteenth. However, it differs from its companion volume in several significant respects. The first difference is its focus on Christianity in the southern Vietnamese territories, a place of which Bỉnh had no personal experience. Thus, more so than in the case of his work on the northern region, he was heavily dependent on materials he found in the libraries of Lisbon. Although he does not indicate his sources, his primary reference was likely an early Portuguese work on Asian martyrs by Father Agostinho de Santa Maria, *Rosas do Japam, e da Cochinchina* (Martyrs of Japan and of Cochinchina).[88] Published in Lisbon in two volumes that appeared in 1709 and 1724, *Rosas do Japam, e da Cochinchina* would have offered precisely the type of detail Bỉnh was looking for. Furthermore, the format of this book, with its successive chapters on individual martyrs, likely influenced the way Bỉnh organized his own work. Bỉnh lays out his approach in the second chapter of the book (pp. 22–25), explaining that he is following the order conventionally used in Catholic literature. He will begin with tales of the martyrs, followed by general stories about people of the faith. Having said this, however, Bỉnh does not launch into tales of martyrs but first writes a general chapter on the Nguyễn state's suppression of Christianity over the seventeenth century. This is followed by a chapter on Andre, the man often considered the first Vietnamese convert. Only then does Bỉnh begin to write about martyrs.

In its focus on martyrs and other Vietnamese Catholics, this volume is quite different from the first in the set, which features a more continuous chronological narrative. *Tales of Đàng Trong* is more anecdotic, with stories about the life trajectories of these individuals, typically focusing on the ways in which they came to the faith, the hardships that they endured because of it, and frequently their martyrdom. Also, most of the volume deals with the seventeenth century, in which Roman Catholicism was first established, and then looks at early Vietnamese Catholics, with a strong focus on those who were martyred between the 1620s and the 1660s. Relatively little of the book deals with events after about the 1680s, meaning that its scope is much narrower than that of the volume on Tonkin. This can be explained in no small measure by Bỉnh's source material, for if he did indeed use Agostinho de Santa Maria's *Rosas do Japam, e da Cochinchina*, which was published in the early eighteenth century, its account would have ended in the latter half of the seventeenth century, precisely when Bỉnh's volume itself concludes.

Tales of Annam, Đàng Trong is also distinct from *Truyện Anam, Đàng Ngoài* in another respect. It does not begin with the origins of Christianity or of Roman Catholicism. Instead, Bỉnh starts the volume with a historical and geographical introduction to the Đàng Trong region, focusing on the history of its earlier incarnation as the kingdom of Champa and its gradual annexation by the Vietnamese.[89] Nor, like the volume looking at Tonkin, does this one culminate with the trajectory of Bỉnh's own life into the early decades of the nineteenth century. Instead, the concluding four chapters of the volume focus primarily on political history. They summarize the events of the last three decades of the eighteenth century, during which the two Vietnamese realms were reunited, and then survey the reigns of the first two monarchs of the Nguyễn dynasty, taking the account well into the

1820s. Bình must have been relying on published accounts and newspaper reports to write of events extending at least as far as 1822, three years into the reign of the Minh Mạng emperor. In particular, he discusses that emperor's reluctance to engage in commerce with the French, and his initiation of a policy to restrict European trade for fear of its domestic political repercussions, and because of a growing concern about Christianity.[90] The discussion of the emperor's growing xenophobia, as Bình understood it, was driven by his concern that Vietnam might follow the trajectory seen in Japan in the sixteenth century. There, as Bình knew from his collection of Japanese history books, the shoguns became anxious about European merchants and the religion they had brought with them.[91] The result was a closure of the country, the expulsion of European residents, and the execution or forced renunciation of Japanese Christians.

BÌNH'S LAST YEARS: ONE CONCLUDING TALE AND A FINAL FAREWELL

After finishing the second of the two *Tales of Annam* volumes in 1822, Bình virtually stopped writing. In the preceding seven years he had written nine thick volumes, and now he rested from his labors. He continued to make desultory notes in his *Nhật trình*, where he maintained his brief summaries of annual events for the next two years, stopping in 1824 with a last entry about the death of his remaining companion, Brother Trung. Aside from Trung's death, most of the entries dealt with European and Portuguese political developments, likely gleaned from reading the *Gazeta de Lisboa*. Bình was now freed from any responsibility he might have felt toward his companions, for it is likely that he had nursed each in his final years. Bình's only remaining ties were to the community he had left behind and the future generations he imagined to be his eventual readership. Why Bình stopped writing at this juncture is unclear. He does not comment on it, nor does he write of any change in the rhythms of his life. For the next six years, Bình's only writing was in his *Notebook That Transmits and Records All Matters,* where he updated the list of books in his personal library, drafted a complete list of the notebooks he had written, and continued to record the number of masses he said and how much he was being paid for them.

While we do not know what now occupied his time, Bình's existence, like that of many in Portugal, was increasingly affected by the reemergence of political and military clashes. In a life that had already experienced repeated episodes of warfare, Bình's final years were marked by fallout from the political confrontations that had shaken Portugal during the liberal revolution of 1820. The postrevolutionary political landscape had remained tense, and bitter debates had continued about the country's political future. The constitutionalist reforms had opened up new possibilities for governing the realm, but strong monarchist and conservative clerical sentiments remained. The death of King João VI in 1826 renewed these debates and eventually sparked a succession crisis that pitted one of his granddaughters against one of his sons, Prince Miguel. Miguel had returned from Brazilian exile to serve as regent for his young niece, Queen Maria II, but by 1828 he opted to seized power for himself. This instigated a struggle between the conservative Miguel and the forces of liberalism headed by his older brother, Pedro, who in 1831 abdicated his throne in a newly independent Brazil to challenge his brother. Warfare between the two sides continued for the next three years. Most of the fighting took place in distant Porto in northern Portugal, but the repercussions were strongly felt in Lisbon. Throughout these clashes, Bỉnh lived, as he probably would have wished, in a Lisbon firmly in the hands of the staunchly conservative Migueliste forces, whose leader had shown sympathy for the Jesuits and had raised the possibility of their return to Portugal.[92]

But even as he lived in the midst of this swirling political chaos, in 1830 Bỉnh ended his six-year writing hiatus to take on a final literary project. This was another volume in the *truyện* tradition, a work entitled *Tales of Saint Anne* (*Truyện bà Thánh Anna*). Why Bỉnh broke his long literary silence is unclear. It is possible that he had come across a volume that inspired him. Or perhaps this was an unpaid debt he felt the time had arrived to repay. Whatever the case, he set to work on this volume and completed most of it within a year. *Tales of Saint Anne* is on the scale of his other books of "Tales," at more than six hundred pages. An important contribution to the Vietnamese hagiographical tradition, it is also significant for giving some indication of Bỉnh's frame of mind at this late stage of his life. Most notably, it suggests that Bỉnh still felt the connections to his community and had not forgotten that they had dispatched him to Europe. Writing in the book's preface, as he always did, to identify himself as the author, Bỉnh continued to represent himself in terms of his identity as an envoy, not merely as a priest or resident of Lisbon, or any of a number of possible options: "I am Father Bỉnh, who traveled as an envoy of the Christians of the Jesuit order of the country of Annam, and have produced this book in the city of Lisbon, the capital of the country of Portugal, in the year 1830." Clearly, even at this late stage in his life, his identity was still framed in terms of his mission and his connection to the Vietnamese Catholics who had dispatched him to Europe more than three decades earlier. With the completion of his *Tales of St. Anne*, Bỉnh presumably returned to the routines of the previous six years.

Then, in late January 1832, the rhythms of Bỉnh's life were shattered when he suffered a near-fatal accident in his residence. Early on the morning of January 29, 1832, Bỉnh awoke to participate in ceremonies celebrating the feast day of Saint Frances de Sales. As he was climbing out of bed, however, he fell and struck his head so violently that he was temporarily immobilized. As it was still dark, there was no one else awake, and because his apartment had thick walls and a heavy door, no one could hear his faint cries for help. After lying on the floor for a while, Bình summoned the energy to drag himself back to his bed. He sprawled there in severe pain until morning, when he finally began to hear voices in the corridor. At this point he slowly crawled out of his bed and dragged himself to the door, using his remaining strength to pull it open. The priests who saw him there immediately carried him back to bed and called for help even as they began to perform the last rites. Although the doctors who arrived were able to stabilize his condition, they were convinced that Bình would not recover.

Yet Bình, who had already endured so much in his life, did not succumb to the injuries sustained in the fall. Although he was forced to spend nearly three months in bed, to endure repeated (and expensive) visits from doctors, and to undergo an extensive course of therapy, Bình gradually began to improve. As he wrote about this time of his slow recuperation and its attendant expenses: "I had to lie on my bed for three months, and each day the two doctors came to visit me, and thus I had to expend large amounts of money, because each time that a doctor came I had to pay one *quan*, three *tien*, and twenty *dong*, and as for the medicine, someone from the house would have to go to buy that, and thus I also had to pay money at the pharmacy."[93] After being bedridden for months, Bình was finally able to take some tentative steps on his own and eventually to stand by himself. He reported that by the end of that first month out of bed (likely May of 1832) he was even strong enough to perform masses again, though one suspects only within the Congregation house itself.

At this point he also tried to resume to work on the *Tales of St. Anne*. This, however, proved more than his strength would permit. Even the simple act of moving pen across paper was proving a challenge, as the uneven scrawl of his final written entry suggests. Consequently, Bình appended his farewell message to the final page of his *Tales of St. Anne*:

> Once I had finally recovered and was able to leave my bed, I was initially unable to stand, but eventually I was able to take my first step, and at the end of the month was able to perform a mass by myself, and I wished to concern myself with finishing this book in praise of Saint Anna. But I was unable to write because my hands still trembled, and for this reason at the end of the month of January in the year 1833, I ended it. I, the priest Bình sign my name, and give thanks to the Virtuous Lord Jesus, and the Very Blessed and Virtuous Mother Maria, and the Blessed Saint Anna. Amen.[94]

It was an appropriate send-off for a chronicled life that began with the precise self-introduction offered on the opening page of the *Sách sổ* notebook and now came to a close on the final page of his last written work. Having penned this farewell, Bình now likely anticipated his own death. But this was not something he feared,

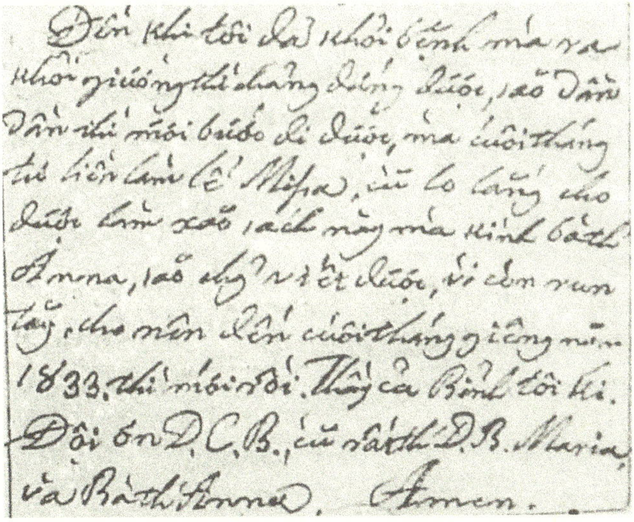
Đến khi tôi đã khỏi bệnh mà ra
khỏi giường thì chẳng đứng được, sau dần
dần thì mới bước đi được, mà cuối tháng
tư liền làm lễ Missa, cũ lo lắng cho
được làm xong sách này mà kính bà thánh
Anna, sau chẳng viết được, vì còn run
tay, cho nên đến cuối tháng giêng năm
1833. thì mới rồi. Thầy cả Bỉnh tôi kí.
Đội ơn Đ.C.B., cũ rất thánh Đ.B. Maria
và Bà thánh Anna. Amen.

FIGURE 26. The last known writing by Philiphê Bỉnh is this short message of farewell on the final page of his *Tales of Saint Anne*.

for he recognized its place in the circle of life. As he wrote in one of his notebooks: "One should not fear death, because one only dies once and no one can escape it. Whether one dies at home in one's own country or one dies in a foreign country, one should be content, for all this means is that the soul has been set free."[95] Bỉnh's soul was set free not long after this last farewell, probably in March of 1833. He was seventy-seven years old.[96]

EPILOGUE

In some respects, Bính was remarkably fortunate to die when he did. Less than a year after his death, in 1834, the Portuguese state formally dissolved all religious orders and congregations within the nation, including the Oratorians with whom Bính had been housed.[1] Not only were the priests dismissed from their religious institutions, but their residences were seized by the state and sold off or redistributed in a variety of ways. Had Bính lived beyond 1833 he would have faced the trauma of being rendered homeless institutionally and physically. The Casa do Espirito Santo, in which he had resided for the last twenty-six years of his life, did not escape the fate of other Portuguese religious houses, for it too was taken over by the state. Bính's former home then began a series of transformations, serving first as office space for the new Republican regime, and then as a philharmonic society, a club for aristocrats, and a hotel whose name changed repeatedly from Europa to Universal to Gibraltar and finally dos Embaixadores.[2] After this series of ventures into hostelry, the building suffered its second substantial destruction (the first having occurred in the great 1755 earthquake) in a fire that gutted its interior on September 29, 1880.[3] Once repairs were completed, the building was reopened as a department store bearing the imposing name "Companhia dos Grandes Armazéns do Chiado."[4] This store would remain the building's tenant for nearly a century, serving several generations of Lisbonites and representing a kind of commercial anchor of the Chiado district. Yet another fire, this one in August of 1988, destroyed the building's interior but spared its historic facade, allowing the space to be restored and brought back into commercial use. Today it continues, as it has since the 1890s, to be a retail center, now featuring a variety of boutique stores, all anchored by the French megastore

FNAC. And, in a nod to its earlier days, it is now home to a hotel, the deluxe Hotel do Chiado.

While Bỉnh's death spared him from homelessness, at a deeper level it marked the end of the Padroado lineage of Vietnamese Roman Catholicism in the Portuguese Jesuit tradition. His journey to Lisbon had reflected the deep commitment of that particular group of Catholics to a distinctive way of practicing their faith, even as this community shared a common Christian tradition with others living in Tonkin. Their story, as reflected in Bỉnh's life and writings, revealed fundamentally new ways of being Vietnamese, ones shaped by multiple geographies: political, physical, temporal, and cultural. Just as some Vietnamese of the sixteenth and seventeenth centuries had been transformed by relocating from the Red River Vietnamese heartland to the southern frontier regions of Thuận Hóa and Quảng Nam, so too Vietnamese Catholics had experienced profound dislocations of their individual and collective identities. The Vietnamese pioneers who moved south were transformed by this geographical displacement in which the new spaces, cultures, climates, and realities of these territories produced a significant shift in how they understood themselves. Vietnamese Catholics, on the other hand, found new ways of being Vietnamese without ever leaving their home region in Tonkin. For them, the new identities and cultural relationships they embraced were more in the mind than in the land. Yet this new identity also reflected a profoundly geographical dimension. The physical and ideological landscapes they inhabited had been remade. They found themselves grouped in congregations, parishes, and apostolic vicariates; they found themselves linked to the networks of the global Catholic Church through Macao to Goa and Rome; they found themselves connected to new genealogies and new sacred landscapes stretching across the lands of the Bible and the European lands of the Christian expansion; and they were now embedded in new temporal structures that shaped both the rhythmic cycles of their annual celebrations and their understanding of the unidirectional flows of linear time.

Bỉnh's story demonstrated as well the crucial importance of geographies of national and ecclesiastical boundaries and networks in shaping Vietnam's Catholic communities and in affecting the ways the communities responded to these powers. The presence of competing religious orders and congregations influenced how Vietnamese understood the allegiances that their new faith expected of them. At the same time, the missionaries who represented these orders brought with them their distinctive European national backgrounds, both politically and culturally. The contests between the French and the Portuguese, between the MEP and Dominicans and the Jesuits, and between the papacy and the Lisbon court all mattered in significant ways. Though one might think Vietnamese converts would not be concerned with these higher-level conflicts, this was not the case. The conflicts had concrete manifestations in the mission field itself, and Vietnamese Catholics found themselves forced to choose sides, or at least to make sense of disputes whose origins often remained murky.

Among the consequences of these national politics in the mission fields were battles over language and its relationship to the faith. As was discussed in chapter 2, contests over the use and pronunciation of words often became heated and even virtually unresolvable. Indeed, one of the primary impulses of Bỉnh's mission to Lisbon was his community's refusal to change how they said the word *grace* and to relinquish the accommodating Portuguese version of *garasa* in favor of the *graça* or *gratia* that the Spanish Dominicans insisted upon. This case illustrated the complex politics of religious language generally but also suggested the ways in which the national origins of European missionaries could be of considerable relevance to their congregants. Just as significantly, it demonstrated the degree to which Catholics might become extremely attached to their ritual practices and strongly resistant to suggestions by ecclesiastical authorities that they had been speaking words incorrectly and would need to alter their pronunciation. Indeed, debates about the renderings of liturgical language continue to the present, with uncanny echoes of those that roiled Bỉnh's community of Padroado Christians in eighteenth-century Tonkin. When, in 2011, the Catholic Church once again modified its translations of certain terms and concepts from Latin into English to more precisely bridge the gap between the two languages, the process provoked a substantial backlash. As had happened more than two centuries earlier in Tonkin, Catholics who had become comfortable with long-standing ritual practices and their language complained of unnecessary and overly complex new terminologies.[5] Notably, people were unhappy with now being forced to pronounce the tongue-twister "consubstantial with" instead of the direct phrase it had replaced in the Nicene Creed: "one with." Such complaints about uncooperative tongues and difficult-to-pronounce words carry echoes of the eighteenth-century Vietnamese case, in which precisely such issues were raised by Bỉnh in the context of the pressure that his community was facing.

In his journey to Portugal, Bỉnh stitched together significant portions of Catholic geographies of place and culture. He took the abstraction that was the Portuguese ruler's right under the Padroado authority and sought to make it a vital reality for his community. His presence in Lisbon and use of the trading networks that spanned the oceans between Tonkin and Europe created a connection between these two remote places. But it was not merely the fact of his presence at the court in Lisbon that mattered; rather, it was his ardent and relentless advocacy for his community for more than a decade. Then, when it had become impossible to pursue his mission, Bỉnh turned his energy to writing projects, ones designed to aid those he had left behind as well as future generations of Vietnamese Catholics. He recorded their Christian past, made accessible the histories of global Catholicism, and carefully noted his observations of life in Lisbon in the hopes that these might somehow be useful to future travelers. In short, he never forgot where he had come from or who had sent him. He remained a man who straddled the two worlds of Annam and Portugal, a reluctant exile who sustained his ties to his homeland by continuing to remember his community, follow the news reports from Asia, and, most of all, write in Vietnamese to the end of his life.

The Padroado community's demise, followed by Bình's own death, marked the end of particular chapters in this long episode of Vietnamese Catholicism but not the conclusion of the story itself. The distinctive tale of the Padroado community now flowed into the common story of the Catholics of Tonkin, who continued to grapple with the vicissitudes of life as a minority. They dealt, too, with the growing political complexity and eventual instability of the nineteenth century. It was a century that began with the rise to power of the Nguyễn clan over their longtime rivals, the Tây Sơn. During the reign of the first Nguyễn emperor, Gia Long, Catholics were permitted to continue their religious practices, though, as we saw in chapter 6, most bore the burdens of labor and military service along with other Vietnamese. The coming to power of the Minh Mạng emperor in 1820 marked a different era, as the new emperor's emphasis on orthodoxy in state ideology left little room for practices seen to be at odds with Confucian norms.[6] Minh Mạng's suspicions of Catholics and particularly of European missionaries led to periodic crackdowns and the public execution of Catholic priests. The religious history of this period from 1802 to the 1840s has been carefully studied by Jacob Ramsey in *Mandarins and Martyrs: The Church and the Nguyen Dynasty in Early Nineteenth-Century Vietnam* (2008), which details these complex tensions. Circumstances only became more complicated and for a time more difficult for Catholics as French pressure grew by the middle of the nineteenth century. As Catholics became linked in the popular imagination with the Europeans attacking the Vietnamese lands, the French invasion and territorial expansion prompted large-scale massacres of Catholic communities in the north-central part of the country. Once the French established full colonial control in the South and protectorates over the Center and the North, Catholics saw a growing measure of protection from persecution, though the taint of association with the French lingered. However, by the end of the nineteenth century, and then into the twentieth, this situation began to change, as Charles Keith has so elegantly shown in his *Catholic Vietnam: A Church from Empire to Nation* (2012). As Keith argues, the Vietnamese Catholic Church gradually transformed itself from a captive institution dominated by French clerics to an increasingly autonomous church led by Vietnamese priests determined to chart their own path. In some ways, one might see this as the culmination of a process that began with Philiphê Bình's own assertive engagement with Roman Catholic traditions, for he too had displayed an independence from European church authority. Bình's determined pursuit of a new bishop for Tonkin and his literary insistence upon the significance of an indigenous Catholic history in his homeland were precursors to the emergence of a distinctly Vietnamese and Vietnamese-led Roman Catholic Church.

In the course of the ecclesiastical reinvention unfolding within the Vietnamese church during the later colonial period and the early postcolonial era, an event took place with a profound historical resonance for Bỉnh's story. In 1957 the first Jesuit priests returned to Vietnam, more than 180 years after the order's dissolution. While Bỉnh had rejoiced at the Jesuit restoration in 1815, and had expressed optimism that this might mean a rapid return of the order to his native land, his hopes had been dashed, and he did not live to see its return. The first Jesuits coming back to Vietnam created a community for themselves in the southern hill town of Đà Lạt, in what was then the Republic of Vietnam. These priests founded a pontifical seminary, which was eventually transformed into the Pontifical College of St. Pius X.[7] This seminary/college began training Vietnamese in the Jesuit tradition, and slowly Jesuits began to set down roots in Vietnam once again. By 1975 there were eleven Jesuit priests in the country, and in 2007, when Vietnam marked the fiftieth anniversary of the order's reestablishment, their ranks had grown to thirty-eight.

It was perhaps appropriate that it was in Đà Lạt, the home of these newly ordained Jesuit priests, where another of Bỉnh's wishes would be realized, namely the return of his writings to his homeland. The man responsible for this was Father Thanh Lãng, who was born in Tonkin in 1924 less than twenty-five miles from where Bỉnh had been ordained in 1793. Father Thanh Lãng had then traveled to Europe (to Rome), where he was ordained as a priest before receiving a PhD in literature in Switzerland. It is likely that during his studies in Rome Father Thanh Lãng learned of Bỉnh's writings from Father Georg Schurhammer, who had discovered them during his exhaustive research on the history of the Jesuits. Recognizing their profound significance for Vietnamese Catholics in general, and for the history of Vietnamese Jesuits in particular, Father Thanh Lãng became determined to find a way to publish at least some of Bỉnh's notebooks. After returning to Vietnam in 1957, he was eventually able to secure funding from the Asia Foundation, which allowed him to publish Bỉnh's notebook of miscellany, *Sách sổ sang chép các việc*, in a photo-reproduced version in Đà Lạt in 1968. Although *Sách sổ* was only a small fraction of Bỉnh's voluminous output, its publication constituted the long-delayed realization of Bỉnh's wish that his writings be sent to his homeland.[8] In arranging for *Sách sổ* to be published, Father Thanh Lãng had revived what had once been a dead end in Vietnamese church history, linguistics, and cultural study. As he forcefully argued in an introductory essay, Bỉnh had made major contributions in all of these realms.[9] The return of at least one of his notebooks to Vietnam helped rescue Bỉnh from obscurity, restoring him to the flow of history.

The return of the Jesuits, followed by the return of one of Bỉnh's notebooks, marked the beginnings of a growing awareness of Bỉnh's life and his role in the history of Vietnamese Catholicism. His contributions have been remarked upon

FIGURE 27. According to a local resident, this newly restored family plot contains the graves of Binh's two sisters and a brother. Although this is impossible to confirm, the dates on the grave markers are consistent with Binh's. Author's photo.

by a number of Vietnamese church historians, who have situated his life within the context of the trajectory of Catholicism in the eighteenth and nineteenth centuries. His writings have been the subject of several Vietnamese-language academic works, including an article examining the content of his collection of letters and poetry and a book exploring his role in the development of the romanized Vietnamese script.[10] Awareness of Bình's role in Vietnamese Catholic history has also trickled back to his home community of Ngải Am. When I visited the village in 2010 asking about Bình, a local resident not only had heard of him but claimed to be a member of his family lineage. He then led me through the nearby fields to a well-tended burial plot in which, he told me, were buried two of Bình's sisters and one of his brothers. The plot had obviously recently been rebuilt in impressive fashion, and one suspects that knowledge of Bình's place in local church history had something to do with it.

As I completed my first draft of this project, an unprecedented event in the history of Catholicism immediately brought to mind Father Bình. The election of Pope Francis on March 12, 2013, marked the first time in history that a member of the Jesuit order had been elevated to the highest office in the church. My first thought on learning of this event was how Bình would have rejoiced at this news and likely commemorated it with a poem. The selection of a Jesuit priest, and one from the former Padroado mission regions of South America, would seem to suggest a complete vindication of Bình's stalwart defenses both of his beloved Jesuit order and of his community and its commitment to that order's traditions. Bình had been both a defender of the Jesuits and a firm believer in the office of the papacy and the ultimate authority of the pope. That a member of this order, once disestablished by the pope himself, could be raised to the position of pontiff suggested, perhaps, the ultimate act of contrition on the part of the church. No longer suspects, or threats to the institutional order, Jesuits could now be trusted with the keys to the palace.

APPENDIX 1

Time Line

1759		Philiphê Bỉnh is born in Hải Dương, Tonkin (northern Vietnam).
		Jesuit order is disbanded in Portugal and its overseas territories.
1773	July 21	Jesuit order is disestablished worldwide by Pope Clement XIV.
		Last delegation of European Jesuits arrives in Tonkin, among them an Italian priest, Father Alexandre-Pompée Castiglioni.
1775		Philiphê Bỉnh leaves home to become a catechist of Father Castiglioni.
1777		Father Castiglioni makes plans to return to Europe, but his departure is halted by social unrest.
1778		Padroado community holds discussions about sending a delegation to Europe to request a bishop for Tonkin.
1780	July	Father Onofre Villiani and catechists Thiều and Cuyên depart for Europe.
1787	April 19	Bỉnh's mentor Father Castiglioni dies after a six-month illness.
	Nov./Dec.	Fathers Thiều and Cuyên return from Europe, join MEP mission.
		Philiphê Bỉnh enters the seminary at Bùi Chu/Trung Linh.
1789		Both apostolic vicars of Tonkin die within months of each other.
1790		New apostolic vicars are appointed, but neither man is consecrated as a bishop.

1792	Sept.	Father Jacques-Benjamin Longer, the apostolic vicar of Western Tonkin, is finally consecrated as a bishop. The ceremony is conducted in Macao by Bishop Marcelino José da Silva.
1793	April	Bishop Longer consecrates his counterpart, Father Feliciano Alonso, as a bishop.
	October	A three-man delegation of Padroado Catholics, Brothers Lịch, Trung and Nhân, travels to Macao.
	Nov. 30	Philiphê Bỉnh is ordained as a priest, along with five other seminarians, in a ceremony conducted by both apostolic vicars.
1794	June	Brother Ngẩn is sent to Macao to replace Lịch.
	Sept.	Bỉnh and Brother Liễn depart for Macao.
1795	Jan. 15	Bỉnh books passage to Goa for himself and Brother Nhân; Bỉnh is denied permission to travel to Goa by the bishop of Macao; Liễn takes his place.
	Jan. 20	Brothers Nhân and Liễn depart for Goa en route to Europe.
	Jan. 24	Bỉnh departs Macao for Tonkin via Canton.
	May 20	Bỉnh finally reaches Tonkin and begins a six-month period of additional fund-raising and ministry.
	May	Liễn and Nhân arrive in Goa and are housed by its archbishop; he sends them back to Macao after eight days.
	Late Oct.	Liễn and Nhân arrive in Macao after trip from Goa via Bombay and Malacca.
	Nov.	Philiphê Bỉnh travels to Macao a second time.
1796	Feb. 14	Philiphê Bỉnh and Brothers Nhân, Ngẩn, and Trung depart for Europe on an English ship, the *St. Anne*
	May 8	Bỉnh's group arrives at St. Helena and transfers from the *St. Anne* to a Portuguese vessel, the *Grão Pará*.
	June 1	The *Grão Pará* departs St. Helena for Lisbon in a large convoy.
	July 26	The Vietnamese delegation arrives in Lisbon and is housed with the Oratorian congregation at the Necessidades convent.
	August 7	Vietnamese delegation meets with the Portuguese ruler at Queluz palace.
1797		Bỉnh suspends his mission while Portugal is in a diplomatic crisis with Spain.
1799	July 15	Dom João reluctantly accepts appointment as prince regent of Portugal.

1800		Vietnamese men fall ill and on the advice of physicians make several trips to the hot baths at Caldas da Rainha, northwest of Lisbon.
	March	Pius VII is elected pope.
1801	October 22	The Portuguese ruler appoints Manuel Galdino as bishop of Tonkin.
	Nov. 11	Galdino's appointment to Tonkin is rescinded and transferred to Macao.
1802	March 26	Brother Liễn dies in Macao after a lengthy illness and expensive hospitalization.
		Brother Trạch travels to Macao to replace Liễn as Brother Thuyên's companion.
	April	Dom Alexandre de Sousa Holstein departs for Rome on Bỉnh's behalf and with the crown prince's authorization.
	May	Bishop Lorenzo Caleppi arrives in Lisbon as the new papal nuncio.
	Nov. 21	Dom Alexandre presents Bỉnh's petition to Pope Pius VII, but the pope defers matter to his nuncio in Lisbon.
	Nov. 22	Brother Nhân becomes the first member of Bỉnh's delegation to die.
1803	April 30	Bishop Galdino departs Lisbon for Macao.
	Sept. 7	Galdino arrives in Macao to take over his bishopric.
1804	January	Galdino confiscates the remaining Jesuit monetary assets.
	March	Galdino forces Brothers Thuyên and Trạch to board a boat to return to Tonkin.
1805	May	Bishop Delgado (apostolic vicar of Eastern Tonkin) reports that the remaining Padroado Catholics have now all accepted the authority of the apostolic vicars.
		Dom João sends a new emissary to the Vatican on Bỉnh's behalf.
1807	May	Bỉnh travels to the Mafra palace to petition the Portuguese ruler.
	June	Bỉnh, Trung, and Ngân move from Necessidades to Casa do Espirito Santo in the Chiado district, in the center of Lisbon.
	Nov. 29	Dom João flees Lisbon to Brazil as Napoleonic armies reach the city's outskirts; Bỉnh is denied permission to join him.
1808	Jan-Aug.	The French occupy Lisbon.
1814	Aug 7	Pope Pius VII announces restoration of the Jesuit order; Bỉnh celebrates with a commemorative poem.

1815		Bỉnh begins his literary project with the *Book of Exemplary Tales*.
1817	May 22	Brother Ngần dies.
1818	April	Bỉnh is given permission to travel to Brazil; he purchases tickets for the boat trip, but Trung falls ill and the trip has to be postponed.
1820		The Portuguese constitutionalist revolt challenges monarchy and the church; a constitutional convention meets in the Necessidades convent's library.
1821	July 3	King Dom João VI returns to Lisbon from Brazilian exile.
1824	Sept.	Brother Trung dies.
1830		Bỉnh writes one last collection of tales, *Tales of Saint Anne*.
1832	Jan. 29	Bỉnh suffers a nearly fatal fall in his room and is slowly nursed back to health.
1833	Jan.	Bỉnh records his last entry in the back of his *Tales of St. Anne*.
	Mar/April	Bỉnh dies at the age of seventy-seven.
1834		Portugal disestablishes all religious orders and congregations; the Casa do Espirito Santo is nationalized and subsequently undergoes a series of transformations from private club to hotel.
1839–55		Bỉnh's writings are acquired by the Vatican Library and added to Borgia collection.
1880s		Casa do Espirito Santo is transformed into the Grand Magasins do Chiado.
1951		Father George Schurhammer, SJ, writes an article describing his discovery of Bỉnh's writings.
1957		The first Jesuits return to Vietnam and establish a seminary in Đà Lạt.
1968		Bỉnh's writings finally return to Vietnam with publication of his *Sách sổ* in Đà Lạt through the efforts of Father Thanh Lãng.
1988	August	The Casa do Espirito Santo site suffers a huge fire and is rebuilt to become a boutique indoor mall.
2013	March 12	Pope Francis is elected to the papacy—the first Jesuit pope.

APPENDIX 2

Cast of Characters

[DATES GIVEN WHEN KNOWN]

Vietnamese Clerics

John Thiều—part of the delegation that traveled to Rome with Onofre Villiani in 1781; he was ordained as a priest in Rome and spent time in Paris at the MEP seminary before returning to Vietnam in 1787.

Bảo Lộc (Paul) Cuyền—part of the delegation that traveled to Rome with Onofre Villiani in 1781; he was ordained as a priest in Rome and spent time in Paris at the MEP seminary before returning to Vietnam in 1787, where he served the Christians of the French mission.

Philiphê do Rosario Bỉnh (1759–1833)

Thome (Thomas) Nhân (1760–1802)—traveled to Lisbon as part of Bỉnh's delegation to the Portuguese court; later became the first member of the Vietnamese delegation to die there, at the age of forty-two, after a lengthy illness. A native of Nghệ An, he had begun to serve the church at the age of twelve and had studied Latin at Kẻ Vĩnh, where Bỉnh had also studied; later he continued his education at Kẻ Bắc; he became one of Bỉnh's companions to Lisbon.

Phanchico (Francisco) Ngân (1770–1817)—a native of Nghệ An, and the youngest member of the delegation to Europe, he traveled to Macao in 1794 and from there took part in the ill-fated trip to Goa with Simão Liên the following year. Later he traveled to Lisbon as part of Bình's delegation to the Portuguese court. He died in 1817 at the age of forty-seven, after what Bình describes as a fifteen-year illness.

José Trung (1759-1824)—traveled to Lisbon as part of Bình's delegation to the Portuguese court; the longest-surviving of Bình's companions, Trung died in 1824 at the age of sixty-five.

Simaõ (Simon) Liễn (1752-1802)—traveled to Goa in 1794 with Phanchico Ngân; never fully recovered from the difficulties of the journey. He was to have joined the 1796 delegation to Portugal, but he was too ill to travel and was forced to remain behind in Macao to await Bình's return. Died in 1802 at the age of fifty after a lengthy hospitalization.

Brother Lịch—a member of the initial delegation sent by Bình to Macao in 1793. After a brief stay in Macao, he abandoned his countrymen, entered the French MEP house, and later returned to Tonkin, where he sold Catholic devotional products purchased in Macao.

Bảo Lộc (Paul) Thuyên—traveled to Macao at some point in 1796 and was companion to Liễn between the departure of Bình's delegation in 1796 and Liễn's death in 1803.

Brother Trạch—sent by the community to Macao upon their learning of Brother Liễn's death in 1802; he remained with Brother Thuyên until both were forcibly expelled by Bishop Galdino in early spring of 1804.

OTHER ASIAN CLERGY: DOMINICANS, APOSTOLIC VICARS, BISHOPS, ARCHBISHOPS

MEP Clergy and Bishops

Claude-Françoise Letondal (1753-1813)—the MEP procurator in Macao during the period when Bình was passing through on his way to Europe. Letondal had taken on the post in 1785. He raised significant obstacles to Bình's progress through Macao, including preventing his departure in 1794. He played a key role in sustaining various Catholic colleges around Asia and was instrumental in helping to establish a new college in Georgetown on the island of Penang in 1807. Traveled extensively, including to Manila, the Malay Peninsula, and even Mexico, looking out for Catholic interests.

Jacques-Benjamin Longer (1752-1831) (known to Vietnamese as Gia)—apostolic vicar of Western Tonkin in the years 1792-1831; he was one of the two clerics who ordained Bình to the priesthood in 1793.

Dominican Bishops

Bishop Manuel Obelar (1734–89) (known to Vietnamese as Cố Khâm)—a Spanish Dominican priest who was appointed apostolic vicar of Eastern Tonkin in 1776, a position he served until his death in 1789; he trained at the University of Salamanca and later entered the Dominican order in 1758.

Bishop Feliciano Alonso (1732–99) (known to Vietnamese as Phê)—apostolic vicar for Eastern Tonkin from his ordination in 1793 until his death in 1799; he co-ordained Bỉnh with Bishop Longer and was responsible for excommunicating Bỉnh and the members of his community for refusing to accept his episcopal rulings.

Bishop Ignacio Delgado (1761–1838)—a Spanish Dominican cleric who succeeded Bishop Alonso as the apostolic vicar of Eastern Tonkin; he held this position from 1799 until he was killed in the course of anti-Catholic persecution during the reign of the Vietnamese Minh Mạng emperor in 1838.

Jesuit Clergy

Father Onofre Villiani (active 1750–80s) (known to Vietnamese as Cố Hậu)—a long-serving Portuguese Jesuit who had been sent to Rome in 1760 to recruit more Jesuits after the order was abolished in Portugal. He brought back a large group of priests to Tonkin in 1773 and upon his return became the de facto father superior of the Padroado priests. He was then again selected to accompany the Vietnamese priests John Thiều and Paul Cuyển on their mission to Rome in 1781, after which he remained in Europe, electing not to make the long journey to Tonkin for a third time.

Father (Tulano) Agostinho Carneiro (1722?–1802) (known to Vietnamese as Cố Định)—a Portuguese and the last European Jesuit loyalist cleric in Tonkin. Relatively little is known about him, though he was apparently active in the Vietnamese mission field for nearly half a century, from 1755 until his death.

Father Nuncio Horta (1722–1801) (known to Vietnamese as Cố An)—a Neopolitan priest who arrived in Tonkin in 1760 and was one of the last two surviving Jesuits sustaining the Padroado community.

Father François Antoine (?–1773)—a French Jesuit priest who served as the order's father superior in Tonkin until his death in 1773; responsible for dispatching a delegation to Rome in 1760 to request more Jesuit priests.

Father Alexandre-Pompée Castiglioni (1736–87)—known to Bỉnh as "Father Luis," Castiglioni was the man who took on the young Vietnamese as a catechist and guided him on his early spiritual path. He was the scion of a Milanese noble family, had entered the Jesuit order at the age of twenty-two after rejecting the marriage his father had arranged for him, and arrived in the Tonkin mission field in 1773 as a member of the last contingent of Jesuits to Vietnam.

Bishops, Nuncios, and Archbishops Elsewhere in Asia

Bishop Marcelino José da Silva (1749-1830)—bishop of Macao from 1790 until his resignation in September of 1802; he then returned to Portugal, where Bỉnh met him again.

Bishop Manuel Galdino (1769-1831)—Franciscan priest selected as bishop to Tonkin in October of 1801, only to have the position changed to Macao. After some delay he was ordained to the position in March of 1803, and after less than two years in Macao he was appointed coadjutor archbishop of Goa in August of 1804. He took over that post upon Manoel de Santa Catarina's death in 1812 and served in it until his own death in 1831.

Giovanni Baptista Marchini (? -1821?)—the papal nuncio to Macao starting in 1786; the man to whom the Jesuit loyalists' assets in Macao were surrendered in early 1804, shortly before Thuyên and Trạch were deported to Tonkin. He remained in this post until at least 1821.

Archbishop Manoel de Santa Catarina (1726-1812)—a Carmelite who served as the archbishop of Goa from 1783 to 1812; he was in that position when Brothers Liễn and Ngân traveled as far as Goa in 1795 and was involved in forcing them to return to Macao. He was later joined by Manuel Galdino as coadjutor before Galdino assumed the archbishopric upon Catarina's death.

OTHER FIGURES IN MACAO AND EN ROUTE TO EUROPE

José Manuel Pinto—governor-general of Macao between 1793 and 1797, and then again from 1800 to 1803. Bỉnh had sought his assistance but was blocked by circumstances and the intervention of Bishop Marcelino.

Rodrigo da Madre de Dios—priest in Macao who ran the order house of St. Paul, where Liễn stayed. He also held the Jesuit funds that the Vietnamese were preserving, until Bishop Galdino forced him to surrender them in 1803.

FIGURES IN LISBON AND EUROPE

Portuguese Royalty and Their Representatives

João VI (1767-1826; r. 1816-22)—crown prince and later king of Portugal, regent to his mentally incompetent mother Queen Maria I. He was the target of Bỉnh's appeals because of his authority vested by the papally granted Padroado Real, the right to appoint bishops to territories in Asia. João became the crown prince of Portugal after the death of his older brother in 1788 and de facto head of state in 1792 when his mother went insane; he formally became prince regent in 1799. He then left for Brazil in November of 1807. With the death of Maria I in 1816 in Rio de Janeiro, he finally became king of Portugal as João VI. Returned to Lisbon in 1821, shortly before his death.

Carlota Joaquina (1775-1830)—queen consort of João VI and wife/consort of the crown prince. Daughter of the Spanish royal house, she married her husband at the age of ten and gave birth to a large number of children, some by her husband and others not. Bỉnh met her on his first trip to Queluz in August of 1796. It is unclear if there were any other direct meetings, though he saw her at subsequent court gatherings.

José (II) Francisco Miguel António de Mendonça (1725-1818)—patriarch of Lisbon from 1786 to 1818. His formal appointment was as archbishop of Lisbon, but he also held the honorary title of patriarch, which was established in the early eighteenth century. He was the man who formally granted Bỉnh the right to serve as a priest, say masses, and hear confessions during his time in Portugal.

Dom Alexandre de Sousa Holstein (1751-1803)—Portuguese envoy to Pope Pius VII in 1803, he carried a message and appeal from Bỉnh but died shortly after an unsuccessful meeting with the pope.

Tomás Xavier de Lima Teles da Silva (1727-1800)—the Marques de Ponte de Lima, former prime minister of Portugal (1786-88). He was the person initially assigned to look after Bỉnh's affairs upon the arrival of the Vietnamese delegation in 1796, and he continued to carry out this task until his death in 1800.

Manuel do Cenáculo Vilas Boas (1724-1814)—Archbishop of Evora, appointed by the Portuguese ruler to assist Bỉnh in his dealings with the papal nuncio in early 1803; when he did not succeed, he returned to Evora.

Oratorian Clergy

Antonio Alvares (1753-1807)—Oratorian priest and native of Lisbon. He was an acquaintance of Bỉnh's who wrote a petition to the throne in early 1802 strongly supporting the Vietnamese position regarding Portuguese Padroado authority to appoint a bishop to Tonkin.

José Pegado de Azevedo (1750-1812)—Oratorian priest and native Lisbonite who had joined the congregation in 1778. Upon their arrival in 1796, he worked with the Vietnamese delegation in polishing the rough drafts of their early petitions to the Portuguese court. In July of 1801 he left the Oratorian order house when he was elevated to the position of bishop of Angra (in the Azores).

Teodoro Almeida (1722-1804)—head of the Oratorian congregation in Lisbon until his death; he had been an important scholar and teacher of science. His strong defense of the religious orders and congregations led to an extended exile under pressure from Pombal.

Popes and Papal Representatives

Pope Pius VII (1800-1823)—pope noteworthy for rebuilding the Catholic Church after the chaos of the French Revolution and the Napoleonic Wars. In 1803 he received and deflected an appeal from Binh to permit the Portuguese ruler to appoint a bishop to Tonkin, a petition delivered by Dom Alexandre de Sousa Holstein. Later, in 1814, he restored the Jesuit order.

Bishop Bartolomeo Pacca (1756-1844)—subsequently consecrated as a cardinal in 1801, Bishop Pacca arrived as the nuncio in Lisbon on March 21, 1794, and served in the position until his return to Rome to join the Curia in 1801. He was the Vatican's primary defender of the system of apostolic vicars in Tonkin and successfully undermined Binh's project to persuade the Portuguese ruler to appoint a bishop to Tonkin.

Bishop Lorenzo Caleppi (1741-1817)—arrived in Lisbon in the spring of 1802 as the second papal nuncio to Portugal during the time of Binh's residence there; he continued Cardinal Pacca's project to block Binh's undertaking and unsuccessfully attempted to lure the Vietnamese delegation to Rome. He later joined the Portuguese royal family in exile in Brazil.

APPENDIX 3

Texts Used by Bỉnh in His Writing Projects

Based on comments and notes scattered through his writings, a picture emerges of at least some of the titles that Bỉnh read and drew from for his literary production. The majority of the texts he used for his research were in Portuguese or Latin. It is clear that at some point he must have had access to some texts in Chinese as well as in the Vietnamese demotic script, though these were probably things he had seen either in Macao or prior to his departure from Tonkin. Among the texts that Bỉnh used are the following:

- *Dictionarium Annamiticum, Lusitanum, et Latinum* [Annamite, Portuguese, and Latin dictionary] (Rome, 1651) by Alexander de Rhodes, which Bỉnh copied out as one of his early writing exercises.
- *Cathechismus* (Rome, 1658), by Alexander de Rhodes, which he also copied out in part.
- *Peregrinação* [The travels (of Mendes Pinto)] (Lisbon, 1614), by Mendes Pinto, which Bỉnh translated in part into Vietnamese.
- *Vita Francisci Borgiae, tertij Societatis Iesu generalis* (The life of Francis Borgia, third general of the Society of Jesus] (Antwerp, 1598), by Pedro de Ribadeneyra.
- *De civitate Dei* [The city of God] (fifth century), by Augustine, which Bỉnh cites on p. 20 of his *Sách gương truyện*.
- *Speculo magno* [The grand vision??] (Basel, 1571), by Lorenzo Ventura (cited in *Sách gương truyện,* p. 127), which was an early work on alchemy.
- Numerous texts by Geronimo Maiorica. While Bỉnh does not cite particular ones, they must at least have included the two following works:
  a) *Ông Thánh I-na-xu Truyện—Ông Thánh Phan-chi-cô Xa-vi-e Truyện* [The story of Saint Ignatius—The story of Saint Francis Xavier]
  b) *Các thánh truyện* (Stories of the saints), in 11 vols.

- *Historia et relatione del Tunchino e del Giaponne* [History and description of Tonkin and of Japan] (Rome, 1665), by Giovanni Marini.
- *Relação da prizão, e morte dos quarto veneraveis padres da Companhia* [An account of the imprisonment and death of four venerable fathers of the Company] (Lisbon, 1738), by José da Costa or Manuel de Campos, cited in "Missionario do Tunkim," in an untitled volume of miscellanea (Ms. Borgiana Tonchinese 10, 1813?, Biblioteca Apostolica Vaticana), 1–2; Bỉnh copies substantially from this book about martyrdoms in Tonkin in 1737.
- *Imagem da virtude em o noviciado da Companhia de Jesus do Real Collegio do Espirito, Santo de Evora do Reyno de Portugal: na qual se contèm a fundaçam desta Santa Casa, vida de feu fundador, & mais servos de Deos, que nella, ou foraõ mestres, ou discipulos* [Images of virtue in the novitiate of the Company of Jesus ...] (Lisbon/Coimbra, 1714), by Antonio Franco; cited by Bỉnh in an untitled volume of miscellanea (Ms. Borgiana Tonchinese 10, 1813?, Biblioteca Apostolica Vaticana), 178–79. A history of the early years of the Jesuits at the Portuguese court.
- *Vida de S. Ignacio de Loyola fundador da Companhia de Jesus* [The life of St. Ignatius of Loyola, founder of the Company of Jesus] (Lisbon, 1718), by Francisco de Mattos, cited by Bỉnh in an untitled volume of miscellanea (Ms. Borgiana Tonchinese 10, 1813?, Biblioteca Apostolica Vaticana), 252.
- *Methodo para bem comprender a historia das papas, que contem o que se passou de mais particular em seus pontificadas* [Method for understanding the history of the popes, and relating the most noteworthy occurrences of their pontificates] (Lisbon: Na Officina de Miguel Mansescal, 1719), by Francesco Ferram De Castello Branco (translation from the French).
- *Da affeicao, e amor, que devem ter a Maria Virgem Santissima May de Jesus, Deos e Homem, todos redemidos por seu Filho* [Of the affection and love that should be given to the Most Blessed Virgin Mary, Mother of Jesus, God Incarnate, and all redeemed by her Son] (Coimbra, 1742), by Juan Eusebio Nieremberg.
- *Alma instruida na doutrina e vida Christa* [Instructions to the soul on the doctrines and life of Christ] (Lisbon, 1699), by Father Manoel Antonio Pinheiro Fernandes.

While Bỉnh did not typically provide bibliographical details for his volumes or cite sources for his various anecdotes, he sometimes referred to the texts on which he must have relied. A notable example of this is in the preface to his collection of tales about St. Francis de Borgia (*Truyện Ông Thánh Phanchicô Borja*). Here he discussed the various authors who had previously written books about Borgia in a number of European languages. He cited no fewer than eleven authors of previous accounts, including Dionisio Vasques, Peter Ribadeneira, Andre Escoto, Virgilio Cepari, Philip Glisolfi, Eusebio Nieremberg, Verjur, Daniel Bartholi, Alvaro Cienfuegos, Matteo Ricci, and finally the one author who had previously written about Borgia in Vietnamese, Geronimo Maiorica.[1]

ABBREVIATIONS

AMEP	Archives of the Missions Étrangères de Paris, Paris
IL	Philiphê Bỉnh, *Truyện Ông Thánh Ignacio de Loyola lập Dòng Đức Chúa Jesu* [Tales of Saint Ignatius of Loyola establishing the Order of the Virtuous Lord Jesus], 1819, ms. Borgiana Tonchinese 5, Biblioteca Apostolica Vaticana.
MP	Philiphê Bỉnh, *Truyện nhật trình Ông Fernad Mendes Pinto* [Tales of the travels of Fernando Mendes Pinto], 1817, ms. Borgiana Tonchinese 20, Biblioteca Apostolica Vaticana.
NT	Philiphê Bỉnh, *Nhật trình kim thư khất chính chúa giáo* [Golden book recording a journey to seek an official religious leader], 1796–1826, ms. Borgiana Tonchinese 7, Biblioteca Apostolica Vaticana.
PB	Philiphê Bỉnh, *Truyện Ông Thánh Phanchicô de Borja* [Tales of Saint Francis de Borgia], 1820, Ms. Borgiana Tonchinese 4, Biblioteca Apostolica Vaticana.
PX	Philiphê Bỉnh, *Truyện Ông Thánh Phanchicô Xavier* [Tales of Saint Francis Xavier], 1818, ms. Borgiana Tonchinese 6, Biblioteca Apostolica Vaticana.
SA	Philiphê Bỉnh, *Truyện bà Thánh Anna* [Tales of Saint Anne], 1830, ms. Borgiana Tonchinese 18, Biblioteca Apostolica Vaticana.
SGT	Philiphê Bỉnh, *Sách gương truyện* [Book of exemplary tales], 2 vols., 1815, ms. Borgiana Tonchinese 9, 16, Biblioteca Apostolica Vaticana.
SS	Philiphê Bỉnh, *Sách sổ sang chép các việc* [Notebook that transmits and records all matters], 1822–32, ms. Borgiana Tonchinese 3, Biblioteca Apostolica Vaticana.
TAĐN	Philiphê Bỉnh, *Truyện Anam* [Tales of Annam], vol. 1, *Đàng Ngoài* [The Outer Region], 1822, ms. Borgiana Tonchinese 1, Biblioteca Apostolica Vaticana.
TAĐT	Philiphê Bỉnh, *Truyện Anam* [Tales of Annam], vol. 2, *Đàng Trọng* [The Inner Region], 1822, ms. Borgiana Tonchinese 2, Biblioteca Apostolica Vaticana.

NOTES

INTRODUCTION

1. Bỉnh's own writings never mention his family or clan name. The information regarding the likelihood of his family name having been Nguyễn Văn comes from local residents with whom I spoke on a 2010 visit. They also suggested that the family had been forced to change their clan name to Nguyễn Hữu during a later period of religious persecution. Members of this clan continue to live in the area, and I was shown around by a man who claimed to be part of Bỉnh's extended lineage.

2. Roland Jacques, *Portuguese Pioneers of Vietnamese Linguistics* (Bangkok: Orchid Press, 2002), 51–54.

3. Several French scholars have worked to preserve memories of the Portuguese connections to Vietnam in the early modern period. Pierre-Yves Manguin's *Les Nguyen, Macau et le Portugal: Aspects politiques et commerciaux d'une relation privilégiée en Mer de Chine 1773–1802* (Paris: EFEO, 1984) reveals the crucial economic and political linkages that the Vietnamese and Portuguese maintained via the Lusitanian commercial hub at Macao. Roland Jacques has written several volumes on the crucial role played by the early Portuguese missionaries in spreading Catholicism in Vietnam, including *Portuguese Pioneers* and *Les missionaires portugais et les débuts de l'Église catholique au Viêt-nam*, vol. 1 (Reichstett, France: Định Hướng Tùng Thu, 2004).

4. A detailed discussion of the grant's historical context and subsequent contestations can be found in Teotonio R. de Souza and Surachai Chusriphan, "Padroado," in *A Dictionary of Asian Christianity*, ed. Scott Sunquist (Grand Rapids, MI: Wm. Eerdmans, 2001), 623–27.

5. The Spanish in particular were aggressive in their interpretation of the agreements and were quite willing to ignore them when circumstances permitted.

6. For more on the growing tensions between the papacy and the weakened Portuguese monarchy, see Charles Boxer, *Four Centuries of Portuguese Expansion, 1515–1825: A Succinct Survey* (Berkeley: University of California Press, 1969), 64ff.

7. Pope Paul V had, by 1608, already formally ended the Portuguese monopoly on sending missionaries to Asia, thus opening the way for Spanish missionaries to operate freely in the region, including their prominent outpost in the Philippines.

8. As recently as the 1980s these treaties were invoked in the context of international territorial disputes, as in the case of the Argentine conflict with Great Britain over the Falkland Islands.

9. Trương Bá Cần, *Lịch sử phát triển công giáo ở Việt Nam* [A history of the development of Catholicism in Vietnam], vol. 1 (Hà Nội: Nhà Xuất Bản Tôn Giáo, 2008), 26.

10. P. Manuel Teixeira, *As missões portuguesas no Vietnam*, vol. 14 of *Macau e a sua diocese* (Macau: Imprensa Nacional, 1977), 295n1.

11. Jacques, *Missionaires portuguais*, 52. There is in fact considerable uncertainty about the first missionary contacts with Vietnam. Trương Bá Cần notes that in 1586 two Spaniards may have made it to Quảng Nam, though there is some debate on this (see *Lịch sử phát triển*, 26–27). Even more tangentially, St. Francis Xavier is said to have anchored along the Vietnamese coast three times between 1549 and 1552, though never actually setting foot on Vietnamese soil (*Lịch sử phát triển*, 25). Trương Ba Cấn even cites a later nineteenth-century Vietnamese court chronicle that speaks of a Westerner named I-nê-xu who was preaching Christianity in several hamlets in 1533, though it is unclear precisely where this took place. The incident to which he refers can be found in *Khâm định Việt sử thông giám cương mục*, ed. Viện Sử Học (Hà Nội: Nhà Xuất Bản Giáo Dục, 1998), 720.

12. Trương Bá Cần, *Lịch sử phát triển*, 26–37.

13. For a useful brief summary of the initial missionary work of the various European religious orders in Southeast Asia, see Tara Alberts, *Conflict and Conversion: Catholicism in Southeast Asia, 1500–1700* (Oxford: Oxford University Press, 2013), 23–33.

14. Boxer, *Four Centuries*, 233ff.

15. On Vietnamese jurisdictional hierarchies, see Đặng Phương-Nghi, *Les institutions publiques du Viêt-Nam au XVIIIe siècle* (Paris: EFEO, 1969), 77–89; for a concise contemporary description by a European missionary, see a letter from Father M. Le Pavec to his parents in *Nouvelles des missions orientales reçues à Londres, par les directeurs de Séminaire des Missions Étrangères, en 1793, 1794, 1795 & 1796* (Paris: Séminaire des Missions Étrangères, 1797), 79.

16. An array of (especially) nineteenth-century Vietnamese gazetteers attest to these name changes and territorial and administrative adjustments. A good example is the state-directed geographical project named the *Đại Nam nhất thống chí*, which is a province-by-province examination of, among other things, the administrative hierarchies of places along the length of the country. See *Đại Nam nhất thống chí* [The unification records of the Great South], trans. Phạm Trọng Điềm (Huế: Nhà Xuất Bản Thuận Hóa, 1996), 3:448–49. See also Đào Duy Anh, *Đất nước Việt Nam qua các đời: Nghiên cứu địa lý học lịch sử Việt Nam* [Vietnamese territory throughout time: Research into the historical geography of Vietnam] (Huế: Nhà Xuất Bản Thuận Hóa, 1994).

17. Alain Forest, *Les missionaires français au Tonkin et au Siam, XVIIe–XVIIIe siècles*, vol. 2, *Histoires du Tonkin* (Paris: L'Harmattan, 1998), 126.

18. One can only imagine the anxiety that this might have raised among Vietnamese civic officials had they been aware of this. They would have found not only that the lands they controlled now were being repartitioned by a group of foreigners but, equally troubling, that these foreigners were laying claim to authority over the Vietnamese who lived in these territorial divisions. Most indications are, however, that Vietnamese administrators were unaware of the nuances of Catholic administrative authority. Rather, they viewed the issue of Catholicism more broadly in terms of what they regarded as a socially and politically threatening religious doctrine being spread by outsiders.

19. For a detailed European description of Vietnamese religious practices in the eighteenth century, see Adriano di St. Thecla's *Opusculum de sectis apud Sinenses et Tunkinenses* [A small treatise on the sects among the Chinese and Tonkinese], ed. and trans. Olga Dror (Ithaca, NY: Cornell Southeast Asia Program, 2002). On Buddhism in particular, see 183–216.

20. Thongchai Winichakul, *Siam Mapped: A History of the Geobody of a Nation* (Honolulu: University of Hawaii Press, 1994).

21. John Smail, "On the Possibility of an Autonomous History of Southeast Asia," *Journal of Southeast Asian History* 2, no. 2 (July 1961): 72–102.

22. Charles Boxer, *The Portuguese Seaborne Empire, 1415–1825* (1969; repr., Manchester: Carcanet, 1991), 247.

23. Li Tana, *Nguyen Cochinchina: Southern Vietnam in the Seventeenth and Eighteenth Centuries* (Ithaca, NY: Cornell Southeast Asia Program, 1998), 12–13; Keith Taylor, "Surface Orientations in Vietnam: Beyond Histories of Nation and Region," *Journal of Southeast Asian Studies* 57, no. 4 (November 1998): 949–78, and "Nguyen Hoang and the Beginning of Vietnam's Southward Expansion," in *Southeast Asia in the Early Modern Era*, ed. Anthony Reid (Ithaca, NY: Cornell University Press, 1993), 64–65.

24. George Schurhammer, SI, "Annamitische Xaveriusliteratur," in *Sonderdruck aus Missionswissenschaftliche Studien, Pr. Festgabe Joh. Dindinger, O.M.I.* (Aachen: W. Metz, 1951), 300–314.

25. Laurel Thatcher Ulrich, *A Midwife's Tale: The Story of Martha Ballard* (New York: Vintage Books, 1991).

26. Ulrich expands on her project and approach in "Interviews with Laurel Thatcher Ulrich," a compilation of the questions and answers from three interviews by Laurie Kahn-Leavitt, September 1991, October 1993, and March 1994, accessed August 17, 2012, http://dohistory.org/book/100_interview.html.

27. Roxana Waterson, "Introduction: Analysing Personal Narratives," in *Southeast Asian Lives: Personal Narratives and Historical Experience*, ed. Roxana Waterson (Singapore: NUS Press, 2007), 3.

28. Ibid., 31.

1. PHILIPHÊ BỈNH AND THE CATHOLIC GEOGRAPHIES OF TONKIN

1. *SS*, 1–2. Bỉnh's list is problematic, not only because he mentions eight arrivals and gives only seven names, but also because most other sources list far fewer men in this contingent. Montezon's detailed 1858 history of the Jesuits in Vietnam lists only two men who arrived in 1773, Joseph Candia and Alexandre-Pompée Castiglioni (395); other than that, it lists

only Horta as arriving between 1760 and 1764. It records no other Jesuits arriving at this time. Jesuits, Fortuné de Montezon, Ed Estève, Alexandre de Rhodes, Joseph Tissanier, and Metello Saccano, *Mission de la Cochinchine et du Tonkin avec gravure et carte géographique* (Paris: Charles Douniol, 1858).

2. Trần Công Hiến and Trần Huy Phác, *Hải Dương phong vật chí* [Records of the customs and peoples of Hai Duong] (Hà Nội: Nhả Xuất Bản Lao Động, 2009), 63–64.

3. See *Đại Nam nhất thống chí*, 3:431. The temple is found on early twentieth-century maps of the province but no longer appears to be extant.

4. Phan Huy Chú, *Hoàng Việt địa dự chí* [Geographical records of the imperial Việt] (Huế: Nhà Xuất Bản Thuận Hóa, 1997), 95–97.

5. Trần Công Hiến and Trần Huy Phác, *Hải Dương*, 147.

6. K. Taylor, "Surface Orientations," 961.

7. *Đại Nam nhất thống chí*, 3:448–49.

8. See also Ngô Thì Nhậm, "Hải Dương chí lược" [Summary records of Hải Dương], in Ngô Thì Nhậm, *Ngô Thì Nhậm toàn tập* [Collected works of Ngo Thi Nham] (Hà Nội: NXB Khoa Học Xã Hội, 2004), 533–36, which talks about Nguyễn Bỉnh Khiêm.

9. Trần Công Hiến and Trần Huy Phác, *Hải Dương*, 253, 248.

10. Forest, *Missionaires français*, 3:149.

11. On the Jesuit project in Japan, see Andrew Ross, *A Vision Betrayed: The Jesuits in Japan and China, 1542–1742* (Maryknoll, NY: Orbis Books, 1994).

12. For a brief discussion of the effective linkage between Catholicism and the Portuguese who brought it, see Nola Cooke, "Strange Brew: Global, Regional and Local Factors behind the 1690 Prohibition of Christian Practice in Nguyễn Cochinchina," *Journal of Southeast Asian Studies* 39, no. 3 (October 2008): 398–99.

13. Alberts, *Conflict and Conversion*, 78–79.

14. Forest, *Missionaires français*, 2:126.

15. David Mitchell, *The Jesuits: A History* (London: MacDonald, 1980), 162.

16. Adrien Launay, *Nos missionaires, précédés d'une étude historique sur la Société des Missions-Étrangères* (Paris, 1886), 17, quoted in Peter Phan, *Mission and Catechesis: Alexandre de Rhodes and Inculturation in Seventeenth-Century Vietnam* (Maryknoll, NY: Orbis Books, 1998), 67.

17. Boxer notes that the first secretary of the Propaganda Fide, Francesco Ingoli, had been a strong opponent both of Portugal and of the Jesuits and had sought ways to erode their power. While he was no longer in the position by this time, it is likely that this attitude carried over even after his retirement. Boxer, *Portuguese Seaborne Empire*, 235.

18. Teixeira, *Missões portuguesas*, 165; Mitchell, *Jesuits*, 162, suggests that de Rhodes himself proposed this solution.

19. For a comprehensive discussion of this in the earlier Vietnamese context, see Cooke, "Strange Brew," 384.

20. The history of the MEP has been documented in numerous studies, the most well known of which were produced in the late nineteenth and early twentieth centuries by Adrian Launay, including *Histoire générale de la Société des Missions Étrangères* (1894; repr., Paris: Missions Étrangères de Paris, 2003). The best modern account with a focus on its projects in mainland Southeast Asia is Forest, *Missionaires français*.

21. Schurhammer, "Annamitische Xaveriusliteratur," 305.

22. A concise summary of the MEP's creation and expansion into Vietnam and of the Jesuit resistance can be found in Jacob Ramsay, *Mandarins and Martyrs: The Church and the Nguyen Dynasty in Early Nineteenth-Century Vietnam* (Stanford, CA: Stanford University Press, 2008), 18–20.

23. Teixeira, *Missões portuguesas*, 183.

24. Of these men, the largest group (fifteen) had been Portuguese and another eleven had been Italian, a reminder that not all Padroado missionaries were Portuguese, though all served under ultimate Portuguese oversight.

25. Forest, *Missionaires français*, 2:135–48.

26. Teixeira, *Missões portuguesas*, 186.

27. Boxer, *Four Centuries*, 239.

28. Ibid., 243.

29. For more on Marini (and many others), see D. Basilio Sebastian Castellanos de Losada, *Biografía eclesiástica completa* (Madrid: D. Alejandro Gomez Fuentenebro, 1863). Marini's brief biography is in 18:275–76.

30. Texeira, *Missões portuguesas*, 186–87.

31. Forest, *Missionaires français*, 2:157.

32. Jacques de Bourges to the Sacred Congregation, September 19, 1700, cited in Forest, *Missionaires français*, 2:157. The "Kingdom of Bao" is a reference to the so-called "Bau Lords," an autonomous family-run fiefdom in Hưng Hóa, northwest of Thăng Long, established in the 1520s.

33. Ramsay, *Mandarins and Martyrs*, 19.

34. The year 1696 was, ironically, when the Jesuits finally managed to return to Tonkin.

35. Like its Eastern counterpart, the Western Tonkin Vicariate would remain under the continuous authority of a single religious community and a single nationality for nearly the next two centuries. French MEP clerics occupied the position of apostolic vicar and later that of bishop from 1678 until the appointment of the first non-MEP and non-French bishop in 1950. For details, see David M. Cheney, "Archdiocese of Hà Nội," Catholic Hierarchy, n.d., accessed August 25, 2015, http://catholic-hierarchy.org/diocese/dhano.html.

36. On the Jesuits in China, see David E. Mungello, *Curious Land: Jesuit Accommodation and the Origins of Sinology* (Honolulu: University of Hawaii Press, 1989); Liam Brockey, *Journey to the East: The Jesuit Missions to China, 1579–1724* (Cambridge, MA: Belknap Press, 2008); Ross, *Vision Betrayed*.

37. Hilario Ocio, OP, and Eladio Neira, OP, *Misioneros dominicos en el Extremo Oriente, 1587–1835* (Manila: Orientalia Dominicana, 2000), 16.

38. Ibid., 575.

39. Forest, *Missionaires français*, 3:37n39; the Bible story is found in 1 Kings 3:16–28.

40. Teixeira, *Missões portuguesas*, 184ff.

41. *SS*, 117; *TAĐN*, 56–57.

42. Forest has a detailed description of this episode, including discussion of the various papal briefs and decrees—he argues (*Missionaires français*, 153) that the brief requiring the Jesuit withdrawal was actually issued in 1678, that it finally arrived in 1680, and that the Jesuits did not leave (or at least some of them) until 1682 (161).

43. *TAĐN*, 81. See the passage in Exod. 32:1–5.

44. Forest, *Missionaires français*, 2:162–63.

45. A good introduction to Pombal's life and career can be found in Kenneth Maxwell, *Pombal: Paradox of the Enlightenment* (Cambridge: Cambridge University Press, 1995).

46. An account of Pombal's role in suppressing the Jesuits can be found in Sydney F. Smith, *The Suppression of the Society of Jesus* (Leominster: Gracewing Press, 2004), 5–17; see also A. R. Disney, *A History of Portugal and the Portuguese Empire* (Cambridge: Cambridge University Press, 2009), 1:298–305. Bỉnh himself discusses it in *TAĐN*, 318–19, 329–30.

47. *TAĐN*, 320.

48. *PX*, 578–79; Bỉnh discusses Villiani's arrival in Tonkin in *TAĐN*, 333. According to Trương Bá Cần (*Lịch sử phát triển*, 545), before setting off for Rome Villiani had decided to join the Capucin order, apparently to enable him to persuade priests of that order to move into the territory in which he was operating.

49. Their arrival dates are given in Trương Bá Cần, *Lịch sử phát triển*, 539–40. Some sources give Carneiro's nationality as Spanish—see Trương Bá Cần, *Lịch sử phát triển*, 539n123, though most agree he was Portuguese.

50. *NT*, 225.

51. Teixeira, *Missões portuguesas*, 484–85. There is some confusion about when Father Carneiro died, but an 1809 journal entry by Bishop Longer appears to confirm that this last Jesuit priest in Tonkin died in 1802. *Nouvelles lettres edifiantes des missions de la Chine et des Indes orientales* (Paris: Chez Ad. Le Clere, 1823), 8:279.

52. A brief summary of this sequence of events can be found in Disney, *History of Portugal*, 1:298–305, though Disney argues that Pombal never seriously considered creating a separate national Portuguese church but rather sought greater autonomy from Vatican political dictates.

53. Trương Bá Cần, *Lịch sử phát triển*, citing a letter by an MEP priest, Father Serard, 542; Bỉnh reports that news of the dissolution of the order reached Tonkin in 1774 (*SS*, 3).

54. *SS*, 24–25.

55. Jesuits et al., *Mission de la Cochinchine*, 335.

56. P. de Ravignan, *Clément XIII et Clément XIV: Volume supplémentaire, documents historiques et critiques* (Paris: Julien, Lanier, 1854), 384.

57. Phan, *Mission and Catechesis*, 104.

58. For more on the institution of "catechists" as established by Alexandre de Rhodes, see ibid., 101–6.

59. Details of these hardships of flooding, famine, and popular unrest can be found in *Đại Việt sử ký tục biên* [A continuation of the historical records of Đại Việt], trans. Ngô Thế Long and Nguyễn Kim Hưng, ed. Nguyễn Đổng Chi (Hà Nội: Nhà Xuất Bản Khoa Học Xã Hội, 1991), 438ff.

60. *TAĐN*, 351–52. See *PX*, 579; also Đỗ Quang Chính, *Dòng tên trong xã hội Đại Việt, 1615–1773* [The Jesuit order in Vietnamese society, 1615–1773] (Wichita Falls, TX: NXB Tôn Giáo, 2006), 440.

61. *SS*, 6.

62. *SS*, 13.

63. *SS*, 6.

64. Bỉnh briefly describes their trip in *TAĐN*, 358–59.

65. *TAĐN*, 360–61.

66. *TAĐN*, 359–60.
67. Their story is told in some detail in *TAĐN*, 359–79.
68. *TAĐN*, 360.
69. *TAĐN*, 365.
70. *SS*, 14–15.
71. For more on the role of catechists as crucial intermediaries between priests and populations, see Phan, *Mission and Catechesis*, 101–6.
72. Forest, *Missionaires français*, 1:181ff.
73. Ibid., 2:124ff.
74. Jean-François Le Roy to Georges Alary, July 23, 1782, AMEP, vol. 691, p. 272, cited in Forest, *Missionaires français*, 2:152–53.
75. De Rhodes had specifically produced the text for instructional purposes, and it was printed in a side-by-side bilingual version juxtaposing Latin with romanized Vietnamese, thus making it accessible to students acquainted only with romanized Vietnamese and those with more advanced language skills. Phan (*Mission and Catechesis*, 107–202) discusses this text, its origins, and its content at great length and gives an English translation of the original.
76. Forest, *Missionaires français*, 3:151ff.; see also Alberts, *Conflict and Conversion*, 124–28, discussing some of the teaching texts used in Siam, which were likely used in the seminaries in Tonkin as well.
77. Teixeira, *Missões portuguesas*, 492–93.
78. *TAĐN*, 304–5; Bình records the full story of Trêu, his career as a priest and his martyrdom, on pages 300 to 318.
79. *TAĐN*, 379–80.
80. A brief summary of Alonso's tenure as bishop between 1793 and his death in 1799 can be found in Trương Bá Cần, *Lịch sử phát triển*, 501–4; his life and career are described in the invaluable register of Dominican missionaries in Asia produced by Ocio and Neira, *Misioneros dominicos*, 365–66.
81. Longer would hold his post until his death in 1831, a tenure of more than forty years. For an excellent brief biographical account of his life, see "Jacques Benjamin Longer," AMEP, n.d., accessed July 27, 2012, http://archives.mepasie.org/notices/notices-biographiques/longer.
82. *TAĐN*, 382.
83. *TAĐN*, 426.
84. *SS*, 29–30, 87.
85. *TAĐN*, 302–3.
86. *SS*, 29–30.

2. A CATHOLIC COMMUNITY IN CRISIS

1. Unauthored, undated document that appears to be a 1786 or 1787 recapitulation of events in Tonkin over the previous decade, AMEP, vol. 691, p. 989; see also *SS*, 3.
2. Louis Roux to Pierre-Antoine Blandin, June 16, 1786, AMEP, vol. 691, p. 735. Castiglioni wrote four separate letters, all dated July 8, 1786, to various correspondents in Europe and Macao: AMEP, vol. 691, pp. 710–11 (to Jean-Joseph Descourvières), 714–21

(to Pierre Blandin), and 855–59 (to unnamed), and AMEP, vol. 700, pp. 1295–1301 (to Claude Françoise Letondal).

3. Those executed included one Spanish Dominican priest and four Vietnamese Catholics; there would be one more execution in 1798, that of Jean Dat (see Montezon's account of that execution in Jesuits et al., *Mission de la Cochinchine*, 404). A more detailed account of Dat's life and death is in Louis Beaulieu, *La Salle des Martyrs du Séminaire des Missions Étrangères* (Paris: Charles Douniol, 1865), 69–75.

4. Details can be found in George Dutton, *The Tây Sơn Uprising: Society and Rebellion in Eighteenth-Century Vietnam* (Honolulu: University of Hawaii Press, 2006), 44, 79, 97.

5. Jacques Benjamin Longer to Claude Françoise Letondal, July 17, 1791, AMEP, vol. 700, p. 1473.

6. Charles de la Motte to Denis Boiret, June 19, 1793, AMEP, vol. 692, p. 450.

7. Pierre Eyot to Pierre-Antoine Blandin, June 19, 1793, AMEP, vol. 692, p. 444.

8. Philippe Sérard to Pierre-Antoine Blandin, June 5, 1793/May 28, 1794, AMEP, vol. 692, p. 517.

9. Pierre Eyot to Pierre-Antoine Blandin, August 6, 1794, AMEP, vol. 692, p. 560. "Xứ Nam" refers to the region centered on the city of Nam Định.

10. Dutton, *Tây Sơn Uprising*, 191.

11. Locations of the MEP missionaries in 1794: Le Pavec in Xứ Đoài; Tessier in Xứ Thành; Langlois in Kẻ Sóc, Kẻ Rùng, and Bổ Bắt; Bissachere in Bác Vàng, Nam Xang, and Kẻ Chuôn; de la Motte in Kẻ Sở, Iên Chuyên, and Kẻ Vôi; and Eyot in Kẻ Trình, Thanh Liêm, and Bình Lục.

12. Trương Bá Cần, *Lịch sử phát triển*, 503.

13. Lê Ngọc Bích, *Nhân vật công giáo Việt Nam, thế kỷ XVIII–XIX–XX* [Figures in Vietnamese Catholicism, eighteenth, nineteenth, and twentieth centuries] ([Thành Phố Hồ Chí Minh]: n.p., n.d.), 370.

14. *Đồng khánh địa dự chí* [The Dong Khanh gazetteer], ed. Ngô Đức Thọ, Nguyễn Văn Nguyên, and Philippe Papin (Hà Nội: EFEO, 2003), 1468, 1471.

15. Indeed, the fact that he had held this position also explains his later and repeated complaints about the seizure of Jesuit properties after his departure. Although he had left for Europe, the reports that he later received regarding the gradual expropriation of Jesuit properties made him aware of what had been going on. He would have seen this not merely as an attack on the Jesuit order generally but also as an affront to his own past curatorial responsibilities.

16. *TAĐN*, 404.

17. See *TAĐN*, 404–5.

18. *TAĐN*, 305.

19. Bỉnh later wrote that he had not imagined that this departure would eventually lead to his traveling overseas. *TAĐN*, 408.

20. *NT*, viii.

21. Bỉnh later wrote that he saw people wearing a version of it in Lisbon, where no clergy considered it to be improper; *SS*, 47.

22. *NT*, ix; this episode is also discussed in *TAĐN*, 402–3.

23. *TAĐN*, 402–3.

24. Vicente Rafael, *Contracting Colonialism: Translation and Christian Conversion in Tagalog Society under Early Spanish Rule* (Durham, NC: Duke University Press, 1993), 28–29.

25. Tara Alberts, "Catholic Written and Oral Cultures in Seventeenth-Century Vietnam," *Journal of Early Modern History* 16 (2012): 384.

26. Brian Ostrowski, "The Nôm Works of Geronimo Maiorica, S.J. (1589–1656) and Their Christology," PhD diss., Cornell University, 2006, 47. The terms used here are themselves transliterations into the romanized Vietnamese of the original *nôm* characters.

27. I will return to Maiorica in chapter 8, when I discuss Bỉnh's writings within a tradition, begun by Maiorica, among others, of composing "tales" to popularize elements of the Catholic faith for Vietnamese audiences.

28. Jacques-Benjamin Longer to Claude-Françoise Letondal in Macao, September 18, 1796, AMEP, vol. 701, p. 181. For an extended discussion of Vietnamese imperial tabooing practices, including a brief discussion of those implemented by the Tây Sơn leaders in the late 1780s and early 1790s, see Ngô Đức Thọ, *Nghiên cứu chữ húy Việt Nam qua các triều đại / Les caractères interdits au Vietnam à travers l'histoire*, trans. Emmanuel Poisson (Hà Nội: Nhà Xuất Bản Văn Hóa, 1997).

29. Similiar issues had occurred in China, where Tara Alberts writes of a Jesuit priest, Prospero Intorcetta, who noted that his Chinese students had difficulty pronouncing the letters "B," "D," "R," and any digraphs, and would spontaneously alter these letters and insert vowels into diagraphs to make them more pronounceable. Alberts, "Catholic Written and Oral Cultures," 399.

30. *TAĐN*, 401–2.

31. For an example of this, see Geronimo Maiorica, *Các thánh truyện (tháng giêng)* [Tales of the Saints (January)] ([Thành Phố Hồ Chí Minh?]: n.p., 1997), 484 (23 in original pagination).

32. *NT*, viii or ix; Bỉnh also discusses this issue in some detail in *TAĐN*, 401ff.

33. *TAĐN*, 418.

34. Trương Bá Cần, *Lịch sử phát triển*, 547n150.

35. Rafael, *Contracting Colonialism*, 72.

36. *NT*, introduction (n.p).

37. *NT*, 231–39.

38. Cited in Alberts, "Catholic Written and Oral Cultures," 396–97.

39. *TAĐN*, 423.

40. *TAĐN*, 424.

41. This is the first time that Binh depicts himself as Moses, but it is not the last. It is clear that Bỉnh considers himself in terms of a chosen leader of the members of the Jesuit loyalist community. He is the liaison with the "pharaoh"—Bishop Alonso—the source of the community's suffering.

42. *TAĐN*, 427–28.

43. *TAĐN*, 402–3.

44. See, for example, a letter from the bishop of Gortyne to Pierre-Antoine Blandin, June 18, 1801, AMEP, vol. 693, p. 483. The later bishop of Macao Manuel Galdino would also regularly refer to the community as "schismatics" in his correspondence (e.g., Bishop Galdino to the Portuguese ruler, n.d., cited in João Francisco Marques and José Carlos Lopes de

Miranda, *Arquivo secreto do Vaticano: Expansão portuguesa, documentação*, vol. 2, *Oriente* (Lisbon: Esferada do Caos, 2011), 170.

45. Bishop Obelar to Nuncio Marchini in Macao, May 20, 1801, cited in J. Marques and Miranda, *Arquivo secreto*, 168.

46. *NT*, viii.

47. In 1924 the region was renamed from Vicariate of Eastern Tonking to Vicariate of Hải Phòng.

48. *TAĐN*, 414.

49. *TAĐN*, 408.

50. *NT*, 205; Paul Cuyền to Bỉnh, September 1795.

51. In his writings, Bỉnh described the process for deciding to send an envoy to petition the Portuguese ruler and noted that when there was an important undertaking at hand councils should be convened to decide how to carry out the task, in this case the recruitment of a bishop from overseas (*TAĐN*, 695–98). He also compares the Vietnamese case with that in Ethiopia, also a country without a Christian ruler, whose Catholics sent a delegation to the pope (Paul III) to request a bishop. The pope agreed but passed the issue over to the Portuguese ruler, as he was the one with responsibility for that region, so it was the Portuguese ruler who selected a bishop in response to the Ethiopian request. For another brief description of the selection process, see Bỉnh, *PX*, 579.

52. *NT*, 94, entry for 1815.

53. Moreover, letters from Vietnamese Catholics written to the Seminary of the Missions Étrangerès in Paris over the eighteenth century suggest that this awareness of a wider world was not restricted to Catholics in the Padroado community but extended to Vietnamese Christians elsewhere in Tonkin and Cochinchina. Examples of such letters include Visente Liem, June 9, 1786, AMEP, vol. 691, pp. 1006–8; Visente Liem, July 18, 1787, AMEP, vol. 691, p. 1036; anonymous, August 18, 1787, AMEP, vol. 691, pp. 1056–57; Benedictus Dinh, June 24, 1789, AMEP, vol. 692, p. 49; Visente Liem, July 4, 1789, AMEP, vol. 692, p. 127; Benedictus Dinh, June 3, 1790, AMEP, vol. 692, p. 227; Paulus Tinh, Augustinus Tran, and Jacobus Nhuong, June 28, 1793, AMEP, vol. 692, pp. 460–61.

54. Jacques, *Portuguese Pioneers*, 58n50.

55. The authority of metropolitan archbishops over the bishoprics under their purview are limited by canonical law, but that law does provide for general oversight "to see that faith and ecclesiastical discipline are carefully observed" (Code of Canon Law).

56. The suffragan connection meant that the archbishop had the authority to preside over meetings featuring representatives from the ecclesiastical provinces, including his own seat and those of the suffragan dioceses. He could also temporarily fill the bishopric until a formal replacement was named. The suffragan status did not give the archbishop any formal administrative authorities over the bishop at Macao.

57. Jean Jacques Guérard to Pierre-Antoine Blandin, June 5, 1793, AMEP, vol. 692, p. 527.

3. JOURNEYS: MACAO, GOA, AND LISBON

1. Kate Jellema, "Returning Home: Ancestor Veneration and the Nationalism of *Đổi Mới* Vietnam," in *Modernity and Re-enchantment: Religion in Post-revolutionary Vietnam*, ed. Philip Taylor (Singapore: Institute of Southeast Asian Studies, 2007), 80.

2. Liam Kelley, *Beyond the Bronze Pillars: Envoy Poetry and the Sino-Vietnamese Relationship* (Honolulu: Association for Asian Studies and University of Hawaii Press, 2005).

3. The Vietnamese court envoys would certainly have been able to communicate using the lingua franca of written Chinese, while Bỉnh had learned some Portuguese and would also have been able to conduct at least rudimentary communication in the written lingua franca of premodern Catholicism, Latin.

4. For a detailed and fascinating exploration of this genre and the men who composed it, see Kelley, *Beyond the Bronze Pillars*.

5. *TAĐN*, 382.

6. *NT,* 1. Their journey, like those that followed, likely took place on a relatively small Chinese vessel, which routinely sailed between Macao and the northern Vietnamese coast. These were typically trading boats, navigated by men with intimate knowledge of the dangerous passage through the pirate- and bandit-infested waters linking the two places. See, e.g., Vachet, cited in Launay, *Histoire générale*, 2:475.

7. *TAĐT*, 159.

8. *TAĐN*, 382.

9. *TAĐN*, 384.

10. Letondal's position as procurer for the MEP was essentially that of an intermediary between the European headquarters of the congregation and its Asian outposts. Information, money, and instructions would be channeled through his office. Most of the other missionary organizations with projects in Asia had individuals with similar responsibilities also posted to Macao. For an excellent brief biography of Letondal, see "Claude François Letondal," AMEP, accessed August 28, 2016, http://archives.mepasie.org/fr/notices/notices-biographiques/letondal. The AMEP website, http://archives.mepasie.org/, also contains biographies of many other MEP missionaries.

11. *TAĐN*, 388–89.

12. *TAĐN*, 428. Bỉnh reported that Brother Lịch and his partner sold out their entire supply shortly after their arrival in Tonkin.

13. *TAĐN*, 429.

14. *SS*, 100–103.

15. *TAĐN*, 507.

16. *TAĐN*, 437–38.

17. The dates are all given in *NT,* 1–2. The description of the route and the time required for the various forms of transport are given in *TAĐN*, 437.

18. The overall population estimate comes from Disney, *History of Portugal*, 2:337, who cites Brian Vale, *Independence or Death! British Sailors and Brazilian Independence, 1822–25* (London: I. B. Tauris, 1996), 119–20; the estimate regarding the number of Christians is from Manguin, *Nguyễn, Macau*, 1.

19. For some background on this Jesuit church, see C. Guillén-Nuñez, *Macao's Church of Saint Paul: A Glimmer of the Baroque in China* (Hong Kong: Hong Kong University Press, 2009).

20. Peter Mundy, *The Travels of Peter Mundy in Europe and Asia, 1608–1667*, 5 vols. (Cambridge: Hakluyt Society, 1905–36), cited in Boxer, *Portuguese Seaborne Empire*, 353. For another good description of the church, see Michael Cooper, SJ, *Rodrigues the Interpreter: An Early Jesuit in Japan and China* (New York: Weatherhill, 1974), 271–72.

21. Cooper, *Rodrigues the Interpreter,* 271, describes the Jesuit structures as being left derelict after the order's demise.

22. *TAĐN,* 437.

23. For a detailed study of the trading patterns that brought Vietnamese products to markets in Macao during the late eighteenth century, see Manguin, *Nguyen, Macau.*

24. See, e.g., G. V. Scammell, "European Exiles, Renegades and Outlaws and the Maritime Economy of Asia c. 1500–1750," *Modern Asian Studies* 26, no. 4 (1992): 641–61.

25. *TAĐN,* 445–46.

26. *TAĐN,* 440–41.

27. *SS,* 128, and *NT,* 2, both report the 120 *patacas* sum.

28. The detail of the boat's preliminary movement offshore with its captain is found only in a brief summary of the event contained in *MP,* 22.

29. *TAĐN,* 443–44; *NT,* 2–3.

30. This was likely at the behest of Father Letondal.

31. *TAĐN,* 444–45.

32. *NT,* 431.

33. *TAĐN,* 446. At least this is how Bỉnh relates the episode. It is unclear whether the translator's error was innocent, as Bỉnh suggests, or a cautious attempt to ensure that he would not run afoul of the local religious authorities.

34. *MP,* 23.

35. *TAĐN,* 461.

36. *TAĐN,* 462.

37. Bỉnh reported that on his trip to Macao this journey had taken just thirteen days, but with much more favorable conditions, and in a smaller boat that could travel more swiftly (*TAĐN,* 465).

38. *TAĐN,* 467.

39. An Lang is located a few kilometers up the Red River from the river mouth at Cửa Ba Lạt, south of Nam Định and south-southwest of Hà Nội.

40. *TAĐN,* 528–29.

41. The archbishop had taken up his post in 1784 and would hold it until 1812, his twenty-eight-year tenure making him the longest-serving archbishop of Goa.

42. *TAĐN,* 456; this sequence of events is also summarized by Bỉnh in *SS,* 57.

43. *TAĐN,* 459; see also the much later *SA,* preface, n.p., and *NT,* 4. Bỉnh, clearly recalling his protracted struggle with the French MEP clerics, scornfully wrote in *TAĐN* that while Frenchmen who called themselves Catholics had stolen and looted all of the men's possessions, here was this Dutchman, an atheist who had taken two wives and yet who acted in this compassionate manner toward them.

44. Dates are approximate, based on Bỉnh's report that the men had been in Goa for 8 days, then spent 8 days sailing to Bombay, 20 days to find a ship, 40 days sailing to Malacca, 20 days in Malacca, and another 40 days sailing back to Macao, a total of 136 days (*NT,* 4–5). Bỉnh later recites this list of travel times to the Portuguese ruler in one of his first memorials (*NT,* 229).

45. *TAĐN,* 504–5.

46. Details are found in *SS,* 32–40.

47. TAĐN, 490–91.
48. Dutton, Tây Sơn Uprising, 194–95.
49. TAĐN, 498.
50. SS, 36–37.
51. NT, 202.
52. SS, 5.
53. NT, 203–4.
54. Ocio and Neira, Misioneros dominicos, 366.
55. SS, 43.
56. TAĐN, 515.
57. On the problems with pirates in these waters and the Chinese efforts to suppress them, see Dutton, Tây Sơn Uprising, 215ff. See also Dian Murray, *Pirates of the South China Coast, 1790–1810.* (Stanford, CA: Stanford University Press, 1987), and Robert J. Anthony, *Like Froth on the Floating Sea: The World of Pirates and Seafarers in Late Imperial South China* (Berkeley, CA: Institute of East Asian Studies, 2003).
58. SS, 57; Bỉnh also describes this meeting in MP, 24. What Bỉnh is not clear about is the situation of Trung and Ngân, who continued to wait in Macao. That they were unable to provide for their returning compatriots suggests that they too had been reduced to penury.
59. SS, 57.
60. TAĐN, 527.
61. For some background on Brother Thuyên, see TAĐN, 683–84, and MP, 25.
62. TAĐN, 533. Years later, Bỉnh would meet Bishop da Silva again upon the bishop's return to Lisbon. In an extended conversation, the bishop indicated that his efforts to prevent their departure for Lisbon had been, at least in part, a misunderstanding rather than a deliberate act of sabotage. See TAĐN, 537–39.
63. Although it was not required of foreign visitors, probably more than a few Vietnamese wore their hair in this fashion to blend in and take advantage of the relative anonymity that being taken for Chinese afforded them.
64. SA, 562; in the preface Bỉnh also writes: "Therefore, the third time he told me, 'On the fourteenth day of the second month [this is lunar], which is the first day of the Lenten fasting season, you must go together with him [?] and submit a letter in which you promise that you will return to Annam.' But I did not go because the twelfth was a Saturday, and then when I had already finished eating lunch, I immediately brought the other three men with me, and we left the city of Macao, going together to board a 'guest ship,' and we then rowed out to the head of the mountains."
65. TAĐN, 523.
66. An excellent study of piracy in these waters in the late eighteenth century is Murray, *Pirates*.
67. TAĐN, 534.
68. Date is by inference. It seems clear, however, that Bỉnh's reference to the sixth day of the first month is to the lunar calendar, for this agrees precisely with Febuary 14 in the solar calendar, and he gives the date "the fourteenth of the second month" elsewhere in his writings (preface to SA). Bỉnh later records the date as March 13 in an April 25, 1800, letter to the community in Tonkin (NT, 276).

69. *TAĐN*, 535.

70. *TAĐN*, 535.

71. St. Anne was held in particularly high regard among Europeans at this time as a special protector of ocean travelers. In his journals, Bình commented on the fact that Europeans gave their vessels auspicious names, such as those of saints, as a method for warding off danger, and noted that this differed from Vietnamese practice, in which boats were never given names (*TAĐN*, 540). Years later he would write a lengthy volume on the life of Saint Anne by way of recompense for her apparent intervention on behalf of his delegation. *SA* (563–64) includes more detail on the significance of the St. Anne rescuing them.

72. *SA*, preface, n.p.; *TAĐN*, 536.

73. *SS*, 59–60. Another brief account of the events surrounding their finding passage to Europe is in *NT*, 6–7.

74. *TAĐN*, 539.

75. *SA*, preface, n.p.

76. *NT*, 437.

77. *NT*, 7. The journey is described, with varying degrees of detail, in several of Bình's notebooks. There is a brief version in *NT*, 6–8, a slightly more detailed one in *SS*, 107, 128–29, and a much longer one in *TAĐN*, 532–55.

78. *TAĐN*, 548.

79. *TAĐN*, 540–41. The following description of Bình's journey is taken from *TAĐN*, 540ff.

80. Bình wrote of this storm in a letter home to his community on April 25, 1800 (*NT*, 276).

81. *NT*, 440.

82. "Thế gian này thì tròn như quả bòng" (*TAĐN*, 542). *Dặm* is conventionally translated as "kilometer" or "mile" and is derived from the Chinese distance measure the *li* (里), which is roughly 590 yards in length. Clearly, Bình's 6,000 *dặm* is more metaphorical than precise, as the distance is closer to 12,000 nautical miles.

83. *NT*, 438.

84. *TAĐN*, 550–51.

85. *TAĐN*, 556–57.

86. *NT*, 441.

87. *TAĐN*, 546.

88. While certainly fast, such speeds were not uncommon. Nineteenth-century clipper ships could easily cover 250 nautical miles a day, with the record being nearly double that in a twenty-four-hour period.

89. Historical details on St. Helena can be found in Stephen Royle, *The Company's Island: St. Helena, Company Colonies and the Colonial Endeavour* (London: I. B. Tauris, 2007); Margaret Stewart Taylor, *St. Helena: Ocean Roadhouse* (London: Robert Hale, 1969); E. L. Jackson, *St. Helena: The Historic Island, from Its Discovery to the Present Date* (London: Ward Lock, 1903); T. H. Brooke, *A History of the Island of St. Helena, from Its Discovery by the Portuguese to the Year 1806* (London: Black, Parry, and Kingsbury, 1806).

90. See *SS*, 129, 317. The former page describes the various expenses of the entire journey, noting that while the men were ultimately afforded free passage to Europe, this did not mean that they did not incur expenses.

91. *TAĐN*, 546; *SS*, 158.
92. *TAĐN*, 551–52.
93. For more on the French naval and privateer attacks on shipping along the coasts of Portugal, Spain, and northern Africa, see Patrick Crowhurst, *The French War on Trade: Privateering, 1793–1815* (Hants: Scolar Press, 1989), 63–68.
94. Ibid., 31.
95. *TAĐN*, 556.
96. *TAĐN*, 556–57.
97. The fifty-three-day figure is given in *SS*, 61–62.
98. *SS*, 62. The unescorted trip to Lisbon may have reflected a sense on the part of the British that the passage was relatively secure, for there were times during this period when "British warships were sent to provide additional protection in the areas to the west and the areas near ports in Portugal were also protected by convoy escorts who remained in the vicinity of the ports between seeing their charges safely into harbour and bringing them home" (Crowhurst, *French War on Trade*, 50).
99. Bình gives this arrival date in a letter he later wrote back to the community on April 25, 1800 (*NT*, 276); also *TAĐN*, 555.
100. *SS*, 62, 128. As noted earlier, however, some ancillary expenses had not been covered by their captains, mostly while the ship was at anchor in St. Helena, and to a lesser extent while it had earlier taken on supplies along the Malay Peninsula.
101. *SS*, 63. *Pataca* was the Portuguese translation of the Spanish *peso*, the silver coin widely used as a standardized currency unit in the Americas and beyond to Asia. Bình here refers to a bronze coin, perhaps based on the silver valuation, though establishing a conversion is difficult.

4. ARRIVAL IN LISBON AND FIRST ENCOUNTERS

1. For a brief discussion of the tower and its significance, see Malcolm Jack, *Lisbon: City of the Sea, a History* (London: I. B. Taurus, 2007), 47–48.
2. The following day was another holiday in Spain and Portugal, the feast day of Saint Jacob.
3. *NT*, 443.
4. Estimates of the death toll vary considerably, from twenty thousand to forty thousand. At the upper end of this range it would have killed nearly 20 percent of the city's population. See Maxwell, *Pombal*, 24.
5. The literature on the earthquake is extensive. A good recent study is Mark Molesky, *This Gulf of Fire: The Destruction of Lisbon, or Apocalypse in the Age of Science and Reason* (New York: Knopf, 2015). See also Theodore E. D. Braun and John B. Radner, eds., *The Lisbon Earthquake of 1755: Representations and Reactions* (Oxford: Voltaire Foundation, 2005). Another recent but more popular account is Nicholas Shrady, *The Last Day: Wrath, Ruin, and Reason in the Great Lisbon Earthquake of 1755* (New York: Viking Books, 2008).
6. A late eighteenth-century summary of Pombal's reconstruction efforts can be found in J.-B.-F. Carrère, *Voyage en Portugal et particulierement a Lisbonne* (Paris: Chez Deterville, 1798), 14–19.

7. The largest in order were London, Paris, Naples, and Vienna. Similar in size to Lisbon at this time would have been Amsterdam (around 205,000) and Moscow (200,000-248,000).

8. Adriano Balbi, *Essai statistique sur le royaume de Portugal et d'Algarve, comparé aux autres états de l'Europe: Et suivi d'un coup d'oeil sur l'état actuel des sciences, des lettres et des beaux-arts parmi les Portugais des deux hémisphéres*, vol. 1 (Paris, 1822), 266.

9. SS, 158, where Bình describes this sartorial strategy to emphasize their unusual appearance.

10. The Marques was a senior member of the crown prince's inner circle and had earlier served briefly as prime minister for Queen Maria I.

11. I thank Barbara Watson-Andaya for pointing this out to me. On the Oratorian mission project in Asia, see Sebastiio Rego, *The Apostle of Ceylon: Fr. Joseph Vaz, an Oratorian Priest, 1651-1711* (Calcutta: Catholic Orphan Press, 1897), and Arthur C. Dep, *The Oratorian Mission in Sri Lanka, 1795-1874: Being a History of the Catholic Church, 1795-1874* (Ja-ela: Dep, 1987).

12. *NT*, 8-9.

13. This monastery was built in 1598 and was subsequently reconstructed several times, notably after a large-scale fire in 1898. In 1834, upon the dissolution of religious orders in Portugal, the monastery was converted to the national parliament buildings, a function it continues to serve to the present day.

14. *TAĐN*, 561.

15. *TAĐN*, 566.

16. *TAĐN*, 567.

17. *TAĐN*, 568.

18. Cristina Castel-Branco, ed., *Necessidades: The Gardens and Enclosure* (Lisbon: Livros Horizonte, 2002), 55.

19. A nineteenth-century description noted of the compound that "it has beautiful gardens, but the structure [itself] is small, narrow, inconvenient, and insufficient to house the court: the majority of this palace has been converted into a convent, and the previous king, Don Joseph, presented it to the preachers of the Oratorian congregation; and the rest is occupied by private individuals, whom the queen permits to reside there." See Carrère, *Tableau de Lisbonne*, 109.

20. Manuel Côrte-Real, *O Palácio das Necessidades* (Lisbon: Ministério dos Negócios, 1983), 23-26.

21. A good description of the gardens is found in Castel-Branco, *Necessidades*, 59-60.

22. Among its prominent British visitors was the future George IV of England. Shortly after Bình moved out, the Duke of Wellington (Arthur Wellesley) requisitioned the Necessidades compound as his residence while organizing the defense of Portugal against the Napoleonic forces between 1809 and 1812. With the disestablishment of the orders in 1834, the Necessidades site fell under the authority of the Portuguese state, and today it serves as the home of the Portuguese Ministry of Foreign Affairs.

23. *NT*, 449.

24. Mitchell, *Jesuits*, 167.

25. See Henry Frederick Link, *Travels in Portugal, and through France and Spain* (London: T. N. Longman and O. Rees, 1801), 223; Samuel J. Miller, *Portugal and Rome c. 1748-1830: An Aspect of the Catholic Enlightenment* (Rome: Università Gregoriana, 1978), 356; for a concise

biography of Bishop Caetano, see "São Caetano," in *Portugal: Dicionário histórico*, ed. Esteves Pereira and Guilherme Rodrigues (Lisbon: J. Romano Torres, 1904-15), www.arqnet.pt/dicionario/saocaetano_fi.html; for that of Bishop de Melo, see "Melo (D. José Maria de)," in Pereira and Rodrigues, *Portugal*, www.arqnet.pt/dicionario/melojosemaria.html.

26. The similarities between the Oratorians and the Jesuits had also not been lost on the Marquis de Pombal, whose antipathies toward the Jesuits also extended to their Oratorian rivals. Like the Jesuits, the Portuguese Oratorians suffered in the 1760s under pressure from Pombal. As head of the order, Almeida bore the brunt of the prime minister's attack. In the face of Pombal's relentless pressure, Almeida was ultimately forced into a decade-long exile in France beginning in 1768. He continued his scientific work there until Pombal's ouster by the new Portuguese ruler, Queen Maria I, in 1777, whereupon he returned to Lisbon. See Robert Southey, *Journals of a Residence in Portugal, 1800-1801, and a Visit to France, 1838*, ed. Adolfo Cabral (Oxford: Clarendon Press, 1960), 10.

27. Miller, *Portugal and Rome*, 167.

28. This brief summary is taken from Francisco Contente Domingues, *Ilustração e catolicismo: Teodoro de Almeida* (Lisbon: Colibri, 1994), and from "Teodoro de Almeida (1722-1804)," Science in Portugal: Characters and Episodes, 2004-5, http://cvc.institutocamoes.pt/ciencia_eng/p47.html, which offers a brief overview of this book.

29. Cited in Disney, *History of Portugal*, 1:299; see also A. H. de Oliveira Marques, *History of Portugal*, vol. 1, *From Lusitania to Empire* (New York: Columbia University Press, 1972), 413, and Castel-Branco, *Necessidades*, 55. The Oratorian pedagogical approach was viewed as a preferable modern alternative to what was seen as an overly metaphysical and abstract Jesuit educational model. The Oratorian teaching institutions focused strongly on instruction in science, history, literature, and mathematics and paid far less attention to subjects such as philosophy in which the Jesuits specialized.

30. Governo de Portugal, "Palácio das Necessidades," n.d., accessed September 14, 2016, www.palaciodasnecessidades.com.

31. *TAĐN*, 325.

32. Disney, *History of Portugal*, 1:317.

33. *Essai statistique sur le Portugal* (Bordeaux, 1810), 42.

34. Marcus Cheke, *Carlota Joaquina: Queen of Portugal* (Freeport, NY: Books for Libraries Press, 1969), 11.

35. Disney, *History of Portugal*, 1:312.

36. M. M. Busk, *The History of Spain and Portugal from B.C. 1000 to A.D. 1814* (London: Baldwin and Cradock, 1833), 233.

37. This sequence of events is clearly described in Jenifer Roberts, *The Madness of Queen Maria: The Remarkable Life of Maria I of Portugal* (Chippenham: Templeton Press, 2009), 102-6. Bishop Caetano had been her confessor for nearly three decades.

38. Ibid., 107.

39. Ibid., 1.

40. Neill Macaulay, *Dom Pedro: The Struggle for Liberty in Brazil and Portugal* (Durham, NC: Duke University Press, 1986), 8.

41. Carrère, *Tableau de Lisbonne*, 150-51. An 1827 French account of his reign is similarly skeptical of his political abilities, seeing him dominated by his ministers; see *Histoire de Jean VI, roi de Portugal* (Paris: Ponthieu, 1827), 11ff.

42. Roberts, *Madness of Queen Maria*, 119. While João VI had essentially taken charge in 1792, he was not formally appointed as regent until seven years later, on July 15, 1799.

43. Macaulay, *Dom Pedro*, offers a good, brief description of the princess, her interests, and her temperament, 7–9.

44. Save, perhaps, the Spanish crown, which held a similar papally granted authority for the territories ostensibly under Spanish domination.

45. A near-contemporary and rather critical description of Mafra is found in James Wilmot Ormsby, *An Account of the Operations of the British Army and of the State and Sentiments of the People of Portugal and Spain during the Campaigns of the Years 1808 and 1809* (London: James Carpenter, 1809), 45–49. Ormsby cites, with considerable doubt, reports that the hunting park consisted of ten thousand walled acres.

46. Macaulay, *Dom Pedro*, 8.

47. *TAĐN*, 569.

48. The following account of their first audience with the ruler is taken from *SS*, 164–67, *TAĐN*, 570–73, and *NT*, 9–10.

49. For an early nineteenth-century description, see Richard Barnard Fisher, *A Sketch of the City of Lisbon and Its Environs; with Some Observations on the Manners, Disposition, and Character of the Portuguese Nation* (London: J. Ridgway, 1811), 65–66.

50. A visit to the gardens in 2006 found them in a state of some neglect, particularly the sections more distant from the palace proper, though the grounds proximate to the palace were well tended.

51. *SS*, 128.

52. *SS*, 165.

53. *SS*, 165–66.

54. *SS*, 167.

55. *TAĐN*, 572.

56. *SS*, 167–68.

57. It is unclear who would have issued such a letter, and Bỉnh does not say.

58. Roberts, *Madness of Queen Maria*, 6.

59. *TAĐN*, 582.

60. *SS*, 170; see also *TAĐN*, 581. Bỉnh reports that the decree issued regarding this can be found in *NT*, 2:399.

61. *SS*, 173. Bỉnh provides a detailed description of these court ceremonies and protocol on 170–73.

62. *NT*, 278; letter of April 25, 1800.

63. Evidence for this is found in *SS*, in which Bỉnh includes copies of two certificates made out by fellow priests that refer to him as "Felippe do Rosario, Enviado da Christandade do Reyno de Tunkim," 624–25.

64. *NT*, 278.

65. *SS*, 158.

5. INVOKING THE PADROADO: BỈNH AND PRINCE DOM JOÃO

1. An official translation of the 1791 letter into Portuguese can be found in Manguin, *Nguyen, Macau*, 231–32.

2. *TAĐN*, 576–77.

3. I use the term *petition* here, which best reflects the nature of the documents Bỉnh was presenting to the ruler. The Vietnamese term *tấu* that Bỉnh uses in his writings might also be translated as "memorial," which is the standard translation in the Vietnamese context for such documents presented to a ruler. Given the different context (i.e., Europe) in which the term is being used, I prefer *petition*.

4. José Pegado de Azevedo was an Oratorian priest and native Lisbonite who had joined the congregation in 1778. He left the Oratorian order's house in July of 1801 when he was elevated to his bishopric in the Azores.

5. *NT,* 231–38.

6. Bỉnh's writings routinely referred to missionaries using their nationalities as a shorthand for their respective religious affiliations, as in a June 18, 1798, letter in which he wrote: "It is because the French and Spanish priests carry out many senseless acts that the Christians endure such suffering" (*NT,* 225).

7. It is unclear why Bỉnh speaks of there being five ordained seminarians, as in all of his other writings he speaks of there having been six.

8. Boxer, *Four Centuries,* 234.

9. It is noteworthy that in later years (*NT,* 285) Bỉnh would continue to refer to the Dominican spiritual leader as "the Spanish bishop," indicating the degree to which the man's nationality (rather than his religious affiliation) mattered to Bỉnh.

10. Given its importance, Bỉnh took particular care to protect his one bargaining chip, and his letters to the community leaders back in Tonkin between 1800 and 1803 frequently reminded them to continue carefully to protect this property, because he was essentially promising the ruler that it would be there for any returning Portuguese clerics. See *NT,* 273, 1803; see also letter written in the tenth month of 1801 (*NT,* 290) and letter written on January 22, 1802 (*NT,* 249).

11. *NT,* 238.

12. On Pacca's firm resolve regarding the concession of authority to the Portuguese court, see Miller, *Portugal and Rome,* 365.

13. Paulus Tĩnh, Augustinus Trân, and Jacobus Nhượng to Pierre Blandin, June 28, 1793 (AMEP, vol. 692, 460–61).

14. There are a few exceptions. The most prominent such geographical pairing may have been the juxtaposition of Hồ Quý Ly's joint capitals of Tây Đô and Đông Đô in the late fourteenth century.

15. John Whitmore, "Cartography in Vietnam," in *History of Cartography,* vol. 2, *Cartography of the Traditional East and Southeast Asian Societies* (Chicago: University of Chicago Press, 1994), 481.

16. Dror's introduction to Adriano di St. Thecla, *Opusculum de sectis,* 58, points out that in Chinese texts references to "the West" were typically to India.

17. Cuong Tu Nguyen, *Zen in Medieval Vietnam: A Study and Translation of the "Thien uyen tap anh"* (Honolulu: University of Hawaii Press, 1997), 5b.

18. *NT,* 12.

19. *NT,* 12. The references to going to the palace would probably have been to larger events sponsored by the court at which many other visitors would also have been in audience, rather than the private audiences at which he could make formal presentations of his issue.

20. Bỉnh recorded the dates of these audiences: October 1, 1796, June 21, 1798, August 8, 1799, June 10, 1800, December 11, 1800, September 10, 1801, April 27, 1803, May 30, 1805, and May 15, 1807.

21. Carrère, *Tableau de Lisbonne*, 215-22, provides a caustic description of physicians and their approach to treatment in Lisbon of the 1790s.

22. SS, 132.

23. TAĐN, 711.

24. NT, 14.

25. SS, 130.

26. James Cavanah Murphy, *A General View of the State of Portugal; Containing a Topographical Description Thereof* (London: Cadell and Davies, 1798), 21-22. For a good contemporary description, see Henry Frederick Link, *Travels in Portugal*, 269-71.

27. SS, 131; Carrère, *Tableau de Lisbonne*, has a description of carriages and their rental, 67-69. Bỉnh noted that not all of the men traveled to the springs on each occasion and that he himself went not as a patient but as an aide to his friends (SS, 131-32).

28. SS, 424-25.

29. SS, 130.

30. TAĐN, 72ff.

31. NT, 452.

32. Letter written by Bỉnh back to the community in Tonkin in 1803; see NT, 253-55. He does not specify the nature of the treatment that brought about this remarkable recovery.

33. TAĐN, 710-11. Barbara Watson Andaya pointed out to me that his illness might also have been either dyshidrotic eczema, or dyshidrosis, both of which produce blisters on the soles of the feet and/or the palms of the hands and can be caused or exacerbated by stress or anxiety.

34. Angelo Pereira, *D. João VI, príncipe e rei*, vol. 1, *A retirada da família real para o Brasil (1807)* (Lisbon: Empresa Nacional de Publicidade, 1953), 58.

35. NT, 213.

36. NT, 14.

37. Some sources suggest that he left his post in 1801, but Pacca's own memoirs (86) indicate that he left in June of 1802, thus overlapping briefly with his replacement.

38. Pacca wrote an account of his tenure as nuncio to Lisbon, later published as Bartolomeo Pacca, *Notizie sul Portogallo: Con una breve relazione della nunziatura di Lisbona dallánno 1795 fino allánno 1802* [Notices regarding Portugal: With a brief account of the nunciature to Lisbon from the year 1795 until the end of the year 1802] (Velletri: Domenico Ercole, 1836). He later penned a memoir of his career as cardinal; see Bartolomeo Pacca and George Head, *Historical Memoirs of Cardinal Pacca, Prime Minister to Pius VII* (London: Longman, Brown, Green, and Longmans, 1850).

39. As Miller notes, "Pacca feared that even the slightest open concession would mean the loss of the small gains he had made during his nunciature" (*Portugal and Rome*, 365).

40. Bỉnh, unfortunately, did not preserve a copy of this letter in his records.

41. NT, 16-17.

42. This was the so-called War of the Oranges, in which a Spanish show of force led to the occupation of Olivença, followed by an agreement to negotiate a settlement, the Treaty

of Badajoz, in which Portugal ceded territory and agreed to bar British vessels from its ports. Miller, *Portugal and Rome*, 364; see also Macaulay, *Dom Pedro*, 3.

43. P. Manuel Teixeira, *Bispos e governadores do Bispado de Macao*, vol. 2 of *Macau e a sua diocese* (Macau: Imprensa Nacional, 1940), 293.

44. While he later developed a reputation as a man of great charity who gave away much of his possessions and regular income, the fact that his stay in Macao ultimately proved but a brief stepping-stone to the more prestigious and powerful position of archbishop of Goa suggests that his ambitions continued to drive him. On his reputation as a man of charity, see ibid., 294.

45. *NT*, 19.

46. *NT*, 463.

47. *NT*, 464.

48. *NT*, 19.

49. *NT*, 20. The term *Virtuous Teacher* is here a reference to Galdino himself.

50. *TAĐN*, 686–87.

51. Teixeira, *Bispos e governadores*, 296.

52. "Vua đứng ngầy, thi phô ông Toa Thánh sấp mình xuống dưới chân, mà Vua cúi đầu xuống thì phô ông Toà Thánh nhảy lên tren cổ" (*TAĐN*, 687).

53. *NT*, 21.

54. Teixeira, *Bispos e governadores*, 296.

55. See *TAĐN*, 688. Notice of the appointment eventually appeared in the Portuguese newspaper of record, the *Gazeta de Lisboa*, on February 9, 1802.

56. Teixeira, *Bispos e governadores*, 295–96.

57. Ibid., 297.

58. Ibid.

59. *TAĐN*, 691.

60. *TAĐN*, 691.

61. A brief biography can be found in Innocencio Francisco da Silva et al., *Diccionario bibliographico Portuguez*, vol. 1 (Lisbon: Na Imprensa Nacional, 1858), 84.

62. Antonio Alvares, *Memoria sobre o Real Padroado da Corte de Portugal nas missoes do reino de Tunkin / por Antonio Alvares, da Congregacao do Oratorio de Lisboa, feita em 21 de Janeiro de 1802 e Resposta que deu o procurador de Coroa, Joao Antonio Salter de Mendonca, em 9 de abril do mesmo anno; tudo copiado da colleccao de manuscriptos de Julio Firmino Judice Biker, e por este publicado* (Lisbon, 1802).

63. Alvares's description of the trip to Goa, for example, includes details virtually identical to those Bỉnh reported in his own notebooks (ibid., 8).

64. While an important figure in his own right, Dom Alexandre is perhaps best known as the father of the first Duke of Palmela, a Portuguese diplomat who would later be significantly involved in shaping Europe's post-Napoleonic political landscape.

65. *TAĐN*, 590–91.

66. The complexities of this relationship have been studied in great detail in Miller, *Portugal and Rome*.

67. Cited in ibid., 347. The female monarch referred to in the oath was Queen Maria I.

68. At least this is how Bỉnh reported it. He wrote in *NT*: "Trẩy đến thành Genova, thì vợ liền sinh, vì vậy phải ở lại đấy mấy tháng" (23; He traveled to Genoa, where his wife gave

birth, and thus had to remain there for a number of months). Several of Bỉnh's 1803 letters also describe this sequence of events.

69. TAĐN, 589–92. This is apparently Bỉnh's paraphrase of the pope's statement to the Portuguese envoy.

70. Alan J. Reinerman, "Pius VII (1800–1823)," in *The Great Popes through History: An Encyclopedia*, ed. Frank J. Coppa (Westport, CT: Greenwood Press, 2002), 2:447.

71. Several sources (e.g., Miller) suggest that Pacca had left Lisbon in 1801, but in his own memoirs he gives his departure date as May 1802 (see Pacca, *Notizie sul Portogallo*, 86). When the Portuguese royal family fled to Brazil in late 1807, Caleppi was among those who traveled with them. He continued to function as papal nuncio to the Portuguese court throughout much of its lengthy exile in Rio de Janeiro and eventually died in his South American post in 1817.

72. TAĐN, 688–89.

73. TAĐN, 690.

74. TAĐN, 690.

75. TAĐN, 710–11.

76. In *NT*, Bỉnh provides a detailed account of Nhân's illness and then a three-page biography (26–31). The first to die in Europe had been the unnamed Vietnamese priest brought from Macao back to Rome in 1760 (see chapter 3 above).

77. TAĐN, 718. The description of Nhân's death and the rituals surrounding it is found on 714–18.

78. *NT*, 31.

79. Vatican Secret Archives, Arch. Nunz. Lisbona 33 (3), fol. 32–32v, cited in Marques and Miranda, *Arquivo secreto*, 171.

80. *NT*, 31–39. He also mentions Caleppi's efforts to lure them in a letter written to Tonkin in 1803 (*NT*, 258–59).

81. *NT*, 35. These promises seem unlikely on their face, given the nuncio's repeated arguments that Tonkin already had enough bishops, so it is likely this was nothing more than a ruse.

82. *NT*, 281; letter written on April 29, 1803.

83. TAĐN, 592–93.

84. TAĐN, 595–96; this assumes that 18 van = 180,000 and 19 van = 190,000.

85. Bỉnh does not precisely date this project, but from his notebooks it appears that it was developed in this year.

86. It is true that the first Nguyễn emperor, Gia Long, was quite tolerant of the presence of Christian missionaries. He had had close personal connections with French clergy during the Tây Sơn wars and had entrusted his eldest son to Bishop Pigneaux Pierre de Béhaine for the 1787 mission to the French court to seek assistance. See, e.g., Ramsey, *Mandarins and Martyrs*, 20ff.; also Charles Keith, *Catholic Vietnam* (Berkeley: University of California Press, 2012), 4–5.

87. *NT*, 285.

88. The scheme is laid out in *NT*, 286–87.

89. TAĐN, 601.

90. As was typical of him, Bỉnh was impressed by these amounts and recorded them in his notebooks: two hens, seven pounds of beef, and twelve boxes of tea were sent on a daily basis (*TAĐN*, 603).

91. *TAĐN*, 605-6.
92. *TAĐN*, 604.
93. *TAĐN*, 608.
94. *NT*, 46-47, describes the Vietnamese petition and Bình's record of the official response.
95. *TAĐN*, 607.
96. A. Marques, in *History of Portugal*, vol. 1, notes that plans for such an exile in case of invasion dated back to the Seven Years' War in the middle of the eighteenth century (427).
97. Patrick Wilcken, *Empire Adrift: The Portuguese Court in Rio de Janeiro, 1808-1821* (London: Bloomsbury, 2004), 30.
98. *NT*, 54.
99. Roberts, *Madness of Queen Maria*, 127.
100. William Bradford, *Sketches of the Country, Character and Costume in Portugal and Spain Made during the Campaign, and on the Route of the British Army in 1808 and 1809* (London: John Booth, 1812), 3.

6. WAITING FOR BÌNH IN TONKIN AND MACAO

1. Details of the political fragmentation of the regime are found in Dutton, *Tây Sơn Uprising*, 194-95.
2. For more on this, see ibid., especially 192-96.
3. Launay, *Histoire generale*, 2:324-25. Regarding the shifting landscape for Catholics, see, e.g., bishop of Gortyne to Pierre-Antoine Blandin, June 18, 1801, AMEP, vol. 693, p. 483.
4. Ramsay, *Mandarins and Martyrs*, 47-48.
5. Thuyên and Trạch to Bình, September 17, 1803, *NT*, 384-85.
6. Dutton, *Tây Sơn Uprising*, 166-70. These hardships are also reported in missionary letters of the time. See, for example, a letter from M. Eyot in Tonkin to his superiors in Paris, dated July 9, 1804, in which he describes hard labor imposed upon the populations in Tonkin with large numbers of workers dying from exhaustion, in *Nouvelles lettres edifiantes*, 8:239-40.
7. Bình writes that there were four volumes in the *NT* series, and he occasionally refers to documents that he recorded in the other three, but it is unclear whether these were each used for particular types of documents or by what criteria he had divided their contents.
8. *NT*, 282.
9. Teixeira, *Bispos e governadores*, 203.
10. For each of the letters that he received and recorded in his notebooks, Bình indicated the date on which it had reached him, while the letters themselves were dated, giving a sense of their transit time.
11. Guérard to Toulon, August 3, 1804, AMEP, vol. 701, p. 573; a biography of Guérard, "Jean-Jacques Guérard," can be found at AMEP's website, accessed May 14, 2014, http://archives.mepasie.org/notices/notices-biographiques/gua-c-rard.
12. *NT*, 220.
13. *NT*, 221. He gave similar assurances in another of the letters he wrote at this time, also dated April 25, 1800 (*NT*, 278).
14. *NT*, 221.

15. Letter of October 9, 1801 (*NT*, 267).
16. Letter of May 1800 (*NT*, 268-71); letter of 1801 (*NT*, 245-46); letter of January 22, 1802 (*NT*, 248-49); letter of 1802 (*NT*, 250-52).
17. Letter of May 1800 (*NT*, 268-71).
18. Letter dated only as 1801 (*NT*, 243-44).
19. *NT*, 243-44.
20. Letter of May 1800 (*NT*, 268-71), addressed to "các quan viên bổn đạo nam nữ thuộc về con chiên Dào ta."
21. *NT*, 217-19. No date given, but certainly after 1800.
22. Jacques-Benjamin Longer to Claude-Françoise Letondal, November 17, 1801, AMEP, vol. 701, 465-66.
23. Jacques-Benjamin Longer, Bishop of Gortyne, to Toulon, February 14, 1804, AMEP, vol. 701, p. 539.
24. These would have been written by Bỉnh sometime in the summer and fall of 1798 and then presumably sent off sometime on a ship leaving Lisbon in the spring of 1799 (*NT*, 363-65). Written on November 26, 1800, at the house of Saint Paul, in Macao. Signed by Simao Xavier Liển and Paulo Maria Thuyên. Liển and Thuyên later reported that Bỉnh's letters of 1799 and 1800 finally reached them in September of 1801 (*NT*, 366).
25. Liển and Thuyên to Bỉnh, September 25, 1801 (*NT*, 366-70).
26. *NT*, 366-70.
27. September 25, 1801 (*NT*, 367-68). The writers did note that some people recognized that any such church fires would be the actions, not of the Holy Spirit, but of rival church authorities or their supporters.
28. September 25, 1801 (*NT*, 367-68).
29. Bishop Longer to Pierre-Antoine Blandin, June 18, 1801, AMEP, vol. 693, p. 483.
30. Wenceslao Đầu to Bỉnh, 1800(?), received by Bỉnh in July 1802 (*NT*, 371-372).
31. Manguin, *Nguyen, Macau*, 3-4. For more on this insitution, see Boxer, *Portuguese Seaborne Empire,* 288-89 and 290-91, which discusses the process by which the wealthy made amends for their iniquities by donating money to the miseracórdias.
32. October 3, 1802, written by Thuyên and Trạch (*NT*, 375-79); further details in *NT*, 24-25.
33. October 3, 1802, written by Thuyên and Trạch (*NT*, 375-79). The term they use for "peso" here is *đồng bạc*.
34. Letter written March 25, 1804 (*NT*, 284).
35. Trạch was from the village of Thượng Miêu in the region of upper Xứ Nam and had in his youth been a follower of Fathers João, Nghiệm, and Tuán (*TAĐN*, 684-85).
36. *NT*, 375-79.
37. Letter written on April 29, 1803 (*NT*, 281).
38. Reported in a letter by Thuyên and Trạch, dated the seventeenth day of the ninth month of 1803 (*NT*, 380-92).
39. Teixeira, *Bispos e governadores*, 297.
40. Letter of September 17, 1803 (*NT*, 381ff.).
41. Ibid.
42. Ibid.

43. *TAĐN*, 691; *NT,* 40. Marchini was the nuncio in Macao from 1786 until 1820.
44. *SS*, 128.
45. *TAĐN*, 691.
46. Guérard to Toulon, August 3, 1804, AMEP, vol. 701, p. 573.
47. Vatican Secret Archives, Arch. Nunz. Lisbona 33 (3), fol. 28–28v, cited in Marques and Miranda, *Arquivo secreto*, 170.
48. Bỉnh wrote that Galdino had sent a Spanish priest to Tonkin to investigate and force compliance, likely a reference to the new Dominican apostolic vicar, Bishop Delgado (*TAĐN*, 691).
49. Teixeira, *Bispos e governadores*, 303.
50. Ibid., 298.
51. Ibid., 302–3.
52. Casimiro Christovam Nazareth, (*Mitras Lusitanas no Oriente II: Catálogo chronologico-historico dos prelados da egreja metropolitana de Goa e das dioceses suffraganeas* (Lisbon, 1913), 346, cited in Schurhammer, "Annamitische Xaveriusliteratur," 307.
53. *TAĐN*, 691; Galdino's November 1805 letter expressing surprise at their failure to return is in Vatican Secret Archives, Arch. Nunz. Lisbona 33 (3), fols. 48–49, cited in Marques and Miranda, *Arquivo secreto*, 172.
54. *NT*, 383–84.
55. *NT*, 383–85. It is possible that the Cụ Triệu cited here is Bỉnh's old friend, whom he wrote about as "Trệu."
56. Vatican Secret Archives, Arch. Nunz. Lisbona 33 (3), fol. 30, cited in Marques and Miranda, *Arquivo secreto*, 170.
57. Teixeira, *Bispos e governadores*, 303.
58. The succession of bishops to Macao, along with basic date information, can be found at "Diocese of Macao," n.d., accessed August 30, 2012, www.catholic-hierarchy.org/diocese/dmacu.html. Bishop Chacim served in Macao until his death in 1828.
59. *TAĐN*, 692.
60. Vatican Secret Archives, Arch. Nunz. Lisbona 33 (1), fols. 40–46v, cited in Marques and Miranda, *Arquivo secreto*, 172.
61. Trương Bá Cần, *Lịch sử phát triển*, 549n153.
62. Vatican Secret Archives, Arch. Nunz. Lisbona 33 (1), fols. 17–18v, cited in Marques and Miranda, *Arquivo secreto*, 119.

7. LIFE IN LISBON AND THE CASA DO ESPIRITO SANTO, 1807–33

1. *SS*, 133.
2. A detailed history of the district can be found in Manuel Maria Múrias, *Chiado do século XII ao 25 de Abril* (Lisbon: Nova Arrancada, 1996).
3. Dejanirah Couto, *História de Lisboa* (Lisbon: Gotica, 2006), 207–8; for more on café culture and its manifestation in the eighteenth and early nineteenth centuries, see Jack, *Lisbon*, 134–38.
4. *SS*, 551.
5. *SS*, 416–18.

6. José Hermano Saraiva, *História de Portugal*, 7th ed. (Lisbon: Biblioteca da Historia, 2004), 306.

7. W. F. P. Napier, *History of the War in the Peninsula and in the South of France, from A.D. 1807 to A.D. 1814* (1862; repr., New York: AMS Press, 1970), 1:108.

8. Saraiva, *História de Portugal*, 306.

9. Though the amount available for the French had been dramatically reduced by the flight of the court and its entourage, which featured most of the country's wealthiest citizens carrying off as much as half of all of the money in circulation. See John Grehan, *The Lines of Torres Vedras: The Cornerstone of Wellington's Strategy in the Peninsular War, 1809–1812* (Staplehurst: Spellmount, 2000), 9.

10. *NT*, 53–64.

11. James Wilmot Ormsby, *Account of the Operations*, 88–89.

12. *NT*, 55.

13. *NT*, 55ff. In fact, the absent ruler eventually gave orders to resume royal funding for Bỉnh and his companions' housing and other expenses and arranged for retroactive payment of their earlier expenses.

14. *NT*, 51–52.

15. *NT*, 52.

16. *NT*, 56; Wilcken, *Empire Adrift*, 86ff.

17. *NT*, 52.

18. Ibid, 53–64.

19. Dutton, *Tây Sơn Uprising*, 46; Ngô Gia Văn Phái, *Hoàng Lê nhất thống chí* [The unification records of the imperial Le] (Thành Phố Hồ Chí Minh: Nhà Xuất Bản Văn Học, 1998), 108–9.

20. *NT*, 54; "Bản Quốc Ký Sự," Viện Hán Nôm, Hà Nội, A. 989, 99a–b; elsewhere, in his *SS*, Bỉnh also mentions the famines of 1777 and the fact that these led many people to join rural rebellions (3).

21. *NT*, 45.

22. Christopher Hibbert, *Wellington: A Personal History* (London: HarperCollins, 1997), 69. Among the many histories of the Peninsular Wars that offer substantial detail are Roger Parkinson, *The Peninsular War* (London: Hart-Davis MacGibbon, 1973); Nicole Gotteri, *Napoléon et le Portugal* (Paris: Bernard Giovanangeli, 2004); and Julian Paget, *Wellington's Peninsular War: Battles and Battlefields* (London: Leo Cooper, 1990). There are numerous memoirs and other personal accounts of these campaigns as well.

23. Hibbert, *Wellington*, 69–70.

24. *NT*, 60–62, provides some details of the Napoleonic conflicts.

25. See, e.g., Parkinson, *Peninsular War*, 41–42; Gotteri, *Napoléon et le Portugal*, 205ff.

26. *NT*, 63.

27. Lieut.-Gen Sir William Warre, *Letters from the Peninsula, 1808–1812* (London: John Murray, 1909), 39.

28. Bỉnh offers a brief summary of these military clashes between 1807 and 1812 in *TAĐN*, 610–16.

29. See, for example, August Ludolf Frierich Schaumann, *On the Road with Wellington: The Diary of a War Commissary in the Peninsular Campaigns*, ed. and trans. Anthony M. Ludovici (New York: Alfred A. Knopf, 1925), 342ff.

30. On the British occupation of Portugal, see M. D. D. Newitt, *Lord Beresford and the British Intervention in Portugal, 1807–1820* (Lisbon: Impr. De Ciencias Sociais, 2004).

31. *SS*, 597.

32. See David G. Marr, "Concepts of 'Individual' and 'Self' in Twentieth-Century Vietnam," *Modern Asian Studies* 34, no. 4 (2000): 774–81.

33. On the link between modernity and the autonomous individual and writing about the self, see Waterson, "Introduction," 7–8.

34. *SS*, 524–28.

35. *SS*, 371–72.

36. *SS*, 407–8. Santarem is a small town north of Lisbon that Bỉnh visited at least once during his residence in Portugal.

37. *SS*, 409–10.

38. Bỉnh never makes clear what unit of currency he refers to with the word *tiền*.

39. This served as an opportunity for Bỉnh to comment that in Lisbon parishioners were free to go anywhere they wanted to have their confessions heard, unlike Vietnam, where one of Bỉnh's chief complaints regarding the apostolic vicars was their efforts to place restrictions on where people could go to say their confessions.

40. *SS*, 383–84.

41. As an 1822 study reported, "The Royal School of the Congregation of the Oratory was established in the house of the Blessed Spirit [Casa do Espirito Santo], where it is tended by religious of the same order as that of the royal hospice of Our Mother of Necessidades. Latin grammar is taught there to a large number of students." Balbi, *Essai statistique*, 68.

42. *SS*, 421–22.

43. Unfortunately, Bỉnh does not make it clear whether the men shared rooms or had separate apartments.

44. Bỉnh reports purchasing thirty earthenware containers in 1819 alone (*SS*, 548).

45. *SS*, 539.

46. *SS*, 550.

47. *SS*, 564.

48. *SS*, 551. Bỉnh noted that this was butter from cow's milk rather than pork fat, which he perhaps knew as a spread from his homeland.

49. *SS*, 135.

50. *SS*, 582ff.

51. Link, *Travels in Portugal*, 205.

52. *SS*, 136–37.

53. *SS*, 49–52.

54. *SS*, 563–64.

55. The content of this paragraph is derived from *SS*, 571–74.

56. *SS*, 569ff.

57. *SS*, 552–53.

58. On Thăng Long (Hà Nội) as a capital and the limits of the pre-twentieth-century Vietnamese urban tradition, see William Logan, *Hanoi: Biography of a City* (Seattle: University of Washington Press, 2000).

59. Thang Lãng, "Thay lời giới thiệu: Một kho tàng văn hóa vô cùng quí giá chưa hề được phát giác" [Words of introduction: A previously undiscovered priceless literary archive], in

Sách sổ sang chép các việc, by Philiphê Bỉnh (Sài Gòn: Viện Đại Học Đà Lạt Xuất Bản, 1968), xix–xxxvi.

60. There were also smaller private libraries belonging to scholars who had come from literary families who might have collected books over the generations. Such collections would have been accessible only to family members or friends. For an eighteenth-century reference to private libraries, see Phạm Đình Hổ, *Vũ trung tùy bút* [Random notes from amid the rains], trans. Nguyễn Hữu Tiến (Thành Phố Hồ Chí Minh: Nhà Xuất Bản Văn Nghệ Thành Phố Hồ Chí Minh, 1998), 35. For more on earlier Vietnamese libraries, see George Dutton, "The Nguyễn State and the Book Collecting Project," unpublished paper for Harvard Conference on Nguyễn Vietnam, 1558–1885: Domestic Issues, 2013, 7, 18ff.

61. Biblioteca Nacional de Portugal, "About the BNP: History," n.d., accessed August 21, 2012, www.bnportugal.pt/index.php?option=com_content&view=article&id=82&Itemid=90&lang=en. The complex had been built on the site previous occupied by the Ribeira palace, which had been destroyed in the 1755 earthquake.

62. Southey, *Journals of a Residence*, 140.

63. *IL*, 412.

64. Balbi, *Essai statistique*, 83–86. See also Link, *Travels in Portugal*, 227–28, who particularly praises the library of the Benedictine monastery of Nossa Senhora de Jesus.

65. Carrère, *Tableau de Lisbonne*, 240.

66. Link, *Travels in Portugal*, 228.

67. For more on Livraria Bertrand, see Mária Costa, *O Chiado pitoresco e elegante* (Lisbon: Municípo de Lisboa, 1965) 191–201.

68. The list is found in his *SS*, 598. The following page includes a list of the books he wrote himself. Together they constitute an inventory of his complete library at the time of his death.

69. *SS*, 455–58.

70. The *crusado* was a coin commonly used in eighteenth-century Portugal.

71. *SS*, 458–60; on the Vietnamese situation, see George Dutton, "Scholars, Courts, and the Examination System in Eighteenth-Century Vietnam," unpublished paper, 2003, 13–17.

72. *SS*, 451ff.

73. *SS*, 153–54; for an interesting counterpart to Bỉnh's descriptions of the medical profession in Portugal, see that found in Carrere, *Tableau de Lisbonne*, 215–21.

74. *TAĐN*, 705.

75. *TAĐN*, 707.

76. He detailed the event in his *NT*, 70–75.

77. *NT*, 79.

78. *NT*, 466.

79. Schurhammer, "Annamitische Xaveriusliteratur," 308.

80. Robert Tombs, *France, 1814–1914* (New York: Longman, 1996), 92–93.

81. Schurhammer, "Annamitische Xaveriusliteratur," 308.

82. *SS*, 135.

83. *SS*, 435.

84. *SS*, 435–36.

85. Vatican Secret Archives, Arch. Nunz. Lisbona 33 (3), fols. 59–60, cited in Marques and Miranda, *Arquivo secreto*, 174.

86. *NT,* 97.
87. This sequence of events is described in *NT,* 101–14.
88. *NT,* 109.
89. *NT,* 110.
90. *NT,* 110.
91. David Birmingham, *A Concise History of Portugal* (Cambridge: Cambridge University Press, 2003), 111–14.
92. *NT,* 104.
93. *SS,* 136.
94. *TAĐN,* 738.
95. *TAĐN,* 738–39. The subsequent quotes come from the same section.

8. THE TALES OF PHILIPHÊ BỈNH

1. *TAĐT,* 82.
2. *TAĐN,* 378.
3. *TAĐN,* n.p. (first and second pages of unpaginated preface).
4. *IL,* 329 (emphasis added).
5. *PX,* 446.
6. *SGT,* 1: preface. Forest, *Missionaires français,* 3:152, cites French priests who commented on the ease with which the Tonkinese Christians were able to memorize and recite liturgical materials.
7. *SS,* 118.
8. *SGT,* 1:3.
9. Laurentino Gomes, *1808: The Flight of the Emperor,* trans. Andrew Nevins (Guilford, CT: Lyons Press, 2013), 28–29.
10. Carrère, *Tableau de Lisbonne,* 228.
11. For a partial list of the printed books that Bỉnh used for his writing project, see Appendix 3.
12. *TAĐN,* 32–33.
13. *NT,* 1.
14. Keith Taylor, *A History of the Vietnamese* (Cambridge: Cambridge University Press, 2013), 120.
15. To be competent in this writing system, people had to learn the Chinese writing system first; only then could they comfortably write in the new demotic script.
16. Alberts, *Conflict and Conversion,* 124.
17. Jacques, *Portuguese Pioneers,* 52.
18. Ibid., 11–12; see also Gonçalo Fernandes and Carlos Assunção, "The First Vietnamese Dictionary (Rome 1651): Contributions of the Portuguese Patronage to the Eastern Linguistics," *Tạp chí khoa học ngoại ngữ / Journal of Foreign Language Studies,* no. 41 (2014): 3–25. I thank Raul Máximo da Silva for sending me a copy of this article.
19. For more on the early history of the romanized *quốc ngữ* script in Vietnam, see Đỗ Quang Chính, *Lịch sử chữ quốc ngữ, 1620–1659* [A history of the *quốc ngữ* script] (Sài Gòn: Ra Khơi, 1972); see also Jacques, *Portuguese Pioneers,* esp. 51ff., and Phan, *Mission and Catechesis,* 28–36.

20. Jacques, *Portuguese Pioneers*, 80. Whether this is a valid comparison is unclear, for Jacques speaks of "literary production" for *nôm*, while his total for *quốc ngữ* is "works printed" in that script.

21. A significant minority still continued to write in the older vernacular script of *chữ nôm*, which had once dominated Catholic writings, and Bỉnh himself wrote some liturgical materials in it, making it clear that even by this relatively late date *quốc ngữ* had not entirely displaced the demotic script within Catholic communities.

22. A detailed comparison of the orthographic transformation of the writing system can be found in Jacques, *Missionaires portugais*, 348–73. This reveals the relatively modest amount of change that occurred from the 1630s to the present time.

23. *SS*, first page of volume (n.p.).

24. *SGT*, 1:3.

25. Stefan Tanaka, *New Times in Modern Japan* (Princeton, NJ: Princeton University Press, 2004), 4ff.

26. The field of geographical temporality suggests the importance of understanding time as a social and cultural construct. Jon May and Nigel Thrift, eds., *TimeSpace: Geographies of Temporality* (New York: Routledge, 2001); see also Robert Levine, *A Geography of Time: The Temporal Misadventures of a Social Psychologist, or How Every Culture Keeps Time Just a Little Bit Differently* (New York: Basic Books, 1998). Useful also for its exploration of the socially constructed nature of time in a Southeast Asian context is Janet Hoskins, *The Play of Time: Kodi Perspectives on Calendars, History, and Exchange* (Berkeley: University of California Press, 1997).

27. This was not the only such alternative temporal schema in effect for Vietnamese, however, for Buddhism also has its own distinctive marked times, most notably centered on the birth of the Buddha and other key events in his lifetime, though unlike Catholic times, these were linked to phases in the lunar calendar.

28. A useful early discussion of these calendrical occurrences in the Vietnamese ritual year is by a seventeenth-century Catholic, Bento Thien, and can be found in George Dutton, Jayne Werner, and John Whitmore, eds., *Sources of Vietnamese Tradition* (New York: Columbia University Press, 2012), 223–26.

29. Forest, *Missionaires français*, 3:151–52, discusses the fierce competition to distribute new calendars.

30. *SS*, 391. Naming Day commemorates Jesus's circumcision and naming, though it has also come to be a day for celebrating the motherhood of the Virgin Mary.

31. *SGT*, n.p. (in preface).

32. There is an obvious disjuncture here between the number of years since Jesus's birth, 1802, and the year in which Bỉnh wrote this book, 1815. Some of the other figures are also inconsistent, such as the date of the disbanding of the Jesuits, which would also put the table's creation at 1802. I can only surmise that this was carelessness on Bỉnh's part or that the table was drafted over time and was not edited in its final version.

33. Pope Pius VII was actually the 251st pope. Bỉnh does not give the number of years from time of event to the present for this entry.

34. *MP*, 2.

35. *SS*, 300.

36. A direct comparison with the original shows just how little of it Bình actually translated. See Fernão Mendes Pinto, *The Travels of Mendes Pinto*, ed. and trans. Rebecca Catz (Chicago: University of Chicago Press, 1989).

37. Gen. 11:1-9.

38. *MP,* 170. The story of the Tower of Babel has long intrigued modern scholars of language, for it is regarded as a crucial moment at which a failure to communicate dramatically manifests itself. See, for example, Lydia Liu, *Translingual Practice: Literature, National Culture, and Translated Modernity in China, 1900-1937* (Stanford, CA: Stanford University Press, 1995), 20; and Jacques Derrida, *Psyche,* trans. Joseph Graham (Stanford, CA: Stanford University Press, 2007), 191-225.

39. Paulus Tĩnh et al. to Paris, June 28, 1793, AMEP, vol. 692, pp. 460-61.

40. *TAĐN,* fourth page of unpaginated preface.

41. *SS,* 28.

42. *TAĐN,* 81.

43. *NT,* 269.

44. *TAĐN,* 531.

45. *NT,* 92; the Bible story is found in 1 Sam. 18:6-16.

46. *TAĐN,* 389; the Bible story is found in 1 Sam. 20:42.

47. *TAĐN,* 404; the Bible story is found in 1 Sam. 21:12-15.

48. Job 1-2.

49. *SS,* 316.

50. *TAĐT,* 29-30.

51. *NT,* 395-97.

52. *NT,* 224-26.

53. *NT,* 282-87.

54. *TAĐN,* 632-33.

55. Olga Dror, *Cult, Culture, and Authority: Princess Liễu Hạnh in Vietnamese History* (Honolulu: University of Hawaii Press, 2007), 16-17.

56. For a brief background discussion, see Cao Thi Nhu Quynh and John C. Schafer, "From Verse Narrative to Novel: The Development of Prose Fiction in Vietnam," *Journal of Asian Studies* 47, no. 4 (November 1988): 758-60. A modern English translation is Ly Te Xuyen, *Departed Spirits of the Viet Realm,* trans. Brian E. Ostrowski and Brian A. Zottoli (Ithaca, NY: Cornell Southeast Asia Program, 1999). Scholars have suggested that the text may also date from the Lý dynasty, though it has also been ascribed to a fourteenth-century literatus, Trần Thế Pháp. The earliest dated version of the text is from 1492; Lại Nguyên Ân and Bùi Văn Trọng Cương, *Tự điển văn học Việt Nam* [Dictionary of Vietnamese literature] (Hà Nội: Nhà Xuất Bản Giáo Dục, 1997), 262. Liam Kelley has produced a recent modern English translation; see Vũ Quỳnh, comp., *Lĩnh Nam chích quái liệt truyện* [Arrayed tales of selected oddities from south of the passes] [1492], trans. Liam C. Kelley et al., Viet Texts, accessed September 22, 2014, https://sites.google.com/a/hawaii.edu/viet-texts/.

57. The *Truyện kỳ mạn lục* was substantially based on an earlier Chinese work, *Tiễn đăng tân thoại* [燈新話 New tales by the trimmed lamp]. Lại Nguyên Ân and Bùi Văn Trọng Cương, *Tự điển văn học Việt Nam,* 636.

58. For an English translation and commentary, see Cuong Tu Nguyen, *Zen in Medieval Vietnam*.

59. Ostrowski, "Nôm Works," 59, gives a chart of twenty-two volumes probably written by Maiorica that are no longer extant.

60. Maiorica, *Các thánh truyện*, 488 (original page 19).

61. Philiphê Bỉnh, "Missionario de Tunkim," in untitled volume of miscellanea, Ms. Borgiana Tonchinese 10, 1813?, Biblioteca Apostolica Vaticana, iv–xiv.

62. Bỉnh likely gleaned some of his information about Maiorica from the work of Giovanni Marini, a Jesuit priest who was a contemporary of Maiorica and who left an account of him and of the history of the church in Vietnam. Bỉnh notes that this account was first published in Rome in 1663 and subsequently translated into other European languages. Bỉnh must have seen it, for he quotes from it in *TAĐN*, 31. Giovanni Marini's work is *Relation nouvelle et curieuse des royaumes de Tunquin et de Lao* (Paris: Chez Gervais Clouzier, 1666).

63. *The Tales of Saint Anne* is unlike the other three volumes. Not only is it not focused on a figure associated with the Jesuit order, but it is not even historical. Rather, it is essentially apocryphal, telling the life of the mother of Mary, a figure not mentioned in the Bible who appears only in the later Apocrypha. Despite this, Bỉnh still managed to assemble a book of more than six hundred pages of tales about her.

64. *PB*, preface.

65. *TAĐN*, unpaginated preface.

66. *TAĐN*, unpaginated preface.

67. *SGT*, 1:2. See also Ostrowski, "Nôm Works," 59.

68. *SGT*, 1:2.

69. *SGT*, 1: unpaginated preface.

70. *SGT*, 1:215.

71. *SGT*, 1:216.

72. Hippolyte Delehaye, *The Legends of the Saints*, trans. Donald Attwater (Portland, OR: Four Courts Press, 1998), 54.

73. *PX*, unpaginated preface.

74. João de Lucena, *Vida do Padre Francisco Xavier*, 2 vols. (Lisbon: União Gráfica, 1959).

75. *PX*, 447.

76. *PX*, 584.

77. *PB*, 631–722.

78. Ibid., 589.

79. *TAĐN*, ninth page of unpaginated preface.

80. *TAĐN*, title page.

81. *TAĐN*, first page of unpaginated preface.

82. *TAĐN*, third page of the unpaginated preface.

83. *TAĐN*, 436–37.

84. See Nguyen, *Zen in Medieval Vietnam*, 25ff.

85. *TAĐN*, 12ff.

86. *TAĐN*, 18–19.

87. While historical, these tales are also clearly didactic, designed to tell the community of Catholics where they came from and the kinds of challenges they have faced, and

particularly to remind them of those who gave their lives as martyrs for the faith. As in European writings about the history of Vietnamese Catholicism there is a strong element of martyrology in Bỉnh's collections of "tales."

88. Agostinho de Santa Maria, *Rosas do Japam: Candidas açucenas . . . colhidas no jardim da Igreja do Japaõ . . . em as vidas das muyto Illustres Senhoras, D. Julia Nayto, D. Luzia da Cruz, ou Caraviaxi, & D. Thecla Ignacia, ou Muni, & de suas companheiras*. (Lisbon: Na Officina de Antonio Pedrozo Galram, 1709).

89. *TAĐT*, 2–7.

90. *TAĐT*, 691.

91. Ibid. Bỉnh wrote (690) that he owned three volumes of tales about Japan ("truyện Nhật Bản").

92. Isabel Nobre Vargues and Luís Reis Torgal, "Da revolução à contra-revolução: Vintismo, cartismo, absolutismo. O exílio político," in *História de Portugal*, ed. José Mattoso (Lisbon: Editorial Estampa, 1998), 5:63–76.

93. *SA*, 598.

94. *SA*, 599.

95. *TAĐN*, 694.

96. It is possible that Bỉnh was a victim of a large-scale cholera outbreak in Lisbon that year. The epidemic was particularly virulent in Lisbon between April and October of that year, and it killed more than thirteen thousand people. See Rui Cascão, "Demografia e sociedade," in Mattoso, *História de Portugal*, 5:371.

EPILOGUE

1. This was a consequence of the conclusion of the civil war between the two Braganza royal family princes in favor of Prince Pedro and his liberal Republican allies. One significant consequence of Pedro's victory was a substantial curtailment of the church's power.

2. Costa, *Chiado pitoresco e elegante*, 62.

3. Ibid.

4. Ibid.

5. See, e.g., Mitchell Landsberg, "New Translation of Prayers Is Rooted in Catholic Church's Past," *Los Angeles Times*, November 25, 2011, 4.

6. On Minh Mạng's attitude toward Christians, see Minh Mạng Emperor, "Comments Regarding Christianity," in Dutton, Werner, and Whitmore, *Sources of Vietnamese Tradition*, 325–28. For more on the emperor in general, see Choi Byung-Wook, *Southern Vietnam under the Reign of Minh Mang (1820–1841): Central Policies and Local Response* (Ithaca, NY: Cornell Southeast Asia Program, 2004).

7. Nguyen Cong Doan, "Jesuits: Fifty Years in Vietnam," *Province Express*, July 11, 2007, www.express.org.au/article.aspx?aeid=3153.

8. It is worth noting, however, that his book was published in the southern part of the then-divided Vietnamese territories and that it could not be circulated to his native Tonkin until after the war had ended in 1975.

9. Thanh Lãng, "Thay lời giới thiệu."

10. Nguyễn Phương Trang, *Dấu ấn tiếng Việt trong Sách Sổ Sang Chép Các Việc (1822) Chuyên Khảo* [Hallmarks of the Vietnamese language in the *Notebook That Transmits and Records All Matters* (1822): A monograph] (Thành Phố Hồ Chí Minh: NXB Đại Học Quốc Gia TP HCM, 2015); Võ Xuân Quế, "Philiphê Bỉnh và sách quốc ngữ viết tây: 'Nhật trình kim thư khất chính chúa giáo,'" [Philiphê Bỉnh and a handwritten book in Quốc Ngữ: Daily records and current letters [pertaining to] the request for a primary bishop], *Nghiên cứu lịch sử* 3, nos. 5–6 (1998): 52–58.

APPENDIX 3

1. Bỉnh, preface to *Truyện ou Thánh Phanchicô de Borja*.

BIBLIOGRAPHY

BỈNH'S NOTEBOOKS

Bỉnh, Philiphê. *Alma instruida* [The instructed soul]. 1812. Ms. Borgiana Tonchinese 15, Biblioteca Apostolica Vaticana.

———. *Alma instruida no doctrina* [The soul instructed in the doctrine]. n.d. Ms. Borgiana Tonchinese 13, Biblioteca Apostolica Vaticana.

———. *Lễ luật khuyên anh em trong họ 7 Sự Thương Khó rất thánh Đức Bà* [The ritual laws and exhortations to my brothers of the Seven Sorrows of the Most Blessed Virgin Mary]. 1802. Ms. Borgiana Tonchinese 11, Biblioteca Apostolica Vaticana.

———. *Nhật trình kim thư khất chính chúa giáo* [Golden book recording a journey to seek an official religious leader]. 1796–1826. Ms. Borgiana Tonchinese 7, Biblioteca Apostolica Vaticana.

———. *Phép giảng truyện các đời đ. thánh phapha* [A method for explicating tales of the popes]. 1798–1831. Ms. Borgiana Tonchinese 21, Biblioteca Apostolica Vaticana.

———. *Sách dạy xem lễ Misa* [Book explaining the conducting of the mass]. 1802–10. Ms. Borgiana Tonchinese 19, Biblioteca Apostolica Vaticana.

———. *Sách gương truyện* [Book of exemplary tales]. 2 vols. 1815. Ms. Borgiana Tonchinese 9 and 16, Biblioteca Apostolica Vaticana.

———. *Sách số sang chép các việc* [Notebook that transmits and records all matters]. 1822–32. Ms. Borgiana Tonchinese 3, Biblioteca Apostolica Vaticana.

———. *Truyện Anam* [Tales of Annam]. Vol. 1. *Đàng Ngoài* [The Outer Region]. 1822. Ms. Borgiana Tonchinese 1, Biblioteca Apostolica Vaticana.

———. *Truyện Anam* [Tales of Annam]. Vol. 2. *Đàng Trọng* [The Inner Region]. 1822. Ms. Borgiana Tonchinese 2, Biblioteca Apostolica Vaticana.

———. *Truyện bà Thánh Anna* [Tales of Saint Anne]. 1830. Ms. Borgiana Tonchinese 18, Biblioteca Apostolica Vaticana.

———. *Truyện nhật trình Ông Fernad Mendes Pinto* [Tales of the travels of Fernando Mendes Pinto]. 1817. Ms. Borgiana Tonchinese 20, Biblioteca Apostolica Vaticana.

———. *Truyện Ông Thánh Ignacio de Loyola lập Dòng Đức Chúa Jesu* [Tales of Saint Ignatius of Loyola establishing the Order of the Virtuous Lord Jesus]. 1819. Ms. Borgiana Tonchinese 5, Biblioteca Apostolica Vaticana.

———. *Truyện Ông Thánh Phanchicô de Borja* [Tales of Saint Francis de Borgia]. 1820. Ms. Borgiana Tonchinese 4, Biblioteca Apostolica Vaticana.

———. *Truyện Ông Thánh Phanchicô Xavier* [Tales of Saint Francis Xavier]. 1818. Ms. Borgiana Tonchinese 6, Biblioteca Apostolica Vaticana.

———. Untitled volume of miscellanea. 1813? Ms. Borgiana Tonchinese 10, Biblioteca Apostolica Vaticana.

OTHER PRIMARY SOURCES

Archives des Missions Étrangères de Paris, letters.
"Bản quốc ký sự" [Records of the affairs of our country]. Viện Hán Nôm, Hà Nội, A. 989.
Gazeta de Lisboa, 1796–1807.

PUBLISHED PRIMARY AND SECONDARY SOURCES

Adriano di St. Thecla. *Opusculum de sectis apud Sinenses et Tunkinenses* [A small treatise on the sects among the Chinese and Tonkinese]. Edited and translated by Olga Dror. Ithaca, NY: Cornell Southeast Asia Program, 2002.

Alberts, Tara. "Catholic Written and Oral Cultures in Seventeenth-Century Vietnam." *Journal of Early Modern History* 16 (2012): 383–402.

———. *Conflict and Conversion: Catholicism in Southeast Asia, 1500–1700*. Oxford: Oxford University Press, 2013.

Almeida, A. Duarte de, ed. *As invasões francescas: Reinado de D. Maria I—Regencia do Principe D. João, 1777–1816*. Lisbon: João Romano Torres, n.d.

Alvares, Antonio. *Memoria sobre o Real Padroado da Corte de Portugal nas missoes do reino de Tunkin / por Antonio Alvares, da Congregacao do Oratorio de Lisboa, feita em 21 de Janeiro de 1802 e Resposta que deu o procurador de Coroa, Joao Antonio Salter de Mendonca, em 9 de abril do mesmo anno; tudo copiado da colleccao de manuscriptos de Julio Firmino Judice Biker, e por este publicado*. Lisbon, 1802.

Andre-Marie, R. P. F. *Missions dominicaines dans l'Extrême Orient*. Vol. 2. Paris: Librairies Poussielgue Frères, 1865.

Anthony, Robert J. *Like Froth on the Floating Sea: The World of Pirates and Seafarers in Late Imperial South China*. Berkeley, CA: Institute of East Asian Studies, 2003.

Balbi, Adriano. *Essai statistique sur le royaume de Portugal et d'Algarve, comparé aux autres états de l'Europe: Et suivi d'un coup d'oeil sur l'état actuel des sciences, des lettres et des beaux-arts parmi les Portugais des deux hémisphéres*. Vol. 1. Paris, 1822.

Baltazar, Isabel. *D. João VI: As duas faces do poder*. Lisbon: Roma Editoria, 2009.

Beaulieu, Louis. *La Salle des Martyrs du Séminaire des Missions Étrangères*. Paris: Charles Douniol, 1865.

Bình, Philiphê. *Những bài thơ phụ lục trong nhật trình kim thư khất chính chúa giáo* [Golden book recording a journey to seek an official religious leader]. Reichstett, France: Định Hướng Tùng Thư, 2004.

Birmingham, David. *A Concise History of Portugal*. Cambridge: Cambridge University Press, 2003.

Boléo, Luisa V. de Paiva. *D. Maria I: A Rainha Louca*. Lisbon: A Esfera Dos Livros, 2009.

Bon, M., and M. Dronet. *Manuel de conversation Franco-Tonkinois*. Ke So: Imprimerie de la Mission, 1889.

Borri, Christoforo. *Cochinchina*. 1633. Facsimile reprint, New York: Da Capo Press, 1970.

Boxer, Charles. *Four Centuries of Portuguese Expansion, 1515–1825: A Succinct Survey*. Berkeley: University of California Press, 1969.

——. *The Portuguese Seaborne Empire, 1415–1825*. 1969. Reprint, Manchester: Carcanet, 1991.

Bradford, William. *Sketches of the Country, Character and Costume in Portugal and Spain Made during the Campaign, and on the Route of the British Army in 1808 and 1809*. London: John Booth, 1812.

Braun, Theodore E. D., and John B. Radner, eds. *The Lisbon Earthquake of 1755: Representations and Reactions*. Oxford: Voltaire Foundation, 2005.

Brockey, Liam. *Journey to the East: The Jesuit Missions to China, 1579–1724*. Cambridge, MA: Belknap Press, 2008.

Brooke, T. H. *A History of the Island of St. Helena, from Its Discovery by the Portuguese to the Year 1806*. London: Black, Parry, and Kingsbury, 1806.

Busk, M. M. *The History of Spain and Portugal from B.C. 1000 to A.D. 1814*. London: Baldwin and Cradock, 1833.

Câmara Municipal de Lisboa. *Atlas da carta topográfica de Lisboa: Sob a direcção de Filipe Folque: 1856–1858*. Lisbon: Arquivo Municipal de Lisboa, 2000.

Cao Thi Nhu Quynh and John C. Schafer. "From Verse Narrative to Novel: The Development of Prose Fiction in Vietnam." *Journal of Asian Studies* 47, no. 4 (November 1988): 756–77.

Carrère, J.-B.-F. *Tableau de Lisbonne, en 1796 suivi de lettres écrites de Portugal sur l'état ancien et actuel de ce royaume*. Paris: Chez Deterville, 1798.

Cascão, Rui. "Demografia e sociedade." In *História de Portugal*, edited by José Mattoso, 5:365–77. Lisbon: Editorial Estampa, 1998.

Castel-Branco, Cristina, ed. *Necessidades: The Gardens and Enclosure*. Lisbon: Livros Horizonte, 2002.

Castellanos de Losada, D. Basilio Sebastian. *Biografía eclesiástica completa*. Madrid: D. Alejandro Gomez Fuentenebro, 1863.

Cheke, Marcus. *Carlota Joaquina: Queen of Portugal*. Freeport, NY: Books for Libraries Press, 1969.

Cheney, David M. "Archdiocese of Hà Nội." Catholic Hierarchy, n.d. Accessed August 25, 2015. http://catholic-hierarchy.org/diocese/dhano.html.

Choi Byung-Wook. *Southern Vietnam under the Reign of Minh Mang (1820–1841): Central Policies and Local Response*. Ithaca, NY: Cornell Southeast Asia Program, 2004.

Collins, Francis. *Voyages to Portugal, Spain, Sicily, Malta, Asia Minor, Egypt, &c. from 1796 to 1801: With an Historical Sketch, and Occasional Reflections*. London: Richard Phillips, 1809.

Cooke, Nola. "Strange Brew: Global, Regional and Local Factors behind the 1690 Prohibition of Christian Practice in Nguyễn Cochinchina." *Journal of Southeast Asian Studies* 39, no. 3 (October 2008): 383–409.

Cooper, Michael, SJ. *Rodrigues the Interpreter: An Early Jesuit in Japan and China*. New York: Weatherhill, 1974.

Côrte-Real, Manuel. *O Palácio das Necessidades*. Lisbon: Ministério dos Negócios, 1983.

Costa, Mária. *O chiado pitoresco e elegante*. Lisbon: Municípo de Lisboa, 1965.

Couto, Dejanirah. *História de Lisboa*. Lisbon: Gotica, 2006.

Crowhurst, Patrick. *The French War on Trade: Privateering, 1793–1815*. Hants: Scolar Press, 1989.

Cuong Tu Nguyen. *Zen in Medieval Vietnam: A Study and Translation of the "Thien uyen tap anh."* Honolulu: University of Hawaii Press, 1997.

Đại Nam nhất thống chí [The unification records of the Great South]. Translated by Phạm Trọng Điềm. Huế: Nhà Xuất Bản Thuận Hóa, 1996.

Đại Việt sử ký tục biên [A continuation of the historical records of Đại Việt]. Translated by Ngô Thế Long and Nguyễn Kim Hưng. Edited by Nguyễn Đổng Chi. Hà Nội: Nhà Xuất Bản Khoa Học Xã Hội, 1991.

Daly, Gavin. *The British Soldier in the Peninsular War: Encounters with Spain and Portugal, 1808–1814*. Basingstoke: Palgrave Macmillan, 2013.

———. "A Dirty, Indolent, Priest-Ridden City: British Soldiers in Lisbon during the Peninsular War, 1808–1813." *History* 94, no. 316 (2009): 461–82.

Đặng Phương-Nghi. *Les institutions publiques du Viêt-Nam au XVIIIe siècle*. Paris: EFEO, 1969.

Đào Duy Anh. *Đất nước Việt Nam qua các đời: Nghiên cứu địa lý học lịch sử Việt Nam* [Vietnamese territory throughout time: Research into the historical geography of Vietnam]. Huế: Nhà Xuất Bản Thuận Hóa, 1994.

da Silva, Innocencio Francisco, Brito Aranha, José Joaquim Gomes de Brito, Alvaro Néves, and Ernesto Soares. *Diccionario bibliographico portuguez*. Vol. 1. Lisbon: Na Imprensa Nacional, 1858.

Delehaye, Hippolyte *The Legends of the Saints*. Translated by Donald Attwater. Portland, OR: Four Courts Press, 1998.

Dep, Arthur C. *The Oratorian Mission in Sri Lanka, 1795–1874: Being a History of the Catholic Church, 1795–1874*. Ja-ela: Dep, 1987.

Derrida, Jacques. *Psyche*. Translated by Joseph Graham. Stanford, CA: Stanford University Press, 2007.

Disney, A. R. *A History of Portugal and the Portuguese Empire*. Vol. 1. Cambridge: Cambridge University Press, 2009.

Domingues, Francisco Contente. *Ilustração e catolicismo: Teodoro de Almeida*. Lisbon: Colibri, 1994.

Đồng khánh địa dư chí [The Dong Khanh gazetteer]. Edited by Ngô Đức Thọ, Nguyễn Văn Nguyên, and Philippe Papin. Hà Nội: EFEO, 2003.

Đỗ Quang Chính. *Dòng tên trong xã hội Đại Việt, 1615–1773* [The Jesuit order in Dai Viet society, 1615–1773]. Wichita Falls, TX: NXB Tôn Giáo, 2006.

———. *Lịch sử chữ quốc ngữ, 1620–1659* [A history of the *quốc ngữ* script, 1620–59]. Sài Gòn: Ra Khơi, 1972.

Dror, Olga. *Cult, Culture, and Authority: Princess Liễu Hạnh in Vietnamese History.* Honolulu: University of Hawaii Press, 2007.
Dutton, George. "The Nguyễn State and the Book Collecting Project." Unpublished paper for Harvard Conference on Nguyễn Vietnam, 1558–1885: Domestic Issues, 2013.
———. "Scholars, Courts, and the Examination System in Eighteenth-Century Vietnam." Unpublished paper, 2003.
———. *Tây Sơn Uprising: Society and Rebellion in Eighteenth-Century Vietnam.* Honolulu: University of Hawaii Press, 2006.
Dutton, George, Jayne Werner, and John Whitmore, eds. *Sources of Vietnamese Tradition.* New York: Columbia University Press, 2012.
Essai statistique sur le Portugal. Bordeaux, 1810.
Fernandes, Gonçalo, and Carlos Assunção. "The First Vietnamese Dictionary (Rome 1651): Contributions of the Portuguese Patronage to the Eastern Linguistics." *Tạp chí khoa học ngoại ngữ / Journal of Foreign Language Studies* 41 (2014): 3–25.
Fisher, Richard Barnard. *A Sketch of the City of Lisbon and Its Environs; with Some Observations on the Manners, Disposition, and Character of the Portuguese Nation.* London: J. Ridgway, 1811.
Fletcher, Ian, ed. *Voices from the Peninsula: Eyewitness Accounts by Soldiers of Wellington's Army, 1808–1814.* London: Greenhill Books, 2001.
Forest, Alain. *Les missionaires français au Tonkin et au Siam, XVIIe–XVIIIe siècles.* Vol. 2. *Histoires du Tonkin.* Paris: L'Harmattan, 1998.
———. *Les missionaires français au Tonkin et au Siam, XVIIe–XVIIIe siècles.* Vol. 3. *Organiser une église convertir les infidèles.* Paris: L'Harmattan, 1998.
Gomes, Laurentino. *1808: The Flight of the Emperor.* Translated by Andrew Nevins. Guilford, CT: Lyons Press, 2013.
Gotteri, Nicole. *Napoléon et le Portugal.* Paris: Bernard Giovanangeli, 2004.
Graïnha, Emm. Borges. *Histoire de la Compagnie de Jésus en Portugal (1540–1910).* Lisbon: Imprimerie National, 1915.
Grehan, John. *The Lines of Torres Vedras: The Cornerstone of Wellington's Strategy in the Peninsular War, 1809–1812.* Staplehurst: Spellmount, 2000.
Guillén-Nuñez, C. *Macao's Church of Saint Paul: A Glimmer of the Baroque in China.* Hong Kong: Hong Kong University Press, 2009.
Gunn, Geoffrey. *Encountering Macao: A Portuguese City-State on the Periphery of China, 1557–1999.* Boulder, CO: Westview Press, 1996.
Heyer, Friedrich. *The Catholic Church from 1648 to 1870.* Translated by D. W. D. Shaw. London: Adam and Black, 1969.
Hibbert, Christopher. *Wellington: A Personal History.* London: HarperCollins, 1997.
Histoire de Jean VI, roi de Portugal. Paris: Ponthieu, 1827.
Hoang Anh Tuan. *Silk for Silver: Dutch-Vietnamese Relations, 1637–1700.* Leiden: Brill, 2007.
Hoskins, Janet. *The Play of Time: Kodi Perspectives on Calendars, History, and Exchange.* Berkeley: University of California Press, 1997.
Jack, Malcolm. *Lisbon: City of the Sea, a History.* London: I. B. Taurus, 2007.
Jackson, E. L. *St. Helena: The Historic Island, from Its Discovery to the Present Date.* London: Ward Lock, 1903.

Jacques, Roland. *Les missionaires portugais et les débuts de l'Église catholique au Viêt-nam.* Vol. 1. Reichstett, France: Định Hướng Tùng Thu, 2004.

———. *Portuguese Pioneers of Vietnamese Linguistics.* Bangkok: Orchid Press, 2002.

"Jacques Benjamin Longer." Archives des Missions Étrangères de Paris, n.d. Accessed July 27, 2012. http://archives.mepasie.org/notices/notices-biographiques/longer.

Jellema, Kate. "Returning Home: Ancestor Veneration and the Nationalism of Đổi Mới Vietnam." In *Modernity and Re-enchantment: Religion in Post-revolutionary Vietnam*, edited by Philip Taylor, 57–89. Singapore: Institute of Southeast Asian Studies, 2007.

Jesuits, Fortuné de Montezon, Ed Estève, Alexandre de Rhodes, Joseph Tissanier, and Metello Saccano. *Mission de la Cochinchine et du Tonkin avec gravure et carte géographique.* Paris: Charles Douniol, 1858.

Keith, Charles. *Catholic Vietnam: A Church from Empire to Nation.* Berkeley: University of California Press, 2012.

Kelley, Liam. *Beyond the Bronze Pillars: Envoy Poetry and the Sino-Vietnamese Relationship.* Honolulu: Association for Asian Studies and University of Hawaii Press, 2005.

Khâm định Việt sử thông giám cương mục. Edited by Viện Sử Học. Hà Nội: Nhà Xuất Bản Giáo Dục, 1998.

Koschroke, Klaus, et al., eds. *A History of Christianity in Asia, Africa, and Latin America, 1450–1990: A Documentary Sourcebook.* Grand Rapids, MI: William B. Eerdmans, 2007.

Lacouture, Jean. *Jesuits: A Multibiography.* Washington, DC: Counterpoint, 1995.

Lại Nguyên Ân and Bùi Văn Trọng Cương. *Từ điển văn học Việt Nam* [Dictionary of Vietnamese literature]. Hà Nội: Nhà Xuất Bản Giáo Dục, 1997.

Landsberg, Mitchell. "New Translation of Prayers Is Rooted in Catholic Church's Past." *Los Angeles Times*, November 26, 2011, 4.

Launay, Adrien. *Histoire générale de la Société des Missions-Étrangères.* 1894. Reprint, Paris: Missions-Étrangères de Paris, 2003.

———. *Nos missionaires, précédés d'une étude historique sur la Société des Missions-Étrangères.* Paris, 1886.

Lê Ngọc Bích. *Nhân vật công giáo Việt Nam, thế kỷ XVIII–XIX–XX.* [Figures in Vietnamese Catholicism, eighteenth, nineteenth, and twentieth centuries]. [Thành Phố Hồ Chí Minh]: n.p., n.d.

Lê Quýnh. *Bắc hành tùng ký* [A record of traveling along to the north]. Translated by Hoàng Xuân Hãn. Huế: Nhà Xuất Bản Thuận Hóa, 1993.

Lessard, Micheline. "Curious Relations: Jesuit Perceptions of the Vietnamese." In *Essays into Vietnamese Pasts*, edited by John K. Whitmore and Keith Taylor, 137–56. Ithaca, NY: Cornell Southeast Asia Program, 1995.

Levine, Robert. *A Geography of Time: The Temporal Misadventures of a Social Psychologist, or How Every Culture Keeps Time Just a Little Bit Differently.* New York: Basic Books, 1998.

Link, Henry Frederick. *Travels in Portugal, and through France and Spain.* London: T. N. Longman and O. Rees, 1801.

Li Tana. *Nguyen Cochinchina: Southern Vietnam in the Seventeenth and Eighteenth Centuries.* Ithaca, NY: Cornell Southeast Asia Program, 1998.

Liu, Lydia. *Translingual Practice: Literature, National Culture, and Translated Modernity in China, 1900–1937.* Stanford, CA: Stanford University Press, 1995.

Livermore, H. V. *A New History of Portugal.* 2nd ed. Cambridge: Cambridge University Press, 1976.
Ljungstedt, Anders. *An Historical Sketch of the Portuguese Settlements in China; and of the Roman Catholic Church and Mission in China.* Boston: J. Munroe, 1836.
Logan, William. *Hanoi: Biography of a City.* Seattle: University of Washington Press, 2000.
Lousada, Maria Alexandre. "Public Space and Popular Sociability in Lisbon in the Early 19th Century." *Santa Barbara Portuguese Studies* 4 (1997): 220–32.
Lucena, João de. *Vida do Padre Francisco Xavier.* 2 vols. Lisbon: União Gráfica, 1959.
Ly Te Xuyen. *Departed Spirits of the Viet Realm.* Translated by Brian E. Ostrowski and Brian A. Zottoli. Ithaca, NY: Cornell Southeast Asia Program, 1999.
Macaulay, Neill. *Dom Pedro: The Struggle for Liberty in Brazil and Portugal.* Durham, NC: Duke University Press, 1986.
Maiorica, Geronimo. *Các thánh truyện (tháng giêng)* [Tales of the saints (January)]. [Thành Phố Hồ Chí Minh?]: n.p., 1997.
Mair, Victor, ed. *The Columbia Anthology of Traditional Chinese Literature.* New York: Columbia University Press, 1994.
Manguin, Pierre-Yves. *Les Nguyen, Macau et le Portugal: Aspects politiques et commerciaux d'une relation privilégiée en Mer de Chine, 1773–1802.* Paris: École française d'Extrême-Orient, 1984.
Mantienne, Frédéric. *Mgr. Pierre Pigneaux, évêque d'Adran, dignitaire de Cochinchine.* Paris: Églises d'Asie, 1999.
Marini, Giovanni. *Relation nouvelle et curieuse des royaumes de Tunquin et de Lao.* Paris: Chez Gervais Clouzier, 1666.
Marques, A. H. de Oliveira. *History of Portugal.* Vol. 1. *From Lusitania to Empire.* New York: Columbia University Press, 1972.
Marques, João Francisco, and José Carlos Lopes de Miranda, eds. *Arquivo secreto do Vaticano: Expansão portuguesa, documentação.* Vol. 2. *Oriente.* Lisbon: Esferada do Caos, 2011.
Marr, David G. "Concepts of 'Individual' and 'Self' in Twentieth-Century Vietnam." *Modern Asian Studies* 34, no. 4 (2000): 774–81.
Mattoso, José, ed. *História de Portugal.* Vol. 5. *O liberalismo (1807–1890).* Lisbon: Editorial Estampa, 1993.
Maxwell, Kenneth. *Pombal: Paradox of the Enlightenment.* Cambridge: Cambridge University Press, 1995.
May, Jon, and Nigel Thrift, eds. *TimeSpace: Geographies of Temporality.* New York: Routledge, 2001.
Miller, Samuel J. *Portugal and Rome c. 1748–1830: An Aspect of the Catholic Enlightenment.* Rome: Università Gregoriana, 1978.
Mission de la Cochinchine et du Tonkin, avec gravure et carte géographique. Paris: Charles Douniol, 1858.
Les missions catholiques en Indochine: 1939. Hong Kong: Imprimerie de la Société des Missions-Étrangères de Paris, 1940.
Mitchell, David. *The Jesuits: A History.* London: MacDonald, 1980.
Mitras Lusitanas no Oriente II: Catálogo chronologico-historico dos prelados da egreja metropolitana de Goa e das dioceses suffraganeas. Lisbon, 1913.

Molesky, Mark. *This Gulf of Fire: The Destruction of Lisbon, or Apocalypse in the Age of Science and Reason*. New York: Knopf, 2015.

Monita ad missionarios: Instructions aux missionaires de la S. Congrégation de la Propagande. Paris: Archives des Missions Étrangères, 2000.

Mundy, Peter. *The Travels of Peter Mundy in Europe and Asia, 1608–1667*. 5 vols. Cambridge: Hakluyt Society, 1907–1936.

Mungello, David E. *Curious Land: Jesuit Accommodation and the Origins of Sinology*. Honolulu: University of Hawaii Press, 1989.

Múrias, Manuel Maria. *Chiado do século XII ao 25 de Abril*. Lisbon: Nova Arrancada, 1996.

Murphy, James Cavanah. *A General View of the State of Portugal; Containing a Topographical Description Thereof*. London: Cadell and Davies, 1798.

Murray, Dian. *Pirates of the South China Coast, 1790–1810*. Stanford, CA: Stanford University Press, 1987.

Napier, W. F. P. *History of the War in the Peninsula and in the South of France, from A.D. 1807 to A.D. 1814*. Vol. 1. 1862, Reprint, New York: AMS Press, 1970.

Nazareth, Casimiro Christovam. *Mitras Lusitanas no Oriente II: Catálogo chronologico-historico dos prelados da egreja metropolitana de Goa e das dioceses suffraganeas*. Lisbon, 1913.

Newitt, M. D. D. *Lord Beresford and the British Intervention in Portugal, 1807–1820*. Lisbon: Impr. De Ciencias Sociais, 2004.

Ngô Đức Thọ. *Nghiên cứu chữ húy Việt Nam qua các triều đại / Les caractères interdits au Vietnam à travers l'histoire*. Translated by Emmanuel Poisson. Hà Nội: Nhà Xuất Bản Văn Hóa, 1997.

Ngô Gia Văn Phái. *Hoàng Lê nhất thống chí* [The unification records of the imperial Lê]. Thành Phố Hồ Chí Minh: Nhà Xuất Bản Văn Học, 1998.

Ngô Thì Nhậm. "Hải Dương chí lược" [Summary records of Hải Dương]. In *Ngô Thì Nhậm toàn tập* [The collected works of Ngô Thì Nhậm], 533–36. Hà Nội: NXB Khoa Học Xã Hội, 2004.

Nguyen Cong Doan. "Jesuits: Fifty Years in Vietnam." *Province Express*, July 11, 2007. www.express.org.au/article.aspx?aeid=3153.

Nguyễn Dữ. *Truyện kỳ mạn lục giải âm* [Annotated collection of strange tales]. [Hà Nội: Nhà Xuất Bản Khoa Học Xã Hội, 2001.

Nguyễn Phương Trang. *Dấu ấn tiếng Việt trong "Sách sổ sang chép các việc" (1822) Chuyên khảo* [Hallmarks of the Vietnamese language in the *Notebook That Records and Transmits All Matters* (1822): A monograph]. Thành Phố Hồ Chí Minh: NXB Đại Học Quốc Gia TP HCM, 2015.

Nogueira de Azevedo, Francisca L. *Carlota Joanquina: Cartas inéditas*. Rio de Janeiro: Casa da Palavra, 2007.

Nouvelles des missions orientales reçues à Londres, par les directeurs de Séminaire des Missions Étrangères, en 1793, 1794, 1795 & 1796. Paris: Séminaire des Missions Étrangères, 1797.

Nouvelles lettres edifiantes des missions de la Chine et des Indes orientales. Vol. 8. Paris: Chez Ad. Le Clere, 1823.

Ocio, Hilario, OP, and Eladio Neira, OP. *Misioneros dominicos en el Extremo Oriente, 1587–1835*. Manila: Orientalia Dominicana, 2000.

An Officer. *Letters from Portugal and Spain Written during the March of the British Troops under Sir John Moore*. London: Longman, Hurst, Rees, and Orme, 1809.

Ormsby, James Wilmot. *An Account of the Operations of the British Army and of the State and Sentiments of the People of Portugal and Spain during the Campaigns of the Years 1808 and 1809*. London: James Carpenter, 1809.

Ostrowski, Brian. "The Nôm Works of Geronimo Maiorica, S.J. (1589–1656) and Their Christology." PhD diss., Cornell University, 2006.

Pacca, Bartolomeo. *Notizie sul Portogallo: Con una breve relazione della nunziatura di Lisbona dallánno 1795 fino allánno 1802* [Notices regarding Portugal: With a brief account of the nunciature to Lisbon from the year 1795 until the end of the year 1802]. Velletri: Domenico Ercole, 1836.

Pacca, Bartolomeo, and George Head. *Historical Memoirs of Cardinal Pacca, Prime Minister to Pius VII*. London: Longman, Brown, Green, and Longmans, 1850.

Paget, Julian. *Wellington's Peninsular War: Battles and Battlefields*. London: Leo Cooper, 1990.

Panduro, Lorenzo Hervás y. *Catálogo de las lenguas de las naciones conocidas, y numeracion, division, y clases de estas segun la diversidad de sus idiomas y dialectos: Lenguas y naciones de las islas del los mares Pacífico e Indiano austral y oriental, y del continente de Asia*. Madrid: Administracion del Real Arbitrio de Beneficencia, 1801.

Parkinson, Roger. *The Peninsular War*. London: Hart-Davis MacGibbon, 1973.

Pereira, Angelo. *D. João VI, príncipe e rei*. Vol. 1. *A retirada da família real para o Brasil (1807)*. Lisbon: Empresa Nacional de Publicidade, 1953.

Pereira, Esteves, and Guilherme Rodrigues, eds. *Portugal: Dicionário histórico*. Lisbon: J. Romano Torres, 1904–15. www.arqnet.pt/dicionario/index.html.

Phạm Đình Hổ. *Vũ trung tùy bút* [Random notes from amid the rains]. Translated by Nguyễn Hữu Tiến. Thành Phố Hồ Chí Minh: Nhà Xuất Bản Văn Nghệ Thành Phố Hồ Chí Minh, 1998.

Phan, Peter. *Mission and Catechesis: Alexandre de Rhodes and Inculturation in Seventeenth-Century Vietnam*. Maryknoll, NY: Orbis Books, 1998.

Phan Huy Chú. *Hai trinh chi luoc: "Recit sommaire d'un voyage en mer."* Paris: Archipel-L'Harmattan, 1994.

———. *Hoàng Việt địa dư chí* [Geographical records of the imperial Việt]. Huế: Nhà Xuất Bản Thuận Hóa, 1997.

Pinto, Fernão Mendes. *The Travels of Mendes Pinto*. Edited and translated by Rebecca Catz. Chicago: University of Chicago Press, 1989.

Porter, Jonathan. *Macau: The Imaginary City: Culture and Society, 1557 to Present*. Boulder, CO: Westview Press, 1996.

Rafael, Vicente. *Contracting Colonialism: Translation and Christian Conversion in Tagalog Society under Early Spanish Rule*. Durham, NC: Duke University Press, 1993.

Ramsay, Jacob. *Mandarins and Martyrs: The Church and the Nguyen Dynasty in Early Nineteenth-Century Vietnam*. Stanford, CA: Stanford University Press, 2008.

Ravignan, P. de. *Clément XIII et Clément XIV: Volume supplémentaire, documents historiques et critiques*. Paris: Julien, Lanier, 1854.

Rego, Sebastiio. *The Apostle of Ceylon: Fr. Joseph Vaz, an Oratorian Priest, 1651–1711*. Calcutta: Catholic Orphan Press, 1897.

Reinerman, Alan J. "Pius VII (1800–1823)." In *The Great Popes through History: An Encyclopedia*, edited by Frank J. Coppa, 2:447. Westport, CT: Greenwood Press, 2002.

Roberts, Jenifer. *The Madness of Queen Maria: The Remarkable Life of Maria I of Portugal*. Chippenham: Templeton Press, 2009.

Ross, Andrew. *A Vision Betrayed: The Jesuits in Japan and China, 1542–1742*. Maryknoll, NY: Orbis Books, 1994.

Royle, Stephen. *The Company's Island: St. Helena, Company Colonies and the Colonial Endeavour*. London: I. B. Tauris, 2007.

Santa Maria, Agostinho de. *Rosas do Japam: Candidas açucenas . . . colhidas no jardim da Igreja do Japaõ . . . em as vidas das muyto Illustres Senhoras, D. Julia Nayto, D. Luzia da Cruz, ou Caraviaxi, & D. Thecla Ignacia, ou Muni, & de suas companheiras*. Lisbon: Na Officina de Antonio Pedrozo Galram, 1709.

Santana, Francisco. *Lisboa Na. 2.A metade do xéc XVIII (plantas e descrições das suas freguesias)*. Lisbon: n.p., n.d.

Saraiva, José Hermano. *Breve história de Portugal ilustrada*. Lisbon: Livraria Bertrand, 1981.

———. *História de Portugal*. 7th ed. Lisbon: Biblioteca da Historia, 2004.

Scammell, G. V. "European Exiles, Renegades and Outlaws and the Maritime Economy of Asia c. 1500–1750." *Modern Asian Studies* 26, no. 4 (1992): 641–61.

Schaumann, August Ludolf Frierich. *On the Road with Wellington: The Diary of a War Commissary in the Peninsular Campaigns*. Edited and translated by Anthony M. Ludovici. New York: Alfred A. Knopf, 1925.

Schurhammer, Georg, SI. "Annamitische Xaveriusliteratur." In *Sonderdruck aus Missionswissenschaftliche Studien, Pr. Festgabe Joh. Dindinger, O.M.I.*, 300–314. Aachen: W. Metz, 1951.

Shrady, Nicholas. *The Last Day: Wrath, Ruin, and Reason in the Great Lisbon Earthquake of 1755*. New York: Viking Books, 2008.

Smail, John. "On the Possibility of an Autonomous History of Southeast Asia." *Journal of Southeast Asian History* 2, no. 2 (July 1961): 72–102.

Smith, Sydney F. *The Suppression of the Society of Jesus*. Leominster: Gracewing Press, 2004.

Southey, Robert. *Journals of a Residence in Portugal, 1800–1801, and a Visit to France, 1838*. Edited by Adolfo Cabral. Oxford: Oxford University Press, 1960.

———. *Letters Written during a Short Residence in Spain and Portugal*. London: Longman and Rees, 1799.

Souza, Teotonio R. de, and Surachai Chusriphan. "Padroado." In *A Dictionary of Asian Christianity*, edited by Scott Sunquist, 623–27. Grand Rapids, MI: Wm. Eerdmans, 2001.

Stothert, William. *A Narrative of the Principal Events of the Campaigns of 1809, 1810, & 1811 in Spain and Portugal Interspersed with Remarks on Local Scenery and Manners*. London: P. Martin, 1812.

Tanaka, Stefan. *New Times in Modern Japan*. Princeton, NJ: Princeton University Press, 2004.

Taylor, Keith. *A History of the Vietnamese*. Cambridge: Cambridge University Press, 2013.

———. "Literacy in Early Seventeenth-Century Northern Vietnam." In *New Perspectives on the History and Historiography of Southeast Asia: Continuing Explorations*, edited by Michael Arthur Aung-Thwin and Kenneth R. Hall, 183–98. New York: Routledge, 2011.

———. "Nguyen Hoang and the Beginning of Vietnam's Southward Expansion." In *Southeast Asia in the Early Modern Era*, edited by Anthony Reid, 42–65. Ithaca, NY: Cornell University Press, 1993.

———. "Surface Orientations in Vietnam: Beyond Histories of Nation and Region." *Journal of Asian Studies* 57, no. 4 (November 1998): 949–78.

Taylor, Margaret Stewart. *St. Helena: Ocean Roadhouse*. London: Robert Hale, 1969.

Teixeira, Manuel. *Bispos e governadores do bispado de Macau*. Vol. 2 of *Macau e a sua diocese*. Macau: Imprensa Nacional, 1940.

———. *As missões portuguesas no Vietnam*. Vol. 14 of *Macau e a sua diocese*. Macau: Imprensa Nacional, 1977.

Thanh Lãng. "Thay lời giới thiệu: Một kho tàng văn hóa vô cùng quí giá chưa hề được phát giác" [Words of introduction: A previously undiscovered priceless literary archive]. In *Sách sổ sang chép các việc*, by Philiphê Bỉnh, vii–xxxvi. Sài Gòn: Viện Đại Học Đà Lạt Xuất Bản, 1968.

Tombs, Robert. *France, 1814–1914*. New York: Longman, 1996.

Tran, Anh Q. "Inculturation, Mission and Dialogue in Vietnam: The Conference of Representatives of Four Religions." In *Beyond Conversion and Syncretism*, edited by David Lindenfeld and Miles Richardson, 167–94. New York: Berghahn Books, 2012.

Trần Công Hiến and Trần Huy Phác. *Hải dương phong vật chí* [Records of the customs and peoples of Hai Duong]. Hà Nội: Nhà Xuất Bản Lao Động, 2009.

Tran Van Toan. "Western Missionaries' Overview on Religion in Tonkin (North of Vietnam) in the 18th Century." *Religious Studies Review* 1, no. 3 (October 2007): 14–28.

Trương Bá Cần. *Lịch sử phát triển công giáo ở Việt Nam* [A history of the development of Catholicism in Vietnam]. Vol. 1. Hà Nội: Nhà Xuất Bản Tôn Giáo, 2008.

Truong-Vinh-Ky, P. J. B., and P. J. Honey. *Voyage to Tonking in the Year At-hoi. 1876*. Reprint, London: School of Oriental and African Studies, 1982.

Ulrich, Laurel Thatcher. "Interviews with Laurel Thatcher Ulrich." Questions and answers from three interviews by Laurie Kahn-Leavitt, September 1991, October 1993, and March 1994. Accessed August 17, 2012. http://dohistory.org/book/100_interview.html.

———. *A Midwife's Tale: The Story of Martha Ballard*. New York: Vintage Books, 1991.

Vargues, Isabel Nobre, and Luís Reis Torgal. "Da revolução à contra-revolução: Vintismo, cartismo, absolutismo. O exílio político." In *História de Portugal*, vol. 5, edited by José Mattoso, 57–76. Lisbon: Editorial Estampa, 1998.

Võ Xuân Quế. "Philiphê Bỉnh và sách quốc ngữ viết tay: 'Nhật trình kim thư khất chính chúa giáo'" [Philiphê Bỉnh and a handwritten book in *quốc ngữ*: Daily records and current letters [pertaining to] the request for a primary bishop]. *Nghiên cứu lịch sử* 3, nos. 5–6 (1998): 52–58.

Vũ Quỳnh, comp. *Lĩnh Nam chích quái liệt truyện* [Arrayed tales of selected oddities from south of the passes] [1492]. Translated by Liam C. Kelley et al., n.d. Viet Texts. Accessed September 22, 2014. https://sites.google.com/a/hawaii.edu/viet-texts/.

Warre, Lieut.-Gen. Sir William. *Letters from the Peninsula, 1808–1812*. London: John Murray, 1909.

Watterson, Roxana. "Introduction: Analysing Personal Narratives." In *Southeast Asian Lives: Personal Narratives and Historical Experience*, edited by Roxana Waterson, 1–37. Singapore: NUS Press, 2007.

Whitmore, John. "Cartography in Vietnam." In *History of Cartography*, vol. 2, *Cartography of the Traditional East and Southeast Asian Societies*, edited by David Woodward, 478–507. Chicago: University of Chicago Press, 1994.

Wilcken, Patrick. *Empire Adrift: The Portuguese Court in Rio de Janeiro, 1808–1821*. London: Bloomsbury, 2004.

Winichakul, Thongchai. *Siam Mapped: A History of the Geobody of a Nation*. Honolulu: University of Hawaii Press, 1994.

INDEX

Abraham 236, 244
Africa 13, 69, 93–96, 252, 295n93
Almeida, Teodoro 107
Alonso, Feliciano (bishop) 44, 46, 49–50, 54–56, 70–71, 84–85, 116, 121–22, 126, 177, 238, 287n80, 289n41
Alvares, Antonio 142
Amaral, Gaspar do 227
An Lang 71, 81m 292n39
Annam 21, 23, 29, 35, 50, 52, 54, 56, 60, 67, 69, 87, 92, 104, 106, 114, 117, 125, 145, 150, 153, 180, 190, 193–94, 196, 200, 202–203, 210, 216–17, 219–20, 223–24, 227, 232–33, 235, 237–39, 243–46, 248–49, 252–57, 263
Antoine, François 35
Apostolic vicar 51, 53, 55, 56, 58–63, 69, 84–85, 87, 115, 121–23, 132, 139, 141, 148–50, 159–62, 165–68, 170–72, 174–75, 177–81, 217, 238–40, 261, 305n48, 307n39
Archbishop 63–64, 76, 82–83, 108, 116, 123–24, 132–34, 147–49, 179, 180, 214, 292n41, 301n44
Audience (with ruler) 16, 112–14, 117, 126–27, 131, 151–55, 193
Augustinian (order) 3, 10, 112
Ayutthaya 41
Azevedo, José Pegado de 120, 299n4

Baptism 53, 55–56, 58–59, 115, 150, 196
Barbary pirates 95

Barbosa, Antonio 227
Beijing (see Peking)
Bible (see also Old Testament) 6, 96, 122, 167, 236–37, 240–41, 247, 261, 312n63
Bishop 2, 4, 14, 16–17, 19, 28–31, 33, 39–41, 43–46, 49–51, 53–57, 59–64, 69–71, 75–79, 81–89, 107–109, 111, 113, 115–16, 119–24, 126, 131–42, 144–51, 153, 156, 159, 161–62, 167–68, 170–72, 174–83, 191–92, 195, 213–14, 217–18, 232, 238–41, 263, 299n9, 302n81, 305n58
Boat 16, 27, 29–31, 35, 37, 40, 66, 68–69, 71, 76–83, 86–89, 91–99, 101–103, 141, 149, 156–58, 164–65, 170, 175–76, 189, 191, 208, 213
Bombay 60, 83, 89, 292n44
Books 39, 42, 51, 106, 122, 178, 193–95, 202, 204–207, 216, 219, 222–227, 229, 232, 237, 242–251, 255–258, 266, 308n60, 308n68, 309n11, 312n63, 313n8
Bookstores 183–84, 204, 206
Borders 12, 66, 85, 134, 215
Borgia, Stefano de 220, 243–44, 247, 249
Bourges, Jacques de 31
Boxer, Charles 14
Brazil 2, 3, 7, 17, 19, 34–35, 102–103, 120, 156–58, 182, 184, 187, 189, 192–93, 212–15, 217, 257, 302n71
British 2, 12, 17, 19, 83, 88, 94–96, 134, 157, 158, 166, 188, 191–92, 205, 215, 295n98, 296n22, 301n42

327

INDEX

British East India Company 94
Buddhism 12, 125, 204, 242, 253, 310n27
Bùi Chu 32, 41–42

Caldas da Rainha 128–30
Caleppi, Bishop Lorenzo 145–147, 213, 302n71, 302n80
Cảnh Thịnh 48
Canton 40, 69, 79–81
Carlota Joaquina 110, 115
Carneiro, Augustin 61–62, 115, 121, 139–40, 171–72, 176, 286n49, 286n51
Casa do Espirito Santo 103, 104, 154, 183–84, 199, 206–207, 214, 260, 307n41
Castiglioni, Alexandre-Pompée 41, 42, 45–47, 49–50, 189, 251, 283n1, 287n2
Catechist 38, 39, 41–44, 46, 68–69, 84, 176–77, 286n58, 287n71
Cathechismus 42, 205, 231–32
Cenáculo Vilas Boas, Manuel do 147, 149
Censorship 225
Ceramus (bishopric) 59
Champa 66, 255
Chiado (district) 103, 184–86, 206, 260–61, 305n2
Chronology 215, 232, 243
Chữ Nôm 42, 53, 54, 227
Clothing 17, 61, 71, 83, 86, 88, 115, 117, 160, 199
Cochinchina (see also Đàng Trong) 9, 15, 24, 26–29, 31, 35, 42, 47–48, 53, 75, 84, 161–62, 222, 249–50, 255, 290n53
College of San Juan de Letran 32
College of St. Paul 72–75
Colonialism 12–13, 52, 229, 230, 236, 264,
Commerce 69–72, 85, 189, 250–51, 256
Confession 51, 54, 58–59, 61, 85, 91, 130, 161, 170, 174, 196–98, 228, 245–46, 307n39
Confucianism 6, 24, 43, 67, 68, 162, 226, 237, 247–48, 263
Contracting Colonialism 52
Convert 52, 54, 103, 223, 227, 230, 250, 255, 261
Cruz, Gaspar da 9
Cuyển, Bảo Lộc (Paul) 39–41, 43–44, 61, 114, 118, 232–33

Đại Việt 21, 24, 26–27, 29, 63, 66, 120, 124, 173,
Đàng Ngoài (see also Tonkin) 21, 23–24, 33, 163, 190, 222, 231, 249, 250, 253, 255
Đàng Trong (see also Cochinchina) 15, 21, 33, 102, 222, 240, 249–50, 254–55
Đào Công Chính 24

David 43, 236, 239–40
Davoust, Jean 40
de Lima Teles da Silva, Tomás Xavier 102
Delgado, Ignacio 177–78, 181, 305n48
Deydier, François 29–31
Dom João (see João VI)
Dominican (order) 3, 4, 9, 10, 31–32, 34, 36, 39, 45–46, 48–50, 52, 54–55, 59, 61, 69, 76, 78, 115, 121, 122, 126, 140, 167, 175–76, 238, 240–41, 261–62, 305n48
Donations (see also Gifts) 70–71, 84, 96, 171, 173, 197, 198
Đồng Nai 75
Dutch 83, 292n43
Dutton, John 94

Earthquake 34, 101, 103–04, 154, 184–85, 187, 206, 260, 295n5
East 2, 35, 123–126, 137, 139, 203, 235, 252
East/West 125
Egypt 7, 45, 57, 59, 238, 241
Enoch 217
Envoy 16, 43, 64–68, 78, 82–83, 86, 104–105, 114, 122, 132, 138, 139, 142, 143–47, 153–55, 160–61, 163–64, 169, 178, 183, 193–94, 211, 213, 219, 222, 257, 302n69
Eve 70, 253
Execution 47, 162, 250, 256, 263, 288n3
Exemplar 219–21, 224–25, 232, 240, 242, 244–47, 249, 252,
Exile 2, 7, 35, 57, 59, 66, 108, 156, 182–83, 192–94, 212–15, 218, 221, 223, 238, 239, 241, 254, 257, 263, 297n26, 302n71, 303n96
Eyot, Pierre 48

Famine 38, 47, 48, 306n20
Fesseë (bishopric) 44, 59–60
Fez, Bishop of 44
Fish 26, 75, 79, 93, 96, 128, 201–202
Flood (biblical) 232–33, 235–37, 253
Flood 232–33, 235–237, 253, 286n59
Food 17, 60–61, 69, 75, 79, 83, 89, 91, 93, 95–97, 102, 104, 115, 127, 128, 153, 160, 183, 187–90, 197, 199–203
Forest, Alain 31
Fort James 94
France 6, 19, 48, 95, 109, 112, 140, 145, 187, 190, 212, 247, 257, 297n26
Franciscan (order) 3, 9–10, 112, 134–35, 165, 173, 179
Fund-raising 70–71, 79, 84, 86

Gaballa (bishopric) 59
Galdino, Manuel 134–143, 145–46, 148–49, 165, 172–181, 240, 289n44, 301n49, 305n48, 305n53
Garden of Eden 70, 253
Gazeta de Lisboa 149–50, 205, 256, 301n55
Geography 2, 4, 6, 9–12, 14–16, 18, 23–24, 26, 28, 30–31, 38, 56, 59, 63–65, 67 122–26, 151, 160, 183–84, 193–94, 202, 204, 219, 226, 229, 230, 232, 236–37, 241, 246–47, 252, 25–55, 261–62
Gifts (see also Donations) 70, 84, 113–15, 219, 248
Goa 4, 13, 20, 35, 60, 63–65, 76, 79, 81–83, 86–87, 91, 132, 134, 148, 174, 179–80, 254, 261, 301n44, 301n63
Golden Book (see *Nhật Trình*) 50, 164, 220
Goliath 239
Gonzaga, Cardinal Valenti 37
Gortyna (bishopric) 59
Grace 51, 54–58, 84, 121, 262
Grão Pará (ship) 95–96, 98, 101
"Grocer King" 30
Guangdong 86, 88
Gulf of Tonkin 1, 49

Hà Nội 24, 29, 203, 307n58
Hà Tiên 9
Hải Dương 23, 24, 45
Hải Phong 1, 26–27, 37, 61
Hainan (island) 28, 89
Hair (haircuts) 87, 117, 216
Hats 51, 102, 199
Henry, Duke of Viseu (Henry the Navigator) 101
Herod 49, 238, 241
Hierocaesarea (bishopric) 59
Holstein, Dom Alexandre de Sousa 143–147, 172, 301n64
Holy See (see also Vatican) 40, 75, 115, 136, 145, 148–49, 171, 174, 179, 180, 217
Holy Spirit 53, 167, 170, 304n27
Hospital 128, 173, 181, 211, 228
Hưng Yên 30
Illness 76, 87, 93, 96, 109, 121, 127–131, 152–53, 160, 168, 172–73, 202, 211–213, 216, 223, 300n33, 302n76
Introduction to Devout Life 42
Israelites 7, 59, 167–68, 238–39, 241
Italian (language) 40, 52, 56, 227, 250
Italian (nationality) 10, 31, 37–38, 165, 167, 186, 242, 285n24

Jacob 45, 295n2
Jamestown 94–95
Jesuit (order) 2–4, 6, 7, 16–17, 19, 24, 26–39, 41–43, 48–62, 68–69, 71–76, 79, 84, 85, 106–108, 114–15, 122–23, 132, 138, 140, 145, 150, 159–61, 165–68, 170–71, 174, 176–81, 186, 193–94, 202, 205, 207, 211–14, 220–22, 224, 227, 229–30, 232–33, 235–36, 239–40, 242, 245–49, 253, 257, 261, 264, 266, 297n26, 297n29, 312n62, 63
Jesuit Dissolution 3, 36, 50, 114, 186, 264, 310n32
Jesuit Recall (1682) 33–34, 36, 239
Jesus 49, 60, 70, 167, 212, 217, 223, 232–33, 235, 236, 240–41, 248–50, 253, 258, 310n30
João VI 16, 20, 102–104, 109–112, 114, 119–121, 128, 131–32, 134–139, 141, 143, 145, 147, 151–155, 177–78, 182, 187, 189, 192–93, 196, 214–15, 217–18, 257, 298n42
Job, 240
Jonathan 43, 239,
Joseph 45, 223
Joseph-Marie-Pierre Khuất Văn Tạo (Bishop of Haiphong)
Judas 70, 240

Kẻ Bui 44–46, 49–50, 61
Keith, Charles 263
Kelley, Liam 67
King Solomon 33
Kinh Bắc 42

La Motte, Charles de , 28–30
la Motte, Pierre Lambert de 28–30
Language xii, 27, 38, 42, 51–56, 62, 67, 75, 103, 120, 123, 190, 195, 204, 220, 222, 227, 237, 241–44, 248–52, 262, 266, 287n75, 311n38, 312n62
Last Rites 55, 58, 130, 258
Latin 39, 42, 52–53, 55–56, 220, 227, 250, 262, 287n75, 291n3, 307n41
Lê Dynasty 24, 26, 47
Le Roy, Jean François ,
Lê Tắc 66
Letondal, Claude-Françoise 69, 76–78, 81, 291n10, 292n30
Letters 14, 17, 19, 39, 47, 59, 75, 85, 92, 116–18, 133–34, 142, 149, 150, 163–69, 171–74, 176–81, 192, 208, 221, 228, 238, 251
Lezzoli, Raimondo 31
Li, Tana 15
Libraries 104, 106, 188, 205–206, 256, 308n60, 308n64
Lịch (Brother) 68–70

INDEX

Liễn, Simaõ (Simon) 67, 70–71, 76, 78–79, 81–84, 86–88, 91, 110, 132–33, 143, 148, 160–61, 166–69, 171–73, 175, 203, 211, 216
Lisbon 2, 3, 7, 14–17, 19–20, 34–35, 40, 43, 62, 65, 67, 70–71, 78, 90, 94–95, 97–120, 123, 127–28, 130, 132–34, 136, 139–43, 145–47, 149–54, 156–57, 159–61, 164–67, 169, 170, 172–174, 178, 182–219, 221–26, 231, 235, 237–38, 246–47, 251, 254, 256–57, 260–262, 288n20, 293n62, 295n98, 296n7, 297n26, 300n38, 302n71, 304n24, 307n36, 39, 313n96
London 101, 184, 296n7,
Longer, Jacques-Benjamin 43–44, 53, 168, 171
Lottery 204, 209, 228
Loyola, Ignatius 102, 207, 220, 233, 238, 243, 247
Lý Dynasty 66
Lý Long Tường 66

Macao 4–6, 13, 16–17, 19–20, 27–28, 30, 35, 39, 44, 47, 53, 56, 63–65, 68–92, 94, 115–17, 120, 132–34, 137–42, 145–46, 148–49, 156, 159–81, 192, 194, 202, 208, 211, 221, 239–41, 248, 254, 261, 301n44, 302n76, 305n43, 58
Madre de Dios, Rodrigo da 169, 170, 175–76, 179,
Mafra (palace) 110, 112, 134, 137–38, 151–56
Maiorica, Geronimo 53, 167, 226, 242–248, 252, 289n27, 312n62
Malacca 60, 63, 65, 69, 81, 83, 91, 292n44
Malay Peninsula 81, 83, 89, 94–95, 295n100
Manila 4, 29, 32, 63
Map (also Mapping) 4, 12–14, 20, 64
Marchini, Giovanni Baptista 75, 176, 181, 285n29, 305n43
Maria I 109, 120, 131, 275, 297n26, p. 301n67
Marini, Filipe 30, 251, 312n62
Martinho, Captain Caetano 95
Martyr 32, 43, 62, 75, 219, 233, 240, 249–50, 253, 255, 263, 313n87
Mary (Virgin) 51, 55, 89, 96, 102, 122, 223, 231, 310n30
Mass 56–58, 70, 81, 84–86, 96, 103–104, 112, 116–17, 130, 147–48, 161, 166, 173, 183, 185, 193, 195–97, 201, 203, 220–21, 245, 256, 258
Matthias 70
Mendonça, José (II) Francisco Miguel António de 116
MEP 34, 36, 39–41, 45–46, 48–51, 53, 61, 69–70, 74, 76, 78, 121–22, 124, 140, 142, 161–63, 165, 167, 176, 179, 230, 241, 249, 261, 284n20, 285n22, 35, 286n53, 291n10

Milopotamus (bishopric) 59
Moses 7, 34, 43, 57, 59, 168, 223, 235, 238, 239, 241, 244, 289n41
Mozambique 40
Mt. Sinai 7, 34, 167, 238–39
mũ bàng (hat) 50

Nam Định 31, 44–45, 49, 292n39
Napoleon 2, 16, 19, 65, 119, 131, 145, 156, 160, 187, 190–91, 296n22
Necessidades palace 102–107, 112, 115–16, 118, 131, 147, 151, 153–156, 184, 185, 188, 195, 205, 210, 214, 296n22
New World (the Americas) 7, 156, 182, 188, 208, 213–214, 233
Newspapers 149–50, 204, 256
Ngân, Phanchico (Francisco) 70, 76, 79, 87, 88, 210, 212, 213, 254, 293n58
Nghệ An 42–43, 45
Nguyễn Bỉnh Khiêm 24
Nguyễn dynasty (1802–1945) 21, 150, 163, 249, 263
Nguyễn lords (prior to 1802) 21, 27, 47, 84, 120, 125, 161–62, 170, 173, 175, 250, 255
Nhân, Thome (Thomas) 43, 68, 76, 79, 81–84, 86–87, 91–92, 95, 101, 127–28, 130–133, 147–48, 173, 212, 216, 254, 302n76–77
Nhật Trình 136, 164, 190, 214, 226, 256
Ninh Cơ river 81
Noah 232–33, 235, 253
Notebook of Miscellany (see *Sách Sổ*) Notebooks 17–19, 38, 45, 70, 128, 142, 154, 163–64, 183, 186, 202, 211, 219–20, 223, 226, 228–29, 231, 234, 256, 259, 264
Nova Castella, João de (Portuguese admiral) 94
Nuncio 20, 35, 63, 75, 115, 123, 132–34, 138–42, 145–49, 167, 170, 172, 180–81, 213, 300n38, 302n71, 305n43

Obelar, Manuel 39, 44
Old Testament (see also Bible) 6–7, 34, 122, 201, 222, 236–38, 241, 244, 247
Olissipo 100
Opium 79
Orality 42, 224–25, 229, 242, 252
Oratorians 102–109, 117–18, 120, 127, 130, 142, 147, 153, 155, 166, 183, 185, 193, 195, 196, 198, 200–201, 203, 212, 218, 297n26
Ordination 3, 16, 41–43, 45, 46, 49, 62, 116, 140, 195

Pacca, Bishop Bartolomeo 123, 132–33, 138, 145, 299n12, 300n37, 38, 39

INDEX

Padroado community 3, 6–7, 17, 28, 31, 33, 35–46, 48–51, 54–56, 58–65, 68, 70, 87, 121, 123, 149, 161, 167–69, 174, 177–78, 181, 182, 223, 238–41, 254, 262–63
Padroado Real 3, 7, 9–10, 28–30, 40, 59, 111, 115, 121, 132, 143–44, 153–54, 213, 215
Pallu, François 28–29
Paris xiii, 3, 19, 27–29, 40–41, 101, 124, 148, 150, 163, 184, 238, 290n53, 296n7, 303n6,
Parish 11, 13, 51, 55, 61, 63–64, 108, 124, 181, 184, 186, 197, 198, 230, 261
Patriarch 107, 116, 123, 195, 215
Paz, Vicente Liêm de la 32
Pearl River 71, 79, 81
Peking 60
Penang 272
Persecution (of Catholics) 1, 42, 46–48, 162, 173, 241, 250, 263
Petition 2, 10, 40, 78–79, 117, 119–24, 126–27, 131, 133–34, 136–37, 139, 142–43, 150, 153–54, 156, 163, 171, 175, 215, 221
Phan Huy Chú 24
Phan, Peter 38
Pharaoh 45, 57, 238–39, 241, 289n41
Philippines 7, 31–32, 52, 55, 115, 282n6
Pilgrimage 67, 75
Pina, Fracisco de 227
Pinto, José Manuel 76
Pinto, Mendes 220, 232, 237
Pirates 76, 81, 83, 86, 88, 91, 95, 176, 293n57
Poetry 24, 67, 68, 78, 89, 91–93, 98–99, 106, 130–31, 136, 211, 221, 227
Pombal, Marques de 34–36, 101, 103, 107–109, 132, 184, 205–206, 295n6, 297n26
Pontius Pilate 49, 238, 240
Pope Clement X 30
Pope Clement XI 30, 32, 36
Pope Innocent X 27
Pope Innocent XI 33–34
Pope Pius VII 131, 143–46, 211, 217, 235, 310n33
Portugal 10, 16–20, 26–26–27, 34–35, 40, 59, 62, 65, 69, 76, 81, 86, 92, 95, 98–101, 104, 106–115, 119–21, 123, 131–32, 134, 136, 139–43, 145, 147–49, 154, 156, 158, 160–61, 163, 174, 178, 180, 183, 188–89, 191–96, 201, 203–205, 208–209, 212–15, 221, 223, 225, 232–33, 240, 252, 254, 256–57, 262–63
Portuguese civil war 2, 214–15
Portuguese-Latin-Annamese Dictionary 52, 149, 220, 227

Postal Service 204, 207–208, 228
Praça do Comércio 98, 149
Pronunciation 51, 53–58, 121, 262
Propaganda Fide 28–29, 118, 132, 284n17
Province of Japan 26
Provincia dominicana de Nuestra Señora del Rosario

Quảng Nam 23–24, 190, 233, 235, 261
Quang Trung 48, 190, 232–33
Queen Maria 109, 120, 131
Queluz (palace) 110, 112–15, 119
Quốc ngữ 68, 220, 226–28, 248, 251, 287n75, 289n26, 309n19

Ramsey, Jacob 263
Red River 24, 30–31, 49, 261
Revolution (French) 48, 108, 134
Rhodes, Alexander de 27–29, 42, 52, 149, 167, 205, 221, 227–28, 231–33, 243–44, 251, 253, 286n58, 287n75
Ricci, Matteo 74, 226–27, 243–44, 248–49
Rio de Janeiro 158, 182, 189, 213, 302n71
Robes 101, 147, 151, 212
Rome 4, 10, 13–14, 23–24, 33, 35–36, 39–40, 42–44, 61–62, 64, 106, 114, 118, 132, 138, 140–41, 143, 145–48, 150, 153, 180, 186, 212, 232–33, 239, 247, 250, 261, 264
Rumors 68–69, 170, 178–80
Ruspae (bishopric) 59

Sách Sổ 23, 118, 194, 198, 206, 228–29, 236, 238, 258, 264
Sacrament(s) 4, 41, 46, 53–55, 59, 61, 122, 131, 140, 161, 164, 181, 196–97
Saints 4, 6, 89, 106, 126, 136, 199, 219, 221, 223, 230, 242–47, 250, 294n71
Santa Catarina, Manoel de 180
Santarem 196, 307n36
Schall von Bell, Johann Adam 74
Schism (Schismatics) 3, 46, 57–59, 61, 122, 140, 148, 161, 165, 168, 171, 174–75, 177–78, 181, 289n44
Schurhammer, Georg 17, 28, 264
Seculars 28
Seminary 40–47, 68, 72, 115, 178, 204, 290n53
Seminary of St. Joseph 72
Seneca 242–43, 246
Sérard, Philippe 48
Sewing 92, 95, 200

Sheep (spiritual) 54, 60, 62, 78, 85, 106
Ship (see Boat)
Siam 12-14, 29, 41, 69, 92, 287n76
Siam Mapped 12-13
Silva, Marcelino José da 44, 69, 75-79, 81-83, 139-40, 146, 170, 174
Smail, John 14-15
Sơn Nam 42
Soul 43, 70, 106, 136, 147, 153, 173, 194, 201, 214
Spain 7, 10, 19, 44, 109, 119, 127, 134, 140, 150, 189, 21213, 247
Spanish (language) 52, 54-56
Spanish (nationality) 2, 7-10, 13, 16, 29, 31-32, 36, 45, 48-49, 52, 54-56, 65, 110, 112-13, 115, 120-22, 126-27, 134, 140, 141, 155-56, 158, 160, 180, 190, 192, 262
St. Anne (ship) 89, 91, 93, 95-96
St. Anne 89, 91, 93, 95-96, 221, 243, 257-58
St. Helena 16, 20, 90, 93-95, 103-104
St. Tomas, Jose Huyen de 32
Stipend 160, 182, 188
Straits of Malacca 83, 91
Sumatra 91
"Sun King" 30

Tabooed characters 54
Tagalog 52, 55
Tagus River 98-99, 105, 157, 205, 208
Tales 6, 53, 126, 193, 207, 216, 219ff
Tây Sơn 43, 44, 47-48, 54, 84, 150, 161-163, 170, 173, 179, 189-90, 233, 238, 263, 289n28, 302n86
Taylor, Keith 15, 24
Temporality 6, 229, 233
Ten Commandments 7, 34, 167, 235-36, 238-39, 244-45
Territory 13, 26, 27, 29, 31, 33, 59-60, 89, 162, 167, 196, 253
Textiles 71, 113, 115, 199-200
Thái Bình River 1
Thailand (see Siam)
Thăng Long 4, 24, 26, 29, 30, 203,
Thanh Hoá 27, 37
The Imitation of Christ 42
The Lives of the Saints 42
Thiểu, John 39-41, 44, 114, 118, 232-33,
Thongchai Winichakul 12

Thuyên, Bảo Lộc (Paul) 87, 160-62, 169, 171, 173-76, 179-80
Timetables 230-32, 235
Tobacco 1, 24, 26, 199
Tobias 240
Tonkin (See also Đàng Ngoài) 1-4, 7, 10-19, 21, 23-51, 53, 58-61, 63-71, 75, 79-82, 84, 86-87, 89-90, 96, 111, 114, 116-26, 132, 134-43, 145-46, 148-51, 159, 161-84, 190, 192, 194-96, 200-204, 209, 212-14, 218, 221, 222, 224, 230-31, 235, 237-41, 249-51, 253-55, 261-64
Tower of Babel 235, 237, 253
Trạch (Brother) 162, 173-176, 179-80
Translation 17, 51-53, 78-79, 134, 211, 218, 220, 222, 225, 227-28, 237, 244-46, 248, 251, 254, 262
Treaty of Tordesillas 7-9, 13
Trêu, Manuel Xavier 43, 50, 61
Trịnh lords 21, 26, 32, 44, 47-48, 125, 249
Trịnh Sâm 47
Trung Linh 44
Trung, José 43-44, 68, 79, 87, 96, 212-13, 216-17, 239, 254, 256
Trương Bá Cần 10
Truyện Annam 222, 226, 231, 249, 251-52, 255
Tuệ Tĩnh 66

Ulrich, Laurel Thatcher 18
University of St. Tomas 32

Vatican (see also Holy See) 35, 37, 39-40, 40, 45, 118-19, 132, 138, 141, 143-48, 211
Vessel (see Boat)
Vicariate 11, 13, 25, 28-29, 31-32, 42-45, 49-51, 54, 59, 63, 85, 124, 126, 150, 168, 177, 238, 261
Villiani, Onofre 35, 37-40,

Waters, Roxana 18, 20
Wellington, Duke of 191-192
West 2, 67, 89, 102, 123-127, 136, 150, 165, 190, 196, 200-201, 203, 205, 208, 210-11, 225, 230-31, 252

Xavier, Francis 193, 207, 220, 223-24, 229, 232-33, 235, 238, 243, 247, 248-49, 252, 282n11
Xứ Đông 38, 61

www.ingramcontent.com/pod-product-compliance
Ingram Content Group UK Ltd.
Pitfield, Milton Keynes, MK11 3LW, UK
UKHW041848270225
455670UK00004B/93